CONSTRUCTION ACCOUNTING

CONSTRUCTION ACCOUNTING:
Financial, Managerial, Auditing, and Tax

Third Edition

JAMES J. ADRIAN
Professor, Bradley University
President, Adrian International

DOUGLAS J. ADRIAN
McGladrey & Pullen, LLP

ISBN 0-87563-845-7

Published by

Stipes Publishing L.L.C.
204 W. University Ave.
Champaign, Illinois 61820

to Robert and Helen

TABLE OF CONTENTS

PREFACE

After years of observing and working with numerous construction firms, we have concluded that the use of sound accounting practices is the single most important characteristic of the profitable firm. Successful construction contracting is, in great part, the ability to forecast correctly and control costs efficiently. Fundamental to both tasks is the regular use of good accounting methods.

This book assumes no prior knowledge of accounting, so we have attempted to present accounting and its related practices in an easily understood manner.

For those readers with prior accounting training, the unique characteristics of construction accounting should be of interest. Understandably, the unique characteristics of both the construction process and the businesses themselves result in accounting practices and procedures that differ from those used in other industries. Included in these characteristics are long-term contracts, decentralized accounting, significant dependence of the construction firm on external parties, and poor internal controls. In fact, no business needs accounting more, but practices it less, than the typical construction firm.

This book is meant to interest any construction firm intent on structuring its accounting practices. The objectives are to assist in increasing a firm's profitability while decreasing its risk. Both objectives take into account the relatively low profit margin and high risk typical in construction.

Lending institutions, surety companies, accountants, and other external parties dealing with the construction firm also need a thorough grasp of construction accounting. This understanding is necessary if they are to assist the construction contractor and if they are to evaluate the construction contractor properly. The book attempts to help external parties with both tasks.

An important part of a construction student's training in a college program should include business topics with an emphasis on accounting. Too often, however, such training addresses either the design or the construction supervision phases of the whole process. Design and supervision mainly affect quality-one of construction's three important variables. Accounting in great part addresses the other two variables-time and cost.

Construction accounting is not static. The introduction of automated data processing equipment that utilizes the computer is having a significant impact on construction accounting practices. Management auditing that aims at improving the overall efficiency and profitability of the construction firm is another example of recent change in accounting practice.

Construction Accounting covers the four most widely recognized divisions of accounting: financial, managerial, auditing, and tax. An introductory chapter precedes these four divisions. This introductory chapter cites some of the special difficulties of construction accounting and identifies accounting areas applicable to construction.

Financial accounting and related material are presented in chapters 2 through 8. Of these, 2 through 5 can be considered as a package of basic accounting principles. Some would maintain that chapter 4, on bookkeeping, should come first. I believe, however, that bookkeeping and all its related forms and procedures are better understood if one first has an understanding of the basic accounting relationship and typical accounting transactions. The accounting relationship and accounting transactions are examined in chapters 2 and 3.

Chapters 6 through 8 address the financial statements of the construction firm. These should be of special interest to any external party who has to interpret these financial statements. Chapter 8 illustrates how the use of alternative accounting methods and principles can result in widely varying financial statement results.

Managerial accounting is discussed in chapters 9 through 13. Here the emphasis is on using accounting for future decision making. This contrasts with the widely held view that accounting is merely a means of reporting on past events.

Management information systems and computers are discussed in chapters 9 through 11. The treatment of these topics reflects their increasing impact on the construction firm, project management, and construction accounting. Chapter 11 has been updated from Edition II to reflect the new computer technology and computer software currently available to the construction firm and industry. The chapter should enable the reader to appraise computer software applications relevant to the construction firm and construction project.

The construction firm's dependence on external parties often results in the need for a financial audit. Chapter 14 discusses the unique difficulties of performing a financial audit of the construction firm. In addition to helping external parties perform an audit, chapter 14 assists the construction firm prepare for an audit.

The concept and procedures of management auditing, to include operational auditing, are presented in chapter 15. Unlike the financial audit that focuses only on financial data, the emphasis of management auditing is on improving the efficiency of the operations that in turn dictate financial results. More and more construction firms are recognizing the value of management auditing.

Chapters 16 through 18 address that far reaching aspect of accounting referred to as tax planning. The emphasis of these three chapters is on ways to lessen the negative impact of tax by tax avoidance and deferral. Discussion is limited to the tax areas commonly confronted by the construction firm.

Part 6, Value Added Services, includes three new chapters. These three new chapters recognize the new and changing services provided by accountants to the construction clients. One of the best ways to increase construction firm profitability and reduce risk is to increase job site productivity. Many of the procedures to increase job site productivity are accounting oriented. Chapter 19 provides accounting related topics relevant to increasing job site productivity.

Given the difficult and uncertain nature of the construction process, many construction firms encounter the need to prepare a construction claim to the project owner or designer. A key component of these claims is the quantification of financial damages. In chapter 20, accounting related topics are presented to enable the construction firm to prevent, prepare, and present construction changes and claims.

Finally, given the need to sell the construction firm or to restructure the firm, an valuation of the firm has to quantified. In chapter 21, alternative methods of valuing the construction firm are presented.

The addition of chapters 19–21 recognize the changing business environment of the construction firm and the services provided by the accounting profession. These chapters provide the reader with the tools and procedures to aid the construction firm in a competitive environment.

We would like to thank the staff of Stipes Publishing for their preparation of typesetting and their review of the material. We would also like to thank Sandy, Jim's wife, and Doug's mother for her review of the material and her assistance in typing. Finally we would like to thank the many construction firms that we have serviced. These firms indirectly inspired us to write this textbook.

Peoria, Illinois

JAMES J. ADRIAN
DOUGLAS J. ADRIAN

CONSTRUCTION ACCOUNTING

Part 1
INTRODUCTION

CHAPTER

1
HOW ACCOUNTING IS USEFUL TO THE CONSTRUCTION FIRM

INTRODUCTION

There is probably no type of firm that needs sound accounting practices more than the construction firm. The success of the construction firm is closely aligned to its ability to forecast and control costs. Both of these functions have accounting as their base.

The construction industry has a history of neglecting to perform the accounting function properly. This has proven fatal for many firms, having resulted in bankruptcy as a daily threat to numerous construction firms. Approximately 13 percent of all construction firms fail annually. Listed below are the ten leading reasons for construction firm business failures as determined by Dun and Bradstreet.[1]

Rank	*Reason*
1	Lack of business experience
2	Inadequate project estimating and/or cost control system
3	Inadequate working capital
4	Receivable difficulties
5	Too much competition
6	Insufficient advertising
7	Lack of technical experience
8	Wrong location for service
9	Inventory control
10	Fraud

The business failure reasons listed are in order of their frequency, the first reason given being the most frequent. Many of the reasons can be traced to inadequate use of accounting. For example, each of the four most frequent

[1] "Business Failures," Duns Review, 1976.

reasons relates to a weakness in accounting. Reasons listed as nine and ten are also evidence of less than adequate accounting practices by the construction firm.

INADEQUATE CONSTRUCTION ACCOUNTING

Regardless of the type of business, a profit-oriented firm must perform the basic management functions of marketing (or sales), production, and control. Control is in great part accounting. There is evidence that, of these three functions, control or accounting is the function most neglected by the typical construction firm. Reasons given for the industry's slighting of the accounting functions vary. However, the following are often cited:

1. The construction firm is often understaffed. As such, when it comes to priorities, the firm tends to value the marketing and production functions, which appear to be most essential. However, this often proves to be a dangerous oversight as to the real order of importance.
2. The uniqueness of the industry's product, including its mobility and flexibility of design, makes conventional nonconstruction industry accounting less than totally reliable or beneficial for the construction industry. Undoubtedly construction accounting is somewhat unique and complex. However, the fact remains that a properly designed accounting system is as necessary to the construction firm as it is to any other profit-oriented firm.
3. The construction firm tends to be small, often owned and operated by a single proprietor. In many instances this is an individual who was employed as a craftsman and who has found the way to ownership through marketing efforts. In the proprietor's earlier years as an employee, accounting skills were of little or no value. The result is a slow recognition of the need for an essential management function—accounting.

Past failures of the construction industry to recognize the value of accounting will in all likelihood not persist. Competition and increasing concern of lending and bonding companies about the construction firm's financial risk have placed pressure on the construction firm to become more sophisticated in its approach to the accounting function. This pressure has been overdue. While the pressure may appear at first glance as just another of the many factors weighing on the firm, it may in fact be a blessing in disguise. The firm that is forced to practice sound accounting because of the demands from external parties will obtain numerous internal benefits.

UNIQUE CHARACTERISTICS OF CONSTRUCTION ACCOUNTING

There are several characteristics of the construction firm that result in construction accounting practices and procedures varying significantly from those used by other manufacturing industries. The result is that, what are good accounting practices and procedures for an industry such as the automobile industry may not be good practices or procedures for the construction industry.

Included in the unique characteristics of the construction industry are the following:

1. Construction projects are usually manufactured away from the construction firm's central office. This creates problems in collecting, processing, and effectively using relevant accounting data. It raises questions such as whether the accounting data should be processed at project sites (decentralized accounting) or at the central office (centralized accounting). Related to this characteristic is the fact that the initial accounting data collected at the project site must be collected by production employees. These employees, who are production oriented, often discount the value of accounting and its related procedures. The result is a potential for inadequate collection of needed accounting data.
2. Usually each project a construction firm builds is somewhat singular as to its design and required construction methods. This one-of-a-kind feature results in using a method of accounting referred to as *job-cost accounting*. As compared to the alternative of *process-cost accounting,* job-cost accounting requires more cost traceability practices and procedures. This factor, coupled with the difficulty of collecting and tracing the cost data, creates unique accounting problems. The differences among construction projects also emphasize the need for timely construction accounting data in that, if the data is not timely, it is limited in terms of its use for managing an ongoing project.
3. Often the construction project takes more than a year to complete. Therefore, the construction industry uses methods of recognizing revenue and income referred to as *long-term construction contract methods*. Long-term construction contract methods are discussed in Chapters 3 and 17. Long-term contract revenue-recognition methods are just one example of several alternative accounting methods or practices available almost exclusively to the construction industry.
4. The construction firm's accounting practices are affected in great part by the needs of several external parties. Typically these external parties include lending institutions, surety companies, public agencies, and possibly material suppliers and equipment manufacturers. Each of these parties places various demands on the accounting practices of the construction firm. The result is that the construction firm often is asked to prepare numerous accounting reports over and above those of firms in other industries.
5. The majority of construction firms have few owners, so they are often closely held companies. This characteristic relates to specific financial statement presentation practices and, more importantly, to the tax planning and tax methods most effective for the construction firm. Usually

this feature can be viewed as favorable in that some of the most effective tax planning can be done for the closely held company.

Each of the characteristics listed dictates unique construction accounting practices, procedures, and considerations. These will be highlighted in following chapters. Considering these distinctive features of the construction industry also leads one to the conclusion that it is necessary to know both the industry and accounting principles, practices, and procedures in order to implement the most effective construction accounting. More than once a construction firm has employed an independent accountant's services only to find that the accountant's lack of knowledge of the construction industry resulted in less than desirable performance.

EVOLUTION OF ACCOUNTING IN THE CONSTRUCTION FIRM

The role of the accounting function within the construction firm, and its placement in the organizational structure, varies mainly with the size of the firm. The majority of construction firms are small, often operated by a single owner. It is common for the single proprietor to have his wife serve as bookkeeper or to perform the function himself. The tasks performed by this wife-bookkeeper are often limited to bookkeeping-related functions such as keeping the general ledger, payroll, and payroll tax returns.

As the construction firm grows in size, the accounting role becomes increasingly important. However, evidence indicates that the construction firm is slow to recognize the importance of and the need to increase its accounting personnel. Part-time bookkeeping help may be sought or perhaps the firm may turn to an outside bookkeeping firm to help in the everyday routine. The result is that many construction firms go through a period in which they are in danger of losing control of their financial operations.

As the firm grows in size (with or without a growth in its accounting personnel), it is likely to be confronted with a need for financing or bonding. It is at this time that the firm may be called on to seek a certified public accountant (CPA) to assist in the preparation of reports. The result is audited or unaudited statements. The traditional role of the outside auditing firm regarding the construction firm has been one of performing the financial audit and furnishing tax services.

Recent years have seen public accounting firms extend their traditional audit and tax services to include management advisory services (MAS). The MAS services include designing cost and control systems, forecasting financial results, analyzing a firm's financial position, and aiding other management decisions such as the selection of computer systems. Clearly it is difficult for any one accounting firm to have expertise in MAS as it relates to each and every type of business. The result is that, if the construction firm is to receive the MAS fringe benefits, it should be selective in its choice of accounting firms.

Another aspect of construction firm accounting is that more and more often the firm hires one of its auditing firm's members as its own in-house accountant or controller. This is a natural occurrence in that the auditing firm is likely to cite the need for such an individual and the construction firm, by seeking one of the auditing firm's employees, takes on an individual acquainted with the firm and its set of books.

The controller becomes the financial officer of the firm, and the position is a key one within the firm. Included within the duties of the controller are the normal reporting and interpreting of data, tax administration, economic appraisals, and the overall protection of assets. In many firms the list of duties is extended to overlap with marketing and production-oriented decisions. Given the numerous responsibilities that can be assigned to the controller, the controller's existence is soon justified.

Upon hiring a controller or full-time accountant, the construction firm has not eliminated its need for the outside public accounting firm. The controller is not viewed as an independent party. Thus external parties such as banks will require the construction firm to utilize independent, external auditing personnel such that they can place confidence in the validity of the financial statements. However, a good controller can minimize required auditing time through effective internal-control practices and is free to perform many of the MAS services that are offered for fee by the external accounting firm. As the construction firm grows in size, the internal accounting functions increase. Departmentalization starts to occur with certain individuals assigned the payroll functions, others the payables and receivables, and still others the job-costing function. This specialization by individuals is only feasible for the larger of the construction firms.

DISCIPLINES OF CONSTRUCTION ACCOUNTING

Too often accounting is viewed as being limited to a bookkeeping type of function. This stereotyped view is no doubt due in great part to the number-gathering activities related to generating a payroll and keeping track of accounts receivable and accounts payable. While it is true that accounting includes these necessary bookkeeping-related roles, practical applications of accounting can be traced to many financially-oriented management functions. These applications may be grouped into one of the following disciplines:

1. Financial accounting
2. Managerial accounting or management services
3. Auditing
4. Tax

Financial Accounting

Financial accounting's objective is, in great part, preparing financial statements. These include the income statement and the statement of financial position. Additionally, other financial statements such as a statement of changes in financial position and a statement of work in progress may be prepared on a regular basis.

Financial statements are prepared to satisfy the needs of parties external to the construction firm as well as to serve the needs of the firm's owners. Among the external parties that may require financial data regarding the construction firm are the following:

1. Lenders
2. Sureties
3. Public agencies
4. Clients
5. Suppliers
6. Employees

Of the external parties listed, lenders and sureties are the most common users of the construction firm's financial statements. The construction firm is often very dependent on lending institutions for capital needed to run or expand its business. The financial institutions that lend money are very interested in such factors as the ability of the construction firm to manage, the firm's ability to meet its financial obligations, and the firm's prospects for future profits. The construction firm's financial statments are an important source of information in this regard. Financial institutions also rely on outside sources of information such as the construction firm's past payment of payables record and the overall reputation of the firm.

The construction firm is also very dependent on the surety company which provides the construction firm with needed bonds such as a bid bond or a performance-and-labor bond. To limit their potential liability on a project, potential project owners will often require the prospective contractor to provide these bonds as part of their bid package proposal. Should the construction firm be financially unable to perform its contracted work, the bonding company becomes liable for the work to the project owner. As such the bonding company will probably analyze the construction firm's financial statements before supplying the firm a bond. Because of the high risk nature of contracting, bonds have become increasingly difficult to obtain. Sound financial data and statements can aid in obtaining bonds. In effect, they dictate the amount and type of work the construction firm can perform.

Federal, state, and local governments also require various types of information from the construction firm. The Internal Revenue Service requires information concerning the construction firm's profits, the amount of taxes that the firm owes to the government, and information about the amount of employee taxes withheld. The Social Security Administration requires information concerning the amount of wages earned from the construction firm and the amount of social security taxes withheld. State and local governments may require that sales tax forms be submitted. Other types of reporting may be required from specific states.

The client of the construction firm may also require accounting data from the firm. The accounting data to be submitted to the project owner include billing data, accounts receivable data, and progress reports. A sound bookkeeping system is essential to furnish the owner accurate and acceptable data.

The construction firm purchases a great deal of materials and an inventory of raw materials from a variety of suppliers. If the construction firm makes its purchases on credit, the suppliers usually require information regarding the firm's credit standing and ability to pay. The supplier may obtain such information from external sources such as credit rating agencies. Additionally, it may request accounting information from the construction firm itself.

The construction firm will most likely have to furnish the supplier with accounting data in its routine transactions with the supplier. These include purchase order information which indicates the items and quantities. Additionally, the supplier sends invoices to the construction firm. These invoices become part of the accounts payable accounting data of the construction firm.

The employees of the construction firm are also interested in certain of the firm's accounting data. Labor unions often represent the employees as a group in obtaining the information. Data required include wage levels, fringe benefits, and nonfinancial information such as levels of employment.

Independently of labor unions, employees expect periodic receipt of wage information with detailed data concerning deductions for income taxes, social security, insurance, and union dues. The accounting information system is responsible for providing this routine data.

Other parties external to the construction firm may also request financial data of the firm. Among these are agencies such as Dun & Bradstreet, industry and trade associations, and financial analysts or accountants representing a firm considering a joint venture or merger with the construction firm.

The owners of the construction firm should be vitally interested in financial accounting data. These data provide the means of evaluating the owners' efforts. In addition, the financial data should serve as the basis for the daily and long-term decisions of the firm. Equipment purchase decisions and growth-related decisions are examples of just a few of the many decisions that should be in part based on past financial accounting data.

Financial accounting consists of performing several accounting practices and procedures. Perhaps most fundamental to financial accounting is bookkeeping, which includes payroll, accounts receivable, accounts payable, and general ledger accounting. In order to perform bookkeeping-related functions efficiently, it is necessary to understand fundamental accounting transactions. These include the recognition and appropriate recording of entries for revenue and expense accounts.

The financial accounting function or discipline has as its objective completed financial statements. The form of these financial statements, while somewhat variable in appearance, is structured in part by industry and accepted accounting practices.

Related to the preparation of financial statements is analysis of the firm's financial structure and strength based on the financial statements. This analysis is often done through financial ratio analysis.

Fundamental accounting transaction treatment, bookkeeping, and the preparation of construction firm financial statements are covered in Chapters 2 through 6; financial analysis of the firm based on these statements is discussed in Chapters 7 and 8.

Managerial Accounting or Management Services

The broad nature of accounting for the construction firm is very apparent when one considers the wide-reaching applications of managerial accounting or management services. The management services discipline means different things to different individuals. To some, managerial accounting or management services means only designing and implementing an accounting system to support financial accounting and its objectives. However, to many others the discipline of management services infers much more than accounting systems.

Accounting systems design goes further than the formal "setting up" of the books and accounting cycle for it should recognize its impact on personnel management, planning and scheduling potential, project and company cost, and quality control. If designed properly, the accounting information system can service almost every financial consideration of the firm and have an effect on some considerations that are not normally recognized as being purely financial.

Analyzing the construction firm's cash flow may be considered another application of managerial accounting or management services. Working capital including cash is considered a liquid asset. Too much working capital may often imply a less than desirable rate of return on the firm's assets or equity. The opposite extreme is more typical of the construction firm; that is, the construction firm is characterized by less than adequate working capital. This, coupled with dramatically varying demands for their assets, leads to the inability to meet project and operating cash demands. The ability to identify availability and demand for working capital to include cash is dependent on timely and accurate accounting. Timely reporting is especially important because of the extreme sensitivity of cash-flow demands as a function of time.

Other applicable areas of accounting that may be regarded as part of managerial accounting or management services include determining optimal equipment purchasing and replacing, economical purchasing and controlling of materials, and determining break-even levels of volume and overhead application rates. These applications, along with others, are discussed in Chapters 9 through 13.

Auditing

The construction firm's main reason for hiring a certified public accountant (CPA) revolves around the firm's need for a financial audit. Potential creditors often require the construction firm to have an audit of their books performed as a requirement for extending the firm's credit. Sureties also may request such an audit. Additionally, potential project owners may require audited financial statements from the owner of the construction firm desiring work. This is especially true of public project owners. For example, in order to be eligible for projects over which the Capital Development Board in the state of Illinois has jurisdiction (that is, almost all public construction excluding highway work), the construction firm may have to submit audited financial statements to the board.

When the construction firm holds itself out for an audit, its objective is to obtain a financial clean bill of health. This clean bill of health is in the form of an "unqualified" opinion from the CPA. On the other hand, should the accounting records be in a state of disarray, or if there is evidence of fraud, the construction firm will receive something less than an unqualified opinion. In particular, the CPA will give a qualified opinion (i.e., a "subject to" or "except for") or refrain from giving an opinion. These types of opinions are looked upon unfavorably by external parties.

The fee the construction firm pays for its audit depends on the size of the firm, the detailedness and controls in its accounting records, and the reputation and qualifications of its public accounting firm. The CPA is refrained from performing an audit for a fee that is contingent upon his findings. Rather, the CPA is normally hired on an hourly basis. The CPA will have to perform certain traditional audit procedures (called an audit program) to be satisfied of the validity of the construction firm's financial records. These audit procedures are discussed in Chapter 14.

The construction firm's own internal audit practices can reduce required external CPA audit time. Even if an external audit is not necessary, the internal audit has significant merit. It can expose fraud, cite financial inefficiencies, and aid in evaluating management. Procedures for internal auditing are discussed in Chapter 15.

Tax

Associated with making a profit is the payment of taxes. However, it does not follow that the more profitable or successful firm pays a proportionate increase in taxes. In fact, as is widely publicized, some firms that earn substantial profits may have no tax liability. Perhaps more than in any one industry, the construction firm has substantial tax planning alternatives available to it. Many contracting firms are closely held companies—type of firms that can usually take greatest advantage of tax planning. Additionally, because of the uniqueness of its product, the construction firm has numerous alternative accounting methods available to it. Many of the choices the firm makes can have significant immediate and long-term bearings on the tax liability and reportable income of the firm.

The difference between a firm having a high or small tax liability may in great part depend on its tax planning. There is nothing illegal or unethical associated with a firm attempting to minimize its tax liability as long as it uses acceptable methods. It is the firm that is ignorant of tax planning that is in effect penalized. Clearly the government rewards the firm that practices sound and acceptable accounting to support the use of favorable tax methods.

The income tax formulas and tax rates differ for a proprietorship and a corporation. There are additional differences when one considers the subchapter S corporation which is a modification of the corporate legal structure. Even within a single classification such as the corporate form, the actual tax liability of the firm may be affected by specific provisions. For example, the manner in which profits are distributed and the details of a firm's profit sharing or pension program can play a significant role in determining the tax liability of the firm and its owners.

Another example of the alternative accounting methods that may be used as part of tax planning is the treatment of revenue recognition. Most industries are limited to using a cash or accrual method (or some modification of these methods) of accounting for revenue recognition. Because of the long-term nature of the construction project and the uncertainty of profit or loss, the construction firm can recognize revenue on long-term projects utilizing the percentage-of-completion or completed-contract method of accounting. These methods along with other tax planning practices are discussed in Chapter 17.

Tax planning is not limited to choosing a method or methods for legal structure or recognizing revenue. The choice of accounting method for valuing inventory and depreciating equipment affects a firm's tax liability as well as operating results. Equally important as the choice of accounting methods as to the tax liability and operating results is the firm's pension and estate planning programs. Numerous programs, including the use of profit sharing, annuities, and stock option plans, can serve as a tool for personnel management as well as limiting tax liability and providing for the long-term goals of the owners of the firm. A well thought out tax plan is essential to maximizing the firm's monetary returns for its investment of capital and time.

FOLLOWING CHAPTERS

The remaining chapters in this book are grouped according to the four defined disciplines of accounting as they relate to the construction firm. Financial accounting-related information and practices are presented in Chapters 2 through 8. These are followed by chapters that relate to managerial accounting. Chapters 14 and 15 discuss external and internal auditing of the construction firm. Finally, Chapters 16 through 18 discuss various tax planning topics as they relate to the construction firm.

Part 2
FINANCIAL ACCOUNTING

CHAPTERS

2
RECOGNIZING ACCOUNTING TRANSACTIONS

INTRODUCTION

The recognition of financial transactions is fundamental to the practice of accounting. Every construction firm engages in financial transactions daily: it makes sales, purchases material, pays employees, borrows money, and buys or leases equipment. A *financial transaction* can be thought of as a financial event that results in changes to the firm's financial structure. In turn, the financial structure is characterized by its assets, liabilities, equity, revenues, and expenses. These terms will be described later in this chapter.

Each financial transaction is either external or internal to the construction firm. Examples of external financial transactions include purchasing concrete from a vendor, paying a craftsman's wages, and purchasing a crane. Recognition of depreciation as an expense of owning construction equipment is an example of a financial transaction internal to the firm.

Regardless of whether it is external or internal, each and every financial transaction is recognized in a firm's accounting system. The number and type of transactions that occur are dependent on many factors, including the size of the firm, the type of work it performs, and its legal and financial structure. Typical financial transactions and their accounting treatments are illustrated in this chapter.

FACTORS AFFECTING FINANCIAL TRANSACTION TREATMENT

The treatment of a specific financial transaction in the accounting system is in part the result of several widely recognized generally accepted accounting principles. These principles have been issued by the American Institute of Certified Public Accountants (AICPA).

The *cost principle* indicates that cost is to be the measure of value assigned to the financial transaction. The construction firm, even if it has purchased material or equipment at a bargain price, must recognize the transaction at cost. This removes subjective treatment by different firms. However, the cost principle may also result in a conservative recognition of a transaction's value and, in turn, a conservative view of the firm itself.

The *revenue principle* indicates when a transaction is to be recognized. It establishes different alternatives as to time of recognition. Included in these are the sales basis, the cash basis, the accrual basis, and the production basis. Each method can result in a transaction entering the accounting process at a different point in time. Whatever alternative is used, the *consistency principle* requires that the chosen method be applied the same at all times.

The *matching principle* emphasizes that financial transactions should be recognized in a manner that matches expenses with like revenues. Therefore, when feasible, expenses that are incurred in producing a product that yields revenue should be "matched" to the revenue in the period the revenue is earned.

These four accounting principles, along with others, are very pragmatic and must be applied to diverse sets of facts and conditions. In view of these considerations, some exceptions are to be expected. These are part of the exception principle. The *exception principle* is especially relevant to the construction industry in view of the industry's unique considerations. An example of the application of the exception principle is the construction industry's use of the long-term revenue recognition methods, which include the percentage of completion method.

THE BASIC ACCOUNTING RELATIONSHIP

An understanding of the accounting process and financial transactions will be achieved if the following basic relationship is kept in mind:

$$\text{assets} = \text{liabilities} + \text{net worth} + \text{revenue} - \text{expense}$$

This equality not only prevails at the end of an accounting period, it prevails continuously. After each financial transaction, the five accounting categories—assets, liabilities, net worth, revenue, and expense—must be related using the above equality.

A company's assets may be viewed as all the things that add to the company's value. The liabilities of a company refer to its debts, or all the things it owes. The net worth, sometimes referred to as equity, is the amount of money invested in the firm and the profits retained.

Information regarding the construction firm's assets, liabilities, and net worth is presented in the firm's balance sheet (also referred to as its statement of financial position), which represents the firm's condition at a given date.

Revenue represents the amount of money taken in by the company. An expense is the money spent for things that do not add directly to the company's assets. For example, payment of a utility bill would be an expense as it does not add directly to the company's assets.

Information regarding the construction firm's revenues and expenses is presented in the firm's profit and loss statement (also referred to as its income statement). This statement illustrates whether the company derives a profit or incurs a loss for a specified period of time.

Let us illustrate the equality of assets, liabilities, net worth, revenue, and expense in terms of a particular construction firm. Let us assume we invest $40,000 in the formation of a construction company. We have then created assets of $40,000 in the company. The accounting equality is as follows:

assets = net worth

$40,000 = $40,000

Let us now assume that we buy $30,000 worth of new construction equipment for our company. Rather than pay cash for the equipment, we buy it on credit. We have now increased the assets of our company by $30,000. However, we have created a company liability of $30,000 (we eventually will have to pay for the equipment). The accounting equality is as follows:

assets = liabilities + net worth

$70,000 = $30,000 + $40,000

Let us assume that our newly formed construction company receives a contract for building a construction project. While building the project we have to pay our employees. Let us assume that at the end of a particular week we pay them a total of $3,000. Let us assume that we pay them cash, reducing our company assets by $3,000. We have incurred an expense of $3,000 which has not directly increased our company's assets. The accounting equality is as follows:

assets = liabilities + net worth − expense

$67,000 = $30,000 + $40,000 − $3,000

At the end of the month, the project owner pays us $4,000 for the work we have completed. This $4,000 worth of cash increases our company's assets by $4,000. Likewise, we have had a company revenue of $4,000. The accounting equality now becomes the following:

assets = liabilities + net worth + revenue − expense

$71,000 = $30,000 + $40,000 + $4,000 − $3,000

Obviously a real company would have many more entries during its operation. Each entry would affect the accounting system. However, at all times the relationship would be an equality.

DEBITS AND CREDITS

Accounting practice is to identify each element of the financial transaction as a *debit* or *credit* to the accounting equality. Each term of the accounting equality, including assets, liabilities, net worth, revenue, and expense, is divided into debits and credits.

The reader should be cautioned against attempting to relate any real significance to the words "debit" and "credit." Their significance is limited to the accounting process. There are two fundamental definitions that are part of recognizing financial transactions in the accounting equality: (1) an entry that increases the assets of the company is defined as a debit and is assigned a positive value; and (2) for every debit entry in the accounting equality, there must also be a corresponding credit entry.

As previously stated, the accounting equality, relating a company's assets, liabilities, net worth, revenue, and expenses, must balance after every financial entry. As defined, an asset debit is positive. For the relationship to remain an equality, and for consistency with the asset debit definition and an "equal debit-equal credit" definition, a debit is considered negative and a credit is considered positive if the entry is a liability, a net worth, or revenue. If an entry is an expense, it is positive if it is a debit and negative if it is a credit. Similarly, an asset credit is negative. The described convention of assigning positive or negative values to the various debits and credits in the accounting equality is summarized in Figure 2.1.

Assets		=	Liabilities		+	Net Worth		+	Revenue		−	Expense	
Debit	Credit		Debit	Credit		Debit	Credit		Debit	Credit		Debit	Credit
+	−		−	+		−	+		−	+		+	−

Figure 2.1 Financial Structure of Accounting

Having included debits and credits in the accounting equality, let us now view the equality with respect to the formation of our previously discussed construction company. Originally we invested $40,000 in the formation of the company. The $40,000 increased our company's assets. Thus, the $40,000 is entered as a debit in the asset term of the accounting equality. We, as the investors, have created a net worth of $40,000. Consistent with the accounting model definitions, this becomes a credit entry in the net worth term of the accounting model. The accounting equality is as follows:

assets		=	net worth	
debit (+)	credit (−)		debit (−)	credit (+)
$40,000				$40,000

Having created the company, we purchased on credit $30,000 worth of new construction equipment. The new construction equipment increased our assets by $30,000. Thus, it is entered as a debit in the asset term of the accounting equality. The $30,000 we owe to the seller of the equipment is a liability. Since the equipment was assigned to "debit" in the asset term of the accounting equality, the newly created liability is a credit. The accounting equality is now as follows:

assets		=	liabilities		+	net worth	
debit (+)	credit (−)		debit (−)	credit (+)		debit (−)	credit (+)
$40,000 30,000				$30,000			$40,000

We then performed part of the work on a construction project and paid our workers a sum of $3,000. The payment of the $3,000 decreased our cash and, therefore, our assets. Thus the $3,000 is a credit in the asset term of the accounting equality. The $3,000 was a project expense. Consistent with the fact that the $3,000 was a credit in the asset term of the accounting equality, it is a debit in the expense term. The accounting equality is now as follows:

assets		=	liabilities		+	net worth		−	expenses	
D(+)	C(−)		D(−)	C(+)		D(−)	C(+)		D(+)	C(−)
$40,000 30,000	$3,000			$30,000			$40,000		$3,000	

Finally, we received $4,000 revenue from the construction project owner. The $4,000 increased our company assets by $4,000. Thus, it is a debit. Similarly, the $4,000 is identified as revenue since it was received as a result of our project performance. Because the $4,000 was an asset debit, it is a credit in the revenue term of the accounting equality. The accounting equality is now complete and is as follows:

assets		=	liabilities		+	net worth		+	revenue		−	expenses	
D(+)	C(−)		D(−)	C(+)		D(−)	C(+)		D(−)	C(+)		D(+)	C(−)
$40,000 30,000 4,000	$3,000			$30,000			$40,000			$4,000		$3,000	

Other financial transactions could be entered into the accounting equality. In actuality, the construction firm does not enter its transactions into the described accounting equality as presented. The accounting entries are made in journals. However, these journals and supporting ledgers are based on the described accounting equality.

TYPICAL CONSTRUCTION FINANCIAL TRANSACTIONS

The construction firm engages in many types of financial transactions. Although the type and size of the construction firm plays an important role in characterizing the number and types of transactions, even the relatively small-sized general construction firm takes part in many daily transactions. Material purchasing, labor payment, equipment purchasing, and billings to owners necessitate numerous transactions.

The complexity of discussing typical construction industry financial transactions is increased by the fact that the firm may recognize transactions using numerous variations of alternative, accepted accounting methods. However, basically, the firm may use either a cash method or an accrual method.

Many financial transactions would be recognized by the construction firm at the same point in time and in the same manner regardless of whether the cash or accrual accounting method were used. In particular, any transaction that does not involve a prepaid or accrued item would be handled identically in the cash or accrual methods. As a means of illustrating typical construction firm transactions and of differentiating between the cash and accrual methods, let us consider typical transactions that are part of the everyday business of the construction firm.

Initial Investment

Every construction firm starts with an initial investment of monetary and nonmonetary assets by investors or owners of the firm. Although this initial investment may be very simple as to the accounting recognition (for example, the initial investment of $5,000 by a single investor in his own construction company), the initial transaction may also be very complex. For example, complex partnership investments and corporation stock issues may require several accounting journal entries. However, these complex investment structures are rare in the construction industry and are therefore not discussed in this book.

A large percentage of small construction firms originate with the single investment by one or two individuals in the firm. This investment may be cash, equipment, by cash and equipment. The cash and equipment are considered assets of the newly created firm and the investment is recognized by creating a contributed capital investment account. For example, let us assume that Andy Jackson invests his life savings of $10,000 and his pickup truck in a newly created construction firm. Assuming the truck has a fair market value of $5,000 for an estimated remaining life of five years and is to be depreciated using the straight-line method, the initial accounting entry would be recorded as follows:

Cash	$10,000	
Truck (5-year life, straight-line)	5,000	
Andy Jackson, proprietor		$15,000

It should be noted that the debit entries (those listed first) are equal in amount to the credit entry. Andy Jackson's contributed capital account (referred to as his equity or capital account) is increased when he makes another investment or may be decreased if he decides to make a withdrawal of the invested capital.

Let us assume that instead of Andy Jackson's sole investment, he joins forces with his friend Steve Janko in forming a partnership to start a small construction firm. Andy Jackson's initial contribution is still $10,000 cash and $5,000 for his fair market value truck. Steve Janko's investment is $5,000 cash. Assuming Jackson and Janko are to be credited for their investments, the initial accounting entry would be as follows:

Cash	$15,000	
Truck (5-year life, straight-line)	5,000	
Andy Jackson		$15,000
Steve Janko		5,000

As an alternative to the described partnership agreement, let us assume that Steve Janko has a college education as an engineer and, as such, negotiates with Jackson to own a share of the business that is larger than his contribution. In particular, let us assume that the partnership agreement is such that Janko is to be credited with 50 percent of the firm's contributed capital.

It should be noted that Janko only invests 25 percent of the cash and equipment assets. How then is the accounting entry to be made to recognize a 50 percent ownership? This may be done by one of two alternative accounting entries. For one, the entry may be made using the bonus method: Jackson's capital account is reduced and the amount of reduction is added to Janko's account. The total capital remains unchanged, that is, $20,000.

If Janko is to be credited for 50 percent of the total capital, his final capital account balance should be $10,000. However, he only contributed $5,000. As such, Jackson in effect gives up $5,000 of his investment and transfers it to Janko. The entry would be made as follows:

Cash	$15,000	
Truck (5-year life, straight-line)	5,000	
Andy Jackson		$10,000
Steve Janko		10,000

Had Janko contributed more than 50 percent of the total capital and was to be credited for 50 percent, Jackson, instead of Janko, would receive the bonus.

Instead of Jackson offering Janko a bonus, let us assume that in their agreement they decide that Janko's education is an asset to the firm and they want to treat it as such. This is done by the recognition of goodwill. In the goodwill method, an asset account labeled "goodwill" is debited for the value assigned to Janko's education. In the example in question, the dollar amount of goodwill to be recognized is determined by the fact that Janko's total capital account is to be 50 percent of the total capital. Jackson's capital account remains unaffected at $15,000. Thus, if Janko is to be credited with an equal amount, goodwill recognized must equal $10,000 and Janko's capital account increased $10,000. The entry follows:

Cash	$15,000	
Truck (5-year life, straight-line)	5,000	
Goodwill	10,000	
Andy Jackson		$15,000
Steve Janko		15,000

Unlike cash, which is considered a current asset, and the truck, which is considered a fixed asset, the goodwill is an intangible asset. Such an asset has no physical value, but adds to the earning potential of the firm. Other types of intangible assets include patents and copyrights. Similar to fixed assets, intangible assets are not to remain indefinitely on the firm's financial statements. In particular, intangible assets are to be amortized (part of the value written off as an expense each accounting period). Goodwill is to be written off by consistent charges to an expense account over a period of forty years or less. It should also be noted that the goodwill method illustrated for initial company organization is somewhat inconsistent with the latest published AICPA (American Institute of Certified Public Accountants) opinions. One of the recent opinions states that goodwill should be recognized only when it is purchased. For example, goodwill can be recognized when a firm pays more than the fair market value for the assets of another firm. Assigning goodwill to the "purchase" of an individual's skills is a questionable point. In general, the skills of employees and owners of a firm are not recognized as assets by a firm. For example, a construction firm with well-trained and experienced management certainly has an "asset" in that they add "value" to the firm. However, current accounting practice has not accepted human resource accounting.

The initial entry necessary to recognize the formation of a corporation varies somewhat depending on the complexity and number of shareholders. Generally, common stock is issued for the starting of a corporation. The common stock may be par-value or no par-value stock. Par-value stock has a designated dollar "value" associated with it. Normally the par value is low and the dollar amount received for the stock exceeds the stated par value. The amount received in excess of the par value is referred to as *premium-on-capital stock* and is recognized separately from the dollar amount of the par value of the stock. Even if stock is no par-value stock, it is normally assigned a stated value. As such, it differs little from par-value stock. The par value of stated value of stock has little significance other than it is accounted for separately in the accounting process and some state statutes require a firm to retain the dollar amount of the par-value or stated-value stock. That is, the firm is prohibited from using this dollar amount for paying dividends or buying back issued shares of stock. This dollar amount of required capital to be retained is referred to as legal capital.

A typical corporation stock issuance is recognized as follows:

Cash	$25,000	
Common stock (10,000 shares at $2 par value)		$20,000
Premium on common stock		5,000

Most state statutes prohibit the issuance of stock at less than par value (that is, at a discount).

Debt Capital

Not every construction firm obtains monetary and nonmonetary assets by means of contributed capital. The amount of assets required to start a sizeable firm may exceed the amount of available contributed capital from owners of the firm. Even when equity capital can be obtained, the firm may choose to obtain some of its required assets by means of taking on debt. Such a practice can lead to favorable leverage, that is, higher earnings to investment can be obtained.

Purchasing assets on credit, signing a note payable, financing equipment through a lease (discussed in a following section), and issuing bonds are all examples of obtaining assets by means of debt capital. Issuing bonds as a means of obtaining debt capital is not a common construction industry practice in that this form of raising debt capital is generally available only to large firms. Regardless of whether the construction firm is a proprietorship, a partnership, or a corporation, the required accounting entries for debt capital transactions are the same. Legal and tax differences of a proprietorship, partnership, and corporation are discussed in Chapter 16.

Obtaining debt capital creates a liability to the firm in that the capital has to be repaid (usually with an interest cost) to the lender. Liabilities are normally classified as current or long-term. The AICPA defines a current liability as designating an obligation whose liquidation is reasonably expected to require the use of existing resources properly classified as current assets or the creation of other current liabilities. Perhaps more simply stated, liabilities are debts the firm expects to repay within its operating cycle, which normally can be taken as one year. Typical current liabilities are:

1. Accounts payable
2. Short-term notes payable
3. Advances held as returnable deposits
4. Taxes
5. Bonus obligations

Most current liabilities are not normally recognized in a cash accounting method. As such, typical journal entries are absent in accounting for current liabilities when using the cash method.

The most commonly recognized liability for the construction firm is the purchase of material or supplies on credit. Assuming a purchase of $1,000 of materials or supplies for a given construction firm's inventory, the accounting entry would be as follows:

Materials—inventory	$1,000	
Accounts payable		$1,000

The recognition of short-term notes, advances, taxes, or bonus obligations as a liability would result in an entry similar to the one above.

Because issuing bonds is not a common occurrence for the smaller or middle-sized construction firm, only basic entries for this issuance are discussed. Let us assume that, in order to expand its operations, a relatively large construction firm decides to issue $100,000 in bonds payable in ten years with an annual interest rate of 5 percent. In other words, the construction firm is willing to pay the purchasers of the bonds $5,000 interest each year and repay the $100,000 face value of the bonds after ten years. Assuming that the firm was successful in selling the bonds for exactly $100,000, the accounting journal entry necessary in the construction firm's books would be as follows:

Cash	$100,000	
Bonds payable		$100,000

The annual interest expense to the construction firm would be recognized by the following entry:

Bond interest expense	$5,000	
Cash		$5,000

The above entries assume that the firm would receive exactly $100,000 for the $100,000 face-value bonds. More likely than not, the firm would receive something less or more than the $100,000. If the firm's financial status were sound and the current interest rate for marketable securities were lower than 5 percent, the bond investor would probably be willing to pay more than $100,000 for the bonds. For example, the construction firm might receive $105,000. The $5,000 is referred to as a premium on the bonds. The fact that the bonds sell at a price greater than the face value results in an effective interest rate (referred to as the yield) less than the stated face-value interest rate.

More likely than not, the construction firm will receive less than the expected $100,000, assuming that the 5 percent is the current marketable interest rate. This is because the typical investor views the construction industry as a financially risky investment. Unfortunately, statistics prove the investor correct.

Let us assume that the construction firm receives $95,000 from the issuance of the 5 percent $100,000 bonds. The $5,000 shortage is referred to as a discount on bonds. In effect, the firm is paying a higher interest rate than 5 percent in that it only receives $95,000 instead of $100,000. This higher interest rate can be calculated using yield tables.

Let us arrange this latter transaction in the required journal entries. The issuance of the bonds would be recorded as follows:

Cash	$95,000	
Discount on bonds payable	5,000	
Bonds payable		$100,000

The bond discount account would be amortized along with the annual interest expense journal entry. Assuming a ten-year period of amortization, this would be as follows:

Bond interest expense	$5,500	
Cash		$5,000
Discount on bonds payable		500

In effect, the annual interest expense is increased $500. The above entry has been made assuming straight line amortization of the discount. The accounting entries required for handling the premium on bonds would be similar to those made for the discount on bonds.

Accounting for Cash

Cash is considered a current asset in that a firm will use the cash throughout its operating cycle. Normally, cash is made available to the firm from initial investment (equity investment or from creditors of debt), or from the income from operations. Less frequent in occurrence is obtaining cash from selling one's assets or from selling a portion of the business. Cash obtained as interest from temporary investment of cash (for example, savings accounts, short-term securities, and so on) is debited along with a credit to interest income.

Accounting for cash normally presents little difficulty. There are no estimates required or valuation problems in that the accounting unit of measure is expressed in the monetary unit. The main difficulty in accounting for cash is to provide a means of controlling cash receipts, payments, and petty cash.

The numerous daily cash transactions that are part of running a construction firm and construction project necessitate the existence of one or more petty cash funds. Items such as small hand tools, paper cups, refreshments, and miscellaneous supplies may be purchased from cash in the petty cash fund. Because of the availability of the cash in this type of fund, there has to be concern in regard to controlling cash payments from it.

Two different systems can be used to control a petty cash fund. One system is referred to as a fluctuating-fund system. The initial accounting entry is the same for each of the petty cash systems. Let us assume a firm creates a $500 petty cash fund. The initial accounting entry is as follows:

Petty cash	$500	
Cash		$500

The petty cash account, like the cash account, is considered an asset to the firm. This transaction merely transfers funds from "normal" cash to petty cash.

Accounting control and entries for transactions after the initial transaction vary depending on the system used. Generally, when a fluctuating system is used, an individual in control of the fund is required to maintain a petty cash book. Disbursements are entered in a book that is used as a basic record when the fund is replenished. As disbursements are made, an expense account is debited and the petty cash fund is credited. For example, let us assume that a few small tools costing $40 are purchased from the petty cash account. The accounting entry would be as follows:

Small tools expense	$40	
Petty cash		$40

After a period of time the petty cash fund is replenished by a debit to petty cash and a credit to cash. However, this additional cash is not necessarily equal to the cash disbursements made. It is evident that, when using this approach, the balance in the petty cash account fluctuates.

The nonfluctuation, or imprest, petty cash system is normally preferred in that it is easier to audit than the fluctuating system. Using the imprest system, disbursements are made from the petty cash fund and recorded and summarized in a petty cash book. No accounting debit or credit is made to adjust the initial petty cash entry unless it is desired to increase or decrease the fund. Instead, after the petty cash book is summarized, a check is drawn to the petty cash fund for the exact amount of the expenses. A journal entry is made that debits the appropriate expense accounts and credits cash. For example, let us assume that, during a given time period, the only disbursement from the petty cash fund was the previously described $40 small tools expense. Using the imprest-fund system, the required accounting entry would be as follows:

Small tools expense	$40	
Cash		$40

Other petty cash disbursements would be handled in a similar manner. As can be observed, the petty cash fund does not fluctuate.

Regardless of whether the fluctuating or imprest system is used, the firm should immediately investigate any abnormal overages or shortages. Unfortunately, overages can usually be explained whereas shortages may be difficult to pinpoint and correct. Overages or shortages may be identified by means of a bank reconciliation of cash.

Accounting for Fixed Assets

The typical construction firm has a substantial share of its contributed capital and debt capital invested in fixed assets. Fixed assets are properties and rights that the business retains more or less permanently to use in performing its production operation. Fixed assets such as plant (office buildings, furniture, etc.) and equipment may make up a large percentage of some construction firm's assets. Construction equipment in particular plays an important role in the production process performed by the typical construction company. Earthmovers, cranes, reuseable forms, trucks, and mortar-mixing equipment are just a few of the types of equipment used by the construction firm. Construction equipment is usually recognized by three different classifications: (1) heavy equipment, (2) miscellaneous tools and equipment, and (3) trucks and autos. The large dollar value associated with such equipment has an important impact on the firm's financial statements. The importance of accounting for equipment in the construction industry is evidenced by the fact that the AICPA has published part of an audit guide on the subject matter.

The construction firm normally has several options available to it in regard to the use of construction equipment. It may choose to purchase a piece of equipment, or, as an alternative to purchasing a piece of equipment, the firm may choose to rent or lease it. Several different types of lease agreements may be arranged each of which requires different accounting treatment and each of which has a different impact on the firm's financial statements.

Let us assume a construction firm purchases a piece of equipment. The equipment should be recorded at an asset value equivalent to purchase cost plus any shipment or installation costs. Available discounts, whether taken or not, should be deducted from the equipment's invoice cost. For example, let us assume a firm purchases a $40,000 crane and the manufacturer charges an additional $200 for transporting the equipment. The agreement with the construction firm indicates it will receive a 5 percent discount on the $40,000 if cash is paid when the crane is delivered. However, the construction firm only pays $10,000 upon delivery with the balance due covered by a note payable which is given to the equipment dealer. The journal entry required to recognize the purchase of the crane is as follows:

Equipment—crane	$38,200	
Allowance for discount	2,000	
Cash		$10,000
Note payable (8% annual interest)		30,200

Thus, the crane is capitalized at $38,200. It should be observed that the potential $2,000 discount has been deducted from the $40,000 invoice cost. The lost discount would be recognized as an expense to the construction firm. The journal entry necessary to recognize the expense is as follows:

Discount lost expense	$2,000	
Allowance for discount		$2,000

Occasionally a construction firm will purchase a major piece of equipment on a deferred payment plan. For example, the firm may need to make three annual end-of-year payments of $37,410 in a purchase agreement for a large earth-moving scraper. During this time the going interest rate was 6 percent. To record the scraper at $112,230 (that is, $37,410 × 3) would include in the fixed asset account the interest cost implicit in the contract. Instead, the scraper purchased on a deferred payment plan should be recorded at the equivalent cash price excluding all interest and implicit interest. The interest should be charged to expense and not capitalized as part of the asset.

In order to determine the value at which the asset purchased on a deferred payment plan should be recorded, the present worth of the annual payments has to be determined. The existing interest during the period in which the payments are to be made should be used in determining the present value. For example, for the scraper that was purchased by means of three annual $37,410 end-of-year payments, a 6 percent interest rate yields a present value of $100,000. It is this value at which the scraper should be recorded. The annual interest expense is calculated as 6 percent times the outstanding principle balance to be paid.

Rather than purchase a piece of construction equipment outright, the firm may purchase a piece of equipment by "trading in" an old piece of equipment as part payment for the new equipment. The accounting cost principle requires that the new equipment be valued (i.e., capitalized) as the sum of the fair market value of the old equipment traded in plus any cash given to the seller. Any difference between the book value of the old equipment and its par market value at the date of exchange should be recognized as a loss or gain on the disposition of the equipment.

Let us assume a construction firm trades in an old truck for a new one. The old truck's original cost was $20,000; depreciation to date on the truck is $15,000 (leaving a book value of $5,000). The new truck had a selling price of $25,000. The construction firm traded the old truck and $17,000 cash for the new truck. Since the firm paid $8,000 less cash than the selling price of the new truck, one can assume that the old truck had a fair market value of $8,000. As such, the accounting entry is made as follows:

Truck—new ($17,000 + $8,000)	$25,000
Accumulated depreciation—old truck	15,000

Cash		$17,000
Truck—old		20,000
Gain on exchange of trucks		3,000

The $3,000 gain is reported on the firm's income statement. Any loss on a similar exchange would be handled in a similar manner. The debit to "accumulated depreciation" is required to offset earlier credits to this account. Depreciation accounting entries are discussed in Chapter 18.

It should be noted that the tax law does not recognize a gain or loss when similar assets are exchanged. The accounting entry necessary to be compatible with tax laws would be as follows:

Truck—new	$22,000	
Accumulated depreciation—old truck	15,000	
Cash		$17,000
Truck—old		20,000

The difference between the two entries (financial accounting versus tax accounting) is that in the latter entry the new truck is capitalized as the sum of the depreciated value of the old truck plus any cash paid in respect to the exchange.

Because of the type of work the construction firm performs, it is not unusual for the typical firm to construct some of its own plant. This is particularly true in regard to its home office building, temporary branch offices, and material warehouses. The accounting problem of recognizing general overhead arises when a firm constructs its own assets. Two possibilities exist. For one, the construction firm may construct its plant when in fact it is operating at capacity. That is, all of its personnel are gainfully employed. In this situation, clearly the asset constructed should be charged for additional overhead costs and a share of the firm's general overhead.

In the second situation, the firm may use idle personnel to construct the asset (that is, the plant). The question arises as to whether any of the general overhead should be allocated to the newly constructed asset. Clearly, this general overhead would exist even if the asset were not constructed. Why then should the asset be assigned a portion of these overhead costs? On the other hand, counter arguments can be made for assigning a portion of the overhead to the asset constructed. For example, it can be argued that the asset should include overhead, otherwise loss from idle time is overstated. In addition, consistent with the cost principle, an allocation is necessary if the true cost of the asset being constructed and the firm's other ongoing operations are to be determined. The author favors the allocation of general overhead mainly because of this latter argument. Furthermore, should the cost of constructing the asset exceed the cost at which it could have been externally contracted, proper accounting would require that the excess cost be written off as a period loss and the asset valued at the cost at which it could be externally contracted.

Current accounting practice does not allow accounting entry recognition of the fair market value of equipment or plant owned by the construction company. For example, a construction firm may have built three central offices in 1960 for a cost of $100,000. Twenty years later, after depreciation charges have been made against the initial cost, the central office may have a book value of $25,000. It is this value that is reported in the financial statements. However, because of rapidly increasing inflation in the 1960s and 1970s, the central office may have a current value of $50,000. Many arguments can be made for revaluation of the central office account by "writing up" the asset. However, current practice requires that cost be used as the basis of the asset. Perhaps a continuing high rate of inflation will force the accounting profession to acknowledge the need for price level adjustments.

Equipment repairs and maintenance are a normal occurrence when owning construction equipment. The relevant question in regard to accounting for repairs and maintenance is whether such costs should be capitalized (deducted from income over a period of years) as part of the equipment cost or expensed as a period cost in one year. In general, only those expenditures that add to the production capacity of the equipment should be capitalized. Costs that are expended to maintain the equipment's production level, or to restore the equipment to its normal production level, should be expensed. The end result is that most, if not all, construction equipment repairs and maintenance costs should be expensed rather than capitalized.

Depreciation of Fixed Assets

Fixed assets, including construction equipment, are purchased because of their future revenue-generating potential. As such, as the revenue is generated, a portion of the cost of the asset should be matched periodically with the period revenue. This process is referred to as depreciation accounting. In particular, depreciation accounting is a system of accounting that aims to distribute the cost of a tangible capital asset, less any salvage, over the estimated useful life of the units in a systematic and a rational manner. Depreciation accounting is a process of allocation, not of valuation!

Note should be made of the fact that depreciation must be recognized in a systematic and rational manner. Alternative depreciation methods such as the straight-line method, the declining-balance method, and the sum-of-the-digits method have all been judged systematic and rational. It is possible to use one depreciation method for financial accounting and yet another for tax purposes. For example, several firms use the straight-line method for financial accounting and the declining-balance or sum-of-the-digits method for determining tax liability.

In determining the periodic depreciation charge for a piece of equipment, the initial cost of the equipment, its salvage value, and the equipment's useful life must be determined. As to the useful life, it should be noted that construction firms sometimes purchase equipment for a specific project. When the project is completed, the firm disposes of the equipment rather than retain it for further work. When this is the case, the useful life of the equipment to the construction firm is the term of the project—say eighteen months—and not the physical life of the equipment which may be eight years. The amount to be depreciated should be the equipment's total cost less its estimated salvage at the time of disposal.

Regardless of which depreciation method is used to depreciate a given piece of equipment, the type of accounting journal entry remains the same. For example, let us assume that, using an acceptable depreciation method, a periodic depreciation charge on a given truck is determined as $2,000. The periodic accounting journal entry would be as follows:

Equipment depreciation expense	$2,000	
Accumulated depreciation—truck		$2,000

The dollar value of the entry would depend on the cost of the asset, its useful life, the salvage value, and the depreciation method used.

The firm should use a depreciation method that best matches the utilization of the equipment to the revenue earned. However, the practicality of a given method overrides the matching concept. Several depreciation methods determine the depreciation charge as a function of time. Others determine the depreciation charge as a function of asset usage. Depreciation methods are discussed in Chapter 18.

Accounting for Leases

The large dollar cost associated with the purchase of equipment and the rather specialized characteristics of some types of construction equipment result in the typical firm renting or leasing a substantial portion of its equipment used to build projects. In addition to having less initial negative effect on the firm's cash flow (its liquidity), renting or leasing equipment can result in a smaller unit cost of usage when the firm only needs the equipment for a few select operations, whereas it would remain idle for long periods if it were owned. On the other hand, if equipment is used rather continuously by the construction firm, purchasing the equipment normally results in a much lower cost per unit of usage. However, even when this is the case, the construction firm's cash availability may restrict the firm to renting or leasing a needed piece of equipment.

When equipment is rented, the accounting is relatively simple. The rental cost of the equipment is allocated to particular projects on some reasonable basis such as direct cost of the projects, duration of the projects, equipment time on the projects, or equipment mileage on the projects. The accounting entry to record the allocated cost is made by debiting a project expense account and crediting cash paid for the rental or an account payable if the rental company issues the equipment on credit. Assuming a $2,000 rental cost is paid by a construction firm for the use of a piece of equipment on a single work item, the accounting entry would be as follows:

Project expense—equipment rental	$2,000	
Cash		$2,000

Unlike purchased equipment, equipment rentals do not appear as an asset on the firm's financial statements. However, substantial rental commitments should be disclosed in footnotes to a construction firm's financial statements.

Leasing differs from renting in that leases are normally considered to be for a longer period of time. For example, whereas a construction firm may rent a piece of equipment for a one-month duration, a lease agreement for the equipment might run five or ten years. More important than the duration difference between leasing and renting is the fact that leases may in fact be purchases or options to purchase. Such agreements require accounting recognition that differs from that used for recognition of rental agreements.

Under some circumstances, a lease agreement may actually represent an installment purchase of equipment. While the recognition of such an agreement may sometimes be difficult to detect, it is normally characterized by the following circumstances:

1. When the lease is made subject to the purchase of the equipment at the expiration of the lease for a nominal sum or for an amount obviously much less than its fair value at the time of purchase.
2. When the lease agreement stipulates that the rentals may be applied in part as installments on the purchase price of the equipment.
3. When the rentals obviously are not comparable with other rentals for similar equipment so as to create the presumption that portions of such rentals are partial payments under a purchase plan.

Additional means of determining whether an agreement is a lease or an installment purchase should focus on which party is liable for maintaining the equipment and which party bears the risk of ownership.

In a true lease (sometimes referred to as an operating lease) the owner (the lessor) retains the usual risk of ownership. The lessee's rental receipts are computed to cover the usual ownership cost of depreciation, taxes, insurance, and profit. The lease is normally readily cancelable by the lessor, and no special equipment ownership is given up by the lessor.

Typically the construction firm would prefer to recognize a piece of equipment as a lease rather than a purchase. The purchase requires recognition of a substantial liability. A bonding company or lending institution may look unfavorably at this liability on the firm's balance sheet.

The construction firm's accounting recognition of an operating lease is similar to the recognition of a rental agreement. That is, a debit to rent or lease expense and a credit to cash is recognized. The entry is exactly the same as the one previously made for the described rental payment.

If the firm prepays some of the equipment lease expense (as is often required), that portion which is prepaid should be recognized as an asset rather than as an expense in the period paid. For example, let us assume a construction firm initially pays an equipment leasing firm $4,000 for the lease of a piece of equipment, $2,000 of which is to cover the lease cost in the current period. The accounting journal entry would be as follows:

Lease expense	$2,000	
Prepaid lease expense	2,000	
Cash		$4,000

The $2,000 prepaid lease expense amount would be removed in the following accounting period and an expense recognized.

When an equipment lease agreement is such that it actually is a form of an installment payment purchase, proper accounting treatment requires that the equipment be recognized as an asset and the related indebtedness as a liability. That is, the equipment is to be capitalized and a liability is recognized. This type of recognition is necessary in order to fully disclose the firm's financial position. The accounting entry necessary to capitalize the leased equipment differs depending on whether a straight-line amortization or present-value amortization is used. Since present value is a more exact method it will be illustrated.

Using the present-value method, the accounting entry should debit the equipment account for the present value of the equipment rights and credit a liability to the leasing company. For example, let us assume a construction firm enters into a financing lease whereby it obtains rights to a piece of equipment through five equal end-of-the-year payments of $4,747.93 each. The capitalized amount of the assets should be the total cost paid minus any implied interest costs. Let us assume that the current annual interest rate is 6 percent. The capitalized value of the equipment would be determined by means of the following calculation:

Present value of equipment rights = ($4,747.93) times (4.2124)*
Present value of equipment rights = $20,000

(*Present value of a uniform series for five periods and at 6 percent)

The accounting entry required to recognize the lease purchase agreement would be as follows:

Equipment—leasehold	$20,000.00	
Discount on lease obligation	3,739.65	
Liability—lease obligation		$23,739.65

The discount represents the cost exceeding the calculated present-value cost. It is an interest cost that will be amortized over the period of the lease agreement. Other than the portion of the liability that is due in the current period (i.e., a current liability), the dollar amount of the liability is considered long term.

Additional accounting period entries have to be made to recognize the annual lease payments and to depreciate the asset. However, it should be noted that the period for which these two different entries are to be made may differ. For example, whereas the lease agreement is to be for five years, the equipment may have a useful life of ten years. As such, depreciation is to be recognized over a ten-year period.

Using a present-value amortization of the interest payments, the accounting entries necessary to recognize the payment of the first rental payment follow:

Liability—lease obligation	$4,747.93	
Cash		$4,747.93

It is also necessary to recognize the interest expense:

Interest expense	$1,200.00	
Discount on lease obligation		$1,200.00

The interest expense for the accounting period is calculated as 6 percent times the unpaid balance which, for the first period, is $20,000. In the following period it would be 6 percent times the unpaid balance of $16,452.07 or an interest expense of $987.12.

An accounting entry would be necessary to record the depreciation. Assuming a ten-year life and straight-line depreciation, the accounting entry would be as follows:

Expense—depreciation equipment leasehold	$2,000	
Equipment—leasehold, accumulated depr.		$2,000

Similar entries would be made in the following accounting period.

Revenue and Expense Recognition

Revenue and expense transactions are handled through *nominal accounts*. Nominal accounts are those accounts whose balances are normally transferred (i.e., closed) to other accounts when the books are closed. In particular, revenue and expense accounts are closed to an account commonly referred to as *income summary*. In effect this account is used to summarize all the revenue and expense transactions for a given period of time. The difference between the two types of accounts is reported as profit or loss for the period.

The procedure as to how and when various construction revenue and expense transactions are entered and summarized in the firm's set of books is in part dependent on the firm's choice of accounting method. For example, the percentage-of-completion method and the completed-contract method differ as to when revenue and expenses are summarized into the income account. The effect of the accounting method choice on revenue and expense transaction recognition is discussed in Chapter 3.

Independent of the accounting method choice, certain fundamental revenue and expense transactions are common to each and every firm. Let us first consider common expense transactions.

The construction firm may purchase materials for a specific project or may purchase the material and add it to its inventory. The former transaction is an expense transaction whereas the latter is merely an exchange of asset accounts. Let us consider the expense transaction.

If the firm pays $1,200 cash for the material the transaction would be as follows:

Material expense	$1,200	
Cash		$1,200

A firm utilizing a job-cost accounting system, which identifies material to specific projects, may describe the entry as follows:

Material expense—job 101	$1,200	
Cash		$1,200

A more sophisticated job-cost accounting system may identify material and labor costs to specific segments of work of a project. The following entry would reflect such recognition:

Material expense—concrete slabs—job 101	$1,200	
Cash		$1,200

The latter two types of transactions would be kept in subsidiary job-cost ledgers and summarized via a general ledger material expense account.

More often than not material is purchased on account. In this case the credit entry would be to an accounts payable account rather than the cash account. Assuming material is traced to specific projects, the entry would be as follows:

Material expense—job 101	$1,200	
Accounts payable—Ace Hardware		$1,200

When the invoice is paid, an entry is made to reflect the change in the asset and liability accounts. If the firm were on a cash basis accounting method, the expense would not be recognized until the material bill was paid.

Often the construction firm is given an opportunity to take advantage of a purchase discount when paying for material. For example, if the construction firm pays the material vendor within ten days, it may receive a 2 percent discount from the invoice. The entire bill amount is due in thirty days. This payment agreement should be indicated by the notation 2/10/n30. The recognition of purchase discounts can be handled in more than one manner. The question arises as to whether the failure to take advantage of a purchase discount should create recognition of an expense entitled "purchase discount lost." Let us assume a construction firm has a potential 10 percent discount and fails to take advantage of it on a $1,200 invoice. One means of transaction recognition is as follows:

Materials expense	$1,200	
Cash		$1,200

Alternatively, the lost purchase discount could be singled out through the following entry:

Material expense	$1,080	
Lost purchase discount expense	120	
Cash		$1,200

The latter entry has the advantage of singling out the inefficiencies of the cash disbursement function. The expense "lost purchase discount" is identified as an "other expense" in the firm's financial statements.

If material is purchased for inventory, no expense account is immediately recognized. Assuming the material is purchased on account, the transaction would be as follows:

Material inventory	$1,200	
Accounts payable S & A Hardware		$1,200

Eventually the material may be used for specific projects and an expense would be recognized:

Material expense—job 101	$1,200	
Material inventory		$1,200

The transaction assumes the material is identified as belonging to a specific project rather than individual work segments.

Direct labor costs for a project, like material costs, may merely be identified as labor costs to the firm or may be identified as belonging to specific projects or segments of work. Labor expense entries must include recognition of withholding and FICA taxes. This may be done by means of two separate entries: one to reflect the labor wage expense, and the other to reflect various employer labor tax expenses.

The employer withholds employee taxes from the paychecks it issues. Let us assume that labor payroll is $10,000 for a certain week and employee payroll taxes withheld are equal to $1,800. The following entry would be made:

Labor payroll—job 101	$10,000	
Withholding taxes payable		$1,200
FICA taxes payable—employees		600
Cash		8,200

In addition the employer would be liable for payroll taxes. Assuming they total $900 the entry would be as follows:

Expense—payroll taxes	$900	
FICA taxes payable—employer		$600
FUTA taxes payable—federal		50
FUTA taxes payable—state		250

The FICA tax is social security and the FUTA is unemployment taxes. The employer will have to submit both the employee taxes withheld and its taxes payable to the appropriate agencies. However, when they are paid, an expense entry is not made. Rather the "accounts payable" liability accounts are debited and cash is credited for a like amount.

Supervision and administrative payroll entries would be made in a manner similar to the direct labor expense entries. However, rather than identify the expense as belonging to a specific project or work segment expense account, these labor accounts may be titled "officers' salaries," "administrative salaries," and so on. Like direct labor costs, they will eventually be included in all the expenses that make up the firm's income statement.

Other types of expense transactions besides direct material and labor are recognized in the firm's income statements. The depreciation and lease expense entries were discussed in earlier sections. Additionally, the firm incurs many expense-related transactions that are not always easily traced to specific projects. They are commonly referred to as overhead expenses.

Using job-cost accounting (which is common to construction and is discussed in Chapter 9), overhead is often expensed to specific projects through an application procedure. For example, after estimating total overhead expenses for a period of time, the firm may decide to apply overhead costs to projects at a rate of $1.50 per $1.00 of direct material and labor costs for a project 101 for a period in time. The overhead expense entry would be made as follows:

Overhead applied expense—job 101	$7,500	
Overhead control		$7,500

The overhead control account is an account used to collect and record actual overhead expenditures. For example, assuming $500 of small tools is purchased (and identified as an overhead item), the purchase would be entered as follows:

Overhead control	$500	
Cash		$500

If overhead is being applied correctly, the debits and credits to the overhead control account should equal zero. Otherwise the firm has under- or over-applied overhead. This under- or over-applied overhead should be recognized through an adjustment to the expense accounts of the various projects.

As an alternative to applying overhead to specific projects through formal accounting entries, overhead costs may be merely expensed to specific overhead expense accounts as they are incurred. In this case, the specific account entry would depend on the type of overhead expense incurred. For example, if the overhead item were small tools, the entry would be as follows:

Small tools overhead expense	$500	
Accounts payable—S & A Hardware		$500

Other overhead expenses would be entered in a similar manner.

The point in time at which a revenue transaction is recognized depends on the choice of accounting method. Included in these methods are the cash and accrual methods. Using the cash method, the revenue accounting entry would be as follows:

Cash	$6,000	
Revenue—job 101		$6,000

More often than not, revenue is actually "earned" by the construction firm before the cash is received. The time of billing is often used as the point in time at which the revenue is recognized. The following entry would be made to reflect this occurrence:

Accounts receivable—job 101	$6,000	
Revenue—job 101		$6,000

When the cash is received, an entry is made to reflect the change in asset accounts. In particular, the entry would be made as follows:

Cash	$6,000	
Accounts receivable—job 101		$6,000

This transaction does not affect a revenue or expense account.

A reality of doing business is the fact that the firm may not be able to collect all of its receivables. In order to reflect this, a firm will recognize an expense entitled "bad debt expense." Several procedures for recognition of a bad debt expense exist. One is, the firm may write off the expenses as they are incurred. This is sometimes referred to as the *direct write-off method.* Assuming $500 of receivables were identified as uncollectible, the accounting entry would be as follows:

Bad debt expense	$500	
Accounts receivable—job 101		$500

Rather than utilizing the direct write-off approach, the construction firm may recognize the bad debt expense by using an allowance account. Based on an estimate of monthly or yearly uncollectible receivables, the firm would set up an allowance account. Assuming for a period of time, say a year, that estimated uncollectible receivables are $4,000, the allowance entry would be as follows:

Bad debt expense	$4,000	
Allowance for doubtful accounts		$4,000

This entry recognizes the total estimated expense for the period and sets up a liability allowance account. As particular receivables are judged uncollectible, they are written off through the allowance account. Assuming a $400 receivable is judged uncollectible, the entry would be as follows:

Allowance for doubtful accounts	$400	
Accounts receivable		$400

Similar entries would be made throughout the year as other receivables were deemed uncollectable. If the initial estimate of the bad debt expense was correct, the allowance account will have a zero balance at year end. If the estimate was incorrect and thus a balance exists in the allowance account, the amount can be carried forward to the next period or adjusted to the year's bad debt expense account.

The construction firm may receive revenue from sources other than normal operations. For example, it may receive revenue from interest or from rental of real property. It is common to recognize these nonoperating revenues through "income" accounts. For example, assuming $300 interest is received, the entry may appear as follows:

Cash	$300	
Interest income		$300

Other nonoperating revenues would be reflected in a similar manner. As with operating revenue, if recognition were to be identified before receipt of cash, an account receivable would be debited instead of the cash account.

Closing Entries

As previously noted, revenue and expense accounts are referred to as nominal accounts. A characteristic of nominal accounts is that, at the end of a specified period of time (usually at year end), they are closed and transferred to a *real account*. A real account is normally an asset, liability, or net worth account. The process of closing nominal accounts consists of "clearing out" the dollar amount of debit or credit in the account and thereby bringing the account balances to zero.

Revenue and expense accounts are closed to an "income summary" account. The result is that the income summary account reflects the net income for the period in question. The accounting entry or entries that perform this function are referred to as closing entries.

The closing entry that could be made to close out various expense accounts at the end of the accounting period would be as follows:

Income summary	$24,000	
Material expense		$10,000
Direct labor expense		9,000
Depreciation—building		2,000
Depreciation—furniture and fixtures		500
Bad debt expense		500
Small tools expense		500
Interest expense		500
Taxes		1,000

The actual dollar amounts are assumed. The expense dollar amounts would equal the debit balances in each of the accounts. The dollar amount of the income summary entry ($24,000) is the sum of the expense items being credited.

It is possible to include the revenue entries in the above income summary entry. Alternatively, the revenue entries can be reflected in a separate entry as follows:

Revenue—projects	$22,000	
Interest income	4,000	
Rental income	2,000	
Income summary		$28,000

As with the closing entry for the expense accounts, the dollar amounts of the debited revenue accounts are equal to the credit balance of each of the accounts. The dollar value of the income summary entry is merely equal to the sum of the debit entries.

The sum of the income summary accounts represents the net income (that is, the difference between revenues and expenses) for the period in question. If there is an income summary credit balance, it represents a gain. On the other hand, a debit balance represents a loss.

The income summary account, like revenue and expense accounts, is also a nominal account. It is closed to a real account through a closing entry. In particular, it is closed to *retained earnings* which is a net worth balance sheet account. Using the dollar amount income summary entries indicated, the closing entry would be as follows:

Income summary	$28,000	
Income summary		$24,000
Retained earnings		4,000

The income summary account balance, like the revenue and expense accounts, would now have a zero balance.

The retained earnings account may be affected by paying out of dividends or appropriations of retained earnings to specific restricted accounts. However, none of these transactions are revenue or expense transactions.

CHART OF ACCOUNTS

Financial transactions are typically entered and classified in the accounting process by means of a coding system. A somewhat common convention for classifying financial transactions uses the following number system:

Numbers	*Types of Accounts*
100–299	Assets
300–399	Liabilities
400–499	Net worth—capital
500–599	Revenues
600–899	Expenses

Within this coding system would be several specific account numbers. The set of all the account numbers, or codes, and the names of the accounts they represent is referred to as the *chart of accounts*. For example, the firm's cash might be coded as account 101. This code would be used to group all cash transactions and to provide an order to the listing of specific types of accounts and/or transactions. An entry into the accounting system that pertained to cash could then be as follows:

101—Cash	$3,000	
104—Accounts receivable		$3,000

Several contracting associations or services have published a chart of accounts for their member firms. This is an attempt to standardize the codes used by individual firms. While such a standardization would aid in reducing the fragmentizing that exists in construction accounting, it is also true that each construction firm is somewhat unique.

The type of work a firm performs, the size of the firm, and the extent of detail within its accounting system, all should dictate in part the chart of accounts to be used by the construction firm. The chart of accounts should delineate specific types of transactions and accounts that enable the firm to obtain useful information for making management decisions as well as provide adequate disclosure to external interests. On the other hand, the chart of accounts should be workable. Too many separate codes or accounts may result in excess classification time and may actually lead to errors in recording transactions in that the numerous codes may confuse the individual making the entries.

3
ACCOUNTING ENTRIES FOR REVENUE RECOGNITION

INTRODUCTION

Chapter 2 discussed the accounting treatment of various financial transactions of the construction firm. Omitted from the discussion were the accounting entries for various alternative revenue-recognition methods available to the construction firm.

The construction firm ordinarily has several methods of accounting available to it for determining financial income as well as taxable income. Because of these several alternatives and the controversy surrounding their use, this entire chapter focuses on a discussion of accounting entries for revenue recognition.

The choice of revenue-recognition method used by the construction firm affects both the firm's financial statements and its calculated taxable income. Usually a method that is favorable for one is unfavorable for the other. For example, reducing reportable income by using an available revenue-recognition method may minimize the firm's tax liability. However, this reduction of income may also have a negative impact on the firm's financial statements including a smaller income, less net worth on the balance sheet, and probably less working capital on the balance sheet also. Thus, while the objective of tax minimization might be achieved, the resulting minimization might be made at the expense of causing external parties such as lending institutions and sureties to view the firm's financial statements with disfavor.

Fortunately the above difficulty can be avoided. There is no requirement to use the same revenue-recognition accounting method for both financial reporting and determining tax liability. Often it is preferable to utilize separate methods for the two purposes.

Because it is acceptable to use a revenue-recognition method for financial reporting independent of the method used to calculate taxable income, it is possible to discuss the use of revenue-recognition methods for financial reporting without discussing the impact on taxable income. The impact of revenue-recognition methods on taxable income is discussed in Chapter 17. This chapter is limited to discussing revenue-recognition methods and methods of reporting financial income.

CASH AND ACCRUAL METHODS

A short-term construction project is usually considered one that has a duration of a year or less. Recording revenue and expense for short-term projects presents few problems relative to the recording needed for long-term projects.

Two methods of recognizing revenues and expenses for short-term construction projects are in general usage; these are the cash method and the accrual method. Some construction firms have also devised "hybrid" methods for recognizing revenue that in effect combine elements of the cash and accrual methods.

Usage of the cash and accrual methods is not limited to construction firms. Both are acceptable revenue-recognition methods for almost any type of firm.

The major accounting difference between the cash and accrual methods is the point in time at which the revenue or expense is recognized. This timing difference may have a significant effect on various items in the construction firm's financial statements.

When the cash method of accounting is used, revenue is recognized only when it is received or constructively received. (An example of revenue that is constructively received is interest posted to an individual's savings account that can be drawn upon at any time.) Using the cash method of revenue recognition, a construction firm would not recognize any revenue at the time it billed an owner for work performed. Revenue would be recognized only when the cash itself was received.

Expenses recognized using the cash method of accounting would be limited to those in which cash was actually expended. An exception to this would be noncash expenditures creating an asset having a useful life that extends substantially beyond the close of a firm's operating cycle or a year. Examples of such noncash expenditures that would be recognized in the cash method of accounting would be depreciation and an extended life insurance policy.

The accrual method of accounting recognizes revenue when events occur that fix the *right* to receive revenue and the amount thereof can be determined with reasonable accuracy. Therefore, when a construction firm bills an owner for work performed, revenue is recognized at the time of the billing regardless of the date the amount is actually collected.

The accrual method recognizes expenses when events occur that establish the fact that the construction firm has incurred a liability and the amount can be reasonably determined. For example, when a construction firm purchases material on account from a vendor for building a project, a liability is established; thus, the construction firm recognizes an expense.

When the cash method of accounting is used, income (profit or loss) is calculated as the difference between cash collected and cash expended. Using the accrual method, income (profit and loss) is calculated as the difference between amounts billed to customers and expenditures regardless of whether the expenditures are paid or merely incurred.

Many accounting journal entries would be treated the same using either the cash or accrual accounting method. For example, as noted, depreciation expense would be recognized identically in both methods. However, if cash is not exchanged in a revenue or expense transaction, the accounting recognition would differ depending on whether the cash or accrual method was used.

Consider the purchase of $5,000 of material on account for building a project. If the accrual method were utilized, the journal entry would be

Project material expense	$5,000	
Accounts payable		$5,000

When the vendor was paid the $5,000, the journal entry that would be made using the accrual method would be

Accounts payable	$5,000	
Cash		$5,000

If the cash method were utilized, the journal entry for the material purchase would not be recognized at the time the material was purchased. Because the material is purchased on account and no cash was expended at that time, no accounting journal would be made. When the vendor bill was paid, the cash method of accounting entry would be made as follows:

Project material expense	$5,000	
Cash		$5,000

Note that, regardless of whether the cash or accrual method of accounting is used, the final impact on the construction firm's books would be the same. That is, the firm's books would reflect an expense for material and a lessening of its cash account. While the final result may be the same, the interim results may be significantly different. For example, if an income statement were prepared after the material purchase but before the cash payment to the vendor, using the accrual method it would include an expense for material, whereas, using the cash method, it would not reflect the expense.

Often the cash method of revenue-recognition results in misleading financial statements. The failure to recognize expense incurred but not expense paid, such as the discussed expense for material, can result in a misleading or deceptive financial statement. For this reason, the cash method of accounting for financial reporting is not recommended. The cash method is usually only an excuse for poor bookkeeping that fails to recognize receivables and payables.

Effect on Income Statement of Cash and Accrual Methods

The cash or accrual methods of recognizing revenue and expense can result in widely varying recognized income depending on which method is used. If amounts billed and uncollected are in excess of costs and expenses incurred but not paid, the accrual method of accounting will result in more recognized income than the cash method. On the other hand, if costs and expenses incurred but not paid are in excess of amounts billed and uncollected, the cash method of accounting will result in more recognized income than the accrual method.

In order to illustrate the differing impact of the cash and accrual methods on financial statements, let us consider the data for four different projects as illustrated in Figure 3.1. General and administrative (G & A) expense data are also shown in Figure 3.1. Note that the expenditures shown for each of the four projects are for direct job costs and do not include a portion of the general and administrative expense.

The impact of the cash versus accrual methods for the four projects in Figure 3.1 and the construction company as a whole is illustrated in Figure

SAMPLE CONSTRUCTION COMPANY

	Project A	Project B	Project C	Project D
Total contract amount	$720,000	$1,200,000	$1,400,000	$1,000,000
Cash expenditures to 12/32/X0	600,000	550,000	750,000	600,000
Total expenditures to 12/31/X0	620,000	700,000	800,000	600,000
Estimated expenditures to complete	–	600,000	400,000	300,000
Total estimated expenditures	620,000	1,300,000	1,200,000	900,000
Billings through 12/31/X0	700,000	800,000	800,000	750,000
Cash collectors through 12/31/X0	690,000	700,000	800,000	700,000
Cash G & A expense to 12/31/X0–$150,000				
Total G & A expenses to 12/31/X0–$180,000				

Figure 3.1 Examples of Data for Four Projects

SAMPLE CONSTRUCTION COMPANY
INCOME STATEMENTS

	Cash Method		Accrual Method	
Project A				
Revenue	$690,000		$700,000	
Expense	600,000		620,000	
Income		$90,000		$80,000
Project B				
Revenue	$700,000		$800,000	
Expense	550,000		700,000	
Income		150,000		100,000
Project C				
Revenue	$800,000		$800,000	
Expense	750,000		800,000	
Income		50,000		0
Project D				
Revenue	$700,000		$750,000	
Expense	600,000		600,000	
Income		100,000		150,000
Total project income		$390,000		$330,000
Less G & A expense		150,000		180,000
Net income		$240,000		$150,000

Figure 3.2 Example of Differences between Cash and Accrual Methods

3.2. Naturally the results shown in Figure 3.2 are dependent on the data given. While using the cash method in Figure 3.2 has resulted in significantly more income than the accrual method, the reverse could also be true if different data had been given in Figure 3.1.

Independent of whether the cash or accrual method results in a larger income for a given set of data, note the significant potential difference in the reported income from the two methods illustrated in Figure 3.2. Especially noteworthy is the fact that the cash method can be interpreted as "reflecting" $90,000 of ficticious income in that outstanding payables exceed outstanding receivables by this amount. This $90,000 difference between payables and receivables is reflected in the income reported using the accrual method that is illustrated in Figure 3.2.

The failure to recognize payables and receivables has led many to conclude that the cash method is weak and nonrepresentative of the firm's "actual position." This is true and especially important in regard to the construction firm in that there are usually a significant amount of payables and receivables.

It is also true that some individuals would argue that the accrual method is equally or more misleading than the cash method in regard to recognizing income. This argument also has merit; it acknowledges that construction firms may "overbill" and therefore create ficticious income or may receive invoices from vendors late, which has the effect of lessening the recorded expense. While both of these events are possible, the accrual method usually better reflects the actual income of the firm than does the cash method and is the preferred method of the two for financial reporting.

LONG-TERM CONTRACTS

Because of the large dollar value of the construction project, the relatively complicated and time-consuming construction process, and the construction industry's dependence on weather and seasons, the duration of building a project often exceeds a year or overlaps the construction firm's year end. This, along with the fact that a construction firm may overbill a customer for work performed as of a given date and the difficulty of determining the cost to complete a project, have led to the acceptability of long-term contract methods for recognizing revenue and expense in the construction industry.

The use of long-term contract accounting methods is somewhat unique to the construction industry because of the industry's singular characteristics. Included in long-term contract methods of revenue and expense recognition are the percentage-of-completion method and the completed-contract method.

A long-term contract is generally held to be one that takes twelve or more months to complete. In regard to tax laws, a construction contract may be considered long-term as long as its duration overlaps a company's year end, independent of whether it actually takes twelve months or more to complete. Long-term contracts and taxation are discussed in Chapter 17.

A long-term contract involves the manufacture of a product. Contracts for services performed by architects, engineers, or architectural or engineering firms are also accorded long-term contract treatment.

The discussion of long-term revenue and expense-recognition methods is relevant to both financial reporting and calculating taxable income. In general there are more restrictions on the use of specific long-term methods for financial reporting than there are for calculating taxable income. For example, while the completed-contract method is in great use for calculating taxable income, in financial reporting its use is restricted to instances in which estimates are not dependable (because of inherent hazards) or for short duration projects. In fact, the completed-contract method will probably continue to come under strong attack as a financial reporting method in that many argue it reports misleading financial results. In this sense, the completed-contract method is somewhat like the cash method for recognizing revenue and expense.

Current AICPA financial statement presentation guidelines emphasize the use of the percentage-of-completion method. They argue that a contractor should almost always be able to make reasonably dependable estimates of the extent of project progress. The guidelines indicate the following:

1. The percentage-of completion method: to be used when reasonably

dependable estimates can be made, contract rights and consideration are defined, and the owner and contractor can be expected to perform.
2. Completed-contract method: can be used for short duration projects and those in which inherent hazards exist (and for which, therefore, dependable estimates cannot be made).

The procedures of using each of the methods will now be illustrated.

Percentage-of-Completion Method

The percentage-of-completion method is generally the preferable method for recording income on long-duration projects. Its major advantage is that it recognizes income on a current basis and, as such, results in a more regular flow of income. On the other hand, the method has the disadvantage of dependence on cost estimates, which are subject to uncertainties. The AICPA recommends that the income is to be recognized by determining

1. The percentage of estimated total income that incurred costs to date bear to estimated total costs after giving effect to estimates of costs to complete based upon most recent information.
2. The percentage of estimated total income that may be indicated by such other measures of progress toward completion as may be appropriate having due regard to work performed.

In most circumstances, the first means of estimating income to be recognized will prove appropriate. However, for certain types of projects total incurred costs may not be the best measure of income earned. Where a more meaningful allocation of income would result, the second means of estimating income is to be preferred. For example, in certain circumstances a more appropriate recognition of income may be based on the percentage of direct labor costs expended to the estimated total direct labor costs for the project.

Method 1 is the most commonly used for determining revenue, expenses, and income to recognize. To illustrate the calculation process, let us assume the following project data:

Contract amount	$1,000,000
Cost to date	600,000
Estimated additional costs	200,000
Total estimated costs	800,000
Billings to date	800,000

The percentage of completion based on costs would be calculated as follows:

$$\text{percentage of completion} = \frac{\text{cost to date}}{\text{total estimated cost}} = \frac{600{,}000}{800{,}000} = 75\%$$

The revenue to recognize would be calculated as follows:

(contract amount)(% complete) = ($1,000,000)(.75) = $750,000

The cost or expense to recognize would be the actual amount incurred to date, or $600,000. Therefore, the gross income that would be recognized would be calculated as follows:

Revenue	$750,000
Costs or expenses	600,000
Gross income	$150,000

Note that the audit guide also allows the construction firm to recognize income based on some basis other than total direct cost. For example, if the actual percentage of completion is a function of labor costs only, the labor cost incurred divided by the total estimated labor cost can be justified as the means of determining the percentage of completion and the resulting income.

It may also be that the best measure of the actual percentage of completion of a project is better determined by a means other than cost. For example, one might calculate the linear feet of highway placed to the total feet to be built and determine the percentage of completion. The ability to do this is permitted by the second means stated as an acceptable method by the AICPA.

The use of the percentage-of-completion method is somewhat similar to the use of the cash and accrual methods in that it also recognizes revenue, expense, and income throughout the building of a project. However, it differs in that the percentage-of-completion method attempts to recognize income based on what is "earned" rather than on what is collected in cash or what is billed.

In order to contrast the accrual method and the percentage-of-completion method, let us consider the project D data illustrated in Figure 3.1. Independent of general and administrative expenses, a gross income for project D using the accrual method was calculated as $150,000 in Figure 3.2. The calculation is repeated in Figure 3.3.

The gross income using the percentage-of-completion method of recognizing revenue and expense is also illustrated in Figure 3.3. The difference between the two incomes in Figure 3.3 is because the construction firm has "overbilled" for work it has done. Based on a calculation of costs incurred to date versus total estimated costs, the project is 66.67 percent complete. However the construction firm has billed for 75 percent of its contract amount. Based on the amount of work that is completed, the construction firm should have only billed 66.67 percent of the contract amount, or $666,667.

Using the accrual method of recognizing income, the $83,333 of overbilling appears as income. Using the percentage-of-completion method, the $83,333 of overbillings would appear on the construction firm's balance sheet as a liability in that it is money charged to a customer that is not earned to date.

When the percentage-of-completion method is used, it is very common to have over- or underbillings calculated as part of the income determination. This is primarily because the construction firm may not bill in proportion to

Accrual Method—Project D

Revenue	
Amount billed	$750,000
Expense	
Expenditures incurred	600,000
Gross income	$150,000

Percentage-of-Completion Method—Project D

Expenditures to date	$600,000	
Total estimated expenditures	900,000	
Percentage of expenditures to date	66.67%	
Contract amount	1,000,000	
times percentage complete	66.67%	
Should be billing		$666,667
Expenditures to date		600,000
Gross income		$ 66,667
Actual billing	$750,000	
Should be billing	666,667	
Overbilling	$ 83,333	

Figure 3.3 Accrual Method versus Percentage-of-Completion Method

the percent of expenditures it has incurred to the total estimated expenditures. In addition, the fact that the construction firm cannot totally control the timing of the bills it receives from its material suppliers and vendors also can lead to over- or underbillings.

An underbilling appears as a current asset on the construction firm's balance sheet. It represents a receivable in that it is work performed for which the construction firm has a reimbursement claim from the customer.

An overbilling appears on the construction firm's balance sheet as a current liability. It is a liability in that the construction firm has billed (and may have received payment) for work not yet performed. In this regard the construction firm "owes back" the billing to its customer.

When using the percentage-of-completion method, the accounting journal entries result in recognition of revenue, expense, and income throughout a project. To illustrate accounting journal entries for the percentage-of-completion method of accounting, let us again consider project D data illustrated in Figure 3.1. Let us further assume single revenue and expense transactions to date of $750,000 and $600,000, respectively, as illustrated in Figure 3.1. In reality these two transactions would each be made up of several individual transactions. However, the type of accounting entry made would be the same for each separate transaction.

The $600,000 of expenditures for building project D would be recognized by means of the following accounting journal entry:

Construction in progress—project D	$600,000	
Cash (or accounts payable)		$600,000

Billings by the construction firm to the project owner are debited to "Accounts receivable" and credited to "Revenue billed on construction contracts." The $750,000 billing would be recognized as follows:

Accounts receivable	$750,000	
Revenue billed on construction contracts—project D		$750,000

As the cash is received from the project owner, the accounts receivable account is reduced and cash is debited. For the identified account receivable, this would be done as follows:

Cash	$750,000	
Accounts receivable		$750,000

At given points in time during construction, income would be recognized for a project when using the percentage-of-completion method. For example, this may occur monthly or yearly. For purposes of illustration, let us assume income is to be recognized for project D at the end of year 19X0. The year-end entry based on percentage complete of costs would be

Construction in progress—project D	$66,667	
Income projects—project D		$66,667

The $66,667 of income recognized is calculated as shown in Figure 3.3. It represents the earned profits to date based on the percentage of expenditures to date and the total estimated profit.

When project D is complete, both the "Construction in progress—project D" account and the "Revenue billed on construction contracts—project D" account are closed out. Assuming that income is recognized periodically, the two accounts should offset. The entry made at the completion of the project would be made as follows:

Revenue billed on construction contracts—project D	$1,000,000	
Construction in progress—project D		$1,000,000

In effect the "Construction in progress" account that is being closed includes both expenditures and recognized profit. This is why the total of the account will equal the "Revenue billed" which should equal the total contract amount.

When a loss becomes apparent during construction of a project, proper accounting calls for the recognition of the total estimated loss. The total loss should be recognized at the time it is estimated regardless of the percentage of completion at that point in time. This is consistent with the conservative principle of accounting.

Completed-Contract Method

As indicated in an earlier section, the completed-contract can be used for short duration projects or for projects whose inherent hazards result in the inability to make reasonably dependable estimates. "Reasonably dependable" is a subjective term and has resulted in variations when the method has been used.

In practice, using the completed contract method for financial reporting is somewhat of an admission by the construction firm of a weak job-cost accounting system. The weaker the cost system is in regard to forecasting or controlling costs, the more difficult it is to determine cost to complete and percentage complete to date. However the AICPA suggests that the completed-contract method should not be used as an excuse for a weak cost system. Instead, the method should be used if and when inherent hazards exists in a contract.

When the completed-contract method of recognizing revenue and expense is used, the construction firm recognizes no revenue or expense (or resulting profit or loss) until the completion of the construction project. During construction all costs incurred by the construction firm for building a project are accumulated in a construction in progress account which is an asset account.

Any billings to a customer by the construction firm during construction are recognized as a receivable and an account entitled "revenue billed on construction contracts" is credited. In effect the revenue billed on construction contracts is a liability account until the project is complete and revenue is recognized.

In order to illustrate the accounting journal entries that would be made using the completed-contract method, let us consider the construction project D data illustrated in Figure 3.1. While the expenditures to date would likely be made up of several labor and material expenditures, for purposes of illustrating the journal entry let us assume the expenditure is a single transaction. In reality each of the project expenditures would be made the same. Using the completed-contract method, the accounting journal entry for the $600,000 project D expenditure would be made as follows:

Construction in progress—project D	$600,000	
Cash (or accounts payable)		$600,000

Billings by the construction firm to the project owner are debited to accounts receivable (an asset account) and credited to revenue billed on construction contracts. Assuming the entire $750,000 billing on project D was made through a single billing (as is the case with expenses, this would normally be several transactions), the accounting journal entry would be made as follows:

Accounts receivable	$750,000	
Revenue billed on construction contracts—project D		$750,000

As the cash is received from the project owner, the accounts receivable account is reduced and cash is debited. For project D this would be done by the following entry:

Cash	$750,000	
Accounts receivable		$750,000

No revenue or expense results from the illustrated journal entries. Only when the project is complete would revenue and expense and the resulting profit or loss be recognized. This might occur in the following year or even later. When in fact project D is completed, an accounting entry would be made that closed out the asset and liability "holding" accounts and recognized the profit or loss. In regard to project D the entry would be

Revenue billed on Construction contracts—project D	$1,000,000	
Construction in progress—project D		$900,000
Income on projects—project D		100,000

The effect of the entry would be to reflect $100,000 of income from project D at the point in time when it is complete.

Whereas no income (profit) is recognized until a project is complete when using the completed-contract method, a loss must be reported as soon as it becomes apparent that a loss is to be incurred. This is consistent with the conservative principle of accounting. In fact, the entire expected loss must be recognized, not just the loss incurred to date.

A significant question that occurs when using the completed-contract method relates to when a project is to be considered complete. The date can be very important in that a matter of a few days difference can result in recognition or no recognition of significant revenues and expenses on a financial statement. A project completed on December 28 would be recognized for a December 31 year end. However, if the project is judged "completed" a mere five days later, no recognition on the statements would result.

Audit guidelines suggest that a construction firm should be consistent in its determination of project completion dates. It also suggests that a project is complete when it is *substantially* complete. In the construction industry the term substantially complete usually means that the project is to the point at which it can be used for its intended purposes.

It is noteworthy that the criteria used for determining when a project is complete may vary for financial reporting and calculation of taxable income purposes. Tax law criteria for completion dates are discussed in Chapter 17.

Some individuals would argue that the completed-contract method is a more accurate method of recognizing revenue and expense than the percentage-of-completion method in that the method requires no estimate of profits earned prior to the completion of the construction. These defenders of the completed-contract method argue that only at the time of a project's completion is it possible to determine profits in that prior recognition of profits is based on *estimates* of costs to complete. Given the uncertainty of the construction process, one might question the validity of any estimate of costs to complete a project.

The argument for completed-contract remains weak. While it may have support in that it is not dependent on estimates, the fact remains that the method results in a poor matching of revenue and expense and often results in misleading financial statements. Significant revenues or expenses may be omitted from the income statement during construction. Given this fact, the reader of the financial statements may come to the wrong conclusion regarding the profitability of a given project or the company as a whole.

Income Effect of Percentage-of-Completion Versus Completed-Contract

The accounting difference between the percentage-of-completion and completed-contract methods may be dramatized with the differences in the resulting income statements that can be prepared using the two methods. Differences also appear in balance sheets prepared using the two different methods.

Financial statement presentation is discussed in Chapter 6; however, in order to illustrate the dramatic difference that can result from using one or another revenue-recognition method, we will illustrate a calculation of net income. In effect, the calculation is a form of an income statement.

Let us consider the data for projects A, B, C, and D illustrated in Figure 3.1. The calculations of net income at the end of the year using both the percentage-of-completion and completed-contract methods are shown in Figure 3.4. Note that the total, recognized net income for the percentage-of-completion method is $20,000, whereas using the completed-contract method results in $180,000 loss.

Naturally the numbers illustrated in Figure 3.1 dictate the $200,000 difference in net income. Using different data for the four projects might result in a smaller dollar difference. Also, it is possible that, for a given set of project data, using the completed-contract method might lead to a larger net income than the income derived using the percentage-of-completion method. However, the fact remains that the difference in net income reported using the two methods can be dramatic.

In Figure 3.4 only project A is handled identically as to revenue and expense when using the two revenue-recognition methods. This is because the project is started and completed in the accounting period represented by the statement period.

The recognized loss for project B is also handled similarly using either accounting methods. This is because the project has an estimated loss and proper accounting requires recognition of the total forecasted loss independent of the accounting method used.

Projects C and D bring out the potential dramatic difference between the percentage-of-completion method and the completed-contract method. Neither project is completed at the time of statement presentation. Therefore, no

Percentage of Completion

	Project A	Project B	Project C	Project D	Total
Total revenue	$720,000	$646,155	$933,333	$666,667	$2,966,155
Total expenditures	620,000	700,000	800,000	600,000	2,720,000
Additional estimated loss		(46,155)			(46,155)
Gross profit	$100,000	$(100,000)	$133,333	$ 66,667	$ 200,000
G & A expense					180,000
Net income					$ 20,000

Completed Contract

	Project A	Project B	Project C	Project D	Total
Total revenue	$720,000	–	–	–	$ 720,000
Total expenditures	620,000	–	–	–	620,000
Forecasted loss		$(100,000)			(100,000)
Gross profit	$100,000	$(100,000)	–	–	0
G & A expense					180,000
Net income (loss)					$(180,000)

Figure 3.4 Income Effect of Percentage-of-Completion and Completed-Contract

revenue or project expense (and resulting profit or loss) is recognized in the completed-contract income statement at that point in time. On the other hand, based on the costs expended to date and the total estimated costs, a total of $200,000 of income is recognized on projects C and D. Both projects C and D are 66.67 percent complete based on costs expended to the total expected project costs. Therefore, two-thirds, or 66.67 percent, of the total contract amount is recognized as revenue on the projects.

Because of the $200,000 greater income that results when using the percentage of completion in the year in question, it follows that in a later year, the use of the completed-contract method will result in $200,000 of added income. However, in the year in question, a reader of the statements will observe the net income using one of the methods and may come to an entirely different conclusion regarding the financial strength of the firm than he might if he observed or analyzed the income statement using the other revenue-recognition method.

The financial impact of the two accounting methods is not limited to the resulting income statements. For the data illustrated in Figure 3.1, the increased income for the percentage-of-completion method would carry over to the firm's balance sheet as an improved working capital position relative to that using the completed-contract method. Here, again, the reverse could be true for a different set of project data.

Independent of the different dollar amounts possible, using either of the two accounting methods can affect financial ratios derived from the balance sheet as well as those derived from the income statement. The conclusion is that the reader of the financial statements has to interpret the statements in order to equate a statement prepared using the percentage-of-completion method to one prepared using the completed-contract method. This interpretation or analysis is enhanced by the availability of a work-in-progress schedule. This type of financial statement or schedule is discussed in Chapter 6.

Inspection of Figure 3.4 indicates that the firm's general and administrative expense (also referred to as G & A or overhead) is subtracted from the calculated gross profit to yield the net income regardless of the choice of accounting methods. In other words, in Figure 3.4 the G & A is written off as a period cost (written off in the period incurred).

Some would argue that one is justified in capitalizing some of this expense in a given time period when using the completed-contract method. The argument for this is based on the "matching" principle. Some or all of the G & A expense shown in Figure 3.4 is the result of building projects C and D. Since no revenue is recognized for these two projects in the period in question, one might defend the fact that the related G & A expense should not be recognized until revenue is recognized. One could defend this position and therefore "defer" some or all of the $180,000 of G & A expensed on the completed-contract net income calculation shown in Figure 3.4. Recognition of the G & A as either a period cost (expensed in period incurred) or a product cost (capitalized as part of the asset), whereby it is different, could have been and have been defended in practice. Period cost and product cost are further discussed in Chapter 13. The variability of this G & A treatment when using the completed-contract method is just another example of the numerous alternative accounting methods and procedures used in practice.

4
THE BOOKKEEPING PROCESS

INTRODUCTION

Bookkeeping can be defined as the set of procedures and forms that are used to record all the financial transactions of a firm. The previous two chapters presented the theory and mechanics of specific accounting entries for financial transactions. They illustrated how each transaction resulted in debits and credits to the firm's accounts and how the accounting relationship of assets, liabilities, and net worth remained in balance.

The bookkeeping process in the construction industry is made difficult by the fact that project costs are incurred at a distance from the location at which the accounting for them is done (that is, the home office). Normally, the construction project is not large enough in regard to profit or long enough in regard to duration to justify setting up an entire bookkeeping personnel team at the project location. This is not to say that it has not been done occasionally. On large projects, the construction firm may in fact set up a homeoffice–branch office at the project site. However, it is much more common periodically to send the required bookkeeping cost data from the field office to the home office. This distance between the location of the cost occurrence and that of formulating them creates several control problems. In addition to requiring more forms and procedures, the distance creates problems in regard to the time at which the cost data is received, formulated, and analyzed for control purposes.

In practice, accounting entries are not made directly to an "accounting equation" or directly to a financial statement such as the income statement. Instead, the entries are made to accounting forms that include ledgers and various types of journals. These ledgers, journals, and the procedures used to record data on them are part of the bookkeeping process. We also refer to this process as the firm's *accounting system*.

The appearance and use of ledger and journal forms used by construction firms vary considerably. While one firm may use standardized forms prepared by a publishing company, another firm may "custom" design its forms to meet its own characteristics. This chapter will discuss some of the more commonly used bookkeeping procedures and forms that are applicable to the construction firm.

THE ACCOUNTING CYCLE

The entire accounting cycle is aimed at summarizing and classifying financial data and is completed when financial statements are produced. Preliminary to this producing of financial statements is the completion of the accounting steps illustrated in Figure 4.1.

The first step in the accounting cycle is entering the financial transaction accounting entries. These entries are commonly made in *journals* and summarized into *ledgers,* which is referred to as *posting*. The entries to journals are made daily, whereas the posting process is normally performed monthly. The frequency of the preparation of financial statements varies from monthly, to quarterly, to annually for some construction firms.

JOURNALS

Accounting systems may be classified as either *pen-and-ink* or *computerized.* In a pen-and-ink system, accounting transactions are entered manually on a set of journal forms. In a computerized system, entries can be made directly into a computer input device. In this type of system, the accounting transactions are processed and structured internally within the computer. Computers and computer systems are discussed in Chapter 11.

In pen-and-ink systems, journals serve as the original book of entry for financial transactions. The type of journal system used varies from a simple, two-column journal all the way to relatively complicated journal systems that include several specialized journals. Some of the factors that should be con-

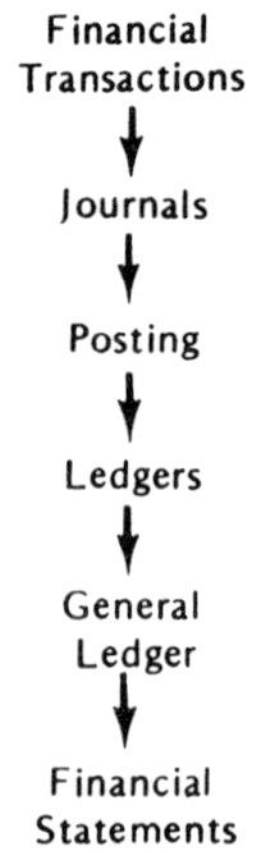

Figure 4.1 The Accounting Cycle

sidered in selecting the type of journal system to be used by the construction firm include the following:

1. The number of bookkeeping personnel.
2. The skills of the bookkeeping personnel.
3. The degree of departmentalization.
4. The size of the firm and the frequency and number of accounting transactions.
5. The type of work the firm performs.
6. The sophistication of the firm's job-cost control system.

Two-Column Journal System

The two-column journal system is used only when the number of a firm's transactions is very small. The form shown in Figure 4.2 is an example of a two-column journal. Each and every entry is made directly into the journals. The debit entry, or entries, for each financial transaction is made in one column while the credit entry, or entries, is placed in the other column. Each entry is coded with the appropriate general ledger account number. If the firm is on a cash basis, only cash transactions are entered into the journal in Figure 4.2. On the other hand, if the firm is on an accrual basis, both cash and accrual entries are made in the journal.

At some point in time each and every entry in the two-column journal is transferred to individual ledger accounts. Usually this would be done monthly. For example, all of the cash entries made in the two-column journal would be located, summarized, and transferred to the cash ledger sheet. Other entries would also be transferred to a ledger using the same procedure. This process is redundant and the time required to do it is excessive unless the firm only has a few financial transactions in a given period of time.

The result is that the two-column journal system is a feasible system only for a small firm. In reality the two-column journal system is more of a "textbook" journal system than an efficient one to be used in practice.

Cash Journal System

The cash journal system is a multiple-column journal. Unlike the two-column journal, columns are provided for grouping specific types of entries. An example of a cash journal is illustrated in Figure 4.3.

The cash journal shown in Figure 4.3 provides columns for both cash paid in and cash paid out of the firm. Therefore, both sales and expenses are recognized in the single journal. Other columns are provided for recording entries that occur frequently for a specific account which reduces the number of postings to the general ledger or the need to group and summarize journal entries in order to post to a ledger. Instead, the specific entries in columns are summed and posted in total to the general ledger at the end of the month.

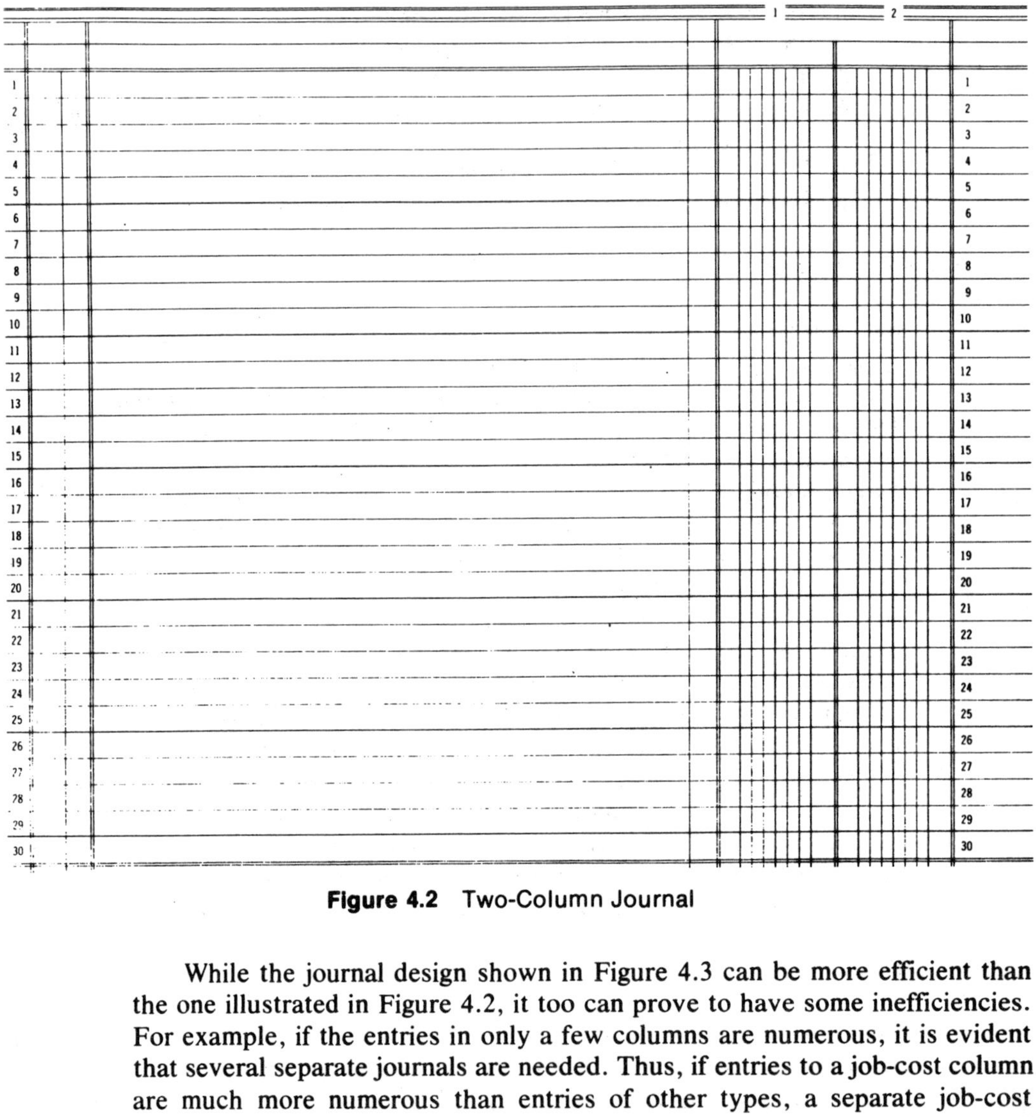

Figure 4.2 Two-Column Journal

While the journal design shown in Figure 4.3 can be more efficient than the one illustrated in Figure 4.2, it too can prove to have some inefficiencies. For example, if the entries in only a few columns are numerous, it is evident that several separate journals are needed. Thus, if entries to a job-cost column are much more numerous than entries of other types, a separate job-cost journal should be considered; otherwise, much of the space in the cash journal will be wasted. In addition, a separate job-cost journal may provide columns for breaking down the specific types of job costs. This breakdown may aid management in planning and controlling its jobs.

Some firms will use a journal similar to that shown in Figure 4.3 but will design the sheet to result in more columns. Then these columns are used to identify components of job costs or may identify specific columns for entering

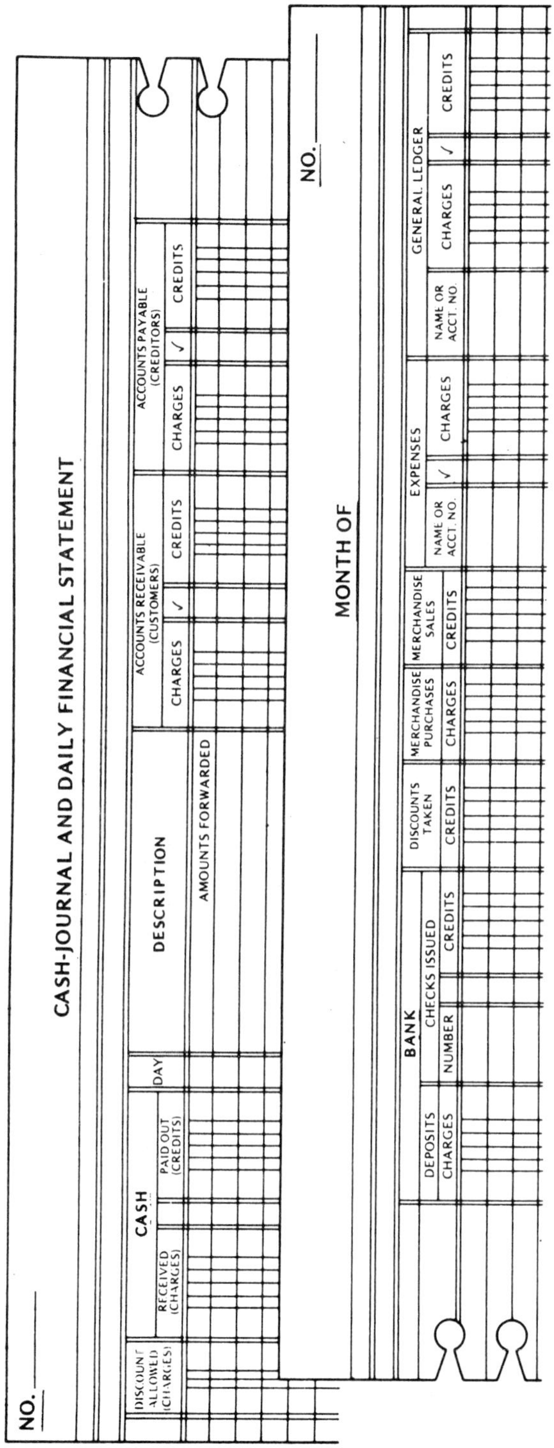

Figure 4.3 Cash Journal

costs to a specific job or jobs. In this way the firm is able to determine the total job costs as well as individual job costs by merely summing the appropriate column entries recorded in the journal.

In practice, the number of columns in a journal, including a cash journal, is dictated by the design of the bookkeeping process, the firm's need for data, and, not to be overlooked, the number of columns available on the forms in use. For example, a firm may set out fourteen column headings merely because it has adopted the use of fourteen-column accounting paper. While this latter reason may seem weak, the fact remains that, for many construction firms, the forms often dictate the accounting practices rather than vice versa. Not that this is correct, but it does remain true.

Other examples of separate journals that may be appropriate include the sales journal and purchase journal. An example of a separate job-cost journal is shown in Figure 4.4.

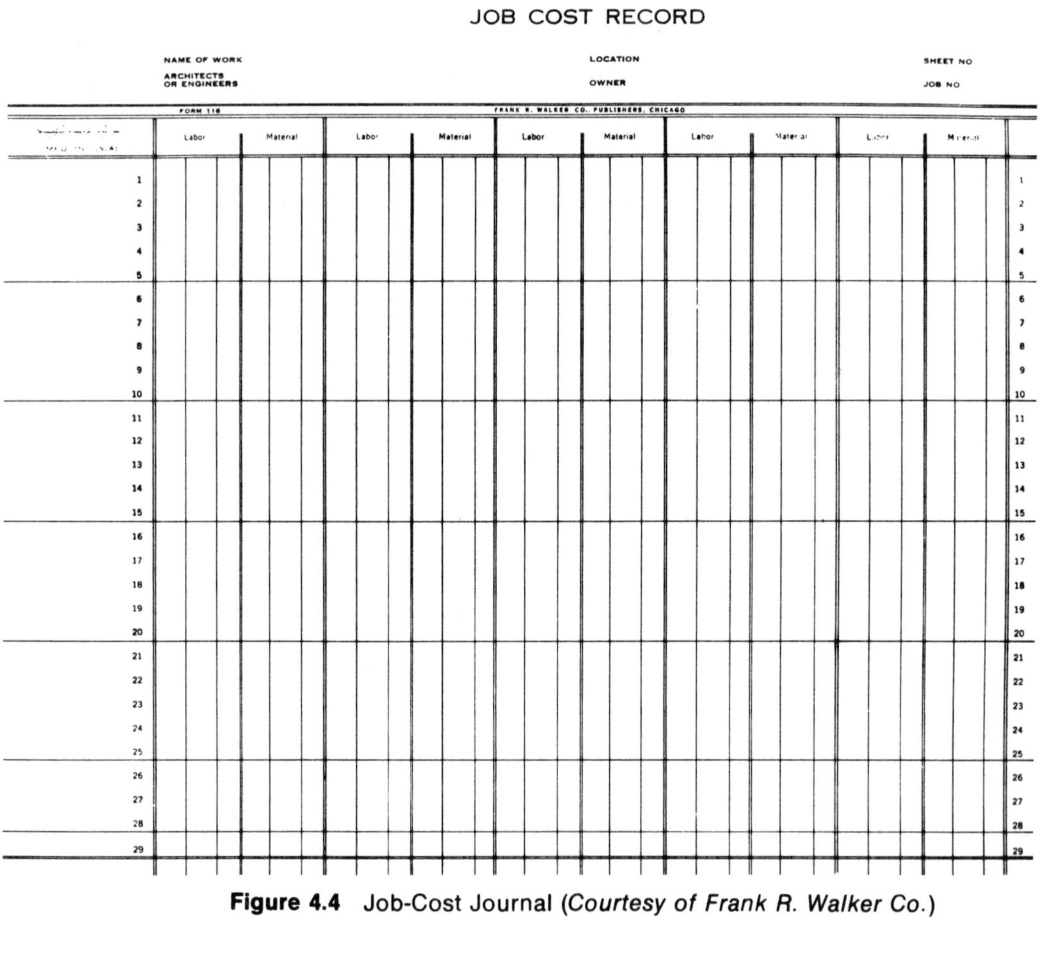
JOB COST RECORD

NAME OF WORK — LOCATION — SHEET NO
ARCHITECTS OR ENGINEERS — OWNER — JOB NO
FRANK R. WALKER CO. PUBLISHERS, CHICAGO

	Labor	Material	Labor	Material	Labor	Material	Labor	Material	Labor	Material	
1											1
2											2
3											3
4											4
5											5
6											6
7											7
8											8
9											9
10											10
11											11
12											12
13											13
14											14
15											15
16											16
17											17
18											18
19											19
20											20
21											21
22											22
23											23
24											24
25											25
26											26
27											27
28											28
29											29

Figure 4.4 Job-Cost Journal (*Courtesy of Frank R. Walker Co.*)

Another sometimes recognized criticism of the journal shown in Figure 4.3 is that once an error has been made, it may be necessary to check numerous transactions in detail to see that cash was entered in the correct column. While this criticism may be justified, one should point out that this is a criticism of all journals, independent of the journal's design.

Receipts and Disbursements Journals

The use of two separate journals for recording revenue and disbursements is referred to as a *two-journal* system or set. Some argue that the two-journal system provides the firm greater analysis potential. This point is debatable. In reality, using a single cash disbursement journal or a set of two journals, including the receipts and disbursements journal, is a matter of personal preference.

An example of a two-journal set is shown in Figure 4.5. The receipts journal has several columns available for entering and analyzing specific journal entries, and a single column for debiting cash. Several columns are available in the disbursements journal for entering and analyzing debit entries, which may include purchases and labor costs. A single column is provided for crediting cash when a disbursement is made.

Both the receipts journal and the disbursements journal shown in Figure 4.5 provide columns for recording accruals including receivables and payables, respectively. As a bill is made out, it may be recorded in the receipts journal by debiting the receivable column shown and crediting the appropriate sales account. When the cash is received, a credit entry is made to the identified receivable column. A debit in equal dollar amount is made to cash. Assuming the firm has no outstanding receivables at a specific point in time, the total of the debit receivable entries should equal the credit receivable entries.

When the construction firm receives a bill from a vendor, it is possible to accrue the related expense by recording the payable in the credit column of Figure 4.5 and debiting the appropriate expense account. When the construction firm pays the recorded bill, an entry is made in the accounts payable debit column of Figure 4.5. Cash is credited for the dollar expense amount.

One argument that can be made for the two-journal set (separate receipts and disbursements journals) versus the single journal is that almost all entries (other than cash) are credits on the receipts journal and debits (other than cash) on the disbursements journal. The fact that one is not mixing many debits and credits on a single page may result in fewer errors in making or summing the individual entries.

It is also true that using two separate journals allows identification of more column accounts in each journal which makes it possible to break down more detail in the journal. For example, given the availability of more columns, a construction firm may distribute labor costs to specific jobs.

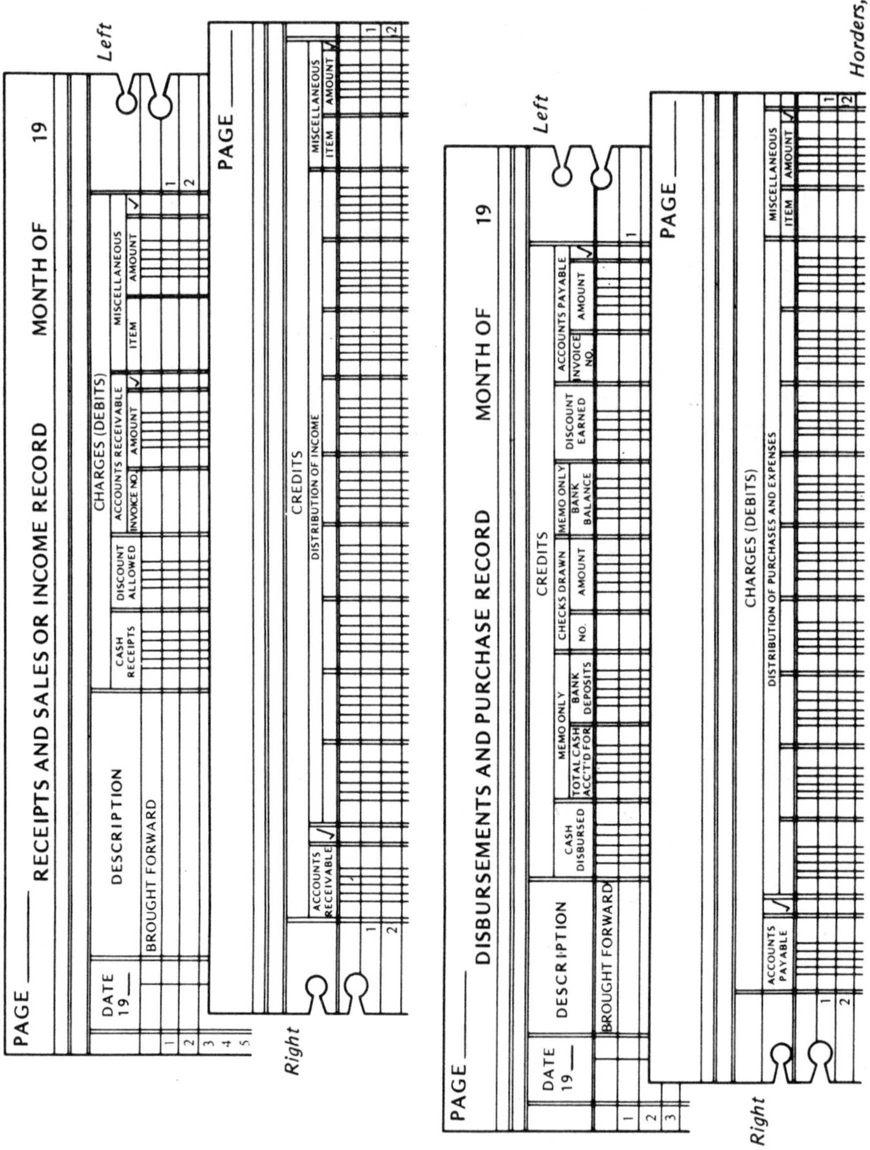

Figure 4.5 Two-Journal Set—Cash Receipts and Disbursements Journal

LEDGERS

A ledger is an accounting form that serves to summarize all the entries to a specific account. The process of summarizing the debits and credits made to a specific account in the firm's journal and the transfering of these amounts to specific ledger is referred to as posting. The actual posting process or timing of the process of posting depends on the form of journals used (the previous section presented several alternative journals). At one extreme a firm may have several journal columns that, in effect, serve as ledgers for specific accounts. Even when this is the case, the firm will probably summarize the accounts using individual ledger forms. The concept of posting from a journal to a ledger is illustrated in Figure 4.6. In practice more journal entries would typically make up the total that is transferred monthly to the ledger account, especially if the ledger account was "cash."

There is usually a ledger form or ledger page in a book for each defined account in the construction firm's chart of accounts. The group of ledger forms or ledger pages is commonly referred to as the firm's *general ledger*. As is true with journals, the construction firm may keep a set of specialized ledgers that support the master or general ledger. These are referred to as *subsidiary ledgers*. Subsidiary ledgers are used to supply details in various selected accounts. For example, rather than keep an accounts receivable ledger for each and every individual firm who owes money to the construction firm, subsidiary ledgers may be used for each with all controlled by the general accounts receivable ledger. The overall receivable ledger is referred to as the *controlling ledger* when it is supported by subsidiary ledgers. The concept of a general ledger supported by subsidiary ledgers is illustrated in Figure 4.7.

Like journals, ledger accounting forms vary in design. One of the more common forms used for a ledger is shown in Figure 4.8. It is referred to as a *debit, credit, and balance ledger*. The date of posting is placed in the "date" column. This usually occurs every month. The "description" column is used to designate the type of entry being made. Usually the description in the column refers to a monthly entry; however, the entry to the ledger form may be an adjusting journal entry (see Chapter 5 for a discussion of adjusting journal entries) that is made when the financial statements are prepared.

The "folio" column serves as a means of referencing the posting entry to a page or series of pages in the journal. This referencing provides a trace to follow when searching for an entry to a source document for a financial transition.

The "debit" and "credit " columns provide columns for identifying the dollar amount of the entry being made. Finally the "balance" column is for keeping a running total of an account balance after each entry is made.

The ledger form illustrated in Figure 4.9 is an alternative to the ledger form shown in Figure 4.8. It is referred to as a *debit, credit, debit balance, and credit balance ledger*. It contains an additional column for listing either a debit or credit balance. If an account can have a debit or credit balance, the

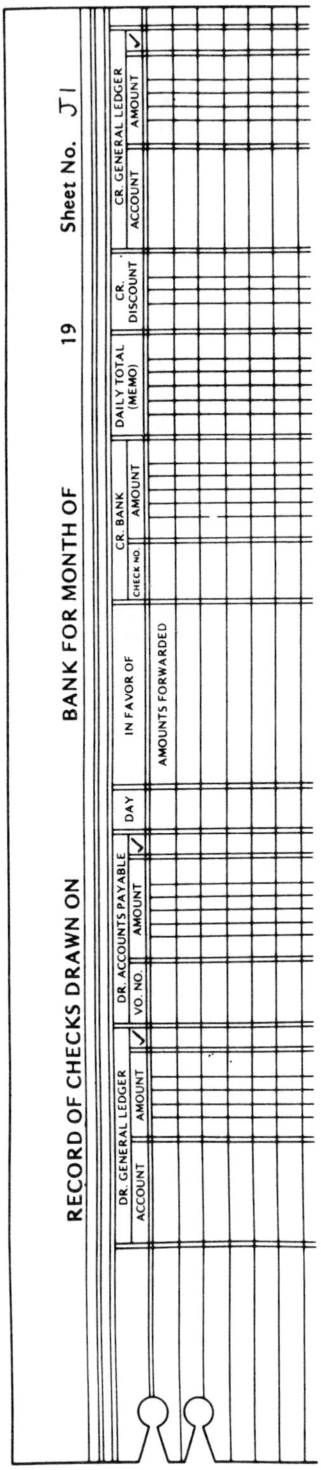
RECORD OF CHECKS DRAWN ON
BANK FOR MONTH OF
19
Sheet No. J1
DR. GENERAL LEDGER
ACCOUNT
AMOUNT
✓
DR. ACCOUNTS PAYABLE
VO. NO.
AMOUNT
✓
DAY
IN FAVOR OF
AMOUNTS FORWARDED
CR. BANK
CHECK NO.
AMOUNT
DAILY TOTAL (MEMO)
CR. DISCOUNT
CR. GENERAL LEDGER
ACCOUNT
AMOUNT
✓

(Back)

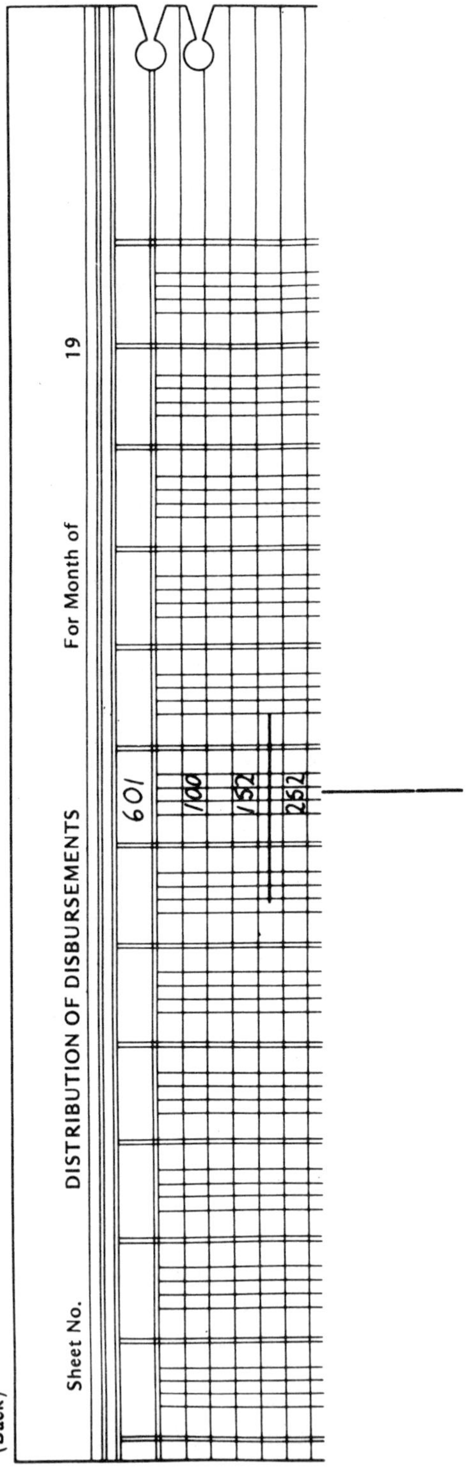
Sheet No.
DISTRIBUTION OF DISBURSEMENTS
For Month of
19
601
100
152
252

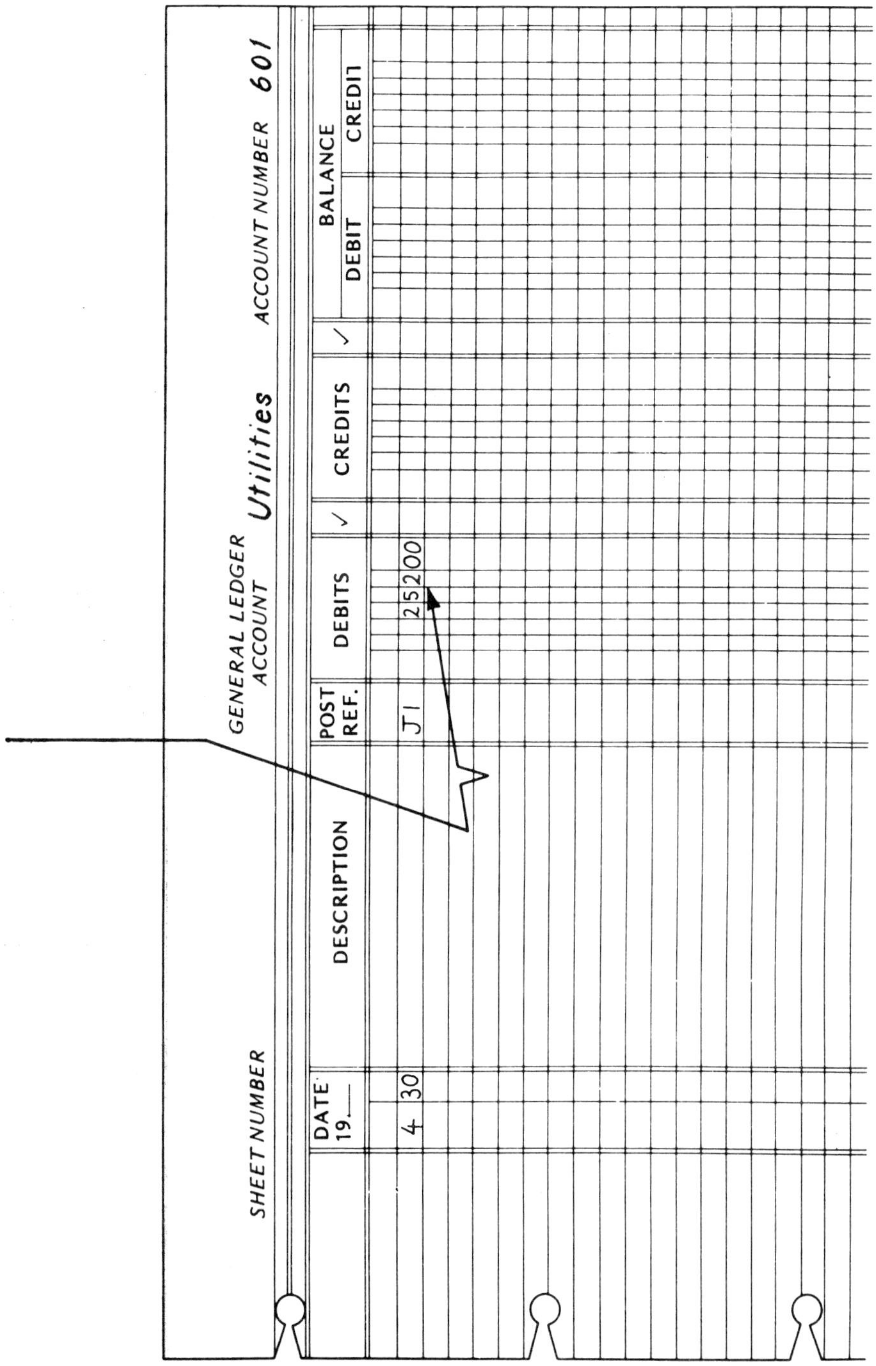

Figure 4.6 Posting to Ledger from Journal

General ledger accounts receivable*

	Debit	*Credit*	*Balance*
May 31, 79	3,520	2,120	1,400 Dr

*Note: Amounts Posted at End of Month

Debits and Credits Summed and Transferred

Accounts receivable ledger**

R. J. Jones Co.

Date	*Type*	*Debit*	*Credit*
5/ 3/79	S	825	
5/18/79	CR		1,450
5/21/79	S	936	

L. Roecker Co.

Date	*Type*	*Debit*	*Credit*
5/ 8/79	S	1,759	
5/21/79	CR		670

**Note: Amounts Posted Daily.

Figure 4.7 Control and Subsidiary Ledgers

ledger form illustrated in Figure 4.9 is preferred over the one shown in Figure 4.8. Given a balance that varies from a debit to a credit as a function of time, the one balance-column ledger is more likely to lead to posting mistakes or reader misinterpretation of the balance.

The ledger forms shown in Figures 4.8 and 4.9 may be bound in a book or appear as individual sheets of paper in a tray designed to hold the sheets. In addition to the ledger forms shown, specialized ledger forms may be designed for specific types of subsidiary ledgers such as ledger forms for recording inventory or equipment. These forms vary in design and use and are not illustrated here. Even when used, these special purpose ledgers function in the same way as a general ledger form; that is, they serve as a means of summarizing a series of journal entries.

BOOKKEEPING FOR CONSTRUCTION LABOR COSTS

Whereas the lack of proper documentation and control of construction materials (discussed in a following section of this chapter) seldom leads to overall project loss, such practices in regard to labor productivity and costs are one of the prime causes for project and company financial loss. Labor is the most variable of all construction costs. Construction project labor bookkeeping is commonly referred to as *timekeeping*. The actual timekeeping process has two objectives. First, it determines the total amount of time for which each worker is to be paid. As such, the process is part of the firm's payroll task. Of equal importance in regard to control and cost accounting is timekeeping's contribution to allocation of labor hours and costs to the various project work items.

The actual timekeeping on a construction project is normally done by project foremen or a timekeeper. Employing a timekeeper is usually not justified on small construction projects; instead, foremen are given the responsibility of daily documentation of worker hours both as to their amount of hours and the allocation of the hours to the performed work items. They do this by recording hours in a small book kept in the pocket or by filling out a timecard at the end of the day. Because such timecards are stored at the field office, there is little chance that they will be lost and, as such, this procedure is preferred. Such a form is shown in Figure 4.10.

If a project is of a size that justifies employing a timekeeper (note: the timekeeper can also be responsible for receiving and protection of project materials), better potential for control results than if foremen are assigned the timekeeping responsibility. The timekeeper generally has more time and is more committed to the timekeeping task than are foremen. In addition, there is probably less potential for collusion between the timekeeper and workers

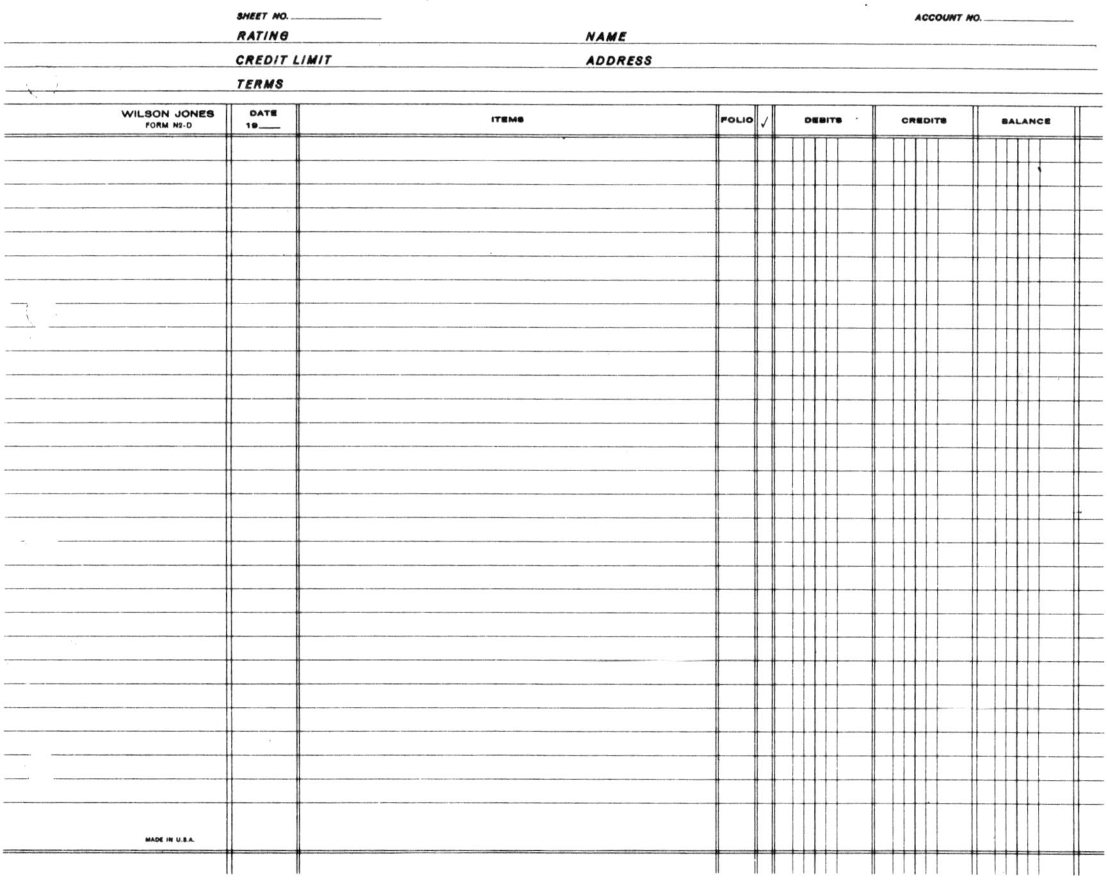

SHEET NO. ACCOUNT NO.
RATING NAME
CREDIT LIMIT ADDRESS
TERMS

WILSON JONES FORM N2-D	DATE 19__	ITEMS	FOLIO	√	DEBITS	CREDITS	BALANCE

MADE IN U.S.A.

Figure 4.8 Debit, Credit, and Balance Ledger

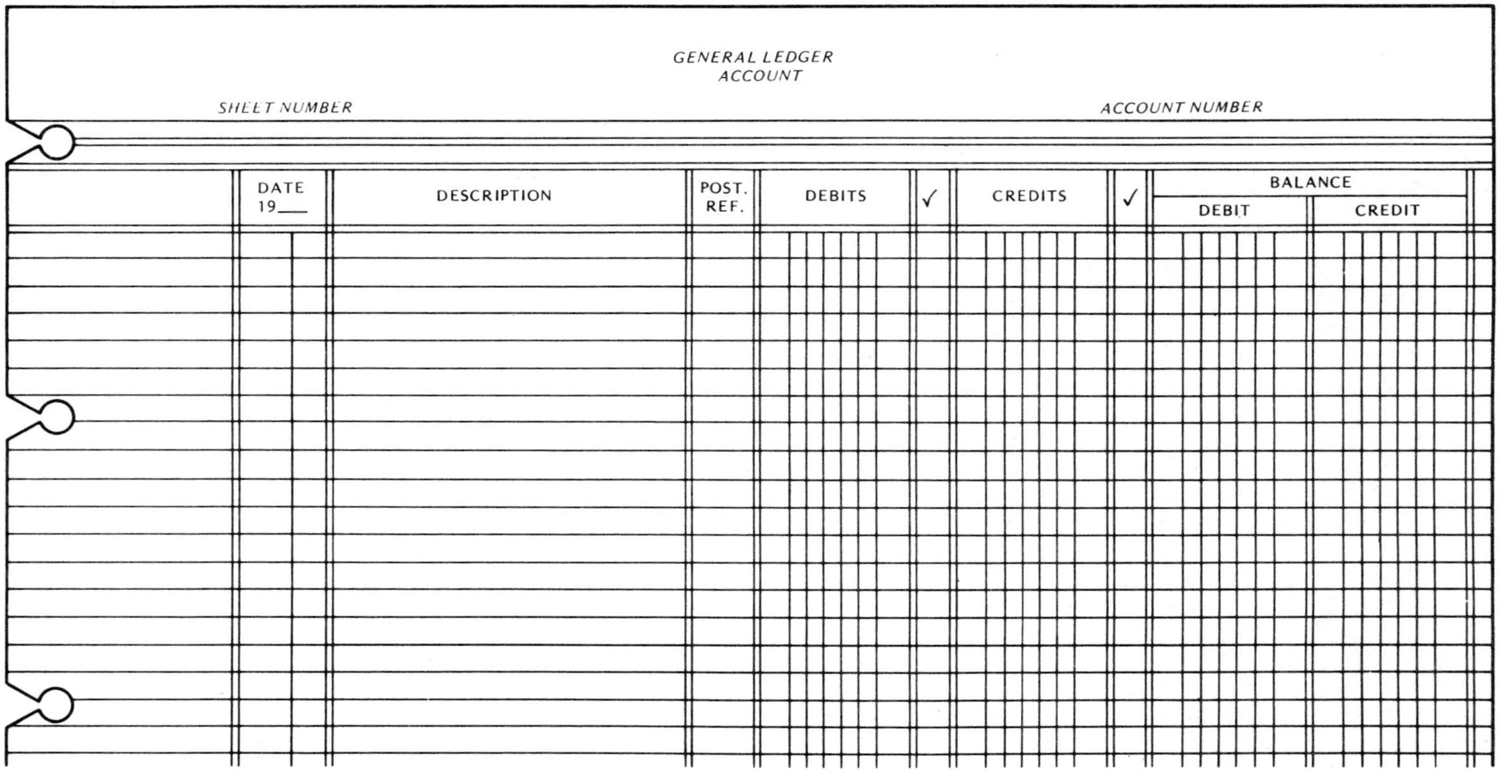

Figure 4.9 Debit, Credit, Debit Balance, Credit Balance Ledger

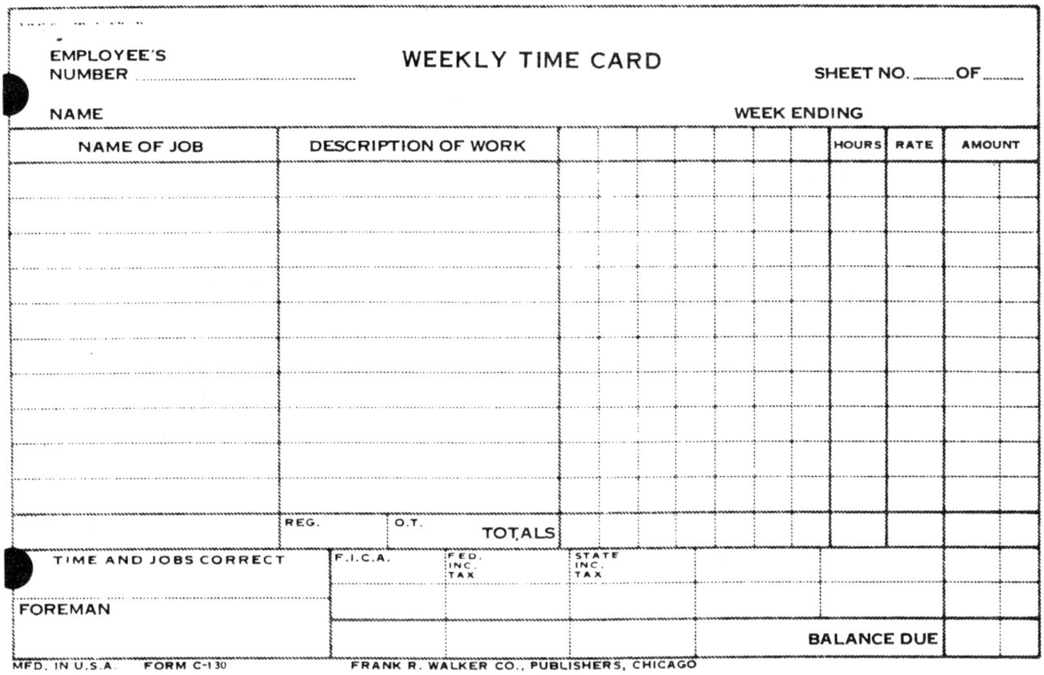

EMPLOYEE'S NUMBER

WEEKLY TIME CARD

SHEET NO. ____ OF ____

NAME

WEEK ENDING

NAME OF JOB	DESCRIPTION OF WORK								HOURS	RATE	AMOUNT
	REG. / O.T. / TOTALS										

TIME AND JOBS CORRECT

FOREMAN

F.I.C.A. | FED. INC. TAX | STATE INC. TAX

BALANCE DUE

MFD. IN U.S.A. FORM C-130 FRANK R. WALKER CO., PUBLISHERS, CHICAGO

Figure 4.10 Labor Timecard (*Courtesy of Frank R. Walker Co.*)

than there is between a foreman and his workers. That is, foremen are often involved in working with their workers and their closeness to them encourages such a practice as the foreman's reporting a worker's hours even though the worker is absent for the time period.

When a project is spread out over a relatively large area, the timekeeper may have difficulty documenting late starting or early quitting of individual workers. In addition, there may be so many workers on the project site that the timekeeper may in fact fail to observe and document the absence of a given worker. Such a failure will lead to documenting and paying wages for which no work is performed. There are several well-known procedures for documenting the starting and finishing time of a worker. Probably the most frequently used timekeeping device used in the manufacturing industry is a timeclock. Workers insert a card into a punch-type device that records the time of the day on the card. Timeclocks have not proved popular in the construction industry for several reasons: the mobility of the construction project, workers' general dislike of them, and the difficulty associated with monitoring such a system.

An alternative to using a timeclock is using a badge procedure. Small metal badges with numbers on them are kept at a central location that is maintained by the project timekeeper. Upon arriving for work, workers pick up their badges with their assigned numbers and pin them on their work uniforms. At the end of the day they return the badges. Such a procedure ensures documentation of workers' presence, starting times, and quitting times. In addition, it brings attention to a given worker's long absences. The main difficulty of the badging system is that workers have to report to a central location to pick up and return their badges. Such a procedure may prove time consuming when the workers are spread out over a project.

An alternative to the badging system is to have workers continuously wear a badge number. This badge is not turned in, but is kept by the worker. While walking the project the timekeeper documents the presence of workers by noting their number. Such a procedure is especially advantageous when many workers are employed and the timekeeper does not know each one by face. While proving useful in documenting the presence of a worker, this procedure does not aid in noting whether a worker starts or quits on time.

Regardless of whether a foreman or a timekeeper is responsible for documenting labor time, occasionally an individual from the home office should visit the construction project to check the foreman's or timekeeper's report as to who is working. This provides a means of control in regard to potential collusion between a worker and the foreman or timekeeper.

Furthermore, regardless of whether the foreman or timekeeper makes out daily timecards, they have to be sent to the home office, preferably daily. At the minimum, they should be sent in weekly. These weekly reports lack the control potential that daily reports offer because the quicker labor inefficiencies or overruns are recognized, the better the change for corrective management. In addition, weekly reports encourage fraudulent reporting procedures—a worker might be laid off on Tuesday and carried on the payroll through Friday due to fraudulent timekeeping.

The daily or weekly labor cost reports turned in by the foreman or timekeeper should indicate both total worker hours and the allocation of the hours to project work items. However, project foremen cannot be expected to document a very detailed analysis of each worker's time, that is, it is awkward to require foremen to account for coffee breaks, inefficient production, and so on. Effectiveness as foremen might be weakened if they are asked to be watchdogs of their workers. This is yet another reason for justifying the employment of a timekeeper on a project.

Payroll Procedures

Once the timecards are received in the home office, the individuals in charge of payroll calculate the net pay due each employee and make the journal entry for the payroll accrual. They also prepare reports required by various laws concerning employees.

In order to prepare payroll checks, the various accrual accounting entries, and required employee reports, several payroll steps must be made. Included in these are the following:

1. Gather attendance times of employee.
2. Use appropriate pay rates established per employee and additional compensation including sick pay, tool allowance, and so on.
3. Group employee hours and multiply by the appropriate pay rates.
4. Distribute employee hours or costs to jobs or parts of jobs (work items) if a job-cost system is used.
5. Calculate deductions from gross payroll including
   a. Withholding taxes
   b. FICA (Federal Insurance Contributions Act tax)
   c. Union dues
   d. Various deductions for funds such as education fund, health and welfare, and so on
   e. Insurance payments for group insurance, hospitalization, and so forth
   f. Deductions for employee advances
6. Prepare the following statements and reports:
   a. Payroll journal
   b. Paycheck
   c. Pay stub or employee's earning statement
   d. Employee's earning record
   e. Forms and reports required of employers regarding income tax withheld and tax due under FICA

Gathering of each employee's time is not totally within the control of the payroll individual or department. The time worked by an employee is determined at the job site when a timekeeper or foreman fills out employee timecards. These timecards are then delivered to the home office. Often the cutoff date is Wednesday, which gives payroll one to two days to prepare paychecks in order to make them available to employees on Friday.

The payroll individual or department cannot be expected to verify all employee hours on the timecard. However, while the major responsibility for correct timecards should be placed on field personnel, the office payroll personnel should inspect the timecards for any obvious mistake or misrepresentations. For example, hours charged to a job that was finished three months ago, or a reported employee time of 70 hours worked in a time period, usually means an error has been made on the source document.

Pay rates for each construction labor craft are usually established by labor union agreements or by agreement with labor at the start of a specific project. These agreements also determine various benefits that must be paid by the employer and the employee. The pay rates are usually set for a defined period of time.

Officer salaries and the pay rates of the professional and office staff present few problems. Often these personnel are on salary and the weekly pay is fixed, independent of hours worked.

The payroll effort required to group and extend employee hours times labor rates depends on the design of the timecards. Some are designed to enable the calculation of the gross pay directly on the timecard. Others require using a worksheet to sum employee hours and extend the hours at the relevant pay rate. This is especially the case when daily timecards are used.

Distributing hours to specific jobs or phases of jobs (referred to as *work items*) supports an effective project planning and control management system. While this distribution of employee hours may be done independently of the payroll function, it is usually more efficient if the distribution is done as part of the payroll process. The design and use of project planning and control management systems are discussed in Chapters 9 and 10.

Once the calculation of an employee's pay is determined, the next step is to calculate various deductions and taxes due that are to be withheld to determine the net pay (the net pay is the amount appearing on the employee's paycheck). Withholding taxes include federal withholding tax and possibly a state or even municipal withholding tax.

The federal withholding tax is required by law. While the tax is the responsibility of the employee, the employer in effect "collects" it by deducting the tax from the employers gross pay and in turn submitting the payment to the federal government. When an employee is hired, he fills out a W-4 form establishing the number of his dependents, which in part has the effect of establishing the amount to be deducted from his gross pay. The form is illustrated in Figure 4.11. The amount of the employee's pay also determines the amount to be withheld. The federal government has standardized charts or tables made available to employers that indicate the amount of tax to be withheld as a function of the gross pay and the number of dependents claimed. The rates in these tables vary according to the tax law in effect at the time. The state and municipal withholding taxes, when applicable, are made in the same manner.

The Federal Insurance Contributions Act (FICA) requires both employer and employee to pay a premium on an employee's wages for the purpose of employee disability, hospital insurance, and retirement benefits. The premium is required on all wages to a maximum established by law. Once an employee earns the maximum in a year, no premium is required on wages in excess of that.

The employer and employee pay equal shares of the FICA premium. The premium rate has varied according to changing tax laws. The employee's share of the FICA premium is deducted from the gross pay. In effect, the money deducted is held by the employer and is submitted to the appropriate collecting agency along with the employer's share.

While no deduction is made from the employee's gross pay, the employer is liable to pay unemployment compensation insurance (UC) for his employees. This premium is paid on employee's wages up to a set maximum, which is significantly less than the maximum used for calculating the FICA premium. The premium rate for any one construction firm depends on several factors including employment records as to layoffs. Given the seasonal characteristics

Form **W-4**
(Rev. May 1977)
Department of the Treasury
Internal Revenue Service

Employee's Withholding Allowance Certificate

(Use for Wages Paid After May 31, 1977)

This certificate is for income tax withholding purposes only. It will remain in effect until you change it. If you claim exemption from withholding, you will have to file a new certificate on or before April 30 of next year.

Type or print your full name		**Your social security number**
Home address (number and street or rural route)	Marital Status	☐ Single ☐ Married ☐ Married, but withhold at higher Single rate
City or town, State, and ZIP code		**Note:** *If married, but legally separated, or spouse is a nonresident alien, check the single block.*

1 Total number of allowances you are claiming	
2 Additional amount, if any, you want deducted from each pay (if your employer agrees)	$
3 I claim exemption from withholding (see instructions). Enter "Exempt"	

Under the penalties of perjury, I certify that the number of withholding exemptions and allowances claimed on this certificate does not exceed the number to which I am entitled. If claiming exemption from withholding, I certify that I incurred no liability for Federal income tax for last year and that I anticipate that I will incur no liability for Federal income tax for this year.

Signature ▶ .... **Date** ▶ ...., **19**.........

.... Detach along this line ....

▲ *Give the top part of this form to your employer; keep the lower part for your records and information* ▲

Instructions

The explanatory material below will help you determine your correct number of withholding allowances, and will assist you in completing the Form W-4 at the top of this page.

Avoid Overwithholding or Underwithholding

By claiming the number of withholding allowances you are entitled to, you can fit the amount of tax withheld from your wages to your tax liability. In addition to the allowances for personal exemptions to be claimed in item (a), be sure to claim any additional allowances you are entitled to in item (b), "Special withholding allowance," and item (c), "Allowance(s) for credit(s) and/or deduction(s)." While you may claim these allowances on Form W-4 for withholding purposes, you may not claim them under "Exemptions" on your tax return Form 1040 or Form 1040A.

You may claim the special withholding allowance if you are single with only one employer, or married with only one employer **and** your spouse is not employed. If you have unusually large itemized deductions, an alimony deduction, or credit(s) for child care expenses, earned income, or credit for the elderly, you may claim additional allowances to avoid having too much income tax withheld from your wages. Please note that alimony is no longer an itemized deduction, but rather is an adjustment to gross income. It may be to your benefit to take the standard deduction in lieu of itemizing deductions because of this change.

If you and your spouse are both employed or you have more than one employer, you should make sure that enough has been withheld. If you find that you need more withholding, claim fewer exemptions or ask for additional withholding or request to be withheld at the higher "Single" status. If you are currently claiming additional withholding allowances based on itemized deductions, check the worksheet on the back to see that you are claiming the proper number of allowances.

How Many Withholding Allowances May You Claim?

Use the schedule below to determine the number of allowances you may claim for tax withholding purposes. In determining the number, keep in mind these points: if you are single and hold more than one job, you may not claim the same allowances with more than one employer at the same time; or, if you are married and both you and your spouse are employed, you may not both claim the same allowances with your employers at the same time. A nonresident alien, other than a resident of Canada, Mexico, or Puerto Rico, may claim only one personal allowance.

Completing Form W-4

If you find you are entitled to one or more allowances in addition to those you are now claiming, increase your number of allowances by completing the form above and filing it with your employer. If the number of allowances you previously claimed decreases, you must file a new Form W-4 within 10 days. (If you expect to owe more tax than will be withheld, you may increase your withholding by claiming fewer or "0" allowances on line 1, or by asking for additional withholding on line 2, or both.)

You may claim exemption from withholding of Federal income tax if you had no liability for income tax for last year, and you anticipate that you will incur no liability for income tax for this year. You may not claim exemption if your joint or separate return shows tax liability before the allowance of any credit for income tax withheld. If you are exempt, your employer will not withhold Federal income tax from your wages. However, social security tax will be withheld if you are covered by the Federal Insurance Contributions Act.

You must revoke this exemption (1) within 10 days from the time you anticipate you will incur income tax liability for the year or (2) on or before December 1 if you anticipate you will incur Federal income tax liability for the next year. If you want to stop or are required to revoke this exemption, you must file a new Form W-4 with your employer showing the number of withholding allowances you are entitled to claim. This certificate for exemption from withholding will expire on April 30 of next year unless a new Form W-4 is filed before that date.

The Following Information is Provided in Accordance with the Privacy Act of 1974

The Internal Revenue Code requires every employee to furnish his or her employer with a signed withholding allowance certificate showing the number of withholding allowances that the employee claims (section 3402(f)(2)(A) and the Regulations thereto). Individuals are required to provide their Social Security Number for proper identification and processing (section 6109 and the Regulations thereto).

The principal purpose for soliciting withholding allowance certificate information is to administer the Internal Revenue laws of the United States.

If an employee does not furnish a signed withholding allowance certificate, the employee is considered as claiming no withholding allowances (section 3402(e)) and shall be treated as a single person (section 3402(l)).

The routine uses of the withholding allowance certificate information include disclosure to the Department of Justice for actual or potential criminal prosecution or civil litigation.

Figure Your Total Withholding Allowances Below

(a) Allowance(s) for exemption(s)—Enter 1 for each personal exemption you can claim on your Federal income tax return* . . .	
(b) Special withholding allowance—Enter 1 if single with 1 employer, or married with 1 employer and spouse not employed** . .	
(c) Allowance(s) for credit(s) and/or deduction(s)—Enter number from line (k) on other side**	
(d) Total (add lines (a) through (c) above)—Enter here and on line 1, Form W-4, above	

*If you are in doubt as to whom you may claim as a dependent, see the instructions that came with your last Federal income tax return or call your local Internal Revenue Service office.

**This allowance is used solely for purposes of figuring your withholding tax, and cannot be claimed when you file your tax return.

Figure 4.11 Form W-4—Employee's Withholding Form

of the construction industry, most firms have relatively poor layoff records and are therefore saddled with a relatively high UC premium. Usually the UC premium consists of both federal and state shares.

Other employee deductions vary depending on the labor union agreement or the agreed-upon regulations for a specific project. More often than not, the employer pays for the labor benefit with no resulting requirement for a deduction from the employee's gross pay. In other words, an employer liability is created, but no deduction is made from the employee's gross pay.

The weekly payroll is accompanied by preparation of the payroll journal, an employee's earnings record, and the paychecks. All three of these forms are prepared at the same time.

The *payroll journal* is a summary report listing the important factors making up each employee's earnings for the payroll period. An example of a payroll journal form is illustrated in Figure 4.12. There is a horizontal line for each employee on which typical items shown are employee's name, hours

PAYROLL SUMMARY

PAGE NUMBER ____________

PAYROLL FOR THE PERIOD ____________ 19 ____ TO ____________ 19 ____________

THE IDEAL SYSTEM COPYRIGHT U.S. PAT OFFICE

IDEAL SYSTEM - FORM S-812

	EMPLOYEE'S NUMBER	EMPLOYEE'S NAME	REGULAR TIME EARNINGS	OVERTIME EARNINGS	OTHER COMPENSATION	TOTAL EARNINGS (A)	DEDUCTIONS FROM EMPLOYEE'S EARNINGS						NET AMOUNT PAID EMPLOYEE (COL. A LESS COL. B)	
							STATE UNEMP. INS. AT ___ %	FEDERAL OLD AGE AT ___ %	FEDERAL WITHHOLDING TAXES	OTHER WITHHOLDING TAXES	OTHER DEDUCTIONS	TOTAL DEDUCTIONS (B)		
1														1
2														2
3														3
4														4
5														5
6														6
7														7
8														8
9														9
10														10
11														11
12														12
13														13
14														14
15														15
16														16
17														17
18														18
19														19
20														20
21														21
22														22
23														23
24														24
25														25
26														26
27														27
28														28
29														29
30														30
31														31
32														32
33														33

Figure 4.12 A Payroll Journal Form

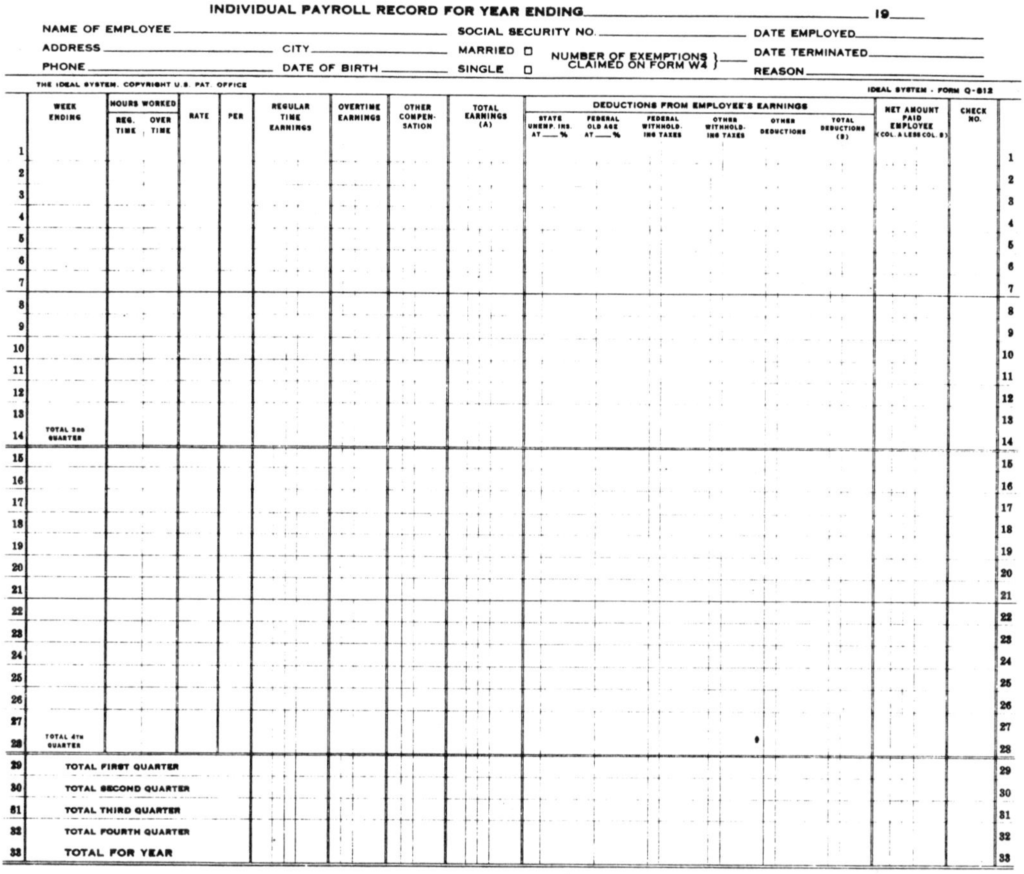

INDIVIDUAL PAYROLL RECORD FOR YEAR ENDING ____ 19__

NAME OF EMPLOYEE ____ SOCIAL SECURITY NO. ____ DATE EMPLOYED ____

ADDRESS ____ CITY ____ MARRIED ☐ NUMBER OF EXEMPTIONS CLAIMED ON FORM W4 ____ DATE TERMINATED ____

PHONE ____ DATE OF BIRTH ____ SINGLE ☐ REASON ____

THE IDEAL SYSTEM. COPYRIGHT U.S. PAT. OFFICE — IDEAL SYSTEM - FORM Q-812

	WEEK ENDING	HOURS WORKED REG. TIME	HOURS WORKED OVER TIME	RATE	PER	REGULAR TIME EARNINGS	OVERTIME EARNINGS	OTHER COMPEN-SATION	TOTAL EARNINGS (A)	DEDUCTIONS FROM EMPLOYEE'S EARNINGS: STATE UNEMP. INS. AT __%	FEDERAL OLD AGE AT __%	FEDERAL WITHHOLDING TAXES	OTHER WITHHOLDING TAXES	OTHER DEDUCTIONS	TOTAL DEDUCTIONS (B)	NET AMOUNT PAID EMPLOYEE (COL. A LESS COL. B)	CHECK NO.	
1																		1
2																		2
3																		3
4																		4
5																		5
6																		6
7																		7
8																		8
9																		9
10																		10
11																		11
12																		12
13																		13
14	TOTAL 3RD QUARTER																	14
15																		15
16																		16
17																		17
18																		18
19																		19
20																		20
21																		21
22																		22
23																		23
24																		24
25																		25
26																		26
27																		27
28	TOTAL 4TH QUARTER																	28
29	TOTAL FIRST QUARTER																	29
30	TOTAL SECOND QUARTER																	30
31	TOTAL THIRD QUARTER																	31
32	TOTAL FOURTH QUARTER																	32
33	TOTAL FOR YEAR																	33

Figure 4.13 An Earnings Record Form

worked, rate of pay, earnings at regular rate, overtime, gross earnings, various deductions, and net pay.

Federal law requires that each employee be given an annual receipt showing FICA taxable wages and tax deducted. Annually each employee is given a W-2 form that reports his gross annual earnings, FICA withheld, taxes withheld, and net pay. In order to efficiently prepare these W-2 forms, an *earnings record* is kept for each employee as part of the payroll process. An example of an employee earning's record form is shown in Figure 4.13. The payroll earnings record for each employee provides a means of keeping a cumulative running total of the employee's total earnings and various deductions.

The employee paycheck that is prepared is usually accompanied by a payroll check stub listing the various deductions from gross pay used to calculate net pay. The information on these stubs is essentially the same as that entered on the employee's earnings record form.

The process by which the payroll journal, earnings record forms, and paychecks are prepared is one of the following:

1. Pen-and-ink methods
2. Payroll pegboards
3. Machine methods

In a pen-and-ink system, the payroll journal, earnings records forms, and paychecks are each prepared by hand separately. Given a relatively small number of employees, this type of manual system can be efficient and inexpensive.

Payroll pegboard systems are widely used by construction firms as well as by other industries. A pegboard system is designed to eliminate making the same entry on all three payroll forms described. Instead, by means of a carbon material coated on the forms, the pegboard system user makes a single entry that is transferred onto all three documents.

An example of a payroll pegboard system in shown in Figure 4.14. Using such a system can save clerical time in performing the payroll function. Often this cost savings can offset the added cost associated with buying the special forms that make up the pegboard system.

Machine-prepared payroll records consist of using bookkeeping machines and computers. After making the source document input into these devices, a payroll journal, earnings record, and the requested payroll reports are prepared mechanically. Bookkeeping machines and computers as they relate to construction accounting are discussed in Chapter 11.

In addition to preparing W-2's for employees, the construction firm must prepare various payroll reports for the Internal Revenue Service (IRS). These reports are prepared directly from the payroll journal and the earnings record reports. The frequency of filing forms depends on the amount of the construction firm's payroll. An example of a required payroll IRS form that a construction firm must submit quarterly is shown in Figure 4.15. The 941 form shown calculates the firm's liability for FICA. Similar types of forms are required for other federal as well as state tax purposes.

In addition to the payroll reports discussed, the payroll department may be required to prepare other reports. For example, labor unions may require payroll reports to accompany health and welfare payments made by the construction firm. Management may also request additional reports regarding turnover, absenteeism, and overtime worked.

BOOKKEEPING FOR MATERIALS AND PURCHASING

The bookkeeping for construction materials has to recognize some of the unique characteristics of the industry. Most construction material is delivered directly to the project site. In other types of manufacturing industries, material is first received by a central receiving location and distributed by means of a

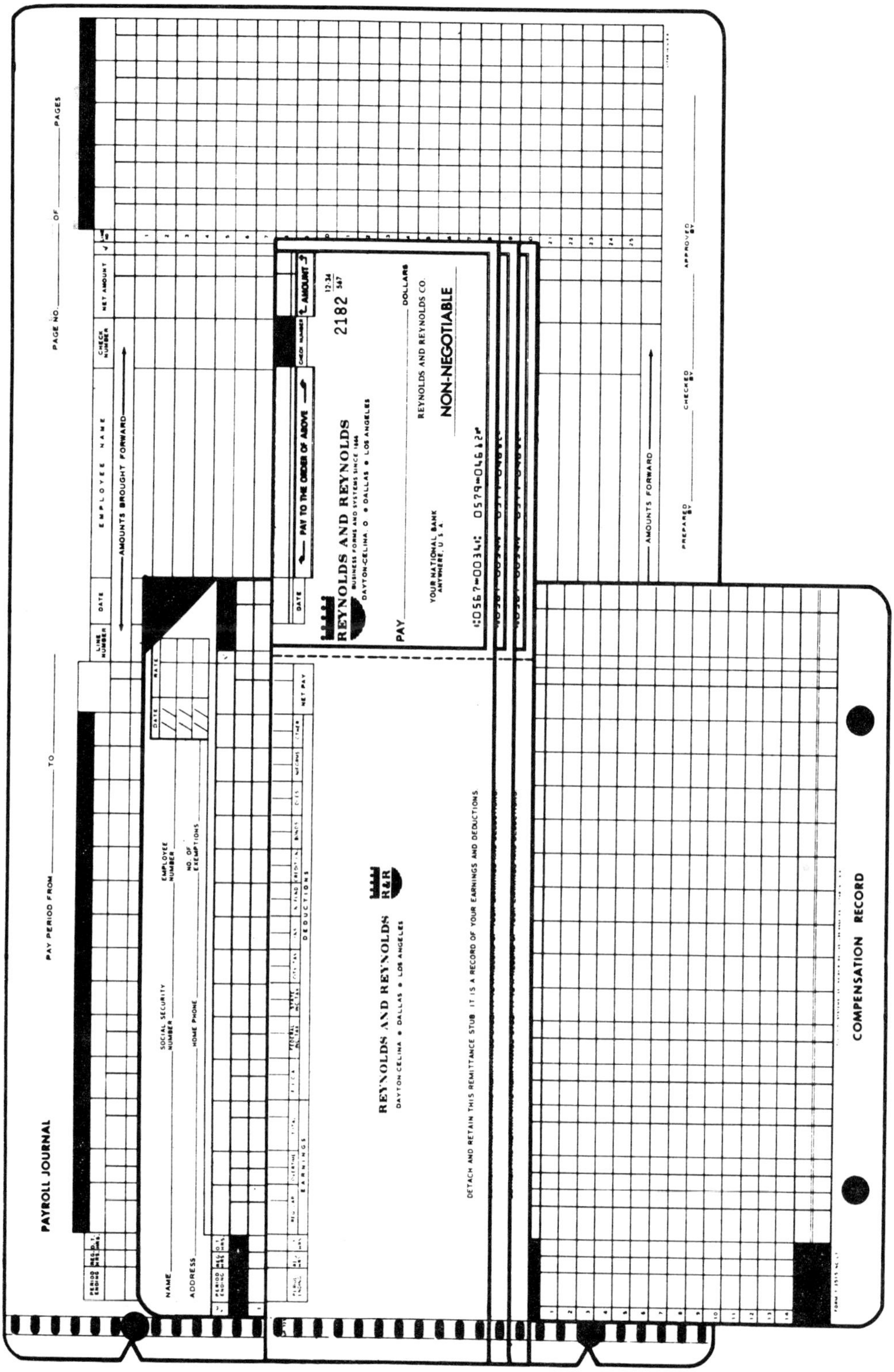

Figure 4.14 One-Write Pegboard Payroll System *(Courtesy of Reynolds and Reynolds Company)*

Form **941**
(Rev. January 1978)
Department of the Treasury
Internal Revenue Service

Employer's Quarterly Federal Tax Return

1 **First Quarter Only.**—Number of employees (except household) employed in the pay period that includes March 12th . . . ▶

2 Total wages and tips subject to withholding, plus other compensation . . . ⟶

3 Total income tax withheld from wages, tips, annuities, gambling, etc. (see instructions) . . .

4 Adjustment of withheld income tax for preceding quarters of calendar year . . .

5 Adjusted total of income tax withheld . . . ⟶

6 Taxable FICA wages paid . . . $ .... multiplied by 12.1% = TAX . .

7 Taxable tips reported . . . $ .... multiplied by 6.05% = TAX . .

8 Total FICA taxes (add lines 6 and 7) . . . ⟶

9 Adjustment of FICA taxes (see instructions) . . .

10 Adjusted total of FICA taxes . . .

11 Total taxes (add lines 5 and 10) . . . ⟶

Record of Federal Tax Deposits (See instructions on page 4)

Deposit period ending:		I. Tax liability for period	II. Date of deposit	III. Amount deposited
Overpayment from previous quarter . . .				
First month of quarter	1st through 7th day . . .			
	8th through 15th day . . .			
	16th through 22d day . . .			
	23d through last day . . .			
A First month total . . .	A			
Second month of quarter	1st through 7th day . . .			
	8th through 15th day . . .			
	16th through 22d day . . .			
	23d through last day . . .			
B Second month total . . .	B			
Third month of quarter	1st through 7th day . . .			
	8th through 15th day . . .			
	16th through 22d day . . .			
	23d through last day . . .			
C Third month total . . .	C			
D Total for quarter (add items A, B, and C)				
E Final deposit made for quarter. (Enter zero if the final deposit made for the quarter is included in item D) . . .				

12 Total deposits for quarter (including final deposit made for quarter) and overpayment from previous quarter. (See instructions on page 4) . . .

Note: *If undeposited taxes at the end of the quarter are $200 or more, deposit the full amount with an authorized financial institution or a Federal Reserve bank according to the instructions on the back of the Federal Tax Deposit Form 501. Enter this deposit in the Record of Federal Tax Deposits and include it in line 12.*

13 Undeposited taxes due (subtract line 12 from line 11—this should be less than $200). Pay to Internal Revenue Service and enter here . . . ⟶

14 If line 12 is more than line 11, enter overpayment here ▶ $ and check if to be: ☐ Applied to next return, or ☐ Refunded.

15 If you are not liable for returns in the future, write **"FINAL"** (See instructions) ▶ Date final wages paid ▶

Under penalties of perjury, I declare that I have examined this return, including accompanying schedules and statements, and to the best of my knowledge and belief it is true, correct, and complete.

Date ▶ Signature ▶ Title ▶

T	
FF	
FD	
FP	
I	
T	

Your name, address, employer identification number, and calendar quarter of return. (If not correct, please change) ▶

Name (as distinguished from trade name) — Date quarter ended

Trade name, if any — Employer identification number

Address and ZIP code

Please file this form with your Internal Revenue Service Center.
(See instructions on "Where to file")

Form **941** (Rev. 1-78)

Figure 4.15 Form 941—Quarterly Tax Report

purchasing department. This latter process facilitates better control of the material costs. Material buying for a construction project is normally planned at the time of estimating a project's cost. This often differs from other manufacturing industries where material buying is planned and carried out throughout the manufacturing process.

Regardless of when construction material is purchased or to where it is delivered initially, the objectives of bookkeeping for material are the following:

1. Control of purchasing
2. Control of receiving
3. Identification of materials to projects and work items
4. Protection against theft, misplacement, and damage.

Construction materials are normally purchased by one of two procedures: (1) the material may be purchased as needed by means of purchase orders, or (2) the material may be purchased for the entire lump sum contract. Purchasing material as needed (initiated by individual purchase orders) has the advantage that many problems associated with protection against theft, misplacement, and damage are eliminated. If the material is to be purchased by purchase orders, the initial request comes from the field. Only authorized personnel should be permitted to initiate a purchase order. More than likely the project superintendent will be responsible for initiating such a request. Purchase requisition forms should be used for initiating this type of material request; such a form is shown in Figure 4.16. A good system is to have triplicate forms such that a copy of the purchase requisition is kept by the field office and a copy is delivered to both the accounting and engineering or planning departments. This will provide the accounting department a means of comparing purchase requests against invoices and receiving statements. In addition, a form will alert the engineering or planning department as to the progress of the project and material usage versus the predetermined project plan.

Let us assume that the material requested in the field is not kept in inventory by the firm. If such is the case, the home office will send a purchase order to the material supplier that is selected. The material supplier will be requested to deliver the material to the job site. The supplier might send the invoice for material ordered to either the home (central office), the field office, or both. Because the field office is removed from the actual purchase or paying of the purchase price, the invoice must eventually be received by the central office. As such, it is preferable if the invoice is sent directly to it.

The next step is the potential bad link in the control process. Because the material is sent directly to the field, it is the field personnel who are responsible for checking to see that the material delivered corresponds to that requested and eventually paid for by the home office. That is, field personnel are responsible for counting or measuring, inspecting, and signing for each incoming delivery. The key to performing this vital step in the control process is assign-

PURCHASE ORDER

TO

ORDER NUMBER

DATE

JOB

PLEASE DELIVER THE FOLLOWING ORDER TO:

SHIP TO

JOB NO.

F.O.B.

TERMS

SHIP VIA

DELIVERY TO BE MADE ON OR BEFORE OR RIGHT IS RESERVED TO CANCEL ORDER

In Accepting Verbal Orders, Purchase Order Number Must be Obtained Before Making Delivery.

QUANTITY	DESCRIPTION	PRICE	AMOUNT

INVOICES MUST STATE ORDER NUMBER AND POINT OF DELIVERY.

PRICES ON THIS ORDER NOT SUBJECT TO CHANGE.

PRACTICAL "STANDARDIZED" FORMS FOR CONTRACTORS FORM 113-A D BY ____________________

FRANK R WALKER CO PUBLISHERS CHICAGO

Figure 4.16 A Purchase Order Form (*Courtesy of Frank R. Walker Co.*)

ing the duty to dependable individuals who make themselves available when in fact the material is delivered.

On large projects this usually creates little difficulty. The project is large enough to justify employing a warehouseman or receiving clerk who is held responsible for the accountability of incoming materials. On the smaller jobs, it is common to allocate this responsibility to the timekeeper. On even smaller jobs, the responsibility is sometimes given to the foreman. These latter two practices, especially the second of the two, are generally less preferable than having a full-time receiving clerk. The fact that the timekeeper or foreman is responsible for other tasks often results in the material-receiving responsibility being viewed as somewhat secondary which can result in a haphazard control procedure. Subcontractors will often arrange with the general contractor to have the general contractor's personnel receive the subcontractor's material. The potential for adequate control is not decreased by this practice.

Whoever is responsible for acknowledging the receipt of materials will normally be requested by the supplier to sign for the material. Since the signature has legal implications (i.e., title passes), the individual signing should first be assured as to the quantity and quality of the material. If the material is inferior, it should not be accepted. In addition, failure to inspect the material in a responsible manner removes the right to later reject the material.

The field office, by way of the individual responsible for acknowledging receipt of construction materials, should account for all materials received for the project in a weekly production report, or perhaps a separate report such as the one shown in Figure 4.17. Here again, the form should be sent to both accounting and the engineering or planning departments. The departments use the report in a continuing evaluation of the project's progress.

The material-purchasing system described implies that all project superintendent requests for materials be in the form of a purchase order sent to the home office. In turn, the home office places the order with a vendor. While this process is to be preferred in that it results in good internal controls on the purchasing function, it may be impractical to implement on a no exception basis. Given the time urgency that often confronts the superintendent performing the production process in the field, the superintendent may have to have the right to purchase some items without approval from the home office. As a practical means of accomplishing this, many construction firms give their superintendents the right to purchase material on credit up to a certain dollar amount without having the permission of the home office. A dollar limit of about $200 is common. Material vendors can be informed of this limit also so that they can serve as another control on a potentially dishonest superintendent.

Even when the superintendent has a right to purchase a small dollar amount of material on account without home office approval, it is important that a record of the purchase at the job site be forwarded to the home office. This is necessary in order to properly record the transaction in the accounting books and in order to validate a vendor's future invoice. One of the biggest

MATERIAL REPORT

JOB DATE

CHARGE TO	MATERIAL RECEIVED AND FROM WHOM	QUANTITY

MATERIALS RECEIVED AND USED

KIND OF MATERIAL						
PREVIOUS						
TO-DAY						
TOTAL						
KIND OF MATERIAL						
PREVIOUS						
TO-DAY						
TOTAL						

PRACTICAL

FRANK R. WALKER CO., PUBLISHERS, CHICAGO FORM P-111

Figure 4.17 A Receiving Form (*Courtesy of Frank R. Walker Co.*)

potential areas of breakdown in an otherwise good accounting system is having to record invoices for which there is no documentation as to the purpose of the related expenditure.

If it is feasible for the firm to maintain a central supply of materials needed for building its various projects, such a system offers the firm a means of better control over purchasing and receiving materials. In addition, through centralization and bulk purchasing, the firm may be able to purchase materials more economically.

The bookkeeping and control process differs when a centralized inventory of materials is kept by the construction firm. Purchase requisitions, sometimes referred to as *stores requisitions*, are still initiated in the field. If an adequate supply of the material is not on hand, the central office may initiate a purchase order to a supplier. However, not every stores requisition necessarily initiates a purchase order. Control of material ordered, received, and sent to projects is now centralized. This is done by individual material accounts referred to as *stores ledgers*. Each type of material is accounted for in subsidiary ledgers referred to as *stores cards* that are, in turn, summarized in the control stores ledger. Purchases are entered into a company register and, when received, are entered in the stores card for the material. Purchases are listed as to their unit price, and, by means of one of several available inventory flow methods, cost levels of inventory are maintained and adjusted for material issues.

The issues of materials as reported by the stores requisition forms are periodically analyzed by the home office as a way of controlling the usage of materials on the various projects. This analysis serves as a means of evaluating project progress.

The fourth objective of bookkeeping for material cost, that of protecting against theft, misplacement, or damage may seem removed from the cost-accounting process. However, the analysis of purchases, deliveries, and issues can be used to alert the firm to this loss of material. Without an effective cost-accounting and bookkeeping system such losses may never be apparent to the firm and they will continue to be accounted for as ordinary project expenses. Determining acceptable material wastage factors is part of an effective cost-accounting system. In addition, protecting material by establishing authorization and security procedures is an important element of the cost-accounting and bookkeeping system. If it is worthwhile keeping an inventory of construction materials, it is worthwhile maintaining adequate protection and control over it. Usually, it is financially rewarding to employ an individual on a project site to receive, protect, and to do general housekeeping for project materials. This is especially true when the project is of a size where there is a large buildup of construction materials on the project site.

MISCELLANEOUS LEDGERS AND ACCOUNTING FORMS

Labor and material bookkeeping predominate the accounting process for the typical construction firm. However, they are not the only areas of interest as

CONTRACT CHANGE ORDER

JOB
CONTRACT JOB NO.

FOR

CHANGE ORDER **No.**

DATE

TO

REVISED CONTRACT AMOUNT

PREVIOUS CONTRACT AMOUNT $

AMOUNT OF THIS ORDER $

TOTAL CONTRACT AND EXTRAS $

The work covered by this order shall be performed under the same Terms and Conditions as that included in the Original Contract.

CHANGES APPROVED

____

By______________________

____

By______________________

AMOUNT OF ORIGINAL CONTRACT $

CHANGE NO.

By______________________

PRACTICAL Form L-101
MFD IN U.S.A.

FRANK R. WALKER CO., PUBLISHERS, CHICAGO

Figure 4.18 A Change Order Form (*Courtesy of Frank R. Walker Co.*)

EQUIPMENT AND DEPRECIATION RECORD

SHEET NO.

KIND OF EQUIPMENT | PURCHASED FROM | SERIAL NUMBER

DESCRIPTION | APPRAISED VALUE

DATE ACQUIRED | HOW ACQUIRED | ESTIMATED LIFE YEARS | DEPRECIATION YEARLY RATE | DATE APPRAISED

FORM 137 | FRANK R. WALKER CO., PUBLISHERS, CHICAGO

PRACTICAL MFD IN U.S.A.

	DATE Mo.	Day	Year	DESCRIPTION	Folio	ORIGINAL COST AND CAPITAL REPAIRS	DEPRECIATION PER YEAR	DEPRECIATION TOTAL TO DATE	PRESENT BOOK VALUE	OPERATING REPAIRS	RENTALS CHARGED OR RECEIVED	
1				MACHINE COST								1
2				ADDITIONAL EQUIPMENT COST								2
3				FREIGHT, TRUCKING, ETC.								3
4				OTHER CHARGES								4
5				TOTAL ORIGINAL COST								5
6												6
7												7
8												8
9												9
10												10
11												11
12												12
13												13
14												14
15												15
16												16
17												17
18												18
19												19
20												20
21												21
22												22
23												23
24												24
25												25
26												26
27												27
28												28
29												29

Figure 4.19 An Equipment Ledger (*Courtesy of Frank R. Walker Co.*)

to keeping a "good set of books" and keeping tight controls on all segments of revenue or expense relevant to the construction firm. Included in these other areas are accounting for sales, receivables, payables, and equipment.

A sales journal is part of the accounting set of books for manufacturing firms. Because of the relatively small sales price of their product, many of these manufacturing firms have to fill many orders from many different customers. The result is that this type of firm often needs a separate sales journal. Usually the construction firm's sales and billing process is limited to a few customers at a time. Therefore, the construction firm has less need for distinct accounting forms or procedures for handling its sales and/or billings.

This is not to say that the construction firm does not need controls in regard to its billing process. However, areas that often prove to be a greater weakness for the construction firm are change orders and collection of billings for sales. All too often a construction firm starts work on a change order before having a signed authorization from the project owner or a representative. On occasion this has led to the construction firm not getting paid for the work it has performed or has resulted in a lengthy dispute that also adversely affects the construction firm.

The potential difficulty cited regarding change orders can be avoided if a formalized change order form is used. An example of a change order authorization form is illustrated in Figure 4.18. Before starting any work on a change order basis, the construction firm obtains an owner's signature or the signature of the owner's representative on the form illustrated. This protects the construction firm in its claim for payment. Equally important is the fact that the change order, when sent to the home office, gives the construction firm a means of recognizing the additional work to be performed in the accounting books.

The control of receivables and payables may be aided by using a properly designed set of journal and ledger forms. Columns in the journal form in Figure 4.5 served the purpose of recording all debits and credits to the receivable and payable accounts. In turn, subsidiary journals and/or ledgers can be designed to support the controlling journal or ledger. This process was illustrated in Figure 4.7.

The construction company will usually have an equipment account that serves to summarize the total dollar amount of its owned equipment. Similarly, the firm will also have a single accumulated depreciation account that summarizes all depreciation taken on individual pieces of equipment.

Some firms also keep individual ledger forms or cards on individual pieces of construction equipment. In this way the firm can trace costs to a specific piece of equipment and determine the unit cost of the equipment and/or other information relevant to using the equipment. An example of an equipment ledger form for this purpose is illustrated in Figure 4.19. Like all ledger forms designed for a specific purpose, the form shown in Figure 4.19 is not universal as to its use in the construction industry.

Other specialized ledger forms are used less frequently in the construction industry. These forms often prove unique to the firm that is using them.

5
ACCOUNTING ENTRIES FOR ADJUSTMENTS, REVERSALS, AND CHANGES

INTRODUCTION

Chapters 2 and 3 illustrated the accounting entries for typical financial transactions of the construction firm. These entries represent a large majority of the entries made by the construction firm. While infrequent in occurrence, the construction firm also has to make accounting entries for adjusting journal entries, reversing entries, and various types of changes. Examples of changes include a construction firm's switching from the completed-contract method of accounting to the percentage-of-completion method, or a change in estimate such as the estimated life of a depreciable asset.

Accounting entries for adjustments, reversals, or changes tend to be more technical and confusing to the construction firm than the accounting entries discussed in Chapters 2 and 3. In fact, more often than not, the reason for a construction firm's books becoming "out of balance" is a mistake or failure to make adjusting, reversal, or changes entries correctly.

While some construction firms rely totally on their external accountant or auditor to assist them in making adjusting, reversing, or changes accounting entries, many other construction firms have to make the entries themselves. Therefore, the ability to make these infrequent entries is as important as the ability to make everyday routine accounting journal entries.

ADJUSTING JOURNAL ENTRIES

Adjusting journal entries are made to recognize unrecorded transactions or incorrect account balances at the time of preparing financial statements. The number of adjusting journal entries needed will depend on the sophistication of the construction firm's accounting process, external events that lead to financial transactions, and the time at which the financial statements are prepared. For example, if the cutoff date for preparing year-end financial statements falls on the same date as the cutoff of the weekly payroll, no adjusting entries are needed for accruing payroll.

The purpose of adjusting journal entries is to change the general ledger records or accounts such that they will reflect the changes and cause them to be reflected correctly on the financial statements. The procedure for securing required data for adjusting journal entries consists of a systematic analysis of the ledger accounts to determine whether their balances represent the actual amount on the particular financial statement date. In many cases the adjustment data is obtained at the end of an accounting period by the application of foresight and the systematic arrangement of the accounts.

Some accounts are more likely to need adjusting journal entries than others. In particular, in order to reflect their account balances correctly at statement time, the following types of accounts should always be analyzed:

1. Depreciation expense
2. Accrued expenses (payroll, interest, etc.)
3. Prepaid expenses
4. Inventory
5. Accrued income
6. Prepaid income

As an example of securing adjustment data, depreciation adjustments may be determined by analyzing subsidiary records of fixed assets. An accrued payroll (an example of an accrued expense) adjusting journal entry may be determined by analyzing payroll records and noting the date of the financial statement.

Some typical adjusting journal entries (a.j.e.'s) at the year-end statement preparation for a construction firm are illustrated in Figure 5.1. The a.j.e.'s represent only a few of many that would often occur when analyzing the accounts of the construction firm.

The first a.j.e. in Figure 5.1 is needed because, while payday was on Friday, January 2 of the following year, on December 31 (a Wednesday) the construction firm was indebted to workers for three days' pay. Therefore, even though no checks were written on December 31, the firm had an accrual expense as of that date.

The second adjusting journal entry made in Figure 5.1 is an example of an a.j.e. that is needed because of an unrecorded entry. Inspection of the firm's checkbook indicates that check#595 was not recorded as an expense. The adjustment has nothing to do with an accrual. Instead, it records an entry that should have been made during the year.

During a period of time, the construction firm records a number of receivables from customers on its books. This is because few customers pay cash. Some of the receivables recorded may never be paid because the cus-

1. Labor expense	602	$7,946.00	
Accrued salaries and wages	319		$7,946.00
(to show wages paid on 1-2-X1 as accrued wages on 12-31-X0)			
2. Miscellaneous expense	629	800.00	
Cash	102		800.00
(to record check #595 written by Ed for sets of plans)			
3. Bad debt expense	610	1,297.67	
Accounts receivable	210		1,297.67
(to write off bad debts per Ed at 12-31-X0)			
4. Accrued interest receivable	209	421.97	
Interest income	592		421.97
(to record accrued interest receivable on certificate on 12-31-X0)			
5. Material costs	603	6,383.00	
Material inventory	112		6,383.00
(to adjust material inventory to physical count at 12-31-X0)			
6. Depreciation expense—trucks	608	2,922.10	
Accumulated depr.—trucks	340		2,922.10
(to adjust accum. depr. to actual)			

Figure 5.1 Adjusting Journal Entries

tomer falls upon bad financial times or has a legitimate dispute with the construction firm. Therefore, it is common practice for the construction firm to analyze its receivables at statement-preparation time and "write-off" those it deems uncollectable. An adjusting journal entry such as that shown as number 3 in Figure 5.1 is required.

Adjusting journal entry number 4 in Figure 5.1 is another example of an accrual adjustment. In this case, analysis of the construction firm's investment accounts indicates the firm has an uncollected receivable in the form of interest as of 12-31-X0. This interest would not have been recorded before the adjusting journal entry.

Because inventory is usually not a significant dollar item for many construction firms, many choose to implement a physical inventory accounting process rather than a perpetual system. While the perpetual system is better for control purposes, the physical system is usually less time consuming as to everyday operations. Given the physical inventory process, a count of material is made at statement-preparation time. An adjusting journal entry is made to record the actual inventory. An example of such an entry is shown as number

5 in Figure 5.1. The result of the entry is to adjust the inventory shown on the construction firm's balance sheet and to recognize the appropriate material expense.

The last adjusting entry shown in Figure 5.1, number 6, is the very common entry made for acknowledging depreciation. The entry is needed because few construction firms make the entry periodically at times between preparation of financial statements. Instead, a "catch-up" depreciation entry is made at the time of preparing financial statements. The dollar amount of the depreciation a.j.e. recognizes the book value of the asset, its remaining life, and the depreciation method used.

Numerous other examples of adjusting journal entries could be given. Because the process of detecting adjustment data for a.j.e.'s is less than scientific, it follows that it is possible to overlook the recording of all necessary a.j.e.'s. When this occurs, the financial statements that follow are not totally correct. When a CPA audits the books of a construction firm, in effect the CPA is saying to external parties as well as the construction firm itself, that all material adjusting journal entries have been made. The word "material" is admittedly a subjective term and is sometimes used as a scapegoat for failure to properly record an adjusting journal entry.

Once all adjusting journal entries are recorded, they are summarized in the adjustments column of the working trial balance. Preparing a working trial balance and financial statements are discussed in Chapter 6.

CLOSING THE BOOKS

Once accounting entries and adjusting journal entries are summarized on the working trial balance, it is possible to prepare financial statements. However, accounting entries do not terminate with the preparation of financial statements. After the statements have been prepared, the ledgers are closed which is commonly referred to as the *closing of the books*. This means that the balances of all the adjusted revenue and expense accounts are transferred to the income summary account. In effect the income summary account represents the profit or loss for the construction firm for the period in question. This amount is transferred to the retained earnings of the corporation or net worth of the proprietorship. The described process of closing the books is illustrated in Figure 5.2. The construction firm would have more revenue and expense accounts to close than those shown in the figure; however the processes would be the same.

The result of the process illustrated in Figure 5.2 is to reset the balances of all revenue and expense accounts to zero. This is necessary in order to divide the financial accomplishments of the construction firm into periods.

REVERSING ENTRIES

Once all entries have been made for preparing financial statements and closing entries have been made to initiate the start of a new reporting period, it is

Year-End Account Balances

Revenue—contract sales	$850,000	Labor expense	$300,000
Interest income	20,000	Material expense	300,000
		Equipment expense	100,000
		Office salaries	50,000
		Depreciation	70,000

Closing Entry #1

Revenue—contract sales	$850,000	
Interest income	20,000	
Labor expense		$300,000
Material expense		300,000
Equipment expense		100,000
Office salaries		50,000
Depreciation		70,000
Income summary		50,000
(to close revenue and expense accounts)		

Closing Entry #2

Income summary	$50,000	
Retained earnings		$50,000
(to transfer profit to retained earnings on balance sheet)		

Figure 5.2 Process of Closing Entries

often convenient to *reverse* certain balance sheet accounts that serve as temporary accounts.

Let us consider adjusting journal entry number one illustrated in Figure 5.1. The entry was made at the time of preparing the financial statements. The entry was as follows:

Labor expense	$7,946	
Accrued salaries & wages		$7,946

The effect of the entry is to record an expense for the construction firm for the year-end 19X0. In addition, a balance sheet liability—accrued salaries & wages—would be created.

When the construction firm closes its books, it will close out the labor expense account balance by crediting the labor expense account and debiting the income summary account. This process was illustrated in Figure 5.2.

Now let us assume that we are into the following year, year 19X1. The construction firm on 1-2-X1 pays its payroll. Let us assume the week's payroll is for $15,000. It might make the following entry:

Labor expense	$15,000	
Cash		$15,000

However, note that, of the $15,000 expense recognized, in reality $7,946 of it was for an expense incurred in the prior year and recognized as an expense in the financial statements for the year end 19X0. In effect, the firm has recognized $7,946 twice. In addition, note that using the procedure described, the balance sheet item—Accrued salaries & wages $7,946—would maintain its balance throughout the 19X1 accounting period.

Naturally the firm might remember that part of the newly created labor expense is for an expense of the prior period and therefore only recognize the difference, $7,054, as a new expense. However, given many of these types of transactions, the construction firm may fall victim to double recognition of entries.

To avoid the possible doubling up of the expense recognized in the prior year and to remove the temporary balance sheet liability account item, the following reversing entry is made after the books are closed.

Accrued salaries & wages	$7,946	
Labor expense		$7,946

This reversing entry removes the balance sheet temporary account and creates a credit labor expense balance for the new year, 19X1. This credit balance will offset a portion of the $15,000 expense when paid in 19X1. The result will be that the recognized labor expense will be as follows:

19X1	$15,000
Less reversing entry	7,946
Labor expense incurred in 19X1	$7,054

By reversing the adjusting journal entry number 1 in Figure 5.1, it is not necessary for the construction firm in 19X1 to remember what the a.j.e.'s were at year-end 19X0. It merely records the 19X1 entry as it would any other entry that occurs in 19X1.

The reversing of entries described is a matter of convenience. The process does away with the necessity of analyzing expense payments made in the new period to determine what portion of each payment belonged to the past period and what part should be charged to the present period.

Usually all balances of accrued accounts and prepaid accounts are reversed including both revenue and expense accounts. However, any reversing entry is for convenience and is not a mandatory account entry. The reversing entry is intended to facilitate subsequent accounting.

ACCOUNTING ENTRIES AND SWITCHING ACCOUNTING METHODS

As will be discussed in a later chapter on tax planning, it is possible to report financial results using one basis or set of books and calculate taxable income using yet another basis or set of books. For example, it may be possible to use the cash basis of accounting for tax and the accrual method for financial reporting. Similarly, the construction firm may adopt the completed-contract method of accounting for tax and the percentage-of-completion method in financial reporting.

A construction firm may also obtain permission to change its method of accounting. For example, after years of using the completed-contract method (for tax and/or financial reporting), the construction firm may choose to switch to the percentage-of-completion method.

Using two sets of books or switching from using one accounting method to another results in the need to understand the accounting entries necessary to make the conversion from one accounting method to another. A firm using two different accounting methods, one for tax and one for financial reporting, does not physically keep two sets of books. Instead, at time of financial statement preparation, they make accounting journal entries that will reflect their accounting records using one accounting method on an alternative accounting method basis. Switching from one accounting method to another for the preparation of financial statements using this method requires only relatively simple adjusting entries. For example, converting from a set of books kept on a cash basis to an accrual basis for the preparation of accrual financial statements can be done using the procedure illustrated in Figure 5.3. The same procedure shown in Figure 5.3 could be used in converting from the accrual basis to the cash basis by working from the bottom of the schedule to the top.

To illustrate some accounting journal entries that would result from switching from one basis or set of books to another, let us assume a construction firm keeps its books on a cash basis and a completed-contract method. Let us further assume that, using the cash method and completed-contract method, the construction firm has the following data regarding five projects at the end of December (the assumed last month of the firm's fiscal year):

Job no.	*Status*	*Contract price*	*Cash collected*	*Billings*	*Mat'l*	*Direct labor*	*Subcontractor's Billings*
102	Closed	$8,000	$1,800	$6,200	$ 650	$5,100	$700
103	Open	9,800	3,000	1,000	400	3,200	500
104	Closed	9,000	1,700	7,300	1,200	6,700	—
105	Open	6,000	700	1,500	300	1,000	—
106	Closed	4,500	4,500	—	550	2,450	—

Furthermore, let us assume that at the end of December no other jobs are ongoing. The "Subcontractor's billings" represent contracts billed to the construction firm we are considering. Also let us assume that the construction firm treats general and administrative costs as period costs. In other words, these costs including office payroll and rent are recognized as expenses on the income statement in the period the expenses occur.

Let us assume that the construction firm wants to portray their financial statements on an accrual basis. This desire to prepare accrual statements may be the result of external parties' (including bankers and sureties) demands to have an accrual statement. The request for accrual statements is based on the

Net income, cash basis		$XXXX
Add:		
Accrued income at end of period	$XXXX	
Prepaid expenses at end of period	XXXX	
Accrued expenses at beginning of period	XXXX	
Prepaid income at beginning of period	XXXX	XXXX
Total		$XXXX
Deduct:		
Accrued expenses at end of period	$XXXX	
Prepaid income at end of period	XXXX	
Accrued income at beginning of period	XXXX	
Prepaid expenses at beginning of period	XXXX	XXXX
Net income, accrual basis		$XXXX

Figure 5.3 Switching Accounting Methods

premise that accrual statements better portray the pluses and minuses of the construction firm.

To change the financial status of projects to an accrual basis requires several entries. Let us consider them individually.

1. The subcontractor's job 102 invoice for $700 has not been paid, and a $200 subcontractor's invoice on job 104 has not been recognized. Since these are liabilities at year end, the following entry is required:

Subcontractors	$900	
Accounts payable		$900

This entry is necessary because, using the cash basis, the entry would not have been made.

2. Using the cash basis, a sale is recognized only when cash is received. However, when using an accrual basis a sale is recognized when a receivable or cash is recognized. Since $6,200 remains unpaid on the closed job 102 and $7,300 remains unpaid on the closed job 104, these amounts are receivables on December 31. The entry required to adjust to the accrual basis is as follows:

Accounts receivable	$13,500	
Sales		$13,500

3. Jobs 103 and 105 are not yet finished. Using the completed-contract method, no revenue or expense should be recognized until the jobs are complete. However, as can be observed from the data given, using the cash basis, $3,000 and $700 of revenue have been recognized from jobs 103 and 105 respectively. In addition, $1,000 and $1,500 are billed (i.e., receivables) on jobs 103 and 105. These amounts are uncollected and unrecognized in the cash basis accounting method. As such, the adjusting entry required is as follows:

Sales	$3,700	
Accounts receivables	2,500	
Billings on jobs in process		$6,200

4. There is no jobs in process account. Rather than charge cash payments as expenses, they should be accumulated in the jobs in process account (i.e., an asset account) in a completed-contract method. The sum of the paid expenses of jobs 103 and 105 (the jobs that are not completed) is $700 and $4,200, and $500 for the material, labor, and subcontractors' accounts. The adjusting accrual entry is as follows:

Jobs in process	$5,400	
Paint and wood		$700
Labor		4,200
Subcontractors		500

The result of the entries made in steps 1 through 4 would be to put the books on an accrual basis. Financial statements prepared on an accrual basis could now be prepared.

ACCOUNTING CHANGES

Regardless of the sophistication of the construction firm's accounting process, situations frequently occur in which changes in accounting methods, estimates, or error corrections must be made. Unlike the routine accounting entries described in Chapter 2, which are handled rather uniformly in practice from one firm to the next, practice has seen a somewhat diverse range of accounting treatment for various types of accounting changes. Only recently, since the accounting profession has set forth several opinions on handling changes, has accepted treatment of changes been defined.

An accounting change can be classified as one of the following three types:

1. Change in accounting principle
2. Change in accounting estimate
3. Change due to discovery of an error

Each of these types of changes is handled somewhat differently as to required journal entries and resulting financial statements.

A change in accounting principle occurs when the construction firm adopts a different, generally accepted accounting principle or procedure from one previously used. An example would be a change from using the straight-line depreciation method to the double-declining depreciation method. Another example would be a change from using the FIFO (First In First Out) method of valuing inventory to the use of LIFO (Last In First Out) for valuing inventory.

A change in estimate occurs when the construction firm becomes aware of more accurate determinations of fact than what was initially estimated in a prior period. An example would be when the construction firm learns that the life of a piece of equipment is eight years rather than the initial estimate of six years. The revised estimate may be made after a few years of using the equipment.

A change due to an error discovery is defined as a change necessitated by the misapplication of facts existing at the time of the initial accounting entry. The misapplication may have been because of oversight or it may have been intentional. An example of a misapplication of facts would be expensing an item of construction equipment in a prior period when the equipment should have been capitalized in that it had an estimated life of three years.

The significant factor about treatment of accounting changes is the impact the treatment has on the financial statements of the construction firm. In particular, the need to recognize an accounting change raises the question of whether it should be handled on the financial statements in the current accounting period, retroactively to prior accounting periods, or prospectively over future accounting periods. The acceptable treatment for the identified types of accounting changes is discussed separately for each type of change in the following sections.

Change in Accounting Principle

A change of accounting principle normally results in a requirement for a catch-up adjusting journal entry. The entry should be fully disclosed to reflect the operational effect of the change. On comparative financial statements, full disclosure and compatibility require that net income and earnings per share data be provided on a pro forma (forecasted) basis, assuming retroactive application.

Let us assume that a construction company has been depreciating its trucks, which cost $200,000 on a straight-line basis over a ten-year life with no expected salvage. After the second year the company decides to adopt double-declining depreciation because it would have tax advantages. The change in accounting principle would have the following effect:

Double declining balance		
Year 1 (200,000 × 0.2)	$40,000	
Year 2 (160,000 × 0.2)	32,000	$72,000
Straight-line recorded		
Years 1 and 2 equal (200,000/10) × 2		40,000
		$32,000

The accounting entry required to recognize the change in accounting principle would be

Adjustment due to depreciation change	$32,000	
Accumulated depreciation		$32,000

The adjustment due to the depreciation change would be recognized as an extraordinary item in the firm's income statement for the current year. In other words, current year treatment is the acceptable accounting treatment.

Change in Accounting Estimate

As previously discussed, an accounting entry may be necessary because of a change of opinion or an error in making an estimate. Because of the many estimates required in the accounting process, making estimate revisions is a common event. For example, the firm may underestimate or overestimate the life of a piece of their equipment. Similarly, they might overestimate the collectability of their receivables. One might treat the change in estimate by a retroactive adjustment or treat it by a prospective (future) adjustment. Current accounting practice favors the prospective treatment.

To illustrate a change in estimate, assume that a piece of construction equipment that cost $12,000 with no expected salvage is being depreciated over a ten-year life. However, on the basis of new information after five years' use, a fifteen-year life appears to be more accurate. The change should be handled by prospective entries. In particular, starting the sixth year, the change would be recognized as follows:

Depreciation recognized to date (10-year life)	= 5 × 1,200	= $6,000
Depreciation to be charged over next 10 years	= 12,000 − 6,000	= $6,000

The depreciation entry for the sixth year and each of the years, seven through fifteen, would be as follows:

Depreciation expense ($6,000/10)	$600	
Accumulated depreciation		$600

In other words, prospective treatment is required. The revised depreciation rate or dollar amount is applied to future years.

More common in occurrence than a change in accounting principle or a change in estimate is a change required because of an erroneous accounting entry. In many cases the error occurs because of less than ideal accounting procedures used by the construction firm. However, it is also true that many of the errors that occur result because of the failure to make correct adjusting journal entries when preparing financial statements. The difficulty of being totally accurate when making adjusting journal entries was discussed earlier in this chapter.

Examples of errors in the accounting process that result in the need to recognize an accounting change are numerous in the construction industry. Included are errors in calculating a percentage of completion, an error in capitalizing an expenditure instead of expensing it and vice versa, and an error in properly classifying an expense. Other errors result from the failure to make an entry. To illustrate this failure, let us consider a construction firm that has been leasing its company headquarters building for a number of years. During the years the company has made significant leasehold improvements to the property. Let us assume they have made $25,000 book-value improvements. The construction company correctly has capitalized the improvements as an asset.

Let us further assume that, as so often occurs, the construction firm changes its office location. Perhaps it builds its own building for its office. As often happens the construction company may have no right to a claim for the improvements it has made to the leased property. Therefore, in effect it forfeits its $25,000 of improvements.

What might happen is that, in switching its headquarters and terminating its lease, the construction firm may fail to adjust the leasehold improvement account. Instead, at financial statement time, it continues to carry the $25,000 as an asset rather than to write it off as an expense.

When the construction firm does detect that they no longer have a $25,000 asset in that it was forfeited when it terminated its lease, an accounting change entry must be made. The type of entry required depends on the time at which the error is detected. Ideally an error is detected before the issuance of financial statements. When this is the case, the error must be corrected by an adjusting entry before issuance of the financial statements. More often than not, an accounting error is not detected until a point in time following the issuance of financial statements. In fact this detection may be several years after the error was initially made.

When an error is detected subsequent to the preparation of financial statements, incorrect account balances should be adjusted to their correct balances and any necessary adjustment should be reported as an "adjustment—correction of error." At the time of preparing subsequent financial statements, the adjustment—correction of error—should be closed to retained earnings and reported as a prior period adjustment (i.e., not appear on the income statement). Regarding comparative financial statements, incorrect financial data for each period reported should be corrected for all subsequently discovered errors. When presenting comparative financial statements, the data for each year being presented should be restated to the correct basis, and any required adjustment should be shown as a prior period adjustment of the retained earnings for the first period being reported.

6
CONSTRUCTION FIRM FINANCIAL STATEMENTS

INTRODUCTION

The entire financial accounting process may be viewed as being aimed at preparing financial statements. While financial statements may be prepared to meet the needs of external parties, the statements can also serve an internal purpose for the construction firm. Specifically, the prepared financial statements can assist the construction firm in making both short-term and long-term decisions. Decisions such as determining whether equipment should be purchased or leased or what type of financing should be obtained for operations or capital expenditures are aided by prepared financial statements.

In practice the frequency of the construction firm's preparation of financial statements varies. As a minimum, financial statements may be prepared annually enabling income tax return preparation and summarizing the year's results.

To satisfy external or internal needs, financial statements may be prepared more frequently than yearly. Quarterly or monthly statements are becoming more common in the industry.

This chapter illustrates commonly prepared construction firm financial statements and the necessary procedures that enable their preparation. While the format and wording of line items on financial statements vary somewhat in practice, the presented statements and supporting schedules are thought to be fairly typical in use and adhere to properly prepared financial statements as established by the AICPA.

TYPES OF FINANCIAL STATEMENTS

The financial statements of a firm may be limited to a *statement of financial position* and an *income statement*. These are by far the most common financial statements prepared in practice. The statement of financial position is more commonly referred to as a *balance sheet*. The income statement is also commonly referred to as the *profit and loss statement* (the P and L statement) or the statement of operations.

Current AICPA guidelines indicate that the correct terminology for the two mentioned statements are the statement of financial position and the income statement. However, the use of balance sheet remains common in practice as an alternative to calling the statement, the statement of financial position. In recognition of this, we will use the term balance sheet. Use of the term income statement has gained in popularity versus use of the term profit and loss statement; therefore, we will use the term income statement or statement of operations.

The balance sheet reports on the assets, liabilities, and net worth, or owner's equity accounts, at a given point in time. On the other hand, the income statement refers to a period of time; it reports on the revenues and expenses for that period. Because the balance sheet presents a point in time, it can be viewed as a snapshot of the firm's financial status, whereas the income statement, which represents a period of time, can be viewed as a film of the financial operation.

If a construction firm desires *audited* financial statements prepared by a CPA, the AICPA requires that a third statement in addition to the balance sheet and income statement be prepared. This is referred to as the *statement of changes in financial position* or, less appropriately, as the funds statement.

In addition to the three financial statements noted, audited financial statements will also include an opinion statement of the auditor, disclosure of significant accounting policies of the audited construction firm, and notes that further describe line items presented on the financial statements.

The construction firm is typically dependent on the financial statement needs of external parties. These external parties include surety (bonding) companies, lending institutions, government agencies, material vendors, and equipment financing companies. Some of these external parties will require financial information or reports in addition to those required to meet the minimum standards of properly prepared, audited financial statements. For example, a statement of work in progress is often requested from the construction firm.

In addition to additional requested financial reports, financial statements are often accompanied by various schedules or statements that support item totals of the previously noted three required financial statements. These schedules or statements usually consist of a statement of general and administrative expenses (also referred to as operating expenses) and a statement of retained earnings. Less frequent in preparation are schedules or statements on amounts due on contract and statements of miscellaneous income such as rental property revenue and expense schedules.

The Working Trial Balance

Preparation of financial statements including the balance sheet and income statement is initiated with the preparation of a *working trial balance* which is also referred to as the *WTB* or sometimes as the *worksheet*.

The WTB is not a financial statement in itself. Instead, it serves as a worksheet for preparing financial statements. The worksheet provides a means of summarizing the account balance of each of the firm's general ledger accounts at the time of financial statement preparation. Each and every account is listed regardless of the account balance. An example of a WTB format for a construction firm is shown in Figure 6.1. Only representative accounts and the debit and credit entries for these accounts are shown.

Following the listing of the account titles and code numbers in the WTB is the balance of the account as adjusted for the end of the previous year. This is followed by the balance of each account as per the general ledger books at the end of the current year.

The balances are shown in the debit and credit columns depending upon whether the specific account has a debit or credit balance. Assuming the firm's set of books are in balance, the debit and credit totals in the WTB should equal one another.

In order to recognize accrual and overlooked accounting entries at the time of preparing financial statements, various adjusting journal entries (a.j.e's) must be made to the firm's set of books. Examples of a.j.e's for a WTB were shown in Figure 5.1. These adjusting journal entries would be recorded in the appropriate columns in the WTB as illustrated in Figure 6.1. Note that not all of the a.j.e.'s are illustrated in Figure 6.1.

The adjusting journal entries listed in the WTB are added to the account year-end balances per book to yield the adjusted account balance. These are also shown in Figure 6.1.

Finally, balance sheet account balances are separated from income statement account balances by listing them in separate columns as shown in Figure 6.1. In order to equate the debit and credit columns in both the balance sheet and income statement, a "plug" number, representing the income or loss for the period, must be determined.

Preparation of the balance sheet and income statement comes directly from the account balances shown on the prepared WTB. Typically, financial statements do not itemize every chart of account dollar balance; instead, several account balances shown on the WTB will be summed and reflected as a single line item.

Balance Sheet

The balance sheet is prepared directly from the working trial balance illustrated in Figure 6.1. The balance sheet accounts listed in the WTB are grouped and presented as line items on the balance sheet at a specific point in time, such as the firm's year end.

The balance sheet, or statement of financial position, reports on the basic economic equation of the firm:

assets = creditor's equity + owner's equity

While individual types of accounts may vary from one firm to the next, the

Sample Construction Co., Inc.
WTB
12/31/X0

Accounts	No.	Trial Balance 12/31 Prior Year		Trial Balance 12/31/X0		Adjustments		Balance Sheet		Income Statement	
		Dr	Cr	Dr	Cr	Dr	Cr	Dr	Cr	Dr	Cr
Petty Cash	101	$ 250		$ 991			$ 800	$ 191			
Cash in Bank	102	5480		4550				4550			
Savings	105	38640		40400				40400			
Accounts Receivable	108	298400		318270				318279			
Material	112			31861			6383	25478			
Accounts Payable	319		$ 58219		$ 57163		7946		$ 65109		
Accrued Workmen's Comp.	325		11205		13058				13058		
Notes Payable	350		93200		81950				81950		
Common Stock	401		95000		95000				95000		
Capital Contributions	450		60000		60000				60000		
Retained Earnings	470		231400		295335				295335		
Contract Sales	501		2300200		2500500						$2500500
Contract Work in Process	503		190400		100500						100500
Time and Material Sales	505		42650		70360						70360
Labor Cost	602	638566		633231		$ 7946				$641177	
Material Cost	603	843780		886221		6383				892604	
Subcontractors	604	410650		360896						360896	
Other Direct Cost	629			11550			800			10750	
Officer's Medical Exp.	721	1750		1885						1885	
Provision for Taxes	780	21950		23800						23800	
		$3510443*	$3510443*	$3560772*	$3560772*	$18293*	$18293*	$889412*	$889412*	$2615210*	$2671360*
										56150	
										$2671360	

*Note: Columns don't foot because only representative accounts are shown. All accounts would be shown in a WTB and column totals would equal those shown.

Figure 6.1 Working Trial Balance

basic economic equation holds true for every firm. For example, the types of owner's equity accounts differ for the individual proprietor and the corporation. However, each type of firm has equity accounts that have the effect of balancing the asset and creditor's equity portion of the economic equation.

The creditor's equity segment of the basic economic equation for a firm is more commonly referred to as the *liabilities* of the firm. When the firm is a corporation the owner's equity segment is commonly referred to as *stockholder's equity*. A fourth category referred to as *deferred credits* sometimes appears in the basic economic equation. However, if possible, its use should be avoided. Because of the infrequency of the need for a deferred credit (an example would be the premium on bonds payable), it will not be considered in this chapter.

The broad-based economic equation is further subdivided into classifications that provide the means of analyzing, interpreting, and comparing the financial statements with past statements and statements of other firms. Although the classifications vary somewhat from one firm to the next depending on the type of firm, the following classifications are typical:

Assets:	Current assets
	Investments and funds
	Fixed assets—tangible
	Fixed assets—intangible
	Other assets
	Deferred charges
Liabilities:	Current liabilities
	Long-term liabilities
Owner's equity:	Contributed capital
	a. Capital stock
	b. Contributions in excess of par
	Retained earnings
	a. Appropriated
	b. Unappropriated

Most of the account classifications are self-explanatory. For example, current assets are those that are readily available and likely to be used in performing the firm's operations in the current account period. Other assets are those assets that do not fit the other asset classifications. In particular, a receivable from one of the firm's officers and a company office that is currently not being used in the firm's production process fit into the other asset category. Deferred charges represent debit balances derived from expenditures but involving a future benefit. They are similar to prepaid expenses except for the fact that the future benefits extend beyond a year's time. A construction firm's organizational costs may be treated as a deferred charge (an asset) rather than being expensed in the year in which they occur. Deferred charges are eventually matched to revenue and expensed.

The difference between appropriated retained earnings and unappropriated retained earnings lies in whether the retained earnings are restricted or not restricted as to being available for payment of dividends and other uses. In particular, some retained earnings may be restricted in the firm's agreement with creditors. The creditors may restrict the payment of dividends in order to assure the creditors that retained earnings are available for bond interest and principle payments.

A typical construction firm's balance sheet position is shown in Figure 6.2. As can be observed from the statement, several accounts unique to the

SAMPLE CONSTRUCTION CO., INC.
BALANCE SHEET
December 31, 19X0

ASSETS

Current assets		
Cash on hand and in bank	$ 45,141	
Accounts receivable:		
Customers	198,224	
Fabricators Co., Inc. (note 1)	7,040	
Steel Erectors, Inc. (note 1)	3,860	
Redi-Mix and Trucking Co., Inc. (note 1)	179	
Investment Co. (note 1)	3,791	
Officers and employees	10,733	
Retained percentages receivable	94,452	
Notes receivable:		
Fabricators Co., Inc. (note 1)	50,000	
Officer	16,000	
Accrued interest receivable	572	
Time and material work not billed:		
Customers	4,383	
Investment Co. (note 1)	571	
Officers and employees	2,459	
Contract equity not billed (schedule B)	28,746	
Inventories of material and supplies—at lower of cost or market	25,478	
Prepaid insurance	2,236	
Prepaid rent	2,000	$495,865
Investments		
Cash value of life insurance	$ 41,279	
Pleasure driveway—district bonds—at cost	6,000	
Lane bonds—at cost	3,000	50,279
Property and equipment (notes 2 and 3)		
Machinery and equipment	$437,585	
Office furniture and equipment	42,270	
Autos and trucks	157,597	
Total—at cost	$637,452	
Less cost charged to operations to date	294,184	343,268
Total assets		$889,412

Figure 6.2 A Balance Sheet

construction industry are a part of the statement. For example, "contract equity not billed" is a current asset account somewhat unique to the construction industry. In effect, it is a type of receivable. As previously discussed, when the costs of projects in progress exceed the billings, the difference is shown as a current asset. It should be noted that a current liability is required to be shown when billings are in excess of costs. No overbillings are assumed in the balance sheet illustrated. When under- and overbillings both exist, they should be shown separately as an asset and a liability on the balance sheet. They should not be netted. The actual calculation of the amounts would probably be shown by means of a note to the financial statement or a supporting

LIABILITIES AND STOCKHOLDERS' EQUITY

Current liabilities		
Accounts payable:		
Trade	$ 48,504	
Erectors, Inc. (note 1)	2,111	
Fabricators Co., Inc. (note 1)	65	
Trucking Co., Inc. (note 1)	12,105	
Retained percentages payable	2,324	
Equipment contracts payable, current installments (net of prepaid interest of $8,046) (note 2)	20,352	
Bank notes payable, current maturities (note 3):		
Unsecured	7,200	
Secured	50,203	
Notes payable—unsecured:		
Officers	41,950	
Others	40,000	
Withheld and accrued payroll taxes	13,058	
Other accrued expense:		
Salaries and wages	70,269	
Interest	3,925	
Property taxes	982	
Estimated liability for income taxes	13,131	$326,179
Long-term liabilities		
Equipment contracts payable, less current installments included above (net of prepaid interest of $11,135) (note 2)	$ 69,615	
Notes payable to insurance companies secured by cash value of life insurance	21,283	
Other notes payable—unsecured	22,000	112,898
Commitments and contingencies (notes 4 and 5)		
Stockholders' equity		
Common stock, $100 par value; 1,000 shares authorized, 950 shares issued and outstanding (note 6)	$ 95,000	
Capital contributed in excess of par value of common stock (note 6)	60,000	
Retained earnings (statement 2)	295,335	450,335
Total liabilities and stockholders' equity		$889,412

Figure 6.2 *Continued*

schedule. A schedule may also be prepared to support the amount listed for plant, property, and equipment.

While the amounts shown in the balance sheet in Figure 6.2 are for a given point in time, comparative financial position statements are sometimes prepared. This is done by showing the financial status of each account listed at the current point in time and at some past point in time such as one year prior. Such statements aid the reader in analysis of the statement.

Income Statement

The income statement is merely the summation of the firm's revenues and expenses for a given period in time. The dollar amounts on the statements also come from a WTB such as prepared in Figure 6.1. The relevant period of time is normally a quarter of a year or an entire year. However, when in need of a bank loan, a firm may be required to prepare an income statement for a period of time as short as a month.

The income statement has grown in significance over the past few years. Whereas creditors and investors of prior years placed their emphasis on the analysis of the firm's financial position statement, the income statement has played an increasingly significant role. Today's investors are primarily concerned with a firm's ability to continually increase its reported annual operating and net income.

As discussed in an earlier section, and as is true in regard to the balance sheet, the form and individual accounts included in the income statement vary in practice. Some statements may report all revenue (operating and nonoperating) first followed by a listing of all expenses, whereas other statements may first list operating revenues and expenses followed by nonoperating revenues and expenses. In addition, some statements may provide a combined income statement and retained earnings statement, whereas in other cases the income statement may be presented independently of the retained earnings statement. The income statement purpose remains the same regardless of the form of the statement which is to yield the net income for the firm for a given period of time. In addition, if the firm is a corporation, a calculation yielding the net income earned per share of company stock (indicative of the firm's rate of return on investment) is made and the earnings per share (EPS) is reported on the income statement.

Typical construction industry accounts summarized in an income statement (also referred to as a *Statement of Operations*) are shown in Figure 6.3. As discussed in an earlier section, the accounts and dollar amounts to be reported in the income statement differ depending on whether the percentage-of-completion or completed-contract method is used for recognizing revenue. The statement shown reflects using the percentage-of-completion method. The income statement shown in Figure 6.3 is for the same firm represented in the balance sheet in Figure 6.2. Note the tie or relation between the income dollar amount and the change in retained earnings on the balance sheet.

SAMPLE CONSTRUCTION CO., INC.
STATEMENT OF OPERATIONS AND RETAINED EARNINGS
Year Ended December 31, 19X0

Sales		$2,671,360
Cost of sales		
Material	$892,604	
Subcontracts	360,896	
Direct labor	641,177	
Equipment rental	20,853	
Other direct cost	10,750	1,926,280
Gross profit on sales		$ 745,080
Indirect cost and operating expense (schedule A)		692,023
Net income on operations		$ 53,057
Other income		
Interest	$ 2,316	
Discounts earned	15,987	
Gain on sale of equipment	890	19,193
Net income before income taxes		$ 72,250
Income taxes		
Provision for income taxes	$ 23,800	
Investment credit	7,700	16,100
Net income for the year		$ 56,150
Earnings per share (note 6) $59		
Retained earnings		
Balance, January 1, 19X0		239,185
Balance December 31, 19X0 (statement 1)		$ 295,335

Figure 6.3 An Income Statement

Operating income is often separated from extraordinary income on the income statement. Extraordinary income is significantly different in character from the typical business activity income of the firm. It has a material effect on income and its occurrence is not expected to recur frequently. A construction firm's selling part of its central office, or condemnation of part of its branch offices, would be considered extraordinary items on the firm's income statement.

Separation of operating income and extraordinary income is important in that a better analysis of the firm can be made. In particular, most of the attention is drawn toward the operating income trend in that extraordinary items, while strongly influencing net income, are viewed as occurring only once. In many cases there is a fine line between what is an operating income item and an extraordinary income item. The situation is made even more complex by the existence of prior period adjustments. A prior period adjustment is something that relates to prior periods and as such is excluded in determining of net income for the current period. Such an item is recognized in the retained earnings statement only. Examples of prior period adjustments (which are rare) include nonrecurring adjustments in income taxes and accounting errors resulting from erroneously entered transactions. The EPS is illustrated in the income statement in Figure 6.3.

Statement of Changes in Financial Position

Not as widely published or recognized as the financial position or income statement, but of increasing significance and frequency, is the statement of changes in financial position. This statement is viewed as essential to the fair reporting of the causes of the changes in the financial position (i.e., the balance sheet) from one period to the next. While the income statement reports changes as a result of operations, it does not reflect all of the financial changes between two consecutive accounting periods. As such, the statement of changes in financial position has grown in acceptance and importance as to potential investors and creditors.

A recent AICPA opinion has made the statement of changes in financial position a necessary statement as part of many published financial statements. The firm only has latitude as to the form of statement it presents. In particular, the statement of changes in financial position can be prepared on a working capital basis or on a cash basis. Regardless of which basis is used, the preparation of the statement of changes in financial position is less straightforward to prepare than the income statement or the financial position statement. Whereas the income statement and statement of financial position are merely the representation of summed accounts, the statement of changes in financial position requires the analysis of transactions and has three specific purposes:

1. To report on all the financing and investing transactions of the firm
2. To report on the generation and application of funds (either on a working capital or cash basis)
3. To report the causes of all the changes in financial position during the period

Like the income statement, this statement represents a period of time.

As indicated earlier, the statement of changes in financial position can be prepared on a working capital or cash basis. Whereas the working capital basis reports on changes in working capital, the cash basis reports only on changes in cash. The difference between current assets and current liabilities represents net available working capital. If working capital is increased, it is said to be generated. If it is decreased, it is said to be applied.

The statement of changes in financial position prepared on a cash basis is useful in the cash planning and cash control that are necessary ingredients of operating a construction firm. The cash basis statement focuses on the critical financing strengths and weaknesses of the firm. In order to illustrate the difference between the two methods, let us consider some examples of transactions and their treatment using each of the two bases. The transactions and their effect on working capital and cash follow.

Transaction			*Cash*	*Working capital*
1. Sell a fixed asset:				
Cash	$5,000		$5,000	$5,000
Note rec.—short-term	4,000			4,000
Note rec.—long-term	10,000			
Accumulated depr.	11,000			
Fixed asset		$28,000		
Gain		2,000		
Total generated			5,000	9,000
2. Borrow from bank:				
Cash	20,000		20,000	20,000
Note payable—short-term		10,000		−10,000
Note payable—long-term		10,000		
Total generated			20,000	10,000
3. Purchase asset:				
Fixed asset	30,000			
Cash		10,000	10,000	10,000
Note payable—short-term		5,000		5,000
Note payable—long-term		15,000		
Total applied			10,000	15,000
4. Depreciate equipment:				
Depreciation expense	10,000		0	
Accumulated depreciation		10,000		0
Total applied			0	0
5. Payoff debt:				
Account payable—short-term	10,000			−10,000
Account payable—long-term	15,000			
Cash		25,000	25,000	25,000
Total applied			25,000	15,000

Other than noticing the different effects of the transactions on working capital and cash, two other points should be noted. First, transaction 1 indicated a gain from the selling of an asset. While this gain is recognized in calculating income, it does not create working capital or cash. Second, inspection of transaction 4 indicates that the depreciation expense (which is used in calculating net income) does not use working capital or cash. These two facts are sometimes used as a means of calculating the change in working capital from operating income. In particular, the change in working capital from net income (i.e., excluding extraordinary items) is calculated as follows:

Net income	$XXX
Plus depreciation	XXX
Minus gain on sale of fixed asset	XXX
Working capital generated by net income	XXX

The point to be made is that depreciation is an expense that does not reduce net working capital (or cash), and an accounting gain from the sale of an asset does not increase net working capital (or cash).

A statement of changes in financial position is illustrated in Figure 6.4. The statement is for the same firm illustrated in Figures 6.2–6.3 and is prepared on a working capital basis. It satisfies the minimum disclosure requirements of the AICPA. As can be observed, it starts by reporting the working capital generated from income before extraordinary items, then goes on to report working capital generated from the extraordinary items. Applied working capital is then reported followed by the total increase or decrease in change in working capital accounts for the period.

Miscellaneous Schedules

The reader of the construction firm's financial statements may require additional information that is not disclosed on the financial statements. This often takes the form of additional financial statements referred to as *schedules*.

The schedules support various line items that are presented on the balance sheet, income statement, and statement of changes in financial position. The schedules supply information to banks and sureties that enhance their ability to analyze the construction firm. The schedules also assist the owners or managers analyze the company's financial position and results of operations which can lead to necessary decisions. Financial statements that include several supporting schedules are sometimes referred to as *long-form* financial statements.

The two most common additional financial statements are the *schedule of indirect cost and operating expense* and the *schedule of contracts in progress*. Other somewhat common schedules or statements are the *retained earning statement* and *schedule of notes payable*.

SAMPLE CONSTRUCTION CO., INC.
STATEMENT OF CHANGES IN FINANCIAL POSITION
Year Ended December 31, 19X0

Funds were provided by		
Operations:		
Net income for the year	$ 56,150	
Charges to operations not requiring funds—depreciation	96,051	
Less gain on sale of equipment (included in proceeds below)	(890)	$151,311
Proceeds from sale of equipment		1,750
New long-term debt	$100,000	
Less current maturities	17,476	82,524
Sale of common stock		10,000
Total funds provided		$245,585
Funds were applied to		
Increase in cash value of life insurance		$ 4,029
Purchase of property and equipment		93,382
Reduction in long-term debt		68,132
East Lane bonds		3,000
Net increase in working capital		77,042
Total funds applied		$245,585

CHANGES IN WORKING CAPITAL

	December 31		
	19X0	Prior Year	(Decrease)
Current assets			
Cash	$ 45,141	$ 54,330	$ (9,189)
Coeur 6% bonds	–	32,550	(32,550)
Accounts and notes receivable	384,279	325,134	59,145
Accrued interest receivable	572	937	(365)
Time and material work not billed	7,413	70,077	(62,664)
Contract equity not billed	28,746	34,604	(5,858)
Inventories	25,478	15,975	9,503
Prepaid expense	4,236	23,521	(19,285)
Income tax refund receivable	–	9,595	(9,595)
Total current assets	$495,865	$566,723	$ (70,858)
Current liabilities			
Accounts and retainages payable	$ 65,109	$168,863	$(103,754)
Equipment contracts payable	20,352	31,449	(11,097)
Bank notes payable	57,403	76,948	(19,545)
Notes payable	81,950	180,950	(99,000)
Billings in excess of equity in uncompleted contracts	–	76	(76)
Withheld and accrued expense	88,234	15,793	72,441
Estimated liability for income taxes	13,131	–	13,131
Total current liabilities	$326,179	$474,079	$(147,900)
Working capital	$169,686	$ 92,644	$ 77,042

Figure 6.4 A Statement of Changes in Financial Position

An example of a schedule of indirect cost and operating expense is illustrated in Figure 6.5. The schedule is for the same firm illustrated in the other financial statements in this chapter. The sum of the indirect costs and operating expenses shown in Figure 6.5 is also shown in the statement of operations illustrated in Figure 6.3. In effect the schedule of indirect cost and operating expense "explains" the total dollar amount shown on Figure 6.3 by itemizing the component costs that make up the total. This itemization provides the reader a means of analyzing what may be a significant expense item on the income statement or statement of operations. In particular, the indirect and operating expenses are typically about 10 to 20 percent of the construction firm's total expense.

The schedule of contracts in process, or work-in-process schedule, is a supporting financial statement somewhat unique to the construction firm. Its purpose is to clarify various items on the balance sheet and to establish the workload at the financial statement date.

An example of a schedule of contracts in process is shown in Figure 6.6. Note that several of the dollar totals on the schedule of contracts in process are shown on the balance sheet shown in Figure 6.2. For example, the sum of the "contract equity not billed" is shown on the balance sheet as a line item.

SAMPLE CONSTRUCTION CO., INC.
SCHEDULE OF INDIRECT COST AND OPERATING EXPENSE
Year Ended December 31, 19X0

Salaries and wages	$151,219
Payroll taxes	53,227
Union welfare and benefits expense	55,896
Travel and entertainment	9,462
Auto and truck expense	74,704
Tools and supplies	23,806
Repairs and maintenance	40,614
Depreciation	96,051
Rent (note 4)	9,750
Officers' medical expense	1,885
General insurance	22,437
Workmen's compensation insurance	24,455
Officers' life insurance	4,036
Office supplies and postage	5,746
Pension plan expense (note 5)	24,795
Legal and accounting	12,239
Advertising	2,383
Dues and subscriptions	1,745
Contributions	1,879
Property and other taxes	2,581
Utilities	7,489
Interest	38,085
Bad debts	17,704
Miscellaneous	9,235
Management fees	600
Total (statement 2)	$692,023

Figure 6.5 A Schedule of Indirect Cost and Operating Expense

SAMPLE CONSTRUCTION CO, INC.
SCHEDULE OF CONTRACTS IN PROGRESS
December 31, 19X0

	Contract price	Contract income earned to date	Contract billing to date	Contract equity not billed	Total estimated cost	Contract cost incurred to date	Estimated cost to complete	Estimated total gross profit
Lutheran Church	$ 68,187	$ 19,000	$ 19,000	$ –	$ 42,700	$ 11,913	$ 30,787	$ 25,487
Storage system	265,139	253,097	253,097	–	218,460	208,411	10,049	46,679
North Street	111,857	106,614	106,614	–	90,318	85,983	4,335	21,539
Tire Co.	160,476	146,311	146,311	–	139,896	127,585	12,311	20,580
Estates Co.	252,721	121,575	121,575	–	237,222	114,104	123,118	15,499
South Avenue	42,966	31,162	31,162	–	39,771	28,516	11,255	3,195
High School	111,343	89,215	89,215	–	95,235	75,521	19,714	16,108
Boat ramp	17,545	17,000	17,000	–	11,882	11,514	368	5,663
Summit	21,183	19,574	19,574	–	19,340	17,870	1,470	1,843
East Avenue	382,774	53,206	24,460	28,746	344,500	47,879	296,621	38,274
Parking lot	108,336	21,016	21,016	–	60,935	11,821	49,114	47,401
State Bank	31,728	28,183	28,183	–	23,020	22,053	967	8,708
Total	$1,574,255	$905,953	$877,207	$28,746	$1,323,279	$763,170	$560,109	$250,976

Figure 6.6 A Work-in-Process Schedule

Because of the relatively long-term nature of the construction project and the relatively large dollar value of the work it performs, it is common for the construction firm to have a significant dollar amount of work in process at any one point in time. Depending on the method of revenue recognition the firm uses, the revenue and related expense of work in process would be reflected differently on the financial statements. The schedule of contracts in process provides the reader a means of interpreting the statements.

Perhaps the greatest need or justification for the schedule of contracts in process relates to the question of the profitability of the work in process. When the dollar amount of work in process is substantial, the potential profit (or loss) of the work can have a large impact on the firm's ability to continue as a going concern. By preparing a schedule such as the one illustrated in Figure 6.6, the statement reader is in a better position to evaluate the financial strength of the company.

Disclosing a firm's work-in-process to external parties is a controversial topic in practice. Some construction firms view this as confidential information and are therefore reluctant to include the schedule of contracts in process in the financial statements that are made available to external parties. There is also a belief that, when hiring an outside accountant to prepare the financial statements, the cost of the service increases significantly when the schedule of contracts in process is prepared. However, this is usually a misconception in that a worksheet similar to Figure 6.6 has to be prepared in order to prepare the income statement, regardless of whether the schedule is printed or not. The fact remains that, without the schedule, the reader of the statements cannot fully analyze the firm's financial strength. Therefore, it follows that a good set of financial statements should include the schedule of contracts in process.

Types of Financial Statements and Additional Disclosure

There are several types or classifications of financial statements. Perhaps the most important classification is audited versus unaudited statements. Preparing audited statements requires disclosure of an opinion paragraph, a statement of significant accounting policies used, and notes that clarify various items in the financial statements. This information is needed in addition to the three financial statements and supporting schedules that have been discussed. Audited financial statements are discussed in Chapter 14.

Unaudited financial statements vary in form and use. Financial statements prepared in-house by the construction firm are usually limited to the statements and schedules presented in this chapter. If a good relationship exists between a construction firm and an external party such as a lending institution, the lending institution may satisfy its analysis needs with these in-house prepared statements.

A construction firm will often engage an independent accountant such as a CPA to prepare its financial statements on a regular basis. This may occur independently of the construction firm's need for audited statements. Unaudited financial statements prepared by an accountant usually take one of two forms. If the financial statements are intended for use only by the owners or management of the construction firm, the statements may be limited to the statements and schedules discussed in this chapter. The accountant should print the following disclosure paragraph on each and every page of the statement:

> These unaudited statements were prepared for management purposes only and do not include a statement of changes in financial position or other disclosures which may be required for fair presentation. We express no opinion with respect to these statements.

This should make it clear that the statements are intended for management only and should not be given to external parties. In part the disclosure paragraph limits the accountant's liability in regard to external parties relying on the statements.

If it is the intent of the owners or management of the construction firm to disclose the statements to external parties, the financial statements should include "notes" that clarify the statements much the same as if they are prepared for audited statements.

Any unaudited financial statements prepared by an independent accountant should clearly disclose the fact that they are unaudited. This is usually done by printing the word "unaudited" on each and every page of the statements. This should put external parties on notice of the fact that the accountant has not taken the audit steps discussed in Chapter 14 that are necessary in order to make an "opinion" on the statements.

7
FINANCIAL ANALYSIS OF THE CONSTRUCTION FIRM

INTRODUCTION

Numerous reasons are given for the high rate of bankruptcy in the construction industry. Blame is often aimed at the potentially inaccurate estimating and lack of project controls that characterize the construction firm. Too often we fail to recognize a firm's inherent financial structure shortcomings. A firm's financial statements, including the balance sheet and income statement, are the means to evaluate its financial structure and analyze its shortcomings.

External parties such as sureties and lending institutions must review and analyze the financial statements of the construction firm in order to avoid being party to a financial failure. The construction firm itself should objectively review and analyze its financial statements. This can lead to profitable decision making and can prevent actions or decisions that potentially lead to failure.

There are few if any types of businesses that are as dependent on external parties as the construction firm. These external parties often rely on their analysis of the construction firm's financial statements as their means of establishing their business dealings with the firm. In many instances, the construction firm's ability to continue as a going concern depends on external parties' interpretation of the construction firm's financial statements. For example, a surety's willingness to write a bond for a construction firm (a bond that may be required to enable the firm to do work) will probably be very dependent on the surety's appraisal of the firm's strength as outlined in the financial statements.

This chapter discusses the construction firm's financial strength as illustrated by the financial statements. Analysis of the statements is discussed along with factors that external parties evaluate in appraising the firm's financial pluses and minuses.

CONSTRUCTION FIRM FINANCIAL STRUCTURE CHARACTERISTICS

Unique external factors tend to shape the total financial structure of the construction firm. Inability to raise equity capital, operating on short-term credit, large amounts of receivables on the books because of the owner's retention of partial payments, and dependence of some firms on large dollar values of equipment all dictate the financial structure. Some of these industry characteristics result in a less than favorable financial structure that contains an undue amount of risk. While any one of these financial factors may not be representative of every firm, they tend to be characteristic of the typical construction firm.

The primary assets of any firm are its cash, receivables, inventory, and fixed assets. Compared to all other industries, the construction firm has a high percentage of its assets in receivables. In addition, compared to the manufacturing industry (of which construction is a part), as illustrated in Figure 7.1, the construction firm has a relatively small percent of fixed assets.

The construction firm's high dependence on receivables results from the typical billing and payment retention procedures. Upon completing various work items, the construction firm bills the owner. However, depending on the owner, actual payment may be slow. Delays of a month or more are common, In addition, when in fact the payment is made, the owner may choose to retain

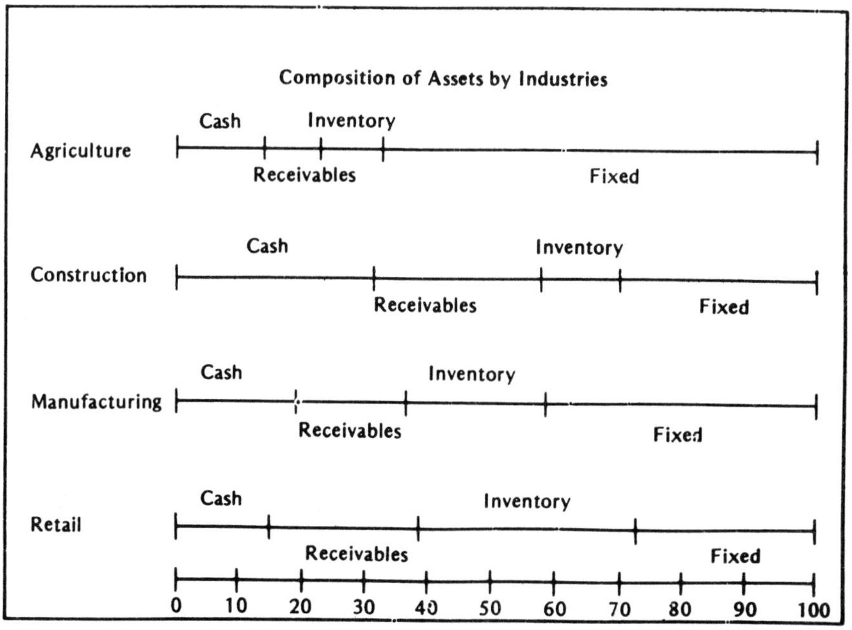

Figure 7.1 Financial Structure of the Construction Firm

part of the payment (typically 10 percent) until the construction project is substantially completed.

Receivables are troublesome assets. For one thing they do not provide the construction firm with an asset that can be used for operations and growth. It is true that the firm can convert them to cash by means of assignment or factoring. However, such procedures are not readily available to the construction firm and, when they are, they are relatively unfavorable because of interest costs. Receivables typically do not aid the firm in resolving any cash-flow problems. In fact a large buildup of receivables is often characteristic of a cash-flow problem leading to bankruptcy.

Unlike receivables in other industries, the construction firm seldom receives interest from the project owner. The owner is in fact using the construction firm's money to finance his project. The uncertainty and risk associated with receivables are other unfavorable financial considerations.

Various construction-related associations have continued their efforts to alleviate the difficulties that are part of the process by which the construction firm is paid. However, by itself the individual construction firm can do little to change the process. As such, the firm has to pay special attention to the control of its receivables which entails adequate collection procedures and an adequate and realistic provision for bad debts.

Inspection of Figure 7.1 also reveals that the construction firm has a relatively large percentage of its assets in cash. The construction firm continually has to have cash on hand to pay for varying amounts of labor and material expenses. While an adequate amount of cash for this purpose is necessary in order to avoid cash-flow problems, the fact remains that cash is not a good income-producing asset.

Cash-heavy firms tend to be nongrowth firms in that income and growth are generated by means of investment in nonmonetary assets such as plant and equipment. The construction firm has to be cautious in using its cash for nonmonetary investments because it needs to have large amounts of cash readily available for operations.

It is difficult to generalize about the construction firm's investment in fixed assets. The amount of such assets within a given construction firm varies from relatively high for the heavy and highway firm to practically nothing for the specialty subcontracting firm. However, as can be observed from Figure 7.1 the typical construction firm has less fixed assets than its counterparts in the manufacturing industry. While this smaller dependence on fixed assets frees cash for other purposes, it is also true that firms with relatively large amounts of investment in such fixed assets tend to be more financially stable.

On the capital side of the construction firm's balance sheet, the firm is characterized by a high degree of debt. Whereas typical manufacturing firms have approximately the same amount of debt capital and equity capital (i.e., invested capital plus retained earnings), the construction firm typically has liabilities in excess of equity capital. This high dependence on debt is not unexpected when one considers the difficulty that the construction firm has with raising investment capital. Typically, the construction firm is relatively small and not in a favorable position to issue stock that provides equity capital.

Usually a large percentage of a construction firm's liabilities are current ones. Normally this means they are liabilities that must be repaid within a duration of a year versus long-term liabilities that typically can be repaid over a period of several years.

The lack of significant long-term liabilities derives from several factors. For one, as with investment capital, third parties viewing the construction firm as risky are reluctant to commit funds to the firm on a long-term basis. Secondly, many construction firms lease their construction equipment by means of a long-term contract. While recent accounting rules will force the recognition of these long-term leases as long-term liabilities (which in effect they are), many balance sheets have not recognized the lease as a liability.

The construction firm's high dependence on current liabilities places it in a position of high financial risk. By definition, current liabilities come due in a relatively short period of time. Should the firm have difficulty making payments because of a slump in its operations or poor cash-flow planning, it may default and become subject to bankruptcy proceedings.

STATEMENT ANALYSIS DIFFICULTIES

In his book *Unaccountable Accounting*, Abraham Briloff poses the question as to whether 1 plus 1 always equals 2 in the accounting profession. Specifically, he draws attention to the fact that alternative accounting methods available to the profession often result in financial statements that are misleading or are open for interpretation.

Alternative accounting methods and means of expressing financial data in financial statements are especially troublesome to the construction industry. Lenders and sureties have fallen victim to misleading financial statements. At the same time, the contractor's ability to continue as a going concern may depend more on the firm's accountant's ability to present financial statements in the most favorable light rather than the firm's technical knowledge or actual financial structure.

To illustrate the significant difference that the choice of accounting method can have on the construction firm's financial statements, let us consider data regarding Sample Construction Co., Inc., a newly started corporation as of January 1, 19X0. The owner of the company started the firm by investing $50,000 cash in the firm of which $10,000 was used to purchase inventory consisting of lumber and masonry and $10,000 was used to purchase 5 percent equity in $200,000 of equipment with an average life of ten years. The owner used an additional $20,000 of his personal cash to purchase a $100,000 building for an office.

Sample Construction Company, Inc. engaged in two projects: project 1 was incomplete at 19X0 year end while project 2 was completed during the year. Data regarding the two projects are as follows:

Project	*Total Contract Price*	*Contract Expenditures to 12/31/X0*	*Estimated Additional Cost to Complete*	*Cash Collections to 12/31/X0*	*Billing to 12/31/Xo*
1	$280,000	$187,500	$12,500	$190,000	$190,000
2	$350,000	$300,000	—	$320,000	$350,000

An additional $15,000 was spent for lumber and masonry units during the year. Lumber and masonry units were in inventory at 19X0 year end. Overhead costs are assumed to be $10,000.

Shown below are two abbreviated income statements.

	Statement 1		*Statement 2*	
Revenue		$612,500		$350,000
Less costs		−487,500		−300,000
Depreciation (equip.)		− 20,000		− 30,000
Depreciation (bldg.)				− 3,750
Beginning inventory	$10,000		$10,000	
Purchases	+15,000		+15,000	
Ending inventory	− 7,500		− 5,000	
Material costs		−17,500		− 20,000
Gross profit (loss)		$87,500		($ 3,750)
Overhead expense		−10,000		− 10,000
Net income before tax (loss)		$77,500		($ 13,750)

Statement 1 reflects a $77,500 profit while statement 2 indicates a $13,750 loss. The interesting point is that both statements are income statements for the same firm, i.e., Sample Construction Company, Inc. for the year 19X0. How can it be that both income statements reflect the same firm? The answer is that different accounting methods are used in statement 1 versus statement 2.

Statement 1 recognizes revenue using the percentage-of-completion revenue-recognition method while the completed contract method is used in statement 2. Both methods are acceptable for accounting purposes. Furthermore, equipment is depreciated using straight-line depreciation in statement 1 while an accelerated-depreciation method is used in statement 2.

Statement 2 reflects the depreciation of the office building. Statement 1 assumes that the owner of the firm chooses to keep the ownership of the office building separate from the construction company. (Note: regardless of whether the office building is held by the individual or the corporation, the fact remains that there is an $80,000 liability for the building.)

The difference in the material cost on the two statements reflects using FIFO inventory costing in statement 1 and LIFO inventory costing in statement 2.

The noteworthy point is that all of the above accounting methods are acceptable ones. By admission, the numbers used are selected to prove a point. However, other alternative accounting methods also result in statement differences. While the balance sheet (statement of financial position) is not shown, the alternative accounting methods would also have a major effect on this financial statement including equity ratios and debt ratios.

The moral of the story is that not all financial statements are equal. The availability of alternative accounting methods emphasizes the need for full disclosures of accounting policies and notes in the financial statements. Only then can the reader analyze and evaluate the financial structure of the construction firm.

FINANCIAL RATIO ANALYSIS

Numerous financial ratios can be developed by dividing one of the many different items in a firm's income or balance statement by another item. The firm can then compare the values of its ratios to the average values of the ratios for its industry and perhaps decide to make an adjustment in its financial structure. Ratio analysis is also used by external parties in evaluating the financial structure and risk of the firm. Sureties and bankers will typically concentrate on what they view as key financial ratios when determining the feasibility of bonding the firm or lending money to the firm.

The financial ratio analysis user should be aware of its limitations. For one, each industry and firm is somewhat unique as to its product, its objectives, and its financial structure. It follows that each firm is somewhat unique as to the values of its ratios. Basing a firm's policies on a specific growth objective may result in its ratios varying from those accepted as average for the industry, although the firm may have a very sound financial structure.

The optimal financial structure for a firm or industry can change over a period of years. What were ideal financial ratios ten or five years ago may not be ideal today. Changes in interest rates, accounting practices, and tax laws are a few of the external factors that can justify changes in the financial structure and financial ratios of the firm.

Perhaps the greatest difficulty with ratio analysis is the fact that a firm can greatly manipulate its financial ratios through transactions that are for this purpose alone. For example, should a firm need to improve its short-term position of current assets versus current liabilities, it can issue long-term debt and thus either raise cash (a current asset) or use the cash to reduce its current liabilities. Similarly, selling fixed assets such as plant or equipment will provide cash that in turn will improve the value of the current ratio to be analyzed by a potential creditor.

A difficulty somewhat unique to the construction industry's use of financial ratios has to do with the alternative accounting methods used by construction firms. Using alternative accounting methods such as the completed-contract method versus the percentage-of-completion method results in different values for certain financial ratios.

Regardless of the problems associated with financial ratio analysis, they continue to be used by the firm and external parties. Specific ratio values are not as important as what the ratios are supposed to indicate. Knowing that a given ratio is indicative of a firm's ability to meet payment on its current liabilities is more important than trying to memorize specific acceptable values of the ratio. In addition, observing the trend of a given ratio's value is useful in that it may flag a potential future financial problem. Observing the ratio as a function of time will also aid in detecting any attempt by the firm to manipulate its ratios.

Whereas certain financial ratios are useful for evaluating the short-term soundness of the firm's financial structure, others are more relevant to evaluating long-term soundness. Thus, potential creditors considering lending short-term loans may be interested in one set of ratios, potential creditors considering lending long-term loans and potential investors of equity capital may be more concerned with a different set of financial ratios. Let us first consider some of the more commonly used financial ratios that relate to short-term financial analysis.

Short-Term Analysis

While not truly a financial ratio, the measure of a construction firm's working capital to its dollar value of work being performed is indicative of its ability to meet commitments as to material purchases and labor payroll. Working capital refers to current assets that are readily transferred to cash. For the construction firm, this consists primarily of cash and current receivables. As a general rule, the construction firm should maintain a 10 to 15 percent ratio of working capital to its dollar workload. A value less than this enhances cash-flow problems.

Creditors focus on financial ratios that center on the relation of current assets to current liabilities and the rapidity with which receivables and inventory turn into cash. Short-term creditors are concerned with the immediate and short-term ability of the construction firm to generate cash for the payment of loan principal and interest. The financial ratios indicative of the construction firm's short-term liquidity or ability to pay are more than often not derived from the firm's balance sheet.

The current ratio is by far the most recognized short-term financial ratio. It is a test of the firm's solvency and indicates the firm's ability to meet current obligations. The current ratio of a firm is derived as follows:

$$\text{current ratio} = \frac{\text{current assets}}{\text{current liabilities}}$$

Typically, lenders of money prefer to see a current ratio of 2:1 or even 2.5:1. However, it is difficult for even the most financially sound construction firm to maintain such a high ratio. The construction firm's high dependence on short-term credit results in a realistic current ratio of about 1.5:1. Any deviation lower than a 1.5:1 ratio should be viewed as an indicator of future solvency problems.

Theoretically, the quick ratio or acid test is an even more severe test of a firm's solvency. Whereas the current ratio includes inventories in determining assets, they are excluded in determining quick assets. The quick ratio or acid test is derived as follows:

$$\text{quick ratio or acid test} = \frac{\text{quick assets}}{\text{current liabilities}}$$

As is true of the current ratio, the quick ratio is derived from line items appearing on the firm's balance sheet.

The quick ratio might be considered as a more critical analysis of a firm's ability to generate cash over a short period of time. Unlike cash, current receivables, and temporary investments, it is sometimes difficult to transform inventory into cash without absorbing a loss on the transaction. As to the construction firm, the difference between the current ratio and quick ratio loses some of its significance because the construction firm is not heavily invested in inventories. This contrasts with other manufacturing industries such as the automobile industry which has a high inventory investment in raw materials. A quick ratio for a construction firm that is less than 1.25:1 or even more critically 1:1 should be viewed with alarm.

The receivable turnover and inventory turnover financial ratios are indicative of a firm's ability to convert receivables and inventory into cash. The ratios are calculated as follows:

$$\text{receivable turnover} = \frac{\text{credit sales}}{\text{average receivables}}$$

$$\text{inventory turnover} = \frac{\text{cost of project}}{\text{average inventory}}$$

Neither ratio is as meaningful in the construction industry as it might be in other industries. The billing and payment process typical of the construction industry dictates the construction firm's collection of receivables. However, should the firm deal in credit sales such as small repair jobs, then the receivable turnover ratio may be indicative of the soundness of the firm's accounting practices as to receivables and its collection procedures. For the most part, the construction firm's receivable turnover depends mainly on the type of owner for which the firm performs work and the duration of projects the firm undertakes. Perhaps the most meaningful use of the receivable turnover ratio for the construction firm is for the firm to observe changes in its own ratio's value with the goal of implementing procedures that improve the ratio's value.

Like the receivable turnover ratio, the inventory turnover ratio is distorted by the fact that the typical construction firm has a relatively small investment in inventory. Since each project is somewhat unique, it is often unwise for the construction firm to build up an inventory of raw materials. However, it should be noted that an incompleted project is in fact inventory to the construction firm. In this context, the inventory turnover ratio can be used to analyze the firm's ability to complete projects on schedule and turn them into cash. However, it should be noted that the value of the ratio will differ significantly depending on the type of accounting method used to recognize project income and project work in progress.

Long-Term Analysis

Although the long-term creditor or investor has to be concerned about the firm's ability to meet its current obligations, it is also concerned about the firm's long-range profitability. Expected income growth, ability to pay future dividends, and the ability to raise long-term funding are of utmost importance to the long-term financial success of the firm. In great part, these long-term success factors are reflected by the firm's income statement.

Of the many financial ratios used for evaluating the long-term financial soundness of the firm, those most used and most relevant to the analysis of the construction firm are as follows:

$$\frac{\text{net profits}}{\text{annual volume}}$$

$$\frac{\text{net profits}}{\text{net worth}}$$

$$\frac{\text{net profits}}{\text{net working capital}}$$

$$\frac{\text{annual volume}}{\text{net worth}}$$

The net profits to annual volume, net worth, and net working capital ratios relate to the earnings rate of the firm as a function of annual volume, net worth, and net working capital, respectively. Net worth equals the owner's invested capital plus any retained earnings. The value of the net profit to annual volume is usually relatively small for construction firms versus other industries. A typical range of financial ratio values for net profit to annual volume is 1.0 to 3.0 percent for construction firms. This "profit margin" is relatively low compared to other industries. Given the relatively high risk of contracting, it is particularly low. However, one must remember that this profit margin or rate of return is a rate of return on the customer's dollar not on the construction firm's investment. In that sense, the ratio or percent cannot be compared to a rate of return associated with equity investment.

The values of net profit to working capital and net profit to net worth for the construction firm tend to be higher than similar ratios in other industries.

Ranges of these ratios for construction firms are approximately 10 to 30 percent and 8 to 22 percent for the net profit to working capital and net profit to net worth, respectively. However, the relatively large values of the ratios are due to the relatively small amount of working capital and net worth of the construction firm rather than a large dollar net profit.

The ratio of annual volume to net worth measures the number of times net worth is turned over in workload. It is indicative of utilization of owner's equity and too low a value may indicate overcapitalization in relation to volume of work performed. Because of the widely varying dollar values associated with types of work performed by different construction firms, the ratio of annual volume to net worth can vary substantially from one firm to the next. As such, as is true of the other financial ratios discussed, the most meaningful use often centers around the firm's comparing the value of the ratio as a function of time. Such a comparison can often flag needed corrective financial adjustments.

In addition to the short-term and long-term financial ratios discussed, numerous other ratios have been used with less frequency to analyze the financial soundness of the construction firm. Included in these are the ratio of fixed assets to net worth, the ratio of net income to project direct costs (i.e., profit margin on cost), and various ratios that are aimed at analyzing the contents of the construction firm's overhead.

INDUSTRYWIDE FINANCIAL RATIOS

Numerous services and associations publish industrywide financial ratio averages. Some of these services and associations limit themselves to publishing ratios for a specific industry while others publish and compare financial ratios of average firms in several industries.

Examples of services that publish financial ratios for several industries include Robert Morris Associates and Dun and Bradstreet. Figure 7.2 illustrates published financial ratio data from Robert Morris Associates regarding general contracting construction. Similar data from the same source regarding a specialty type of contractor are illustrated in Figure 7.3.

Many of the services publishing financial ratios list a range of ratios for a given type of firm. The data that is published is secured from numerous firms resulting in variations in the values of a specific ratio from one firm to the next. The variation is characterized by the range of the financial ratios reported.

In addition to stating a range of financial ratios and an average in Figures 7.2 and 7.3, the ratio values shown in these figures are classified as to the size of the construction firm. By characterizing the ratios by firm size, this can enable the firm to compare itself with a firm of approximately equal size. Comparing the financial ratios of a construction firm to ratios of a firm five times bigger or smaller would result in a meaningless or even misleading analysis.

CONTRACTORS—COMMERCIAL CONSTRUCTION

Under $1MM	$1MM & less than $10MM	$10MM & less than $50MM	$50MM & over	All sizes	RATIOS
1.7 1.2 0.8	1.4 1.2 1.0	1.2 1.1 0.9	1.2 1.0 0.8	1.4 1.2 0.9	Quick
2.0 1.4 0.9	1.6 1.3 1.2	1.5 1.2 1.1	1.4 1.3 1.1	1.6 1.3 1.1	Current
0.2 0.4 1.0	0.1 0.3 0.5	0.2 0.3 0.6	0.3 0.4 0.9	0.2 0.3 0.6	Fixed/Worth
0.7 1.8 4.5	1.1 2.1 3.5	1.4 2.4 3.8	1.5 2.1 3.7	1.1 2.0 3.7	Debt/Worth
11.9 6.3 4.2	9.1 6.6 4.8	8.1 6.6 5.2	15.2 6.7 5.8	9.4 6.5 4.8	Revenues/Receivables
5.7 14.2 −79.0	10.0 17.7 34.5	11.6 23.9 50.7	16.0 24.1 55.1	9.3 17.9 43.2	Revenues/Working Capital
3.3 7.6 17.0	6.2 10.0 15.6	6.8 10.8 16.8	7.7 11.0 17.4	5.7 9.9 16.2	Revenues/Worth
36.4 14.0 −12.1	36.9 17.7 3.4	42.3 23.7 10.1	42.4 29.8 17.8	38.2 19.1 3.4	% Profit Bef. Taxes/Worth
15.6 2.8 −8.4	11.5 5.3 0.8	10.4 7.3 2.9	14.2 10.7 5.1	12.0 5.5 0.6	% Profit Bef. Taxes/Tot. Assets
60583M 133535M	1027313M 406029M	1304410M 511766M	3923819M 934366M	6316125M 1985696M	Contract Revenues ($) Total Assets ($)

M = $thousand MM = $million

Figure 7.2 RMA Financial Ratios for Commercial Contractors (*RMA Annual Statement Studies, Robert Morris Associates*)

Several contracting associations publish average financial ratio data on their membership. This data is openly solicited and firms are usually permitted to submit it anonymously. An example of a contractor association's financial ratio data as determined from a survey of its members is illustrated in Figure 7.4.

CONTRACTORS—ELECTRICAL WORK

RATIOS	Under $1MM	$1MM & less than $10MM	$10MM & less than $50MM	$50MM & over	All sizes
Quick	2.0 1.2 0.8	1.9 1.4 1.0	1.6 1.3 0.9		1.9 1.3 0.9
Current	2.6 1.7 1.2	2.3 1.8 1.4	2.5 1.5 1.2		2.3 1.7 1.3
Fixed/Worth	0.1 0.3 0.8	0.1 0.2 0.4	0.1 0.2 0.6		0.1 0.3 0.6
Debt/Worth	0.5 1.3 2.9	0.7 1.3 2.1	0.7 1.9 3.1		0.7 1.4 2.5
Revenues/Receivables	8.6 6.7 4.8	8.9 6.0 4.7	8.7 6.8 5.0		8.6 6.2 4.8
Revenues/Working Capital	5.0 8.2 18.7	5.9 9.0 13.7	6.8 11.0 17.9		5.7 8.8 15.6
Revenues/Worth	3.7 6.1 12.4	5.0 7.0 10.5	4.9 8.2 12.6		4.5 6.8 11.7
% Profit Bef. Taxes/Worth	36.4 14.9 2.2	37.5 21.9 4.9	38.9 25.2 9.5		37.2 20.0 3.9
% Profit Bef. Taxes/Tot. Assets	15.9 5.1 0.9	14.7 8.5 2.7	15.5 9.1 3.9		15.0 6.7 1.4
Contract Revenues ($) Total Assets ($)	58903M 27745M	420155M 154876M	292824M 111305M	285083M 107104M	1056965M 401066M

M = $thousand MM = $million

Figure 7.3 RMA Financial Ratios for Electrical Contractors (*RMA Annual Statement Studies, Robert Morris Associates*)

Numerous other services or associations publish data similar to that shown in Figures 7.2 through 7.4. Periodicals such as *Engineering News Record* occasionally publish select financial data regarding the financial make-up of the construction industry. This data includes dollar volume of construction firms and salaries of top executives working for construction firms. While not

	Group 1	Group 2	Group 3	Group 4	Group 5	Group 6	Group 7	Industry (Weighted)	Insert Your Ratios
Current ratio (times)	2.76	1.79	2.20	2.00	1.53	1.65	1.45	1.66	
Net fixed assets to net worth (%)	32.76	58.57	21.53	39.43	42.61	44.20	23.15	34.69	
Current liabilities to net worth (%)	45.75	99.05	56.95	71.11	135.11	116.50	178.46	115.34	
Total liabilities to net worth (%)	73.14	147.56	113.61	129.92	176.62	151.99	195.90	150.31	
Funded debt to working capital (%)	28.00	40.45	14.53	41.65	54.47	45.45	17.34	32.44	
Net sales to net worth (times)	3.90	6.78	6.42	5.90	8.17	8.95	8.40	7.34	
Net sales to working capital (times)	4.84	8.60	9.38	8.24	11.29	11.74	10.43	9.51	
Net profit (after taxes) to net sales (%)	5.26	2.70	3.52	2.64	1.07	2.89	1.57	2.39	
Net profit (after taxes) to net worth (%)	20.53	18.32	22.66	15.60	8.75	25.89	13.20	17.57	
Net profit (after taxes) to total assets (%)	12.02	7.40	10.50	7.01	3.16	10.27	4.47	7.05	
Net profit (after taxes) to working capital (%)	25.49	23.26	33.11	21.81	12.09	33.96	16.38	22.76	
Return on investment	12.01	7.39	10.47	7.00	3.16	10.26	4.47	7.04	

Figure 7.4 Published Financial Ratios for Electrical Contractors (Operation Overhead, *National Electrical Contractors Association*)

as encompassing as the data illustrated in Figures 7.2 through 7.4, volume and salary information is segmented financial data and can be used in evaluating how a specific firm stands up to its competitors.

TREND ANALYSIS

The difficulty associated with comparing any one construction firm's financial ratios with published averages for the typical construction firm was discussed earlier. In particular, each firm has its own unique characteristics, including financial characteristics, that limit the usefulness or validity of the comparison.

A meaningful evaluation of the construction firm can usually be made by charting various "key" financial ratios of the firm as a function of time. This is commonly referred to as *trend analysis*.

Trend analysis of financial ratios can lead to early detection of a deteriorating financial structure or a weak link in the overall financial structure of the construction firm. By detecting a potential shortcoming early, the construction firm may be able to make decisions to correct a problem or at least minimize its impact.

A worksheet for performing trend analysis on key financial ratios for a construction firm is illustrated in Figure 7.5. Examples of data for a construction firm are also shown in the figure.

Inspection of the financal data in Figure 7.5 indicates that the firm's profitability has leveled off and actually decreased during the last two years. Even though volume has somewhat increased during the last two, the increase in direct costs and general and administrative expenses of the firm offset the increased volume.

Could the construction firm characterized by the data in Figure 7.5 have foreseen the difficulties of the last two years by analyzing its financial data and financial ratios? The answer to this question is in part yes. Inspection of the first three years of data illustrates that the firm's general and administrative costs were increasing at a rate greater than the firm's gross profit. Given this fact, the firm's total profitability becomes very dependent on the ability to increase volume. Any small decrease or leveling off of volume can lead to a significant decrease in bottom-line profits given a large overhead expense (general and administrative).

A second indicator of potential problems after the first three years that can be detected is the firm's increased dependence on liabilities. In effect these liabilities create a fixed drain on the firm's cash and total profits.

Another danger signal that should have warned the construction firm of potential problems and no doubt was the cause for some of the problems was the negative trend of the firm's current ratio. From a value of 1.6 in year 1, it had decreased to a value of approximately 1.2 by the end of the third year. The construction firm has to be attentive to keeping its current ratio favorable (ideally a value of 1.5 or greater) in order to obtain the bonding necessary to maintain or increase the firm's dollar volume of work. As discussed in a later

Classification General Contractor — Accounting Method % Completion

Name Sample Construction Co. Inc. — Year End 19X5

Location Anywhere, U.S.A. — Legal Structure Corporation

(000's)	X1	X2	X3	X4	X5	
SALES	2,460	2,560	2,830	2,835	2,850	
% SALES GROWTH		4	10.5	1	1	
Labor	800	820	780	810	900	
Matl.	925	900	1,010	1,010	1,040	
Subcont.	500	550	720	765	680	
Gross margin	235	290	320	250	230	
GROSS MARGIN %	9.5	11.3	11.3	8.8	8.0	
General and adm.	133	172	202	218	220	
G & A % SALES	5.4	6.7	7.1	7.7	7.7	
INC. BEFORE TAX	102	118	118	32	10	
INC. BEFORE TAX-%	4.1	4.6	4.2	1.1	0.4	
Admin. salary	24	27	32	38	39	
ASSETS	800	812	830	850	830	
SALES TO ASSETS	3.07	3.15	3.4	3.33	3.43	
EQUITY	350	287	285	280	205	
SALES TO EQUITY	7.03	8.92	9.93	10.12	13.90	
Current assets	520	532	475.8	510	511.5	
Investments	100	110	120	110	120	
Property and eqp.	280	280	354.2	360	338.5	
Accu. depreciation	100	110	120	130	140	
Current liab.	325	380	390	425	465	
Long-term liab.	125	145	155	145	160	
CURRENT RATIO	1.6	1.4	1.22	1.2	1.1	
DEBT TO EQUITY	1.28	1.83	1.91	2.04	3.04	
INCOME TO EQUITY-%	29.1	41.1	41.4	11.4	4.8	
INCOME TO ASSETS-%	12.7	14.5	14.2	3.8	1.2	
SALES TO CUR. ASSETS	4.73	4.81	5.94	5.56	5.57	

Figure 7.5 Trend Analysis with Financial Ratios

section of this chapter, as the current ratio decreases, surety companies become reluctant to bond the construction company resulting in an eventual decrease in the construction firm's volume.

What, if anything, could the construction firm have done after three years to prevent the financial difficulties of the last two years? The firm probably should have attempted to reduce its general and administrative expense. Total profits depend on three factors: volume, direct expense, and overhead costs (general and administrative expense).

The reason the construction firm was unable to increase its volume at a greater rate during the last two years is not clear. Undoubtedly part of the reason was its deteriorating current ratio and inability to maintain or increase bonding. However, the reduction in volume was probably also related to less demand for construction or more competition from competing contractors. The result is that the construction firm is not in total control of its annual volume.

The fierce competition within the construction industry in great part dictates the firm's gross margin (shown as approximately 10 percent for the firm illustrated in Figure 7.5). In other words, the construction firm's direct costs of performing construction work are not totally controllable by the firm. This is not to say that the firm's management cannot use cost-reducing construction methods. However, there are practical constraints including competition that limit the amount of cost savings that can be obtained.

The result is that the most controllable element affecting total firm profits in Figure 7.5 is the firm's general and administrative costs. Attention should focus on this cost because it has continued to grow at a rate faster than volume. More often than not, a construction company is nonattentive to excessive operating expenses during profitable years. The "fat" of the business tends to be overlooked because of the firm's significant profits. However, as soon as volume slows up or decreases, the excess operating expense has a multiplied negative effect on the firm's profitability.

As a minimum, the construction firm should evaluate its overhead expenses annually. This analysis can establish required volume for profitable operations or lead to a necessary reduction in overhead to enable profitable operations. The calculation of break-even volume is discussed in Chapter 13.

Having calculated the break-even volume, the construction firm could direct its marketing efforts to securing the required volume. If this is judged unfeasible, a reduction in operating expense is probably necessary in order to prevent an unprofitable year.

A reduction in overhead expenses may not have been the only management practice that could have improved the results of the last two years shown in Figure 7.5. As noted earlier, the deteriorating current ratio of the construction firm probably leads to some of the problems that surfaced in years 4 and 5. To correct this negative characteristic, several options were open to the firm. First, the owners could have chosen to take less cash out of the firm as salary or as distribution of profits in order to enhance the current ratio. Also, some fixed assets could have been sold, or the firm could have curtailed some of its expenditures for fixed assets. Either of these two actions would have improved the firm's current ratio. The improved current ratio may in turn have led to more volume and more profits.

In summary, many of the favorable or unfavorable financial results of the construction firm do not happen overnight. Analysis of the firm's financial statements and financial ratios for one year to the next can lead to early detection of a future event. This analysis, commonly referred to as trend analysis, can serve to assist the construction firm in managing itself rather than being totally dependent on factors it cannot control.

DEPENDENCE ON SURETY AND LENDING INSTITUTIONS

In order to perform construction work, the construction firm usually has to secure several types of bonds from a surety company. Without the willingness of a surety company to issue it bonds, the construction firm will have no opportunity to contract for work with an owner.

Of the numerous types of bonds often required by the construction firm, the most common one is the *performance bond.* In selling the construction firm a performance bond, the surety company is assuring the potential project owner that the construction project will be completed according to specifications, or else the surety company will compensate the owner for the construction firm's nonperformance. In this regard, the bond serves as "insurance" to the potential project owner.

The surety company is not going to sell the construction firm a bond and take on the risk of being liable for performance if it judges the construction firm as having undue financial risk. This is true regardless of what the construction firm is willing to pay for a bond.

If the surety company does judge the construction firm worthy of bonding, its rate charged for a bond will depend on several factors. One of these is the surety's evaluation of the construction firm's financial strength. Rates charged to a high-risk construction firm may be double those charged to a construction firm with financial strength and a good track record of performance.

Several other types of bonds may be required by the construction firm. The potential project owner may require the construction firm to submit a *bid bond* with its bid for a project. This bond guarantees the potential project owner that the construction firm bidding in a competitive bidding process will not remove its bid once it becomes aware of the bids of its competition. The construction firm may be tempted to do this, to the disfavor of the potential project owner, if it learns its bid is significantly lower than its competitors. The bid bond, like the performance bond, is purchased from a surety company.

The construction firm will usually have to secure a *union wage bond* if it is to carry out construction operations. This bond, given by the construction firm to a union, guarantees the potential project owner that the construction firm will pay union wages and will make proper payment of fringe benefits required by union contract. Without this bond, the potential project owner would be liable to pay the wages and benefits if the construction firm defaulted.

Other bonds that may be required of the construction firm include a *license bond,* a *material payment bond,* and a *self-insurers' workmen's compensation bond.* The ability to purchase any of these bonds also depends on a surety company's willingness to sell it to the construction firm. In turn this willingness depends on the surety's appraisal of the financial strength of the construction firm as presented by the firm's financial statements and financial ratios.

The role of the lending institution or banker in the construction firm's operations is equally as important as the role of the surety. More often than not, the construction firm is dependent on securing several types of financing from the lending institution. For one, because of the common, frequent, late-payment practice of project owners and also because of the practice of owners to hold back a portion of the payment due the construction firm as a retainer, the construction firm often finds it necessary to secure working capital financing. This is especially true during the busy season of the construction firm's business cycle. Many construction firms are small, underfinanced, and unable to finance payroll and material vendors without occasional loans for working capital.

Given the high cost of construction equipment (a single piece of equipment costs as much as $500,000), most construction firms are unable to purchase equipment for cash. Even if they could, it might be unwise in that it could lead to a severe drain on their working capital position. The end result is that equipment financing is needed. While the construction firm may not be limited to looking to the lending institution for equipment financing, they often will use this source of financing.

Construction firms will occasionally require financing for the construction of real estate. The real estate may consist of erecting its own company offices. However, other real estate often is in the form of development property built by the construction firm. A common practice of construction firms is to invest excess profits in speculative houses, apartments, office buildings, and land. In addition to their own equity investment, they often seek external financing. While the construction firm's investment in real estate can prove troublesome (see Chapter 8), the fact remains that more and more firms tend to make this type of investment.

The end result is that the construction firm often needs bank loans or notes in excess of their dollar equity. To this end the construction firm is dependent on the lending institution's appraisal of the construction firm's financial statements.

THE ST. PAUL COMPANIES

ACCOUNTANTS INFORMATION BLANK

Name of Contractor ______________________

Address ______________________

1. Is your firm one of the following? ☐ Certified Public Accounting ☐ Public Accounting
   ☐ Other (Explain) ______________________

2. Please list the professional organizations of which your firm is a member. ______________________

3. How long has your firm represented the captioned contractor? ______________________

4. Do you obtain a written engagement letter from the captioned contractor? ☐ Yes ☐ No

5. Please check the following:	Unqualified	Qualified	Disclaimer	No Opinion – Prepared Without Audit Verification
A. Type of opinion rendered on prior years F.S.	☐	☐	☐	☐
B. Type of opinion rendered on current years F.S.	☐	☐	☐	☐

C. If your opinion on the financial statement is qualified or a disclaimer, what would be required to make your opinion unqualified for the new current year?

____

6. Does your audit cover: Balance Sheet ☐ Yes ☐ No Income Statement ☐ Yes ☐ No

7. Is your Audit Report on the captioned contractor prepared in the formats recommended by the American Institute of CPA's publication "Audits in the Construction Industry"?
   ☐ Yes ☐ No ☐ Other (Explain) ______________________

8. In your Audit Report, do you include the work in progress schedules as recommended and in the suggested format as recommended by the AICPA's publication "Audits in the Construction Industry"?
   ☐ Yes ☐ No ☐ Other (Explain) ______________________

9. Methods of recognizing income:
   ☐ Completed Contract Method ☐ Percentage of Completion Method ☐ Straight Accrual ☐ Other (Explain)
   ____

10. Do you issue a management letter in conjunction with your audit report? ☐ Yes ☐ No

11. Do you prepare interim financial statements? ☐ Yes ☐ No
    If yes, how often? ______________________
    Are they audited? ______________________

12. Do you prepare the contractors tax returns?
    Business ☐ Yes ☐ No Personal ☐ Yes ☐ No

13. What is the method of recognizing income on the business tax returns? ☐ Cash ☐ Straight Accrual
    ☐ Completed Contract Method ☐ Percentage of Completion Method ☐ Same as Financial Statement Reporting
    ☐ Other (Explain) ______________________

14. Is the tax year end the same as the Financial Reporting year end? ☐ Yes ☐ No

15. Does the contractor maintain a double entry bookkeeping system? ☐ Yes ☐ No

16. Basis on which the General Ledger is maintained.
    ☐ Cash ☐ Accrual ☐ Other (Explain) ______________________

24501 Ed. 2-75 Printed in U.S.A. Over

Figure 7.6 An Accountant's Data Form (*Courtesy of The St. Paul Companies*)

17. Please list the "Books of Original Entry": ____________________

____

____

18. Please list all the "Subsidiary Ledgers."

____

____

19. How often are the Subsidiary Ledgers posted? ____________________

20. How often is the General Ledger posted? ____________________

21. How often are trial balances of the General Ledger taken off? ____________________

22. How often are "In House" Financial Statements prepared? ____________________

23. Are the Subsidiary Ledgers reconciled to the related General Ledger control account? ☐ Yes ☐ No

If yes, how often? ____________________

If no, why not? ____________________

24. Is there a Subsidiary Ledger maintained for each construction job for costs and related billings?

☐ Yes ☐ No

If yes, are the Subsidiary Ledgers reconciled to a related General Ledger Control Account?

☐ Yes ☐ No How often? ____________________

If no, what kind of cost records are maintained? Please explain. ____________________

____

25. How often are "Estimated Costs to Complete" analyses prepared by the contractor? ____________________

26. Do you "test" these analyses in your audit? ☐ Yes ☐ No If yes, what auditing procedures did you use?

____

27. To what degree do you find the accounting records and record keeping to be adequate?

☐ Excellent ☐ Good ☐ Average ☐ Poor

28. To what degree do you find the contractors job costs records to be reliable?

☐ Excellent ☐ Good ☐ Average ☐ Poor

29. What improvements in the contractors accounting system and record keeping should the constructor consider making at this time?

____

30. Are the accounting records maintained manually or by machine? Please explain ____________________

____

If by machine, please identify type of equipment. ____________________

Date ____________________ ____________________
Name of Accounting Firm

By: ____________________

Title: ____________________
(To be signed only by Owner or Partner)

I hereby authorize the above accounting firm to answer the above questions to the St. Paul Fire and Marine Insurance Company.

Date ____________________ ____________________
Name of Construction Company

By: ____________________

Title: ____________________

CONCERNS OF SURETIES AND LENDING INSTITUTIONS

When evaluating their willingness to sell a construction firm a bond or give it a loan, both the surety company and the lending institution share common concerns. These include the following:

1. Integrity and personal character of the owners of the construction firm
2. Technical knowhow of the individuals
3. Experience and performance track record of the construction firm
4. Financial strength of the construction firm

The factors are not necessarily listed in order of importance. For the construction firm seeking its first bond or loan, the integrity and personal character of the firm's owners will be especially important. For the ongoing firm, the first three factors become of secondary concern versus the analysis and monitoring of the construction firm's financial statements.

The importance of any of the factors in evaluating the construction firm depends on whether the analysis is being made by a surety or lending institution. Surety companies tend to be less subjective in their analysis than lending institutions. The surety company often avoids making personal opinions. Instead, they stick to established formulas and factors when evaluating the construction firm. This is not to say that factors other than financial ratio and statements are disregarded. Experience and performance along with other factors are weighed in the evaluation. However, the factors and weighting system employed by sureties tend to be more uniform in application from one construction firm to the next compared with lending institutions.

Sureties also tend to be more rigorous in their evaluation of the construction firm than the lending institutions. Perhaps this added rigor is because the average bonding company is likely to understand the construction firm's business better than the typical lending institution. It is also true that the surety company usually has more at risk than the lending institution should the construction firm fail.

Surety companies pay close attention to a few select financial ratios of the construction firm. For example, surety companies generally prefer to limit performance bonds to approximately ten to eighteen times a construction firm's net working capital and approximately ten times the firm's net worth. Modifications to these ranges are made for firms with good or bad experience, track record, and other financial statement characteristics.

On occasion the surety company will request information from the construction firm's accountant as a further tool in evaluating the financial strength of the firm. The intent is that the accountant serves as an independent preparer and analyzer of the construction firm. An example of a form to be filled out by the construction firm's accountant is illustrated in Figure 7.6.

The lending institution tends to be less objective in its evaluation of the construction firm. Personalities and the amount of business transacted by the owners of the construction firm with a bank strongly influence a bank's willingness to extend credit. Financial statements and financial ratios are not disregarded in the analysis. However, there is less uniformity in a lending institution's treatment of two different construction firms than is true of the surety company.

Regardless of who is appraising the financial statements, the construction firm's ability to carry out business with an external party is enhanced if the financial statements and resulting financial ratios are favorable. The high dependence of the construction firm on external parties places even more importance on keeping the financial statements and financial ratios in good light.

8
PORTRAYING THE FIRM IN A FAVORABLE LIGHT

INTRODUCTION

Chapter 7 presented various financial ratios and other financial considerations of the construction firm that concern a surety company, lending institution, and other creditors. The relevancy of various financial ratios was also discussed. However, the fact remains that accounting is by no means a science. Alternative accounting principles and practices often permit the construction firm a degree of flexibility in presenting itself through its financial statements.

Because of this flexibility, sureties and lenders have fallen victim to what some might consider misleading financial statements. At the same time, the construction firm's ability to continue as a going concern may depend more on its ability to present financial statements in the most favorable light rather than on the firm's technical knowledge or actual financial structure.

This chapter will illustrate several methods by which construction firms can improve their financial statements by merely using alternative accounting methods. While the construction firm has to be attentive to portraying itself favorably, it is also important for the firm to remind itself that using favorable accounting methods to portray itself in a good light will seldom help the firm meet its payroll.

SELECTING A YEAR END FOR IMPROVING FINANCIAL STATEMENTS

The date selected as the firm's year end can have a significant impact on the financial statements of the construction firm. This is especially true where workloads vary throughout the year as in midwestern states where winter often brings many construction field operations to a halt.

Choosing a year end that falls at the end of a construction firm's busy production period can result in a better working capital position on the firm's balance sheet than if the firm's year end is established at the end of the construction firm's slow period (for example, at the end of the winter months). The firm's working capital is gradually decreased throughout the winter months because of continuing overhead expenses without offsetting revenue from ongoing projects.

To illustrate the impact of the year-end selection on the reporting of working capital, let us assume the following information regarding a construction firm. The construction firm has fixed overhead of $15,000 per month independent of its production activity. The firm's production process occurs mainly during March through October. During this eight-month period the firm averages $150,000 of revenue per month and $120,000 of direct expenses in each of these months. The firm's starting cash position is assumed to be $30,000.

Calculating the firm's month ending working capital (note: assuming there are no receivables or accounts payable, the only working capital is cash) is shown in Figure 8.1. Note that in each and every year the firm's working capital would be $60,000 greater at the end of October versus the end of February. In other words, an October year-end balance sheet would reflect $60,000 more working capital than a February year-end balance sheet.

Reporting $60,000 more working capital on the firm's balance sheet can prove advantageous to the firm in its dealings with external parties. For example, one rule of thumb used by construction bonding companies is that they will bond a company for ten times its available working capital (note: this is only a rule of thumb and other factors would also be considered). The result could be increased bonding capacity of $600,000 by the increased working capital of $60,000.

The income reported on the income statement for the firm illustrated in Figure 8.1 would only be affected by the choice of the year end in the first

Month	Operating Revenue (Cash) (Inflow)	Operating Expense (Cash) (Outflow)	Monthly Overhead (Cash) (Outlfow)	Initial Cash	Cumulative (1st) (Year)	Cumulative (2nd) (Year)	Cumulative (3rd) (Year)
				$30,000			
January	—	—	$15,000		$ 15,000	$ 75,000	$135,000
February	—	—	15,000		0	60,000	120,000
March	$150,000	$120,000	15,000		15,000	75,000	etc.
April	150,000	120,000	15,000		30,000	90,000	
May	150,000	120,000	15,000		45,000	105,000	
June	150,000	120,000	15,000		60,000	120,000	
July	150,000	120,000	15,000		75,000	135,000	
August	150,000	120,000	15,000		90,000	150,000	
September	150,000	120,000	15,000		105,000	165,000	
October	150,000	120,000	15,000		120,000	180,000	
November	—	—	15,000		105,000	165,000	
December	—	—	15,000		90,000	150,000	

Figure 8.1 Financial Statement Dependence on Year-End Selection

year of selection. In succeeding years the income would be the same regardless of the year-end date. However, even the one-time effect of the year end on the income statement should not be discarded. On occasion construction firms have changed their year end with a resulting one-time benefit to income. This higher reportable income and its positive effect on net worth has been used to increase or enable bonding of a construction firm.

The choice of a firm's year end should not be based totally on the impact of working capital. Other considerations include convenience and tax aspects. For example, if a construction firm is a Subchapter S corporation, it may prove advantageous to choose October 31 as the year end because of the provision for a two and one-half month income-distribution provision.

REAL ESTATE ON THE CONSTRUCTION FIRM'S FINANCIAL STATEMENTS

Construction firms have often invested excess profits from their operations in new and existing rental property such as apartment complexes. Still other construction firms have built rental property on a speculative basis in order to use their idle resources during slack periods in their operational cycle.

Investments in real estate have proven to yield one of the highest and safest rates of returns available to the investor including the construction firm. However, a few words of caution are noteworthy. First, not all real estate has proven to be a good investment. Each investment should be thoroughly examined including recognizing risk factors and analyzing the location, potential rental income, and the liquidity of the investment. Contrary to generally held beliefs, not all investments in real estate have appreciated over the years.

Perhaps a more critical consideration regarding a construction firm's investing in real estate is the effect the investment has on the firm's liquidity. Liquidity is a measure of the availability of a firm's working capital, which in great part is the firm's cash. The more working capital a firm has available, the more "liquid" is the firm. Investing in real estate implies investing liquid assets (cash) in a fixed asset that is not readily convertible into cash that may be needed for daily operations. In addition, debt service payments, such as interest payments on the mortgaged real estate, can have a cash drain on the firm's cash position throughout the year because often the cash inflow from this type of investment is in the form of an end of year depreciation and interest tax write-off.

Having insufficient working capital on hand is very high on the list of reasons for construction firm bankruptcies. Often the firm would be wise to build up its working capital to carry it through possible future operational slowdowns instead of locking it up in fixed assets such as investment property. Real estate remains a good investment, but the construction firm should seek a balance between its investments and its available working capital.

Often overlooked is the negative impact of a construction firm's investing in real property on its financial statements. Let us assume a construction firm

Balance Sheet Before Rental Property Investment

Cash	$ 80,000	Accounts Payable	$ 50,000
Accounts receivable	20,000		
Total current assets	$100,000	Total current liabilities	$ 50,000
Machinery	50,000	Long-term liabilities	$ 80,000
		Total liabilities	130,000
		Net worth	20,000
Total assets	$150,000	Total liabilities and net worth	$150,000

$$\text{current ratio} = \frac{\text{current assets}}{\text{current liabilities}} = \frac{\$100,000}{\$\ 50,000} = 2$$

working capital = $100,000 – $50,000 = $50,000

Figure 8.2a Balance Sheet of Construction Firm—No Real Estate

has a financial structure as illustrated by the balance sheet shown in Figure 8.2a. The current ratio of the firm's assets to liabilities is 2 and its working capital is at $50,000. External parties such as the construction firm's bonding company look to the current ratio and working capital of the firm in evaluating their willingness to bond the firm.

Let us now assume that the construction firm invests $10,000 of its available cash as 10 percent equity in $100,000 of rental property. Let us further assume that, of the $90,000 liability, $5,000 is due in the coming year. The firm's balance sheet at year end would appear as shown in Figure 8.2b.

Analysis of the after-investment balance sheet in Figure 8.2b indicates that the construction firm's current ratio has decreased from 2 to approximately 1.6 and its working capital has decreased from $50,000 to $35,000. Admittedly, the investment may yield an operating cash inflow (revenue minus

Balance Sheet After Rental Property Investment

Cash	$ 70,000	Accounts payable	$ 50,000
Accounts receivable	20,000	Note payable—current portion, rental property	5,000
Total current assets	$ 90,000	Total current liabilities	$ 55,000
Machinery	50,000	Long-term liabilities	80,000
Investment—rental property	100,000	Rental property	85,000
		Net worth	20,000
Total assets	$240,000	Total liabilities and net worth	$240,000

$$\text{current ratio} = \frac{\text{current assets}}{\text{current liabilities}} = \frac{\$90,000}{\$55,000} = 1.64$$

working capital = $90,000 – $55,000 = $35,000

Figure 8.2b Real Estate's Effect on the Balance Sheet

operating expense). However, even if this inflow was initially as large as the cash investment (it is unlikely that it would be this large), the firm is still confronted with the recognition of a short-term liability from the investment for the rental property. This $5,000 liability has the effect of reducing the current ratio and the available working capital.

What has happened is that the rental property investment has created a short-term liability without any compensating short-term receivable. Proper financial accounting does not allow for any recognition of future rental income as a receivable. Many contractors argue that this potential rental income is certain and should be recognized as a current asset. In reality, given a good investment the rental income is likely to occur. However, because of the conservative principle and revenue-recognition principle of proper accounting, this potential income cannot be recognized in a properly prepared balance sheet.

The negative impact of this type of investment on the construction firm's balance sheet would increase as the investments grew in magnitude. While the investments may yield a good return and have little financial risk, the negative impact remains the same.

One might argue that an external party such as lending institution or bonding company would "read through" the balance sheet and in effect give the contractor credit for the potential rental income and its offsetting effect on the recognized liability. While this may occur, it often is presumptious to assume an external party will "interpret" the financial statements. These external parties are often not equipped to do this, or may shy away from such an interpretation in that it may lead to subjective evaluation.

The solution to the problem of rental property's negative impact on a firm's balance sheet is simple. The real estate investment should be made outside the construction firm. Using a separate corporation or going through the owner's personal account can avoid the problem of recognizing a short-term liability with no compensating short-term receivable.

Ideally, the investment in rental property should be made outside the construction firm at the time of the investment. Once the investment is made through the firm, another problem occurs—it is often difficult for the firm owners to remove the rental property from the construction corporation to their personal accounts or another corporation without incurring a significant tax liability. This tax liability and how to possibly avoid it are discussed in Chapter 18.

EQUIPMENT'S EFFECT ON THE BALANCE SHEET

Depending on the type of work a construction company performs, its involvement with equipment varies from having almost none to having equipment costs of up to 50 percent of its direct cost of doing work. Given the high cost associated with purchasing or renting construction equipment, the financial statements of the construction firm that is even moderately dependent on equipment use are greatly affected by the cost of the equipment.

Numerous books and articles have been written on the topic of whether a firm should purchase, lease, or rent its equipment. While the variables relevant to the decision to purchase, lease, or rent are numerous, the decision usually comes down to measuring the amount of expected usage of the equipment in question. The more the expected usage, the more an argument can be made for purchasing because the unit cost of usage becomes more favorable for purchasing versus leasing or renting when the equipment usage is substantial.

Independent of the economics of purchasing, leasing, or renting equipment is the impact of the alternatives on the financial statements of the construction firm. This has to be recognized in addition to the unit cost of usage. Purchasing construction equipment often has an unfavorable impact on the construction firm's balance sheet (statement of financial position) relative to leasing or renting. Because of the large cost of construction equipment (often $50,000 or more), the construction firm usually purchases the equipment by means of a cash downpayment thus creating a liability. The liability is often in the form of a note payable to a bank or equipment vendor with the equipment usually given as security for the note.

While the construction firm's decreasing its cash (by making the downpayment) and creating a liability are offset by creating an asset on the financial statement, it is the classification of the asset and liability that can prove damaging to the construction firm's financial statements. Like the proper accounting used for real estate that was discussed in the previous section of this chapter, a current liability must be recognized on the balance sheet without any offsetting current asset. Recognition of a current liability without recognition of a current asset (in fact, the current assets of the firm are decreased by the cash downpayment) lessens the current ratio and working capital of the construction firm. As noted earlier, external parties often look to the current ratio and working capital in judging the short-term financial strength of the construction firm.

The current portion of the note payable must be recognized as a current liability on the balance sheet. The current portion is the amount of the principal payable within the operating cycle of the firm or a one-year period (usually the construction firm's operating cycle is taken as a one-year period). Since equipment is usually financed over a small number of years (three to ten) relative to real estate financing, the current portion of an equipment note may be around 20 percent or more of the total note payable. The noncurrent portion of the liability would be shown as a long-term liability on the balance sheet.

The purchased construction equipment would be shown at cost as a fixed asset on the construction firm's balance sheet. This is required for financial reporting even though the equipment is to be used in the current year. While the recognized asset adds to the total assets of the firm, it adds nothing to the current section of the balance sheet.

On the other hand, leasing or renting the same equipment may have no effect on the balance sheet other than its indirect effect as an "expense" on the income statement. However, this same indirect effect would also be true of purchased equipment through the recognition of depreciation. While some leases may actually be lease-purchases and therefore must conform to purchase accounting treatment, often leasing or renting result in avoiding the unfavorable impact on the balance sheet that purchasing has. It is for this reason that some firms choose to lease or rent equipment rather than purchase it.

The fact remains that, for equipment frequently used by the construction firm, the unit cost associated with purchasing may be substantially less than that for leasing or renting. Another benefit of ownership is equipment availability and the marketing benefit of having the company's name constantly identified on the equipment.

In an attempt to alleviate the negative effect of purchased construction equipment on the balance sheet, construction firms have on occasion established an affiliated or subsidiary company that purchases the equipment and in turn rents it to the construction firm. For example, a general contractor may establish an equipment rental firm and rent equipment from itself by renting the equipment from the rental company to the general contracting firm. In this way, the general contracting firm, which depends on securing bonds from surety companies, can avoid recognizing a liability. Instead, the equipment rental firm, which has no need for bonding, reflects the current and long-term liabilities and fixed assets on its financial statements.

While one would think an external party such as a lending institution or surety would view both the general contracting firm and its affiliated company as a whole in evaluating the financial strength of the general contracting firm, practice has proven this premise wrong.

Leasing or renting equipment from an affiliated equipment rental company also provides the construction firm the opportunity to regulate the profitability of both companies. For example, a general contracting firm attempting to improve its income and, thus, its balance sheet may establish a favorable rental rate for itself. The rental may be set at a rate that does not cover the operating costs of the equipment such as depreciation, repair, and maintenance. While this practice will result in unfavorable financial statements for the rental equipment company, the rental company might not depend on the financial opinions of external parties.

Establishing affiliated companies and rental rates cannot be made without regard for the tax laws or the imposed restraints on financial reporting. However, enough freedom and flexibility exists in both financial reporting and tax law to result in a significant number of construction firms establishing separate companies for purchasing and operating their equipment.

LIABILITY TERM AND BALANCE SHEET PRESENTATION

Management of construction firms vary from the most liberal to very conservative. Evidence of this range can be seen when it comes to borrowing money. When faced with borrowing money for equipment or other fixed assets, some construction firms will attempt to establish and payoff a note over as short a period as possible whereas other firms will seek a loan that can be paid off in as many years as possible.

For example, a construction firm may agree to a loan repayment of three years on a $50,000 note for a piece of construction equipment, even though a ten-year note is made available. The firm's argument for the three-year note is in great part based on its dislike of debt and the interest associated with it. While it is true that the longer the loan repayment period, the larger the total interest paid, it is also true that the payback period affects the financial statements. This effect should be recognized when establishing the loan repayment period.

While a shorter repayment period will result in less total interest expense than a longer repayment period, the shorter period may adversely affect the firm's balance sheet. This is because the current portion of the note must be recognized as a current liability, and the amount for a short-term loan will be larger than the current portion of a longer-term loan. To illustrate this impact, Figure 8.3 shows the initial current portion of a $50,000 loan at 10 percent for a three-year note and then for a ten-year note. The larger resulting current portion for the three-year note is reflected in a larger current liability on the firm's balance sheet. This liability in turn decreases the firm's current ratio and working capital. The construction firm should evaluate this impact when negotiating the terms of its loans. While the interest may be larger for the longer-term note, proper financial accounting does not require recognition of future interest on the financial statements of a firm.

Establishing a short duration for a loan repayment also imposes a potential financial squeeze on the firm. The shorter the term, the larger the annual or monthly payment. Given the relatively wide variations that occur in the financial operations of the construction firm, the firm may on occasion be too optimistic in evaluating its ability to repay a loan in a short period of time. There is much to be said for having the right to pay over an extended period of time with the option to prepay if desirable. Such a prepayment clause does not increase the recognized current portion of the loan.

Consistent with the objective of decreasing the dollar amount of the current liability section of the construction firm's balance sheet is the "refinancing" of short-term loans or notes with long-term notes. For example, it

$50,000 Loan at 10%

3-Year	10-Year
Annual payment = $20,105.50	Annual payment = $8,137.50
First-year interest = $5,000.00	First-year interest = $5,000.00
First-year principle (current portion) = $15,105.50*	First-year principle (current portion) = $3,137.50*

Figure 8.3 Effect of Loan Term on Current Liability of Balance Sheet

may be possible for a firm to refinance three separate $20,000 notes all payable in the coming year with a single *consolidated* $60,000 note due in six years. This note would remove the current liability by establishing a long-term liability. In addition to the favorable impact on the financial statements, the new note would impose less immediate financial burden on the firm.

RECOGNITION OF OWNER'S INVESTMENT

Construction firms are often started by a single individual or a few individuals. In many cases these individuals have a great deal of optimism, significant technical experience, such as several years as a construction craftsman, and little or no investment cash. The result is that the individual or individuals often borrow money on their personal assets, such as their real estate, as a means of creating cash to start the construction firm. The personal assets serve as security for the loans.

To illustrate the variability of properly prepared accounting financial statements and the impact of a specific transaction on these statements, let us assume the newly formed firm described is a corporation. Let us further assume that two partners established the firm, each borrowing $25,000 from a bank by pledging their homes as security.

The balance sheet of the newly formed construction company is shown in Figure 8.4. It reflects $50,000 in assets and $50,000 in invested capital by the owners. However, what if the owners had started the firm first and then borrowed $50,000 through the company? In this case the $50,000 would be shown as a $50,000 liability on the financial statements as also illustrated in Figure 8.4

The two statements shown in Figure 8.4 are significantly different. The first balance sheet implies that there is $50,000 in "free cash" (nonobligated) in the firm, whereas the second balance sheet infers no free cash because the entire $50,000 is owed as a payable.

Balance Sheet—Contributed Capital Recognition

Current assets		Liabilities	—
Cash	$ 50,000	Total liabilities	$ 0
		Net Worth	
		Contributed capital—partners	$ 50,000
Total assets	$ 50,000	Total liabilities and net worth	$ 50,000

Balance Sheet—Liability Recognition

Current assets		Liabilities	$ 50,000
Cash	$ 50,000	Total liabilities	$ 50,000
		Net worth	0
Total assets	$ 50,000	Total liabilities and net worth	$ 50,000

Figure 8.4 Effect of Owner's Investment

The fact is that, regardless of the balance sheet treatment, the two partners owe the bank $50,000. However, by borrowing the money personally they were able to avoid recognition of a liability on the construction firm's balance sheet. Furthermore, many accountants would agree that the firm's statements would not even have to be footnoted as to the partner's liability to repay the $50,000.

This financial treatment of a transaction should draw attention to the need to look to the financial statements of both the construction firm and its owners when evaluating the firm. However, given the frequent failure of external parties to do just this, the construction firm has been able to present itself in varying financial strength through its financial statements.

OFFICER'S RECEIVABLE AND FINANCIAL STATEMENTS

The construction firm usually has to be very careful to keep sufficient working capital on hand in order to maintain a good relationship with a surety company and/or lending institution. However, at the same time the owners of the firm may desire to take cash out of the firm for their own personal use. One way of taking cash out of the firm is to distribute profits. However, in addition to the tax liability associated with the distribution, this reduces the working capital of the firm because a current asset (cash) is distributed. Given the objective of not weakening their external party relations by lessening their working capital, contractors have on occasion taken cash out of the firm and offset this on the balance sheet by recognizing a receivable—namely an officer's note receivable. More often than not, they also recognize the receivable as a current asset.

Recognition of an officer's note receivable is valid accounting treatment if, in fact, the intent is for the officer to repay the money to the company. If the intent is to pay it back within a year, recognition of a current asset is further justified.

However, many such receivables never do get repaid. Instead, the receivable continues to appear on the statements and in fact the owner may never intend to repay the loan. On occasion the dollar amount of the receivable is significant compared to other balance sheet line items.

The reader of the construction firm's balance sheet has to be cautious in evaluating a receivable that is used to maintain the firm's working capital presentation. The construction firm using this accounting practice will often arouse the suspicion of its creditors, lenders, and surety company.

REVENUE-RECOGNITION VARIATION

Chapter 3 discussed the impact of alternative revenue-recognition methods on both the income and balance sheet statements of the construction firm. For example, the potential dramatic differences from using the completed-contract method versus the percentage-of-completion method were discussed. The reader is referred to Chapter 3 to review those differences.

Even when a revenue-recognition method is chosen, using the method can still result in significant differences in the financial statements. To illustrate this, let us consider the dependence between the reported income on the income statement and the determined percentage-of-completion for a project that is part of using the percentage-of-completion revenue-recognition method. Consider the following data regarding the status of a construction project at its year end:

Contract amount	$2,000,000
Initial estimated direct costs	$1,800,000
Direct costs to date	$1,200,000
Billings to date	$1,300,000

Estimated percentage complete based on cost:
Architect's opinion—64% complete
Contractor's opinion—68% complete
Superintendent's opinion—66% complete

Note that three estimates of the percentage completed vary by only four percentage points. Given all the uncertainties of future construction costs, this variation is relatively minor and can be expected. However, the small variation in these percentages can result in a significant income recognition difference on the firm's income statement at year end. The calculation of this income using the percentage-of-completion method is shown in Figure 8.5

A mere 4 percent difference in the percentage of completion results in a 100 percent difference in the recognized income or profit. In effect, the interim

	Architect's estimate	Contractor's estimate	Superintendent's estimate
% Complete	64	68	66
Billings should be (% complete times contract amount):	$1,280,000	$1,360,000	$1,320,000
Cost to date	1,200,000	1,200,000	1,200,000
Income recognized	$ 80,000	$ 160,000	$ 120,000

	Initial estimate
Initial Estimate of Costs	$1,800,000
Cost to date	1,200,000
% complete	66.7
Billings should be	1,333,333
Cost to date	1,200,000
Income Recognized	$ 133,333

	Billings
Billings to date	$1,300,000
Cost to date	1,200,000
Income recognized	$ 100,000

Figure 8.5 Revenue Methods and Income

profit can be manipulated to reflect the wishes of the individual establishing the percentage of completion. While one can differentiate between a project being 50 percent complete and 75 percent complete, it is questionable if one can differentiate between a few percentage points.

Yet another income results if the percentage of completion is based on the costs expended to date versus the initial estimate. While this method is not recommended because a revision of the initial estimate is usually necessary, the fact remains that yet another income is determined, as shown in Figure 8.5

Given the potential variance in income resulting from calculating percent complete based on cost, some critics argue that billings are a better measure of income to recognize to date. They argue that, if a construction firm is able to bill work, it must have "earned" it. This concept is contrary to accounting principles which acknowledge the fact that a firm may "front end" some of its profit when billing. Nonetheless, if billings were used in the example, yet another income would be recognized, as shown in Figure 8.5

In addition to variations in the reported income on the construction firm's income statement, the firm's balance sheet would also be affected. A statement reader such as a lender is usually in no position to question the percentage of completion and resulting income that is reported. In order to do this, the reader would have to critically evaluate the cost to complete a project. Usually even the contractor cannot do this with 100 percent accuracy.

OWNER SALARY AND FINANCIAL STATEMENTS

A somewhat obvious, but often overlooked, aspect of a construction firm's income statement is the effect of the owner's salary on the statement. Depending on the amount of owner's salary and its classification on the financial statements, it can have varying impact on the firm's reported gross margin, its reported income from operations, and the firm's and owner's taxable income.

Construction firm owners usually take their salary from the firm in the form of either a set weekly payroll check or draws. A draw is either a constant dollar amount at regular intervals, such as weekly, or the owner may make a draw when the money is needed or when the firm has available cash that can be drawn upon. Using draws is to be discouraged, especially for the construction corporation, in that the internal revenue service may view draws as profit distributions and therefore subject to both corporate taxation and personal income taxation.

Regardless of the form the owner's salary takes, the salary an owner may take from the firm varies from a minimum wage or less to a salary that would support a very high life style. The result is that two companies making the same profits will show different bottom-line profits depending on the salary paid to the owner.

To illustrate this point, let us assume that, apart from any owner salary, a construction firm has operating revenue of $1,000,000, direct expenses of

$800,000, leaving a gross profit of $200,000, and general and administrative expenses of $160,000.

Let us further assume that in one situation the owner of the construction firm pays himself an annual salary amounting to $35,000, whereas another contractor pays himself a $15,000 salary. The income statement presentations of the two different situations are described in columns A and B in Figure 8.6. Studying these two income statements would lead one to believe that the column B construction firm is the more profitable in that its profits are shown as $25,000 versus the $5,000 in profits shown in column A. One might conclude that the column B firm is able to generate a profit rate of 2.50 percent on revenue (25,000 divided by 1,000,000), whereas the column A firm has a profit rate of only .50 percent (5,000/1,000,000). One might further conclude that the column B firm is the more efficient which would be wrong. The difference in reported net income is solely because of the differences in owner salary. In reality both firms have made $40,000 independent of owner's salary. In fact, if the firm under discussion is a corporation, the column A firm would probably be better off in that its total tax liability would be less because a firm's profits are taxed twice when distributed, whereas salary disbursements avoid the double tax. The firm in column B might avoid the double tax on its greater profits by declaring some of it as a bonus, which takes on a tax liability as salary.

Regardless of tax considerations, the two different salaries paid in columns A and B result in the potential for an external party to interpret the two income statements differently. Obviously the external party should interpret the income statement by summing the owner's salary and bottom-line profits when evaluating the overall profitability of the firm. However, not all external parties take the time or have the knowhow to do this analysis.

Treatment of owner's salary on the income statement is made more complicated by the fact that some owners may charge some of their time and salary to the direct costs of a project. Such a practice is often consistent with good cost accounting and cost traceability. However, this practice creates further interpretation differences as to the resulting financial statements.

	A	B	C
Revenue	$1,000,000	$1,000,000	$1,000,000
Direct costs	800,000	800,000	810,000*
Gross profits	$ 200,000	$ 200,000	$ 190,000
Gross profit margin	20%	20%	19%
General and administrative expense	$ 195,000†	$ 175,000‡	$ 165,000
Net income	$ 5,000	$ 25,000	$ 25,000
Profit rate %	0.5%	2.5%	2.5%

*Contains a $10,000 owner's salary
†Contains a $35,000 owner's salary
‡Contains a $15,000 owner's salary

Figure 8.6 Effect of Owner's Salary

INCOME STATEMENT 1—OTHER INCOME

Revenue	$2,500,000
Direct expenses	2,250,000
Gross margin	$ 250,000
Operating expenses:	
Depreciation	75,000
Life insurance premium	25,000
Other	152,000
Income from construction operations	($2,000)
Other income:	
Increase cash surrender value	10,000
Net income	$ 8,000

INCOME STATEMENT 2—NETTING EFFECT

Revenue	$2,500,000
Direct expenses	2,250,000
Gross margin	$ 250,000
Operating expenses:	
Depreciation	75,000
Life insurance premium	15,000
Other	152,000
Income from construction operations	$ 8,000
Other income	—
Net income	$ 8,000

Figure 8.7 Effect of Classification

To illustrate the impact of an owner recognizing part of his salary as a direct cost, let us assume that the owner of the construction firm illustrated in column B recognizes $10,000 of his salary as a direct job cost. The resulting income statement is shown in column C of Figure 8.6. Note that, while the bottom-line income remains unchanged, the gross margin of the column C firm has decreased by $10,000 from that illustrated in column B. Once again, if external parties are attempting to analyze the statements of the two firms, they may come to different conclusions regarding the operations.

INCOME STATEMENT TREATMENT OF MISCELLANEOUS INCOME

Accounting practice varies as to how specific types of line items are presented on financial statements. While the dollar amount of a recognized item may be the same, its classification on the financial statements can significantly affect financial ratios.

As an example of the significance of classification, let us consider a firm's income statement and the treatment of the cash surrender value of officer's life insurance. *Cash surrender value* of officers' life insurance is the dollar amount at which a life insurance policy is redeemable at a given time. Many life insurance policies have a cash surrender provision.

As life insurance premiums are made, a firm recognizes an expense for the premiums in its financial books. At the end of the year, the life insurance company adds some of the premiums as a dividend to the cash surrender value of the policy.

To illustrate the differences among alternative financial statement presentations, let us assume that, in the year in question, a construction firm paid a premium of $25,000 for its officers' life insurance policy, but in turn received a $10,000 increase in the cash surrender value of the policy. A common financial income statement presentation for this type of transaction would appear as statement 1 in Figure 8.7. The premium is shown as an operating expense and the increase in cash surrender value is shown as "other income." Other transactions combine with this transaction to yield a $2,000 loss on operations from construction. The reader of this income statement would probably conclude that the construction operations were unprofitable and, if it had not been for the "other income" in the form of an increase in cash surrender value, the company would have lost money.

Another income statement of the construction firm is also illustrated in Figure 8.7. The only difference between the two is that the "increase in cash surrender value" has been offset by the life insurance expense premium with the net amount shown as an operating expense. Netting the insurance premium and cash surrender value increase has a significant impact on the financial statements. While the bottom-line income for the firm is unchanged, a $2,000 loss from construction operations has now been turned into a $8,000 profit. The reader of the statement showing a $8,000 gain will probably come to a significantly different conclusion regarding the firm even though both statements in Figure 8.7 are for the same firm.

Part 3.

MANAGERIAL ACCOUNTING

CHAPTERS

9
MANUAL JOB-COST SYSTEMS

INTRODUCTION

Recent years have seen vastly increasing sophistication in regard to job-cost systems. These systems are aimed at generating financial information and providing management with information from processing financial transaction data. Rapidly increasing construction costs have resulted in the increased importance of management decision-making information. Information for project (the terms project and job are used interchangeably in this chapter) planning and controlling is especially critical. The large dollar amount of the construction project and the numerous factors that dictate project cost and profitability focus attention on job-cost systems.

System is a broad term. In its broadest and most abstract sense, a system is an entity consisting of two or more components, or subsystems, that interact to achieve a purpose. More specifically as it relates to a construction project, a job-cost system is the set of forms, procedures, and communication channels used to document project information, process it, and structure it for project management decisions.

The typical construction firm has been negligent in designing and implementing effective job-cost systems. Numerous reasons for this lack of use are often cited. Some of these were noted in Chapter 1. The reasons do not justify the failure to implement such systems for, if the system is properly designed, the difficulties can be reduced if not eliminated.

This chapter limits itself to relatively unsophisticated manual systems. More sophisticated management systems for total project management are discussed in the following chapter. The increasing availability of computers is having a significant impact on the design and implementation of job-cost systems. Computers and job-cost systems are discussed in Chapter 11.

JOB-COST ACCOUNTING

All too often the construction firm limits itself to tracing its cost only to the firm itself. Such a process is necessary as a minimum requirement for establishing income for purposes of filing a tax return. However, merely identifying costs to the firm results in little potential for project control or, for that matter, determining project profitability during or after completion. As a minimum, the firm should trace project-related costs to the project in question.

There are two accounting processes widely used to determine the cost of a specific product produced. One of these is *job order* or *job-cost accounting* while the other is referred to as *process accounting*. Job-cost accounting is adaptable to firms that produce many types of product, each type of product being unique. Often only one unit of each product type is manufactured. This, of course, is common in the construction industry as each project the construction firm builds usually has unique characteristics. It is for this reason that the construction industry is limited almost exclusively to using job-cost accounting. Process accounting is used by firms engaged in the textile, oil, food, and cement industries.

The job-cost accounting forms and procedures used by various construction firms vary considerably in practice. Job-cost systems range from relatively simple write-it-once systems to sophisticated journal and ledger systems. Regardless of the job-cost system or forms utilized, the theory of job-cost accounting remains unchanged. In particular the job-cost accounting system does the following:

1. Identifies all project-traceable direct costs to the project.
2. Applies nontraceable costs (i.e., those not feasibly traced to a project) to individual projects through a process of allocating costs to projects as a function of a defined cost basis.

The job-cost accounting process is summarized in Figure 9.1. Direct labor and direct material costs are identified and posted to job-cost ledgers. The source document for assessing a project's labor cost is the timecard. The material purchase orders or invoices are the source documents for identifying material costs to specific projects. The accounting journal entries that correspond to the recognition of project labor entries are as follows (also see Chapter 2 for a discussion of journal entries):

Labor cost—project 101	$5,000	
Cash		$5,000

or

Labor cost—project 101	$5,000	
Accounts payable—payroll		$5,000

The first transaction assumes a cash-basis taxpayer. The second journal entry assumes the labor cost is accrued. Regardless of the cash or accrual entry, the "labor cost—project 101" debit entry is posted to the job-cost ledger. Such a ledger is shown in Figure 9.2.

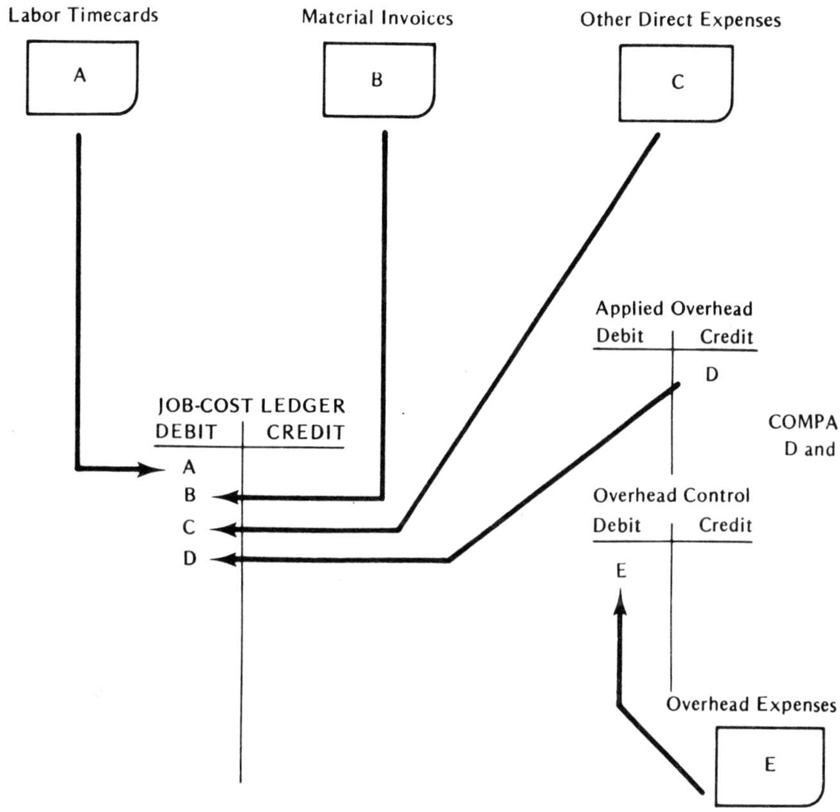

Figure 9.1 Job-Cost System

The accounting entries corresponding to the recognition of the project material entries are as follows:

Direct material cost—project 101	$4,000	
Cash		$4,000

or

Direct material cost—project 101	$4,000	
Accounts payable—supplyman ABC		$4,000

The first entry is in recognition of a cash transaction, whereas the second entry assumes a payable is identified at time of purchase. Regardless, the "direct material cost—project 101" debit entry is posted to the project ledger illustrated in Figure 9.2.

Whenever possible those overhead costs traceable to a specific project should be traced to the project in question. In this way the job-cost ledger reflects all the costs incurred specifically as a result of performance of the

Sample Construction Co., Inc.

Project 101

DATE	DES-CRIPTION	LABOR COST	MATERIAL COST	JOB OVERHEAD COST	APPLIED OVERHEAD COST	SUB-CONTRACTOR COST
6-24-X0		$5,000				
6-25-X0			$4,000			
6-25-X0	BONDS			$9,000		
6-30-X0					$4,500	

Figure 9.2 Job-Cost Ledger

project work. Examples of overhead costs that normally should be traced to a specific project and identified as such on the job ledger are the following:

Bond costs	Project utilities
Insurance costs	Permit costs
Temporary trailers	A/E fees
Project supervision costs	Project finance costs

An example of a journal entry for traceable overhead costs (i.e., often referred to as *job overhead costs*) is as follows:

Bond costs—project 101	$9,000	
Cash		$9,000

As was true of the labor and material costs, the entry may also be made on an accrual basis. The "bond costs—project 101" would be posted to the job cost-ledger illustrated in Figure 9.2.

Overhead costs not easily traceable to a project should be applied to a project's cost ledger as a function of a predetermined base or bases. The base chosen should correspond to how the overhead costs are incurred. For example, it may be that a given firm sees a relationship between project direct cost and nontraceable overhead. The application rate is then determined by making an estimate of both the firm's direct costs and overhead costs not traceable to projects for an equal period of time. For example, assume a firm estimates direct cost (i.e., based on an estimate of volume) for a year's period as $800,000. Similarly based on nontraceable project overhead costs expended in the prior year and recognition of the influence of this year's estimated work volume, this year's nontraceable project overhead costs are estimated as $200,000. The application rate for nontraceable overhead is determined as .25 per $1.00 of direct cost by the following calculation:

$$\frac{\text{estimated nontraceable overhead (1 yr.)}}{\text{estimated project direct cost (1 yr.)}} = \frac{\$200,000}{\$800,000} = .25$$

Let us assume that the $5,000 direct labor cost, $4,000 direct material cost, and $9,000 job overhead cost entries that have been indicated for project 101 represent entries for a given month (such as June). The sum of these direct costs is $18,000. Based on this total, the applied nontraceable overhead cost entry is calculated as follows:

$$\$18,000 \times .25 = \$4,500$$

The journal entry would appear as follows:

Overhead costs—project 101	$4,500	
Applied overhead		$4,500

The "overhead costs—project 101" entry would be recognized in the job-cost ledger as illustrated in Figure 9.2.

The overhead costs-project 101 and applied overhead entries are made independent of the amount of actual overhead expended in the month or period in question. Instead, the actual overhead costs are entered in an overhead control account. Examples of nontraceable project overhead costs include central office costs, marketing costs, entertainment expenses, and so on. An example of a journal entry to recognize an actual nontraceable project overhead cost is as follows:

Overhead control	$3,000	
Cash		$3,000

The application of nontraceable overhead costs is based on estimates. Because they are only estimates (volume, direct costs, and nontraceable project overhead), the amount of overhead applied to projects may not equal the actual incurred overhead costs for a specific period. In this case, the overhead is overapplied or underapplied. If the costs incurred and recognized in the overhead control account are less than those applied to projects through the applied overhead entries, the overhead is overapplied. On the other hand, if the applied overhead recognized in the applied overhead entries is less than the overhead incurred and recognized in the overhead control account, the overhead is underapplied.

The objective of applying overhead is to neither under- nor overapply overhead. This objective is enhanced by accurate estimates and is also made possible by monitoring and correcting the overhead costs and application rate. For example, the firm can analyze monthly any differences between overhead costs incurred and those applied to projects. It may be that a difference occurs because of monthly variation in work volume. However, it may also be that the firm has underestimated the overhead cost for the year. If this is the case, the application rate should be changed to reflect the new estimate of overhead costs. If this is not done, the firm runs the risk of not applying all of its overhead costs to projects. Obviously, underapplying overhead is more damaging than overapplying it. If the costs are underapplied, the firm's profits are fictitious because overhead costs are not totally recognized.

Assuming overhead costs are applied accurately for a given period of time (such as a year), the overhead control account and applied overhead accounts will be equal in amount. At year end they are closed out by debiting the applied overhead account and crediting the overhead control account. If overhead is underapplied or overapplied, the overhead control and applied overhead accounts will not equal. The difference can be written off as a period expense or, more appropriately, prorated to projects in progress and completed projects.

When a specific job-cost ledger reflects only part of the total project cost, the project is considered as *work-in-progress*. The costs that are reflected in the job-cost ledger can serve as the basis for calculating the percentage-of-completion to date as is required for calculating revenue in a long-term contracting method. Completed projects are then transferred out of the work-in-progress accounts. This is done by eliminating them (crediting the account) from the work-in-progress account and transferring them (i.e., debiting an account) to a completed-contract account.

STANDARD COSTS

Work and cost standards are noticeably absent in the construction industry. Such standards are a necessary part of a budgeting and control system. Much of the construction industry's inability to control and substantially increase its productivity can be traced to its lack of work and cost standards.

The concept of standard work and cost can be integrated into the firm's normal costing procedure. For example, the concept of standards is compatible with a job-cost accounting system. Standards outline how a given work package (that is, a construction method) should be accomplished and how much it should cost. As work is performed, actual costs and production are compared with the standard production and costs to reveal variances.

Standard costs can be considered target costs because they are carefully predetermined and should be attainable. They should not be set as ideal standards requiring perfection on the part of management or the individual worker. However, standards should be set such that achieving standard performance is a satisfying accomplishment.

For direct costs, two different types of standards should be determined: one for direct material and one for direct labor. Let us first consider determining standards and analyzing variances for direct material.

Material Standards

A standard amount of material for a given construction method and a standard unit price for the material are first determined. This is probably best accomplished by personnel such as foremen. In more sophisticated firms, a methods department may analyze method material requirements and set the standards. The unit price standard for material is probably best determined by cost-oriented personnel such as those in accounting or estimating.

The amount and cost of the material actually used are compared to the predetermined standards. For example, let us assume we are considering pouring concrete for a 5¾ inch on-grade slab that is 100 feet square. Let us assume that the standard amount of concrete for this slab is 185 cubic yards. This amount is based on the actual volume with a small wastage percentage. The estimating department sets $20 as the standard cost of a cubic yard of concrete delivered to the site. Comparison and analysis of any variances between actual materials and costs and the standards are carried out by means of the format shown in Figure 9.3. The analysis shown in Figure 9.3 assumes

Actual units X actual price	Actual units X standard price	Standard units X standard price
(192) (19.50) $3,744.00	(192) (20.00) $3,840.00	(185) (20.00) $3,700.00

Price variance	Usage variance
$96.00 Favorable	$140.00 Unfavorable

Total variance
$44.00 Unfavorable

Figure 9.3 Material-Cost Variance

that 192 cubic yards of concrete were used for the slab and the unit price of the concrete was $19.50 per cubic yard.

The analysis is carried out by focusing on two variances: purchase-price and usage. The purchase-price variance is calculated by determining the difference between the product of the actual amount of material used and the unit purchase price and the product of the actual amount of material used and the standard unit price. In the example shown, this difference is $96. If the amount of material used times the unit purchase price is more than the amount of material used times the standard unit price, the variance determined is considered unfavorable. That is, this is an indication that the material was purchased at an unfavorable price. Responsibility for this type of variance probably should focus on the purchasing department. This same department should be favorably recognized when the variance is favorable which occurs when the purchase price is less than the predetermined, standard unit price. In the example, there is a favorable purchase-price variance of $96.

The second variance determined in the analysis is the usage variance. It is calculated by taking the difference between the product of the actual amount of material used and the standard unit price, and the product of the predetermined standard amount of material for the work and the standard unit price. In Figure 9.3 this difference is $140. If the amount of material used times the standard price is more than the standard amount of material times the standard unit price, the usage variance is unfavorable. Such an unfavorable variance can usually be traced to excessive material wastage along with poor handling and placing procedures. On the other hand, a favorable usage variance exists when the amount of material used times the standard unit price is less than the standard amount of material times the standard unit price. In the example shown, there is an unfavorable variance of $140. The responsibility for favorable or unfavorable usage variances should be directed at the foreman or job superintendent.

The total material variance may be determined by summing the purchase-price variance and the usage variance. In the example considered, there is a \$96 favorable purchase-price variance and a \$140 unfavorable usage variance resulting in a \$44 unfavorable total variance. It should be noted that merely focusing on the difference between total actual cost and a total standard cost (i.e., the total variance) can be misleading in regard to method efficiency. In the example, the favorable efforts of the purchasing personnel are hidden because of the balancing effect of the inefficient usage of material. Adequate control can only be determined by focusing on the purchase-price and usage variances.

Labor Standards

Determination and analysis of direct labor standards are performed in a manner similar to that for direct material standards—labor-rate and labor-efficiency variances are determined. Construction labor-rate standards are usually set by labor union agreements. As such, they are somewhat outside of management's control. However, while a rate standard may be set, actual dollars of wages spent may exceed the standard, overtime pay being the primary cause for such a difference. In addition, an unplanned change in rates during a project will cause a difference in the predetermined standard and the amount actually paid to workers. This can happen if a union agreement expires during a project and a higher wage is negotiated.

Labor-efficiency standards are controllable; however, they are difficult to set. Disputes over labor efficiency standards are much more likely to arise than are disputes over material-usage standards. Determining appropriate fatigue and rest time for workers has to be considered as well as union work rules. Time and motion studies are the most widely used method of setting labor-efficiency standards. These are usually carried out by personnel acting in a staff position such as an engineer.

The construction industry has not always been receptive to using time and motion studies. Management has sometimes failed to apply such techniques for fear of nonacceptance by the labor unions. In addition, construction managers have argued that it is difficult to set labor-efficiency standards for workers who are performing varying types of work in varying types of environment. There is no question that difficulties arise. However, this does not indicate that adequately trained personnel cannot determine such standards. Latest practices of several of the more informed construction firms indicate that it is possible to set a meaningful labor-efficiency standard. Without such standards, the industry has little means of budgeting and controlling total direct labor costs. Once the labor efficiency standard is determined, project foremen should be held responsible for an efficiency-related variance. Timecards and timecard summaries, as discussed in the previous section on bookkeeping, provide the means of comparing actual labor rates and efficiency with the predetermined standards.

Analyzing direct labor variances is performed by means of a columnar format similar to the one used for analyzing direct material variances. The total direct labor variance is separated into two variances: rate and efficiency. The rate variance for a given work package (i.e., a construction method) is the difference between the product of the actual labor hours used to perform the work and the actual price paid for each hour (i.e., the actual rate), and the product of the actual labor hours used to perform the work and the predetermined standard rate. If the actual hours times the actual rate exceeds the actual hours times the standard rate, the variance is unfavorable. Likewise, if the actual hours times the actual rate is less than the actual hours times the standard rate, the variance is favorable.

Let us assume that 70 actual carpenter hours are used to form 3,000 square feet of vertical walls. In addition, the predetermined labor-efficiency standard is set as 2.5 carpenter hours per 100 square feet. At the beginning of the project a rate standard of $8.00 per hour was used in setting the budget; however, because the union work agreement terminated during the work and a higher rate was negotiated, the average actual rate used for paying labor for the method in question is $9.50.

Given the above information as to forming vertical walls, the rate variance is calculated as shown in Figure 9.4. There is an unfavorable rate variance of $105.

The labor-efficiency variance is calculated as the difference between the product of the actual labor used to perform the work in question and the standard predetermined wage rate, and the product of the standard hours for the work in question and the standard predetermined wage rate. A higher actual hours times standard rate than standard hours times standard rate indicates an unfavorable variance. A higher standard hours times standard rate than actual hours times standard rate indicates a favorable variance. As shown in Figure 9.4, there is a $40 favorable labor-efficiency variance for the form work method previously described. This is based on the fact that, for 3,000

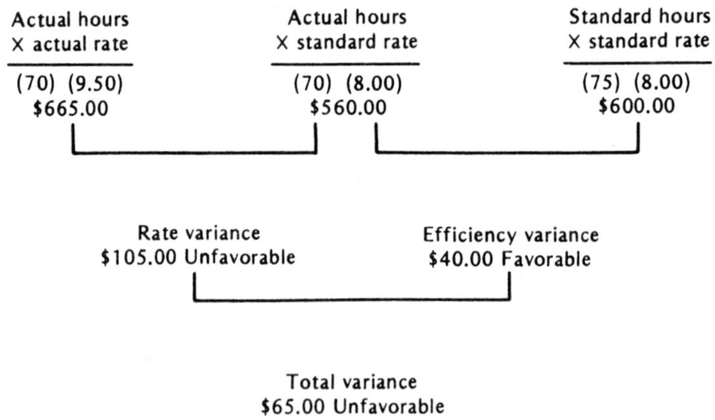

Figure 9.4 Labor-Cost Variance

square feet of formwork, the standard number of hours is calculated as 2.5 times 30 or 75 hours.

The total direct labor variance is the sum of the rate- and labor-efficiency variances. For the example considered, there is $105 unfavorable rate variance and a favorable $40 labor-efficiency variance. As such, there is a $65 unfavorable variance. As is true of the analysis of the direct material variance, it is necessary to focus on each of the two ingredients of the total variance in order to assure adequate control.

Overhead Standards

Determining standards and analyzing variances for overhead recognizes the differences between job overhead and general overhead. For the most part, job overhead is variable in that its amount depends on the volume of work the construction firm performs. On the other hand, general overhead tends to be fixed in that costs such as secretary salaries and maintaining the central office are more a function of time than of the volume of construction projects performed.

The previous section on job-cost accounting discussed using an overhead-control account for comparing overhead costs to the amount of overhead applied. When making use of standard costs, this is done for both variable overhead (i.e., job overhead) and fixed overhead (i.e., general overhead).

Determining and analyzing variances for variable overhead is similar to that discussed for direct material and direct labor. Construction job overhead is applied to a project as a function of a base such as total direct cost, direct labor hours, or direct material cost. Let us assume that a construction firm applies its job overhead to projects as a function of the total direct labor hours estimated for a project. In particular, let us assume that it applies job overhead at a rate of $4 per direct labor hour. The $4 is, in effect, a standard variable-overhead rate. Determining this rate is the responsibility of the cost accounting and engineering personnel.

In addition to setting a standard variable-overhead rate, a standard number of direct hours for performing the method in question must be determined. Because of the definition of the allocation base, this determination is the same as that for the labor-efficiency standard previously discussed.

Unlike the direct material and labor variances, job-overhead variances relate more to the sum of several ongoing activities. For example, actual monthly job-overhead costs might be compared to a predetermined, standard monthly overhead cost. If three methods are being performed during the month, the sum of the direct labor hours incurred on each of the projects is used as a basis for comparing the actual job overhead costs to the standard.

The total variable-overhead variance is made up of a spending variance and an efficiency variance. The spending variance is merely the difference between the actual variable overhead (i.e., job overhead) incurred during the period in question and the product of the actual direct units of the base (e.g., actual direct labor hours) and the standard variable-overhead rate. Let us assume that the previously discussed firm (i.e., the firm that applied job overhead at a rate of $4 per direct labor hour) incurs $8,200 job overhead during a month in which 2,000 direct labor hours of work are performed. As shown in Figure 9.5, the spending variance is calculated at $200. This variance is unfavorable in that the actual job overhead incurred is greater than the actual direct labor hours incurred times the standard application rate.

The variable-overhead efficiency variance is calculated as the difference between the product of the actual direct units of the basis (e.g., actual direct labor hours) and the standard variable-overhead rate, and the product of the standard (budgeted) units of the base and the standard variable-overhead rate. For the previously discussed example, let us assume that the firm set a standard of 1,950 direct labor hours. An efficiency variance of $200 is calculated as shown in Figure 9.5. This efficiency variance is unfavorable in that the actual direct hours incurred times the standard rate exceeds the standard direct hours times the standard rate.

The total variable-overhead variance is the sum of the spending and efficiency variances. For the example considered, both the spending and efficiency variances were unfavorable. As such, a $400 unfavorable total variable-overhead variance is determined. Part of this variance is related to the fact that more direct hours than budgeted were incurred to perform the work in question. The rest of the variance (one-half of it) can be traced to higher than expected job-overhead costs per direct labor hours incurred. This portion of the variance is referred to as the spending variance. Job-overhead control should focus on this variance. The efficiency variance results because of the lack of labor production control.

By definition fixed-overhead costs are not variable. As such, no variation occurs in them as a function of time. Since actual and budgeted or standard

Actual units X actual rate	Actual units X standard rate	Standard units X standard rate
$8,200.00	(2,000) (4.00) $8,000.00	(1950) (4.00) $7,800.00

Spending variance
$200.00 Unfavorable

Efficiency variance
$200.00 Unfavorable

Total variance
$400.00 Unfavorable

Figure 9.5 Job-Overhead Variance

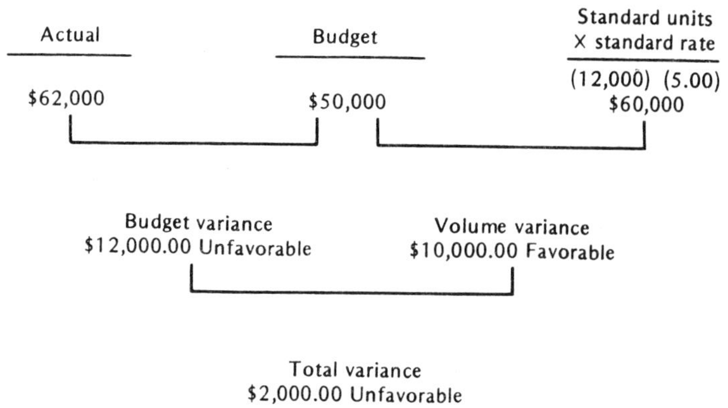

Figure 9.6 Fixed-Overhead Variance

units of the base (e.g., direct labor hours incurred or total direct costs incurred) during the time period may differ, the effective unit of cost applied to the base unit of production may vary.

The total fixed-overhead variance consists of a budget variance and a volume variance. The budget variance is the difference between the actual fixed-overhead costs incurred in a given period of time (e.g., a month) and the budgeted amount of overhead for the time period. For example, let us assume a firm expects to incur an annual general-overhead cost of $600,000. As such, they budget $50,000 of fixed overhead during a given month, but an unfavorable $12,000 budget variance occurs.

As discussed earlier, construction fixed overhead is appropriately allocated on a duration basis. However, within a given month several projects may be ongoing. The monthly overhead budget ($50,000 in the example considered) may be distributed to individual ongoing projects as a function of their total duration or as a function of the amount of work performed on each project during the month. For example, a rate of $5 per direct labor hour might be used. Assume the firm is expecting total labor hours during the year to be 120,000, which is equivalent to 10,000 per month.

A volume variance is calculated as the difference between the monthly budgeted overhead and the product of an actual unit of the base (e.g., 12,000 estimated direct labor hours for the month in question) and the standard rate. As is shown in Figure 9.6, the volume variance is calculated as the difference between $50,000 and 12,000 hours times $5 per hour. Since the budget amount is less than the budgeted hours times the standard rate (i.e., the amount applied to jobs), a favorable volume variance of $10,000 occurs.

Adding the $12,000 unfavorable budget variance and the $10,000 favorable volume variance, a total unfavorable fixed variance of $2,000 is calculated. However, unlike the total variable-overhead variance, not all of the fixed-overhead variance is controllable (i.e., the volume variance). This variance occurs because of seasonal variations in production and is only relevant to product costing. In particular, a volume variance indicates that fixed-overhead costs are not properly matched to a unit of production.

Regardless of whether it is a material, labor, job-overhead or a general-overhead standard, determining the standard and analyzing any variations provide the firm with a means of both budgeting (i.e., project costing) and controlling the budgeted costs. Actual costs are compared to standards and investigating the differences provides indications for corrective management procedures, changes in plans or objectives, or even a change in the standard.

WRITE-IT-ONCE SYSTEMS

Time pressures are always a problem for the construction firm. This is especially true in the case of the small proprietor or small partnership. Because of its limited size, the owner or owners of the firm are required to perform many functions, some of which are often carried out independently of one another. One of these is accounting. Because of the pressures to market its services and perform production, the firm often has limited time for accounting. The result is that the accounting does not get completed or is completed in less than accurate manner.

A *write-it-once* system has been used by small-sized contractors as a job-cost accounting system. It has been proposed that such a system requires the least amount of contractor effort to prepare job-cost ledgers and calculate the sum of them as work in progress.

Write-it-once systems are normally limited to tracing costs to projects because they do not segregate work-item costs and because the general ledger accounts lack detail. Write-it-once systems may not be appropriate for larger contractors. As is true of any accounting system, the write-it-once system is useful to the firm that has accounting needs similar to those provided by the system.

The characteristic of write-it-once systems that differentiates them from more sophisticated general ledger systems is that a single entry results in dual recognition. For example, by posting labor costs to a job-cost ledger, the work-in-process account is automatically updated. This is accomplished by placing the job-cost ledger (which has duplication material on its underside) on top of the work-in-process ledger. A similar approach is accomplished with accounts payable ledgers and a record of invoices.

There are several write-it-once accounting systems that have been designed for construction firms. The companies that have designed the system sell the concept along with the necessary accounting forms and any supporting equipment such as pegboards. Figure 9.7 illustrates a write-it-once construction accounting system. The objective of the system is not only to keep job-cost ledgers up to date, but also to establish control of accounts payable, labor costs, material costs, and subcontract costs. In addition, nontraceable over-

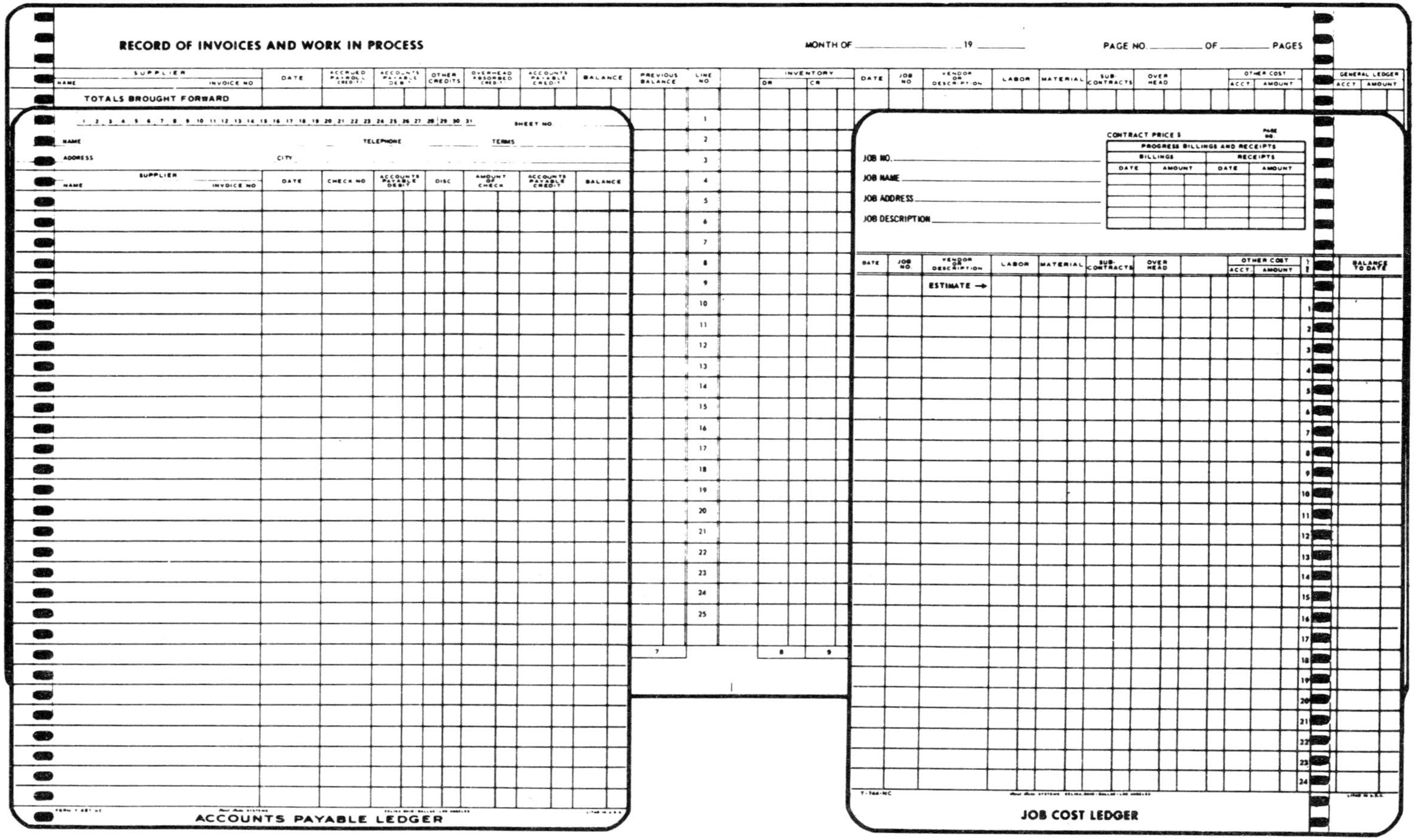

Figure 9.7 One-Write Job Cost System (*Courtesy of Reynolds and Reynolds Company*)

head costs can be recognized using the job-cost ledgers. Fundamental to the write-it-once job-cost system illustrated is the use of the following three forms:

1. Record of invoices and work-in-process
2. Accounts payable ledger
3. Job-cost ledger

No entry is ever made to the job-cost or accounts payable ledgers unless the ledger sheet is placed on top of the record of invoices and work-in-process sheet. In this way the entry made to either ledger is superimposed on the record of invoices and work-in-process. The superimposed forms are lined up by means of a pegboard.

Let us now illustrate how typical entries are made to the write-it-once system. Let us assume a construction firm purchases material for project 101 from ABC Ready Mix Company. The material is bought on account so the construction firm has incurred a liability. Therefore, an accounts payable ledger card for ABC Ready Mix Company is placed on the record of invoices and work-in-process form as illustrated in Figure 9.7. The liability to ABC Ready Mix Company is recognized by crediting the account in the column labeled "credit." The ABC Ready Mix Company ledger serves as a subledger for the general ledger account labeled "accounts payable" shown on the record of invoice and work-in-process form. By placing the accounts payable subledger on the pegboard, the subledger is duplicated in the general ledger.

Intermediate columns on the accounts payable form provide space for recognizing discounts and other deductions from purchase prices. The last two columns of the accounts payable are for calculating the running balance of the individual accounts payable subledger. By superimposing these old and new balances on the record of invoices and work-in-process form, a check can be made of the accuracy of the posting addition.

As checks are written to vendors, their accounts payable subledgers are updated to reflect the debit to their accounts. Again the accounts payable ledger card is placed on top of the record of invoices and work-in-process form before the entry is made. In addition, it is possible to purchase checks that can be placed on top of both the forms. The checks are designed to fit the pegboard. The result is that, by writing it once, simultaneous entries are made to a check, to an accounts payable subledger, and to the general ledger.

Just as a single accounts payable ledger card (i.e., actually it serves as a subledger) is credited for the ABC Ready Mix Company, the construction firm would create a form for each of its vendors. These subledgers can be created for equipment as well as material vendors. Both material and equipment purchased for a specific project and those purchased as overhead items are posted to the accounts payable ledger cards and duplicated on the record of invoices and work-in-process forms.

The concrete the construction firm purchased from ABC Ready Mix Company was assumed to have been bought for use on project 101. Therefore, it is traceable to project 101 and recognized as a job cost in the job-cost write-it-once accounting system. Just as individual accounts payable ledger forms are prepared for each vendor, a job-cost ledger form is prepared for each project. The form for project 101 is also illustrated in Figure 9.7. The purpose of the job-cost ledger is to document those costs traceable or applied to specific projects.

Before placing the job-cost ledger on the pegboard, the name of the project along with other descriptive information including the contract price are written on the job-cost ledger. This is similar to placing descriptive information on the accounts payable ledger forms.

In order to recognize the concrete material transaction for project 101, the job-cost ledger form for project 101 is first placed on top of the work-in-process side of the record of invoices and work-in-process form. Next, the material purchase transaction is entered. This is accomplished by entering the date, job number, vendor and dollar amount in the appropriate column. The reason for entering the job number on the job-cost ledger (which already has the job number written on it) is to duplicate the job or project number (101) on the work-in-process general ledger. In this manner, a reference job number appears on the work-in-process ledger. This provides a means of tracing the entry back to the job-cost ledger.

The effect of entering the material transaction on the job-cost ledger is twofold: (1) a record of the material cost for project 101 is made and (2) the costs identifiable to individual projects are documented on individual project subledger forms (that is, the job-cost ledger forms).

Entering the transaction material to project 101 also has the effect of updating the general ledger account—work in process. The work-in-process account accumulates the costs of all projects in process. It is an asset account and is sometimes viewed as similar to inventory. Because of the duplication characteristic of the write-it-once system, posting to the work-in-process account is made simultaneously with the entry of the transaction to the job-cost ledger.

This transaction represents recognition of a material expense to project 101. If the material was purchased from a vendor other than ABC Ready Mix Company, a different accounts payable ledger form would have been placed on top of the record of invoices and work-in-process form. Likewise, if the material was purchased and used on a project other than project 101, then another job-cost ledger form would have been placed on the record of invoices and work-in-process form. Project labor and subcontractor costs would be entered in the job-cost ledger form and record of invoices and work-in-process in the same manner as the material cost transaction.

Most write-it-once systems have payroll record-keeping systems similar to the accounts payable, job-cost ledger, and record of invoices and work-in-process procedure described. The payroll system includes a payroll register, individual employee payroll cards, and payroll checks designed to be compatible with the forms and pegboard. (An example of a pegboard payroll system was illustrated in Chapter 4.)

As previously noted, no entry is ever made directly to the record of invoices and work-in-process form. An accounts payable or job-cost ledger form must be placed on the form first. In the material cost transaction illustrated, both an accounts payable subledger and a job-cost ledger were affected by the transaction; therefore, both forms are placed on the pegboard.

It is possible that only an accounts payable account or a job-cost ledger is recognized in a transaction; for example, it may be that material is purchased for company inventory rather than for a specific project. In this case the accounts payable recognition would be the same—the transaction would be duplicated on the record of invoices. No job-cost ledger would be placed on the pegboard and no recognition of the material purchased for inventory would be made in the work-in-process account.

It is also possible for an entry to be made to the job-cost ledger form and record of invoices and work-in-process form without any entry to an accounts payable ledger. Examples of these types of transactions include recognizing project equipment costs and allocating overhead to specific projects. If the payroll is processed apart from the record of invoices and work-in-process form, labor costs would be entered to the job-cost ledger form while no accounts payable ledger card would be used in recognizing the transaction.

The last two columns on the record of invoices and work-in-process form are for recognizing a transaction that affects a general ledger account not traced to a project. Both the account number and the dollar amount of the transaction are placed in these columns. An example of a transaction that would be entered in these two columns would be recognizing a liability for a utility expense not traceable to a project. The utility expense code would be identified in the second from last column and the dollar amount in the last column.

Write-it-once systems vary in design. However, many of the principles and information that appear on ledger forms are common to each of the alternative designs available to the construction firm.

GENERAL LEDGER SYSTEMS

Numerous general ledger systems with various forms are available to the contractor. The firm may also custom design its own set of general ledger forms. Regardless of the actual set of forms used, the purpose of the individual ledgers remains unchanged.

The essential form for a job-cost system is the job-cost ledger. It may be titled somewhat differently depending on the system used. The ledger form provides space for listing the date of the transaction, a description of the transaction, and labor, material, subcontract, and miscellaneous expenses. Additionally, there is space for referencing the entry in the folio column. Credit adjustments to the normal debit project expense can be made in the ledger.

Two construction firms may utilize a job-cost ledger form differently. Some firms, especially those that perform small projects with few transactions, may post entries directly to the job-cost ledger form. The corresponding credit entry would then be made to a journal or directly to a general ledger account. For example, if the contractor keeps its books on a cash basis, a material cost transaction would be accompanied by crediting a cash disbursement journal or a cash general ledger form.

Just as a cash disbursements journal may support monthly postings to the cash disbursements (and receipts) ledger, individual job-cost expenses may be initially entered into individual job-cost journals. These individual job-cost journals may be summarized monthly and posted to the job-cost ledger form. Whether journals should be prepared to support individual general ledger accounts depends on the transaction activity of the account in question. An account that has considerable activity probably is more suited to a supporting journal. However, other factors, such as clerical capabilities and overall design of the firm's set of books, relate to the design and need for individual supporting journals.

Work in process at any one point in time may be determined by summarizing the individual job-cost ledgers. As a project is completed, the job-cost ledger is closed and the summarized cost is transferred to the cost of completed projects. In order for the general ledger accounts to balance, both individual job-cost ledgers for projects in process and the summarized costs of completed projects for the period in question must be summarized.

While serving to balance the general ledger accounts, the individual job-cost ledgers serve a more important purpose. In particular, they provide the construction firm a means of analyzing a project's total costs and its components (such as labor, material, equipment, miscellaneous) at any point in time. This analysis can consider the costs to date along with the initial estimate and, in this way, project costs can be controlled and total project profit or loss projected before the completion of the project.

10
MANUAL PROJECT-MANAGEMENT INFORMATION SYSTEMS

INTRODUCTION

More often than not, a construction firm limits the use of its job-cost accounting system to reporting project profit or loss. In reality a job-cost system can be expanded to aid in performing several of the required project-management functions.

Integrating several of the project-management functions by means of cost accounting or a common data base is commonly referred to as a *project-management information system*. Several project-management functions such as project estimating, planning, and control can be integrated into a single process by such a system.

It is common to speak of project-management information systems and computers in the same vein. However, it is possible to design and implement a manual project-management information system that contains all the elements of a more sophisticated automated system. This chapter will discuss the elements of a project-management information system and will illustrate them by means of an example of a manual system.

THE INTEGRATED PROJECT-MANAGEMENT SYSTEM

The construction firm's cost-accounting system can serve as the basis for integrating each component of the project-management operational cycle shown in Figure 10.1. Cost data from ongoing and past projects can be used to aid in controlling ongoing projects and planning and controlling future projects.

Cost and productivity data from a specific project can be traced to alternative cost objects. A cost object is merely an entity for which the firm traces costs; for example, the firm may choose merely to identify the data with the

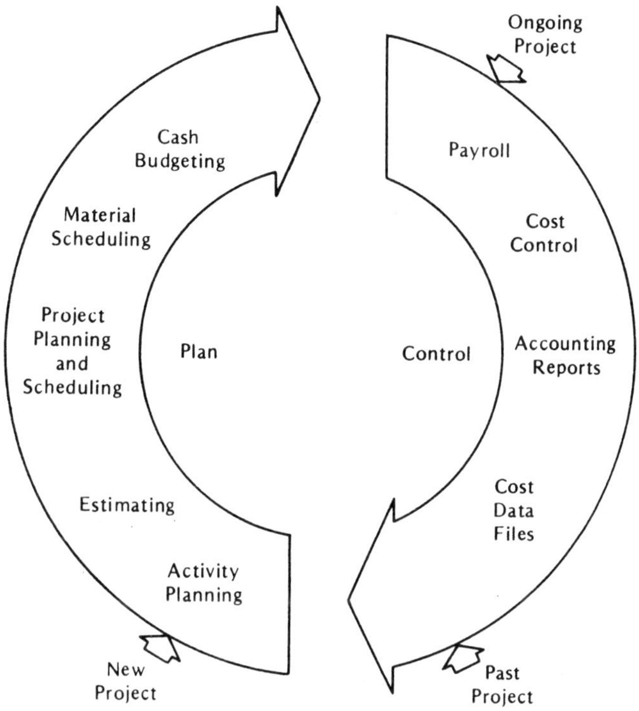

Figure 10.1 Project-Management Operational Cycle

firm itself. Such a procedure creates difficulty in establishing project cost and profitability. In addition, the collected data has little positive input on controlling an ongoing project or planning future projects.

As an alternative to merely tracing project costs to the firm itself, the data may be traced to specific projects. For example, all the direct labor and material costs for a project can be assigned to the project as a cost object. While such a procedure allows evaluation of project profitability, the procedure lacks the cost-accounting sophistication necessary to significantly aid project control and planning.

The most detailed level of project cost and productivity traceability is identifying the data with specific work segments (or work objects) of a project. For example, such a cost-accounting system may single out various labor craft hours and materials used for placing concrete columns, steel beams, or masonry walls for a project. This detailed level of cost identification can help determine the cost and profitability of the overall project and individual work segments. It becomes possible to measure the performance of labor and machines. Ongoing projects can be controlled by comparing progress to plan, while planning future projects is facilitated. Perhaps more important than any of these benefits is that identifying work segment costs helps integrate the essential project-management decision data for numerous required functions.

The benefit to cost ratio for the necessary cost-accounting procedures, forms, and data processing for any one function becomes more favorable.

The concept of integrated project management through cost accounting, which utilizes identification of cost elements for work items, centers on establishing historical cost files for specific segments of work. For the labor segment of cost, the cost files can be structured on a basis of productivity (that is, manhours per unit of work) or unit costs. A cost-accounting system for the construction industry should utilize productivity as the basis. Historical unit cost data (dollars per unit of work) become quickly outdated in periods of rapidly changing labor costs. On the other hand, construction industry productivity has stayed practically constant over the last decade. While this nonincreasing productivity characteristic is detrimental to the profitability of the construction industry, it does result in decreasing productivity records' dependence on time. Historical productivity work files can be easily transferred to unit costs merely by putting in manhour rates. The work files can then serve as a means of providing accurate estimates of cost and duration.

The key to an effective cost-accounting system that facilitates planning and controlling is the definition of work items or segments that are to be the cost objects of the system. The firm has much flexibility in its choice of work items; for example, a firm may identify placing concrete as a single work item, or it may differentiate between placing concrete in columns, slabs, footings, and so forth as distinct work items.

The size of the firm, its data collection and processing capability, and the type of work it performs are a few of the many factors that dictate a manageable and effective set of work items for a firm. The unique characteristics of each construction firm result in the need to custom design a set of work items to the individual firm.

The impact of cost accounting on each of the everyday construction management functions indicated in Figure 10.1 will now be illustrated. Let us assume that the firm has defined work items and has collected labor productivity and material usage data for the work items from the performance of past projects. We will enter the cycle shown in Figure 10.1 at the point of historical work item files.

Activity and Project Planning

The objective of activity planning is determining the optimal combination of resources to be used in performing the required quantity and quality of work for a given work segment of a project. The work segments can be defined to be compatible with cost accounting's work item cost objects. Activity planning addresses determining the best crew size, combination of labor crafts, and types of equipment to be used to perform work.

Too often the construction industry has accepted a traditional mode of performing a construction method. This lack of innovation has weighed heavily on the industry's low productivity. By comparing method productivity for different combinations of labor and equipment, the firm can detect inefficiencies and, in effect, optimize the performance of a method. The result of activity planning should be establishing the number of employees of each type of labor craft to be employed along with the type of equipment to be utilized for the method. Given the determined combination of resources, the work item historical files should predict or plan the following:

$$\text{productivity: } \frac{\text{manhours}}{\text{unit of work item}} \quad \text{or} \quad \frac{\text{units of work item}}{\text{manhour}}$$

$$\text{material: } \frac{\text{quantity of material needed}}{\text{unit of work item}}$$

Activity duration can be established by dividing the work item productivity (assuming the second definition of productivity above) into the units of work to be performed as determined by removing the quantities from the project drawings. This is illustrated as follows:

$$\text{duration} = \frac{\text{units of work item}}{\text{productivity}}$$

The durations become known parameters for the overall project plan, which indicates the relationships among the planned activities. Scheduling techniques such as the *critical path method* (CPM) aid in preparing the project plan. However, it is the cost-accounting data in the form of past project data that determine the fundamental input to project planning.

Project Estimating

No single management function plays a more important role in the firm's financial success than estimating. The secret, competitive bidding process that characterizes the industry emphasizes the need for accurate estimates. Too often the construction firm establishes part of its estimate from "the seat of its pants." With little other than a vague recollection of past performances of the work in question, the estimator is faced with predicting future costs based on hunches and unreliable word-of-mouth information.

Admittedly each time a firm undertakes a new project, it will probably be somewhat unique as to cost factors. However, structured, past project data along with recognition of the project's varying and unique conditions can result in reduced uncertainty in the estimator's project bid.

Past project data regarding individual work items are very useful in estimating. In addition, estimating is interrelated with the activity and project planning tasks. For example, the direct labor cost component of a project can be determined as follows:

$$\text{direct labor cost} = \text{activity duration (hrs.)} \times \frac{\text{crew cost}}{\text{hour}}$$

Estimating the direct labor cost for a new project depends on the same cost-accounting data as used for determining activity durations.

The project estimate is not limited to determining the direct labor cost, but should recognize all the following:

Direct labor cost
Direct material cost
Job overhead
Company overhead
Profit

The project direct-material cost can be established by identifying the quantities of material for individual work items (also referred to as the *quantity take-off* or *quantity survey*), material waste factors as indicated from historical data collected by the cost-accounting system, and the relevant material prices. As is true of identifying direct labor cost, the cost-accounting system can be designed to yield important information for material-cost estimating.

The construction firm often spends numerous hours attempting to be very accurate in its estimate of a project's labor and material costs. All too often this effort is followed by a less than detailed approach to overhead-cost allocation. For example, after determining direct labor and material costs for a project, a construction firm may add 40 percent of the summed direct costs to cover overhead costs and profit. Such a procedure often leads to substantial inaccuracy in the total project bid price. Less than accurate overhead allocation usually can be traced to a firm's lack of a cost-accounting system. Inability to develop an accurate application rate and base along with analysis of the over- and underapplied overhead leads to unprofitable estimates.

Material Scheduling

Closely related to the management functions of planning and estimating is material scheduling. The quantity take-off segment of estimating establishes what materials are to be purchased. Project planning dictates when the material is needed. Cost accounting plays a role in establishing the quantity of material needed by developing wastage factors. Cost accounting also plays an important role in determining when the material is needed by establishing the time required to perform the various work segments.

Traditionally the material-cost component of an estimate was insensitive to the schedule of material for a project. However, recent years have seen widely fluctuating prices for plywood, structural steel, and other materials that comprise a major portion of the construction project. The problem of changing material prices is compounded by the relatively long duration needed to construct the typical project. The result has been that the cost of materials for a project has become an added risk factor in the already high-risk contractor's bid.

The financial risk associated with material costs can be reduced if material needs as a function of time are predetermined by means of a schedule. Such a schedule allows for obtaining materials at advantageous prices by purchasing in advance and taking advantage of discounts. The project plan, schedule, and estimate, all of which are aided by cost accounting, provide the base for preparing a material schedule.

Cash Budgeting

The benefits of preparing cash budgets have been well documented. Regardless of these benefits, the construction firm is often negligent in its preparation of cash budgets. As a result, numerous construction firm bankruptcies can be traced to the lack of preparing and updating project cash budgets.

Much of the project planning and estimating efforts of the construction firm can be summarized by means of a cash budget for the project. Preparing such a budget is part of the study of cost accounting. The components of a cash budget include identifying both the expected dollar amount of cash receipts and disbursements and the time at which various receipts and disbursements occur. The dollar amounts of the disbursements are in great part identified during the estimating process. The dollar amounts of the receipts are determined by the contractor's total project bid.

A project's cash budget is essential for determining financing needs during the project. Because of owner-deferred payment for work performed, owner payment retentions, and low working capital ratios, the construction firm is often faced with the need to secure financing at various points in time during construction of a project. The amount of this financing and the cost of the financing should be determined before a project is bid upon. This is necessary in order to reflect the finance interest cost in the estimate of project costs and subsequently in the project bid. Financing costs are as much a part of project cost as are labor or material costs and identifying them is essential to a profitable estimate and project bid.

The very ability to obtain financing at a critical time in the project schedule often depends on how soon the firm initiates the search for funds. The availability and cost of loan money from financial institutions varies because of many economic factors. Unless a plan exists for obtaining funds in advance, the construction firm may find itself without a source of funds when they are needed.

Preparing a cash budget is facilitated by using a common set of work items. Just as the work items can serve as the base for establishing work segment durations, costs, and material schedules, the cash budget and its supporting schedules can be produced from the defined work items.

Payroll

When a proposed project becomes reality, the role of cost accounting does not diminish. Cost-accounting practices are essential to the ability to control a project's costs and duration. Planning, including estimating and preparing budgets, provides the potential for a profitable project. In fact, it is the control function that brings these potential profits to reality.

The labor component of the control function illustrated in Figure 10.1 begins with the payroll. (The payroll process was discussed in Chapter 4.) Payroll is fundamental to the daily operation of any firm that depends on labor. Preparing employee paychecks, establishing withholding liabilities, and filing required tax forms require the firm to document individual employee hours worked.

The timekeeping duties that are part of the payroll function are often viewed as a necessary evil by the construction firm. The tediousness of the task stems from a narrow-sighted view of the uses of the collected labor time data. Timecards utilized by the construction firm are often limited to documenting total time worked by a given employee. With only a slight modification of the timecard, it is possible to document labor time for specific segments of work performed by the employee. The work segments can be defined in the same way as those utilized for project planning, scheduling, and estimating. In this manner, historical work item files are established from past projects and in turn are used to aid planning and estimating future projects.

As is true of defining the work items used in planning and estimating, practical considerations must guide defining the work items for data collection. Being able to differentiate time for specific work items, the cost of collecting and processing the data, and the benefits to be gained from the processed data all dictate work item definition.

As with labor, cost-accounting procedures can trace material to specific work items. From this collected data, material standards and wastage factors may be established for planning and estimating future projects. Equally important is the role documented material placement per work item data can have in controlling both material and labor costs.

Cost Control

In order to have an effective cost-control program, the trend of the cost must be determined as soon as possible and compared against the progress of the plan such that any required corrective action can be taken. Monitoring of production and costs cannot be overemphasized. If one were to investigate reasons behind many of the reported construction firm failures, lack of control, whether production or cost, would be high on the list of underlying causes.

The need to have a means of quickly documenting and monitoring project production and costs is emphasized by the fact that the construction firm's planned production and costs are often less than accurate estimates. Regardless of the soundness of the firm's planning and estimating practices, numerous factors prevent the plan and estimate from being totally deterministic. The ever-changing environment surrounding the construction work, the variable nature of construction work, and the industry's high dependence on labor productivity all inject uncertainty into the performance of the construction. The result is that plan and performance differences are partly due to lack of control and partly due to a less than accurate plan. Regardless of the cause, early recognition of inefficiencies and deviations from planned progress is essential to corrective management decisions.

Effective project control of labor and material costs can be acquired by documenting material quantities and labor costs for previously defined work items. Let us assume that, for a work item such as placing wall forms, a firm estimates 8,000 square feet of contact area (sfca) of work to be performed. On the basis of historical work item data collected from previous projects, the firm estimates 10 carpenter manhours per 100 sfca of work. The total estimated manhours for the project are therefore calculated as follows:

$$8000 \text{ sfca} \times \frac{10 \text{ manhours}}{100 \text{ sfca}} = 800 \text{ manhours}$$

Let us further assume that inspection of the work after a month indicates that 800 sfca of work is in place. Determining work performed is necessary for progress billings. On the basis of payroll records structured to report labor hours per work items, 200 carpenter hours have been charged to the wall form-related work. Analysis of the in-place material indicates that 10 percent of the work is completed. However, based on an estimate of 800 manhours, the cost-accounting system indicates that 25 percent of the estimated labor hours and cost have been expended. Assuming that labor hours should be proportional to the form work performed, it appears that the contractor is faced with a substantial labor cost overrun.

The discrepancy in the percentages of labor hours versus material placed should receive attention immediately. It may be that it can be explained and is not a reason for alarm. However, it may also be indicative of inefficiencies. Early detection of these inefficiencies can bring corrective management before cost overruns become excessive.

Merely comparing actual costs to estimated costs does not always give good measure of performance. It may be that excessive overtime labor costs are hidden by high labor productivity. Looked at another way, the benefit of high employee productivity may be hidden because of the inefficiencies of management in scheduling work. The point to be made is that effective cost control is achieved by analyzing the factors that make up total cost. With material costs it is necessary to analyze both the purchase price versus the budget price and the amount of material used versus that estimated from quantity take-off. Similarly, the components of overhead costs must be analyzed in order to effectively control the total overhead cost.

Accounting Reports

All too often the construction firm determines project profitability or loss only after all the bills are paid and the final payment is received from the owner.

The lack of cost accounting, and in particular the inability to generate interim financial reports regarding a project, keep the contractor in the dark and uncertain.

Collected material, labor, and overhead data from an ongoing project can serve the control function while providing the basis for interim progress and financial reports. These reports aid the contractor in mapping out its bidding activities, in improving relations with creditors, and perhaps most importantly, in measuring its own performance. Preparing interim reports is a natural outgrowth of data that serve the planning, estimating, and controlling functions.

Collected data that aid control and establish standards for planning and estimating can also satisfy the needs of financial accounting. Documented material, labor, and overhead costs can be summarized and categorized through ledger accounts such that financial statements are prepared directly from the collected data. Financial accounting can be carried out continuously by utilizing the cost-accounting system of isolating project costs.

The strength and internal controls of the firm's cost-accounting system aid the validity of the firm's financial statements. Better recordkeeping, cost-accounting procedures, and control can reduce the rather widely held view of bankers, sureties, and investors that the construction firm's financial information and financial risk is unacceptable.

The cycle illustrated in Figure 10.1 is repetitive. Planned projects become ongoing projects. In turn, the ongoing projects become past projects. Throughout these steps, historical data structured by the firm's cost-accounting procedures continue to be updated. Using this data, each management function illustrated in Figure 10.1 can be performed with increased results and in a manner that supplements performing each other essential function noted.

Defining Work Items

Basic to a project management information system is identifying specific packages of work referred to as work items. The construction firm has much freedom in its definition of specific work items for a given project and for the performance of work on all of its projects. In particular, the problem often arises as to what is and what is not a work item. That is, whereas one firm might choose to define all work related to concrete including forming and stripping as a work item, another firm may choose to identify only placing concrete for all types of concrete work as a work item, and yet another firm may identify placing concrete in a wall as a work item. Clearly the problem of identifying specific work items is one of establishing the degree or magnitude involved.

The definition of the work items dictates the manner in which the estimator takes off quantities and field data are collected. For a given set of drawings, the number of work items the firm establishes as part of the take-off procedure dictates a specific groupings of the items to be identified from the drawings. The broader the scale of a work item, the fewer work items the estimator will single out when taking-off quantities for a project. On the other hand, the broader the scale or scope of work items, the less accuracy will be provided for purposes of determining the cost of performing the project's work. That is, if the estimator takes off all the concrete placement as one work item, the fact that it costs the construction firm more to place concrete in an elevated wall than placing a similar amount in a slab on grade will not be reflected in the estimate. This difference in costs is one major reason why we would want to delineate separate work items for the two different work processes. No single rule or principle can be used to determine what is and what is not a work item. However, if we keep in mind why we are listing separate work items, this will aid us in determining them.

There is a relationship between our costing or pricing of work and determining work packages. If two different types of work require different resources to perform the work, they probably will have different costs for a given unit of work performed on each of the two types of work. Thus, an overall guideline is whenever two or more different resources are required to perform work, we probably are justified in identifying each as a separate work item to reflect the different resources required. However, even this general guideline will not be a practical guideline to solve work item identification in all cases.

In establishing a set of work items that dictate the quantity take-off, one should remember that the work items can prove to be a means of integrating several construction-management functions. If work items are properly defined, they can serve as a means of interrelating project estimating, project planning, project control, and project accounting and payroll functions.

The importance of the relationship between project estimating and the definition of work items is shown in Figure 10.2. In this figure there is evidence that project estimating depends on the compatibility of the work item definitions and the cost data files the firm has gathered from past projects. To illustrate what can happen if the systems are not compatible, let us assume that a construction firm has defined two separate work items: placing concrete

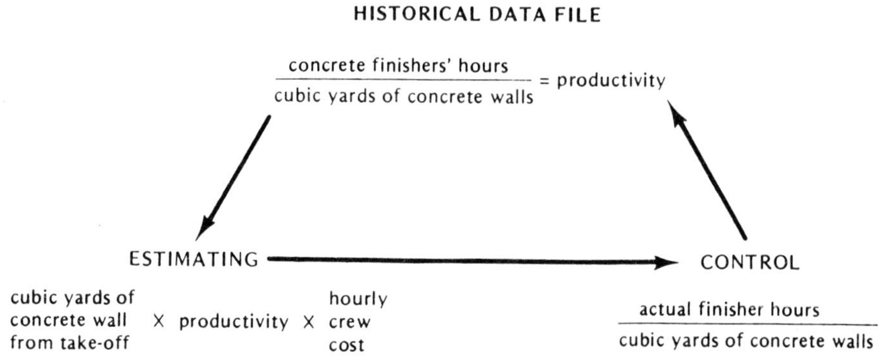

Figure 10.2 Estimating and Historical Data Files

footings and placing concrete walls. The estimator then proceeds to take off the cubic yards of concrete for the two different types of concrete work. This is done recognizing that each type of work may require different costs in regard to pricing a unit of work. Let us further assume that the firm has gathered and structured cost data on placing concrete. No differentiation has been made as to type of concrete placement. When the calculated quantitites for placing the concrete footings and placing the concrete walls are determined, the firm will be forced to use a less than accurate price for the specific work items. The result will probably be an inaccurate estimate.

The definition of work items can also be made compatible with the company's project planning and scheduling system. In particular, it is possible to specify work items such that they can also be defined as project activities on an overall project plan and schedule. When this is done it is easy to transform the cost estimate to a duration that can be used in the project's planning process. This is illustrated in Figure 10.3.

The construction industry is burdened by fragmentation. Work package standards are absent. Units of measure differ for the designer, builder, and material supplier. Using the uniform code as defined by the Construction Specifications Institute (CSI) is a move toward providing a common communication base for the parties involved in the building construction process. Definition of work items for an estimating and control system can be compatible with the CSI division code. Using each division as a broad classification, specific work items can be identified for each. For example, division 3 of the

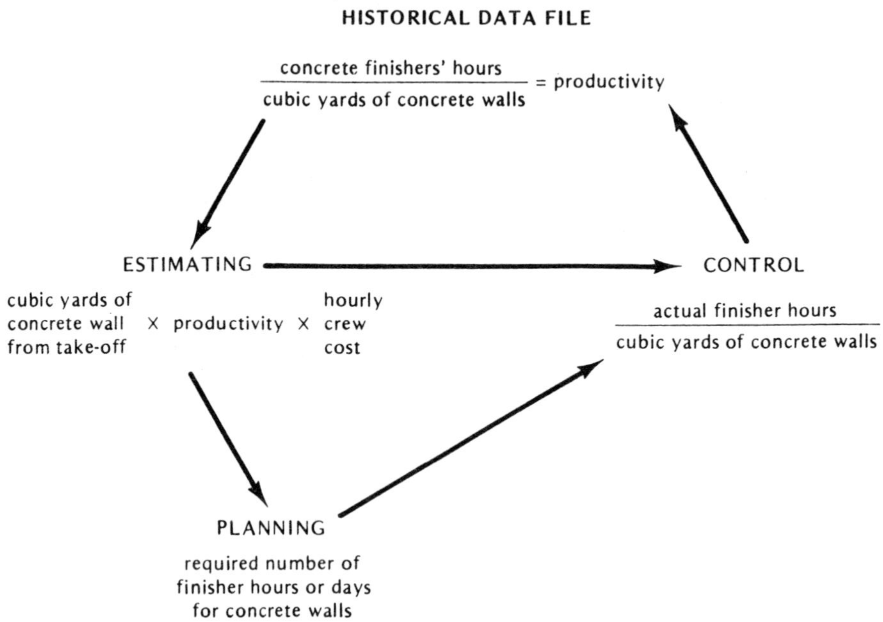

Figure 10.3 Relationship of Project Estimating, Planning, and Controlling

uniform code is identified as "Concrete." With concrete identified as the base, the firm may further define work items as follows:

CF1 Forming concrete beams
CF2 Forming concrete columns
etc.

CC1 Placing concrete in beams
CC2 Placing concrete in columns
etc.

CR1 Place reinforcement in beams
CR2 Place reinforcement in columns
etc.

The code in front of the work item description is an abbreviation that may be indicated on a timecard or used in processing data. The first character (the C here) may be used to identify the division (such as concrete). The second letter is used to aid in identifying the type of work. For example, F may be used to identify Formwork. Naturally the number of work items a firm identifies under any one division depends on the type of work it performs.

The benefit to defining work items consistent with the uniform code is that the firm probably will be better able to relate its data to published cost data averages and systems used by designers. In fact, building construction specifications are increasingly prepared to be compatible with the uniform code.

The uniform code is designed for building construction. A heavy and highway contractor should attempt to define work items using a data base common to heavy and highway construction. Once again the benefits are better communication.

As an alternative to using work items as a means of project control, some construction firms trace costs to project phases or labor crafts. An example of tracing costs to phases might be to trace costs to a specific room or wing of a building. While such a process may aid in controlling the project in question, it offers little as to helping to estimate future projects because usually the design of the building components varies significantly from one building to the next.

As with phase cost identification, tracing and summing labor costs by crafts can be used to help control the project in question. However, as is also true of phase cost identification, summed labor craft costs have little value for future estimating efforts. In conclusion, defining work items as the cost data base or object offers the most potential for both project estimating and control.

MANUAL PROJECT-MANAGEMENT INFORMATION SYSTEMS

The construction firm seeking an effective project-management information system including the collection and processing of historical work item data cannot always afford the luxury of automatic data-processing equipment. However, this does not mean that an effective system of project planning and controlling work item cost is beyond the capabilities of the firm. Through in-depth analysis of the defined work items, data collection forms, and structured procedures, it is possible to obtain a manual work item planning and controlling cost system.

A manual management system for planning and controlling project labor and material costs will now be illustrated. The system emphasizes management data for project planning, estimating, and controlling. In addition, the system will aid the functions of payroll, owner billings, and financial accounting. While cash budgeting and material scheduling are not dealt with by the system, it can be extended to serve these functions.

The previous section discussed the critical task of defining work items. While defining work items is affected by the use or nonuse of automatic data-processing equipment, the importance of selecting work items remains the same regardless of whether the system used is automated or nonautomated.

In order to illustrate a typical system that traces labor and material costs to project work items, we will assume a set of work items has been defined. In particular we will assume the set of forty-four work items shown in Figure 10.4. The list corresponds to what might be used by a general contractor and is not unique. Another general contractor with a different type of work or data collecting and processing capabilities might develop a list that varies from Figure 10.4; nevertheless, a list of about this number of work items is manageable as to the time required to process the project data.

The system to be illustrated is based on productivity rather than unit costs. As such the collected labor data is somewhat insensitive to time. An overview flowchart of the system is shown in Figure 10.5. The system is manual except for payroll which is processed through a computer service bureau, although this too could be carried out manually. However, manual payroll calculations often prove tedious and costly. Computer service bureaus for payroll processing are becoming readily accessible to the construction firm. The firm's bank often provides such a service at little charge.

The integrated management system illustrated in Figure 10.5 is designed to be compatible with the possibility of modifying it to a fully automated system at a future date. While a computer system may not be affordable at a given point in time, it may in the future. A manual system designed with a view toward the future can help minimize conversion costs.

The time at which each of the forms comprising the integrated system is filled out and utilized is indicated in the overview flowchart in Figure 10.5. As will be illustrated, various forms may be used on a daily, weekly, yearly, or end of project basis.

The project management system is initiated with the planning of a potential project. The plan and estimate are the initial management project functions to be performed. If this is the first project for which the system is being implemented, no historical work files would be available from past projects. As

RES 87

WORK ITEM CODES

GENERAL

GS1 SUPERVISION
GC1 CLEAN UP
G01 OTHER

EXCAVATION

EM1 MISCELLANEOUS EXCAVATION
E01 OTHER

CONCRETE

CF1 FORM FOOTINGS
CF2 FORM WALLS–GRADE AND 1st FLOOR
CF3 FORM WALLS–ABOVE 1st FLOOR
CF4 FORM BEAMS
CF5 FORM RECTANGULAR COLUMNS
CF7 FORM SLABS
CF8 FORM STEPS
CF9 FORM DRIVES AND WALKS
CR1 REINFORCING RODS
CR2 REINFORCING MESH
CC1 CONCRETE PLACING–FOOTINGS
CC2 CONCRETE PLACING–WALLS GRADE AND 1st FLOOR
CC3 CONCRETE PLACING–WALLS ABOVE 1st FLOOR
CC4 CONCRETE PLACING–BEAMS
CC5 CONCRETE PLACING–COLUMNS
CC6 CONCRETE PLACING–SLABS GRADE AND 1st FLOOR
CC7 CONCRETE PLACING–SLABS ABOVE 1st FLOOR
CC8 CONCRETE PLACING–STEPS
CC9 CONCRETE PLACING–DRIVES AND WALKS
CP1 CONCRETE PRECAST
C01 OTHER

MASONRY

MB1 BRICK
MB2 BLOCK AND BRICK WALL
MC1 CONCRETE BLOCK–4"
MC2 CONCRETE BLOCK–8"
MC3 CONCRETE BLOCK–12"
MS1 SCAFFOLDING
MT1 TILE, GLAZED
MT2 TILE, CLAY
M01 OTHER

STRUCTURAL STEEL

SS1 STRUCTURAL STEEL
SS2 STAIRS AND RAILING
S01 OTHER

WOOD

WS1 SHEATHING
WF1 FRAMING
WD1 DOORS, JAMBS AND HARDWARE
WT1 TRIM
WM1 MILLWORK
W01 OTHER

Figure 10.4 Work Items for a General Contractor

such, the estimate of manhours for each work item for which there is work would have to come from a source external to the system. However, as the system is applied to projects, these projects would provide the source data for estimating.

Job Estimate Sheet

The first form that is part of the project management system is illustrated in Figure 10.6—the job estimate sheet. The purpose of this form is to estimate the material and labor cost for the project in terms of required material, unit material prices, required labor hours, and labor rates for each of the individual

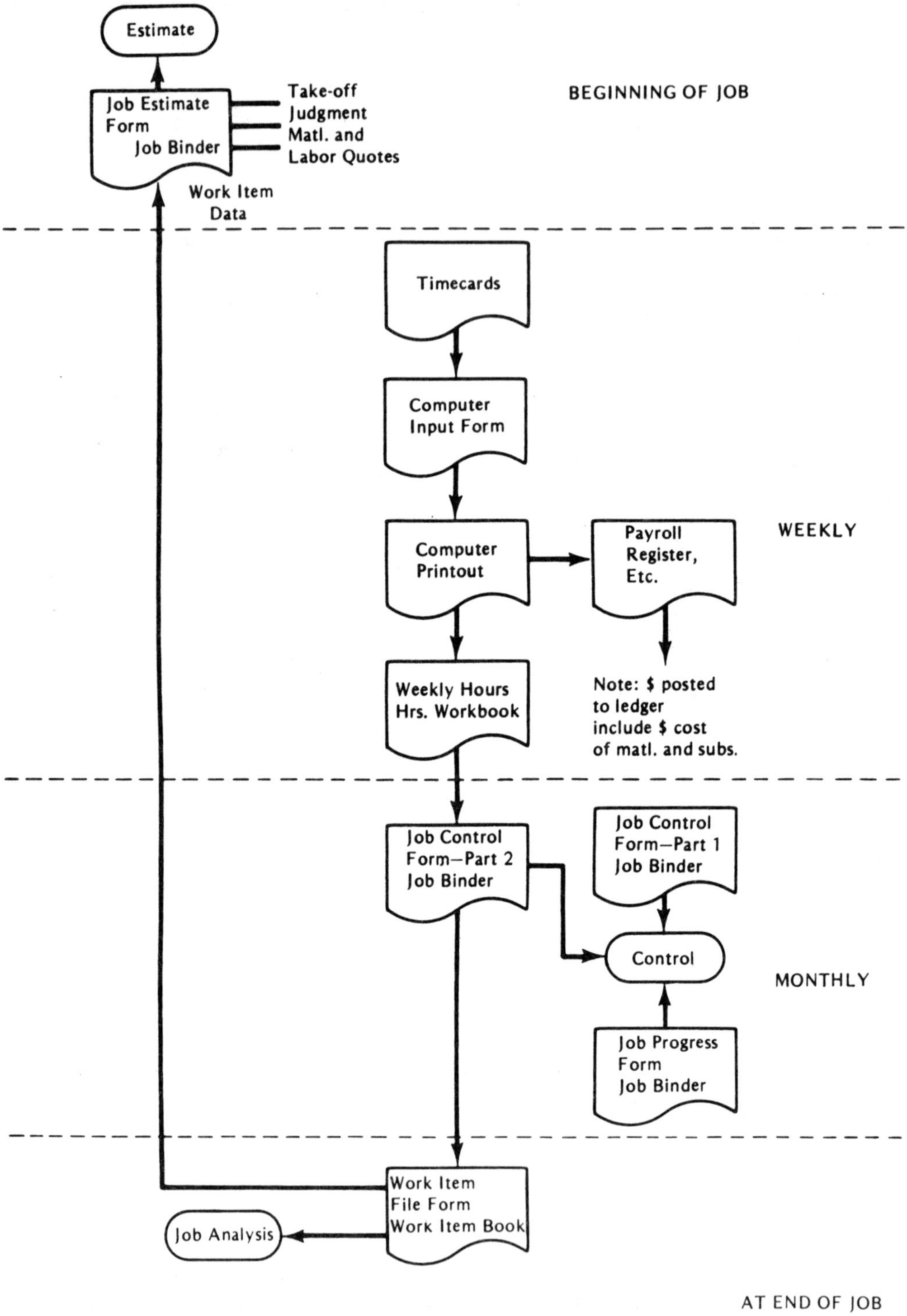

Figure 10.5 Manual Project Information System

JOB ESTIMATE SHEET

ESTIMATOR __________ DATE ________ JOB NAME ____________ CODE ________

WORK ITEM	EST. MATL.	MAT. $ UNIT	TOT. $ MATL.	SUPER-VISION HRS.	CARPENTER			MASON			LABORER			FINISHER			IRON-WORKER			OPER-ENG.			TOTAL LAB. $
					HRS.	$/H	$	HRS.	$/H	$	HRS.	$/H	$	HRS.	$/H	$	HRS.	$/H	$	HRS.	$/H	$	
GS1																							
GC1																							
GO1																							
EM1																							
EO1																							
CF1																							
CF2																							
CF3																							
CF4																							
CF5																							
CF7																							
CF8																							
CF9																							
CR1																							
CR2																							
CC1																							
CC2																							
CC3																							
CC4																							
CC5																							
CC6																							
CC7																							
CC8																							
CC9																							
CP																							
CO1																							
MB1																							
MB2																							
MC1																							
MC2																							
MC3																							
MS1																							
MT1																							
MT2																							
MO1																							
SS1																							
SS2																							
SO1																							
WS1																							
WF1																							
WD1																							
WT1																							
WM1																							
WO1																							

Figure 10.6 Job Estimate Sheet for Manual System

work items. The rows on the job estimate sheet correspond to work items. An abbreviation for a work item is shown in each row. The abbreviations are those shown in Figure 10.4.

After the first column, which identifies the individual work items, the next three columns are used for calculating the work item material costs. The first of these columns, "Est. Matl.," is for listing the quantity of material work to be performed for each work item. These quantities are determined from the take-off of quantities from the project drawings and from recognition of material wastage. For example, for the work item labeled CC1 (i.e., Concrete Placing—Footings), the quantity take-off might indicate that 200 cubic yards of concrete is to be placed. Assuming a 2 percent waste factor (i.e., 4 cubic yards), the cubic yards of concrete work to be estimated is 204. This number is placed in the second column in the CC1 row.

The material price per unit of material is placed in the next column. For concrete work it would be the purchase price per cubic yard. For structural steel it would be the purchase price per ton of steel. The unit of material used for pricing should be the same as that used for the quantity take-off. If the carpentry work is measured in board feet, the material unit price should be entered as the price per board foot.

The material estimate for each work item is determined by multiplying the "Est. Matl." column and "Matl. $ Unit" for each of the work items. The result is placed in the "Tot. $ Matl." column. The total estimated material cost for the project is found by summing all the work item entries in the "Tot. $ Matl." column. It is possible and even likely that, for any one project, there will be several defined work items for which no work is performed. The work item list is designed for the firm and not for any one project. As such, whereas one project may entail all the work items, yet another may contain half or even fewer work items.

A number of columns are used for calculating the estimated labor costs. It is assumed that the firm utilizes seven different types of labor: supervision, carpenters, masons, laborers, finishers, iron-workers, and operating engineers. It is unlikely that all seven types of labor would be utilized for any one work item. In fact, analysis of the work item indicates that no work item would require more than three crafts of labor.

Each of the seven types of labor is listed on the job estimate form. The first column in each of the seven labor categories is for documenting the labor hours required for each work item. These hours can be determined from experience, past records, or external sources such as published cost books.

The estimated hours per work item are multiplied by the dollar rate per hour for the labor in question to yield the labor cost estimate per craft for each work item. The supervision column uses a different approach for handling the entry of the hourly rate. The supervision hourly rate is entered, but it is assumed that this rate is constant for each of the work items and thus is not entered separately for each work item. On the other hand, under each other labor type is a place for multiplying the estimated hours by various labor rates.

This is in recognition of the fact that a given labor craft's rate may depend in part on the type of work being performed.

The total labor cost for any one work item is determined by adding the component labor costs for a single work item. These are placed in the last column of the form. Finally the total labor cost for the project is determined by adding the labor costs for each individual work item as calculated and shown in the last column. A check on the total labor cost is made by adding the individual labor costs from the seven labor columns and summing the total.

The completed job estimate form serves as the basis for future project control. It can be filed in the front of a binder for the specific project. The rest of the binder can be used for filing other project data forms.

Timecard

Ideally, estimated projects become on-going projects. Assuming this to be the case, the next form that is part of the project-management system is the timecard. The purpose of the timecard is to allocate labor hours to work items and to tabulate total labor hours for each worker. The timecard is an essential form in the management system—it serves as the means of collecting essential input data.

Timecards should be designed with attention to ease of use and the timecard's influence on the accuracy of inputted data. Furthermore, the design of the timecard can have a positive or negative effect on worker productivity and motivation.

A timecard designed to be compatible with the system is illustrated in Figure 10.7. The work items and codes shown in Figure 10.4 are printed on the reverse side of the timecard shown in Figure 10.7. The timecard is to be filled out daily and returned to the office weekly for processing. The labor craft foremen probably would have the responsibility for filling out the timecard. It should be noted that the firm's week starts on a Wednesday and ends on a Tuesday. This provides the potential to process the timecards on Wednesday and Thursday and generate payroll checks for Friday.

The front of the timecard provides space for the individual worker's name, labor craft, and the ending date of the timecard period. The front part of the timecard also provides space for documenting labor hours on a given date with regard to individual work items. There is room for documenting work on seven work items in any one week. In addition, there is space for documenting standard, or straight-time hours, and overtime hours. Finally the form provides two ways of calculating and checking the total hours charged for the individual worker in the time period.

The back side of the timecard serves two purposes: (1) a reprint of the system's work items is duplicated on the back of the timecard. This aids in onsite identification of labor hours to specific work items. (2) There is also space for calculating net pay. Hours worked can be transferred to this side of the form, multiplied by the relevant rate, and total earnings calculated. From

NAME ______________________

CRAFT ______________________ WEEK ENDING __________

WORK ITEM		WED	THR	FRI	SAT	MON	TUE	TOTAL
	ST							
	ST							
	ST							
	ST							
	ST							
	ST							
	ST							
TOTAL								

Figure 10.7 Timecard for Manual System

these earnings deductions such as FICA are subtracted to yield net pay. Using the form to calculate net pay is optional depending on how payroll is processed.

The construction firm is normally required to generate payroll checks weekly. If the firm is of even modest size, the number of weekly payroll checks may exceed a hundred. The necessary payroll calculations include adding individual worker hours from the timecard and calculating and subtracting withholding taxes and insurances. Performed manually these calculations can be very time consuming. The clerical time required becomes even greater if the clerk is called upon to add labor craft hours worked for specific work items. This is not to imply that such a procedure is unfeasible. If efficient clerical procedures are developed, manual payroll calculations including distribution and summing of labor hours to specific work items can be accomplished.

However, using a computer service bureau often results in the payroll being generated more economically. Such service bureaus are available to the construction firm through independent operators, time-sharing service companies, or in some cases the firm's bank. In many cases these computer services have the capability of generating a distribution summary of labor hours into specific categories (work items) while producing paychecks and a payroll register.

Let us assume that the system we are describing for project planning and control utilizes a computer printout of labor distribution hours. This distribution sheet for labor hours per work item would be generated weekly as the payroll was produced. If such a service is not utilized, the same information could be produced manually. However, undoubtedly the total cost for performing the manual calulations would exceed the cost of a computer service. The trade-off as to which one would be more favorable in terms of cost obviously depends on the number of employees and timecards that are processed. As the number of timecards increases, the economics become more favorable for using automated data-processing equipment for generating payroll and work hour distribution.

Weekly Hours Form

The next form used as part of this system is a weekly hours form. This serves as a worksheet for compiling labor cost hours as to specific work items for a given month. As noted earlier, the payroll would normally be generated every week. The labor cost hours per work item would appear weekly on the labor distribution form. What is needed is a form to compile the weekly hours into a monthly total. The form, which is designed to be compatible with the work and labor craft items previously defined, is shown in Figure 10.8. As can be seen, the seven different labor types identified with the general contractor in question are listed. Each work item is listed vertically. The first column labeled "BG" under each labor craft is for the beginning total of labor hours from previous months. The following five columns are for transferring the labor hours by work item for each of the weeks in the month. These are taken from the labor distribution forms that were printed as part of the payroll calculations. Finally, the last column labeled "TT" is for adding the beginning hours and hours for each of the weeks in the month in question.

The weekly hours form represents data for a month. Each new month a new weekly hours form would be initiated. The monthly weekly hours form is basically a worksheet that compiles the monthly hours. These monthly hours will be transferred to yet another form for the control function. The responsibility for filling out the weekly hours form lies with the clerical help. The

MONTH ______ WEEKLY HOURS JOB NAME ______ CODE ______

WK ITM	SUPERVISION							CARPENTER							MASON							LABORER						
	BG	W1	W2	W3	W4	W5	TT	BG	W1	W2	W3	W4	W5	TT	BG	W1	W2	W3	W4	W5	TT	BG	W1	W2	W3	W4	W5	TT
[illegible]																												
[illegible]																												
[illegible]																												
[illegible]																												
[illegible]																												
[illegible]																												
[illegible]																												
[illegible]																												
[illegible]																												
[illegible]																												
[illegible]																												
[illegible]																												
[illegible]																												
CR																												
[illegible]																												
[illegible]																												
[illegible]																												
[illegible]																												
[illegible]																												
[illegible]																												
[illegible]																												
[illegible]																												
[illegible]																												
[illegible]																												
CP																												
[illegible]																												
[illegible]																												
MB2																												
[illegible]																												
[illegible]																												
[illegible]																												
MS1																												
[illegible]																												
[illegible]																												
MO1																												
SS1																												
[illegible]																												
[illegible]																												
WS1																												
[illegible]																												
[illegible]																												
[illegible]																												
WM1																												
WO1																												
TOTAL																												

Figure 10.8 Weekly Summary Form

monthly forms can be filed in the job project binder previously described for storing the estimate sheet.

A weekly check of the distribution of hours can be made by adding the column for the week in question and comparing this to the sum of the weekly craft hours as printed in the payroll distribution. Errors found in this comparison should be corrected. More than likely, an error indicates that the clerical help erred in translating labor hours per work item to the weekly hours form.

Job Control Sheet—Part One

The next form that is part of the project-management system is a two-part one: the job control sheet, shown in Figure 10.9. The two-part form is used to control ongoing construction projects. The first part is identified as the estimating part of the form which is used to indicate the estimate of total material and labor hours for each required individual work item. Initially the entries on this part of the form are those that were made on the job estimate form previously shown in Figure 10.6. If there are no change orders, this part of the

MONTH ____________ WEEKLY HOURS JOB NAME ____________ CODE________

WK	FINISHER							IRON WORKER							OPER. ENGR.							TOTALS						
ITM	BG	W1	W2	W3	W4	W5	TT	BG	W1	W2	W3	W4	W5	TT	BG	W1	W2	W3	W4	W5	TT	BG	W1	W2	W3	W4	W5	TT
GS1																												
[illegible]																												
GO1																												
EM1																												
EO1																												
CF1																												
CF2																												
CF3																												
CF4																												
CF5																												
CF7																												
CF8																												
CF9																												
CR1																												
CR2																												
CC1																												
CC2																												
CC3																												
CC4																												
CC5																												
CC6																												
CC7																												
CC8																												
CC9																												
CP																												
CO1																												
MB1																												
MB2																												
MC1																												
MC2																												
MC3																												
MS1																												
MT1																												
MT2																												
MO1																												
SS1																												
SS2																												
SO1																												
WS1																												
WF1																												
WD1																												
WT1																												
WM1																												
WO1																												
TOTAL																												

Figure 10.8 *Continued*

job control sheet will be identical for each of the months. If there are change orders during a project, the entries of the estimated additional material and additional labor hours are placed in the columns labeled "CHG" and "EST," respectively, on the estimate part of the job control sheet.

Job Progress Form

Before we discuss how the second part of the job control sheet is used, we ought to divert our attention to yet another form that is part of the system. This form will provide us the data for the second part of the job control sheet. Each month the construction firm is usually responsible for making a progress report to justify its monthly billings. In some cases this estimate of monthly progress is made in very crude fashion which may result in either overbillings or underbillings. A more accurate estimate of job progress is a benefit of the project-management system being considered. In particular, as part of the process of determining how much work has been done such that the work can

JOB CONTROL SHEET (PART 1) ESTIMATE

MONTH ______________ JOB NAME __________ CODE _______

WORK ITEM	MAT'L. EST.	SUPERV.		CARPENTER		MASON		LABORER		FINISHER		IRNWRKER		OPER. ENG.		TOTAL	
		EST	CHG	EST	CHG	EST	CHG	EST	CHG	EST	CHG	EST	CHG	EST	CHG	EST	CHG
GS1																	
GC1																	
G01																	
EM1																	
E01																	
CF1																	
CF2																	
CF3																	
CF4																	
CF5																	
CF7																	
CF8																	
CF9																	
CR1																	
CR2																	
CC1																	
CC2																	
CC3																	
CC4																	
CC5																	
CC6																	
CC7																	
CC8																	
CC9																	
CP																	
C01																	
MB1																	
MB2																	
MC1																	
MC2																	
MC3																	
MS1																	
MT1																	
MT2																	
M01																	
SS1																	
SS2																	
S01																	
WS1																	
WF1																	
WD1																	
WT1																	
WM1																	
W01																	
TOTAL																	

Figure 10.9a Job Control Sheet for Manual System—Part One

be controlled, the firm can obtain an accurate estimate of progress for billing purposes.

The form used to determine job progress is the job progress form, shown in Figure 10.10. The purpose of this form is to determine each work item progress as determined by job inspection. The estimated progress will be input

JOB CONTROL SHEET (PART 2) PROGRESS

MONTH ______________ YEAR ________ JOB NAME ____________ CODE ____________

WK ITM	ACT. MAT'L. TO DATE	EST. MAT'L. TO DATE	ACT. / EST.	EST. MAT'L. TO DATE / TOTL. EST.	SUP-ERV.		CAR-PENT.		MASON		LAB-ORER		FIN-ISHER		IRON WORK		OPER. ENGR.		TOTAL		
					HRS	%	HRS	%	HRS	%	HRS	%	HRS	%	HRS	%	HRS	%	HRS	%	VR.
GS1																					
GC1																					
G01																					
EM1																					
E01																					
CF1																					
CF2																					
CF3																					
CF4																					
CF5																					
CF7																					
CF8																					
CF9																					
CR1																					
CR2																					
CC1																					
CC2																					
CC3																					
CC4																					
CC5																					
CC6																					
CC7																					
CC8																					
CC9																					
CP																					
C01																					
MB1																					
MB2																					
MC1																					
MC2																					
MC3																					
MS1																					
MT1																					
MT2																					
M01																					
SS1																					
SS2																					
S01																					
WS1																					
WF1																					
WD1																					
WT1																					
WM1																					
W01																					
TOTAL																					

Figure 10.9b Job Control Sheet for Manual System—Part Two

to the job control function and can also aid in billing. It is filled out at the end of each month, typically by the job superintendent.

The columns in the job progress form provide space for updating the monthly progress on one individual form for a year's period of time. The work items are listed vertically in the first column. These are the same work items

JOB PROGRESS FORM

YEAR ______ JOB NAME ____________________

SUPERINTENDENT ____________________ JOB CODE ____________________

WRK ITM COD	JOB MATL. EST.	BEGIN. BAL.	JAN	FEB	MAR	APR	MAY	JUN	JUL	AUG	SEP	OCT	NOV	DEC	END. BAL.
GS1															
GC2															
G01															
EM1															
E01															
CF1															
CF2															
CF3															
CF4															
CF5															
CF7															
CF8															
CF9															
CR1															
CR2															
CC1															
CC2															
CC3															
CC4															
CC5															
CC6															
CC7															
CC8															
CC9															
CP															
C01															
MB1															
MB2															
MC1															
MC2															
MC3															
MS1															
MT1															
MT2															
M01															
SS1															
SS2															
S01															
WS1															
WF1															
WD1															
WT1															
WM1															
W01															

Figure 10.10 Job Progress Form for Manual System

that are used for the estimating and job control. Next, the job material estimate is shown for each of the work items. This estimate of materials would be what was determined in the initial estimate and updated for any change orders. The next column, "BEGIN BAL.," is for carrying over the progress to date when we overlap a year. For example, if in 19X0 the balance of work done for an item was 225 cubic yards, this number would appear in the BEGIN BAL. for the first month of 19X1. As the job superintendent walks the job at the end of the month, he identifies the material put in place in that month. This is done for each work item for which work was done.

There are two different ways of documenting job progress. Both are keyed to the amount of material put in place. One procedure is to document the actual quantity of material put in place at a given time. For example, for concrete-related work items this would mean that the job superintendent would document the actual amount of concrete put in place in a given month. Normally the unit of measure would be cubic yards.

As an alternative to documenting the actual quantity of material put in place in a period of time, the individual making the job progress report could merely document the percentage of work performed in a given period of time. For example, if the entire estimate indicates 100 cubic yards of concrete for a given work item, the individual making the job progress report might establish that approximately 25 percent of the work was completed. Naturally, given this estimate we could determine the cubic yards of concrete put in place. It may be easier for the individual making the job progress report to think of progress in terms of percentages rather than quantities. Either way we should get an accurate estimate of job progress as a function of the individual work item.

The information off the job progress form will be used for job control. Each month after it is used the job progress form can be stored in the individual job binder where it can serve as evidence to back up job progress billing. There is a job progress form for each job and each serves only one job. Naturally, if the project exceeds a year's duration, the design of the form shown results in the need to use more than one job progress form.

Job Control Sheet—Part Two

Let us now return to the job control sheet. We previously discussed part one of the form; let us now discuss the control segment of the form, part two shown in Figure 10.9b. On part two there is space for documenting the materials put in place for each work item on a project to the specified date. In addition, there is space for documenting cumulative hours for each identified craft for each individual work item. The first column, labeled "ACT. MAT'L TO DATE," is used for documenting the actual material identified with specific work items that have been used to date. The source for this information may be the invoices received from material vendors. This information is independent of the monthly job progress report and, in some cases, this information will not be available.

The second column, labeled "EST MAT'L. TO DATE," is used for documenting the materials put in place for each of the work items as indicated in the monthly progress report. The source of this information comes from totaling the material estimated to be in place as determined on the job progress form in Figure 10.10 (thus the job progress form provides input for the job control sheet). The number placed in the column represents a cumulative total to date for the estimated material put in place.

The next column, labeled "ACT./EST.," is used for determining the ratio between the actual material used to date versus the estimated material put in place to date. This division of estimated material into actual material provides us a means of determining a wastage factor, or the fact that some material has been put in inventory and not put in place.

The next column is critical in that it indicates a percentage of material put in place versus the total estimate of material to be put in place. The column is labeled "EST MAT'L. TO DATE/TOTL.EST." Actually this column is merely the division of the second column in the second part of the form divided by the material estimated for the job and shown in the first column of part one of the job control sheet. As such, all the information for determining the percentage of complete material is on the job control sheet. This column will also be used as the basis for evaluating the efficiency of labor performance to date.

Let us now turn our attention to the columns for the seven different labor types. There is a column for each labor category and, under each of these, two additional columns, one labeled "HRS" and one labeled "%." In the HRS column the accumulated labor hours for that craft for a specific work item are shown. The source of the information is the weekly hours form shown in Figure 10.8. Each month a new job control sheet is filled out to reflect the progress as to material and cumulated labor hours for each of the applicable labor categories.

The entries for the percentage column under each labor type are determined by dividing hours shown in the HRS column by the total estimated labor hours for each of the crafts as shown in part one of the job control sheet. The total estimated hours should reflect any additional hours due to change orders that are documented in part one of the form. The result is a calculation of percentage of labor hours expended for each of the labor types for each work item versus the total hours estimated. Based on the assumption that labor hours expended should correlate with work put in place, these percentages should correspond closely to column four which represents the percentage of material put in place versus the total estimate of materials to be put in place for the entire project. A difference in the labor percentage expended versus the estimated percentage of material put in place should be investigated. There may be a good reason for the variance; for example, it may be that the estimated material put in place to total estimated material for the project is a misleading indicator in select instances. Sometimes much of the labor that is required to put in a given amount of material is at the beginning of the work. However, this is not the rule in regard to construction work. It is more likely that the labor expended percentage is higher than the work performed percentage because that labor is inefficient or there is a productivity problem. By comparing the percentage of labor hours to work performed, the construction firm has a mechanism for determining inefficient operations and therefore taking corrective action. This can be done on each work item that is singled out as part of the project-management system.

A column, labeled "TOTAL," is also shown for the accumulation of all the labor hours expended to date. The entry in the HRS part of the TOTAL column is merely the sum of the hours shown in each of the seven different labor types that were used for a given work item. The entries in the % column are merely the hours indicated in the HRS column divided by the total labor hours for a given work item as established in part one of the job control sheet.

Finally, the last column, labeled "VR," can be used for several purposes. It is intended to be an indicator of a total projected variance in regard to the labor hours. It is beneficial to project the total labor hours based on the over- or underestimate of labor hours to date. For example, if the total estimated hours for a given work item were 100 and the work is currently 50 percent complete with an indicated 100 percent overrun, then the projected labor hours shown in the last column would be 200. The bottom row of the job control sheet can be used to calculate the total labor hours by craft for the entire project. This can serve as a check when compared to the hours documented in payroll for the individual crafts.

The job control sheet serves as an important link in the construction firm's ability to control and correct project inefficiencies. The project information that flags project progress as to material and labor is an outgrowth of the data collected in the field. Processing the information and filling out of the job control sheet is a clerical function as the mathematics is limited to addition and division. The monthly job control sheet can be filed in individual job binders which can serve as a single location for filing the project job estimate form, the weekly hours forms, the job progress form, and the job control sheet forms.

Work Item File Form

The benefits obtained from the information placed on part two of the job control sheet are not limited to project control. In particular, the cumulated material and labor performance information can be used for estimating future projects. This is done by using the work item file form shown in Figure 10.11.

The work item file form is designed such that there is a single form for each work item. If the firm has defined forty-four different work items for their project-management systems, then there would be 44 different work item forms. The first column on this form is used to identify the job for which the information in the following columns is being documented. The completion date of the project is placed in the second column of the work item file form. The material put in place for the given work item, as determined from the final job control sheet, is placed in the third column. The next three columns, labeled "C-," are used for documenting the total labor hours expended for three different crafts used on a specific work item. The three columns are in

WORK ITEM FILE

PAGE ______ UNITS ______________ WORK ITEM NAME ___________ CODE _______

JOB	COMP	EST. MAT'L.	C- ______ HRS.	PROD	C- ______ HRS.	PROD	C- ______ HRS.	PROD	TOTAL HRS.	PROD	PROD/CPRD	✓ ENT	CUM. MAT'L.	C- ______ CHRS	CPRD	C- ______ CHRS.	CPRD	C- ______ CHRS.	CPRD	TOTAL CHRS	CPRD

Figure 10.11 Work Item History File for Manual System'

recognition of the fact that probably there will be no more than three labor types per work item, given the definition of work item we have employed. For example, when placing concrete we might utilize laborers, concrete finishers, and carpenters.

The productivity for each labor type is determined by dividing the total hours for that type of labor by the estimated quantity of material shown in column three. The resulting productivity figures would be entered in the columns labeled "PROD." Naturally, if fewer than three labor types are used on a specific work item, then less than three C-columns would be used.

The next column shown on the work item file, labeled "TOTAL," is merely for summing the total hours for all the labor types for the project. The total productivity for all the labor types is the sum of all the labor hours divided by the estimated material for the work item for the project being entered.

The next column, labeled "PROD/CPRB", is used as an indicator column for measuring and evaluating the project's total labor productivity versus the typical productivity for this type of work item as indicated by past projects. Obviously if this were the first project being entered into the system, there would be no number for the denominator in this calculation. However, as time went on and more projects were entered, an average cumulative productivity would be determined and used.

The next column on the work item file has a checkmark in the heading. This column is used merely to indicate whether a given job entry's data would be made part of the cumulative averaging of data for the work item in question. Sometimes a project is performed that has unique factors making that project data unrepresentative of future performances. In that case, the firm may not want to average that data into other productivity data in establishing a norm for the operation; therefore, in that case no entry would be made in the checkmark column. On the other hand, if the data is considered representative, a checkmark would be made.

Assuming that data from a project is to be entered into a cumulative or average set of information, the information would then be added to a running total of previous projects and averaged into calculations for specific labor type productivities and a total labor productivity. The hours and productivity are indicated as cumulative hours and cumulative productivity by a capital "C" in the cumulative calculation columns.

When the firm is faced with determining an estimate for future projects, it can refer to the cumulative data in the individual work item file to aid it in determining the number of manhours for an upcoming project. It may be that, while the cumulative data is of interest, an upcoming project may have characteristics of a previous project that was entered into the system at a prior date. In that case the information for that specific past project may be extremely useful in determining the estimate for that future project. The information on the individual work item file form stays current by continuous updating from new projects. In addition, because the information is productivity data rather than unit cost data, it probably will be current for a relatively long period of time. Productivity information is much less sensitive to change across time than unit cost information.

It should be noted that individual work item file forms are used to collect data from several projects. As such, they differ from the forms previously described that collect data for a specific project. Therefore, the work item file forms are stored and filed in a different manner from the previous forms. In particular, the individual work item file forms can be stored and filed as a group in an individual binder. Specific data regarding a work item can then be traced by merely turning to the specific form. As with work item codes, the firm probably will want to establish codes for specific jobs so it can cross-reference the entries in the work item files to the specific job binders. The form that we have discussed provides space for indicating a code for a specific job. These codes can be designed in many ways, although one with significance aids communication. For example, the job code may indicate in some manner the location of the job and perhaps the year in which the job is either started or completed.

The entire project-management system that has been described and illustrated in Figures 10.4–10.11 repeats itself as the firm undertakes new projects. Data for the new projects come from the performance of past projects while data from ongoing projects is input to the past project data. The cycle is a continuing one. As the firm continues to utilize the system, the data that is part of it becomes more accurate and reliable.

The project-management system described in Figure 10.5 is now complete. Various miscellaneous forms may be designed to supplement the system; for example, the firm may want to design a change order form or an estimate recap form that includes overhead and profits.

The entire system is keyed to productivity; that is, much of the estimating and controlling function is tied to documentation of labor hours rather than labor cost. The benefit of this procedure has been discussed; however, it may be useful for the firm to have a cross-check on a payroll cost to the system of labor hours' documentation. This cost-check can be made easily by adding the labor hours and multiplying by the relevant rate. The result should be a dollar value equal to the dollar value of payroll cost of the individual labor type. This provides a procedure for checking to determine that the payroll function and the estimating and control functions are being performed without error. Differences in labor dollars as documented in the labor hour system versus the payroll process should be investigated and corrected.

11
SELECTION OF COMPUTER SOFTWARE AND APPLICATIONS

WHY THE CONSTRUCTION FIRM IS DEPENDENT ON COMPUTER IMPLEMENTATION

The construction industry and construction firm is in great part an information collection, information processing, and information interpretation business. In order to successfully plan and subsequently control the construction process, the construction firm must collect, process, and interpret vast amounts of information and data. In fact, one might define a construction firm as a manager of information.

The amount of information and data that is part of the construction contracting process is substantial. The fact that the contractor employs a large number of craftsmen results in a complex and time consuming payroll process. The management of the payroll data and information is made more complex by the fact that the construction firm experiences considerable employee turnover, and by the fact that the on-site craftsmen might be employed at numerous locations, perhaps each of which requires different wage scales and payroll deductions.

Owing to the relatively large number of vendors from which a construction firm purchases material or services, the firm's accounts payable system entails a considerable amount of accounts and data entries. One might argue that an effective handling of a construction firm's accounts payable function is in itself a full time job.

General ledger accounting, including payroll, accounts payable, and receivables, is not unique to the construction firm. However, the fact that the contractor's production process is decentralized (projects are constructed at numerous varied site locations) compounds the difficulty of these accounting tasks.

The information needs of the construction firm are not limited to the accounting functions. To be profitable, a construction firm must prepare accurate project estimates, schedules, and cost and time control duties. Each of these tasks requires a significant amount of data/information collection, processing, and interpretation.

The task of data and information management has often overwhelmed the construction firm. The fact that most construction firms are small, closely held companies has resulted in many firms being unable to cope with adequate and necessary data collection and processing. Instead, the construction firm has on occasion focused more on the marketing and sales function and the necessary task of production. Given the firm's insufficient attention to the record keeping and data/information processing aspect of its business, the construction firm has often fallen victim to financial loss on a project and even financial ruin as a firm.

The implementation of the computer and accompanying software has given the construction firm a potential tool for the efficient handling of the vast amount of information that is part of the business. A computer by itself does not solve the information handling tasks of the construction firm. It only provides a tool for processing, manipulating, storing, and printing information. One should remember an often quoted characteristic of the computer: garbage in and garbage out!

While the computer and accompanying software is only a tool, not a solution, for the construction firm, it has and will play an increasing role in the success of construction firms. The increase in computer technology and decreased cost of hardware and software has resulted in the computer becoming affordable to even the small construction firm.

GENERAL LEDGER COMPUTERIZED ACCOUNTING

There is probably no firm that needs accurate and timely accounting than the construction firm. The financial accounting function has been computerized by many construction firms. The computer provides numerous advantages in regard to financial accounting. In addition to eliminating paperwork, computerizing the general ledger process speeds up the process of generating financial statements as well as improving the accuracy of the results. Through computers and telecommunication technology, the construction firm can input data directly from distant job sites and forward timely job cost reports to the job sites in a matter of seconds.

Financial accounting entails the following:

- General ledger accounting
- Accounts payable
- Accounts receivable
- Payroll accounting
- Job costing

The payroll and accounts payable functions are especially troublesome to the construction firm. The large number of transactions for each of these two functions results in a need for considerable personnel time; time that can be reduced significantly through computerization.

There is an abundant number of vendor software available to the construction firm to perform general ledger accounting. An appraisal of alternative vendors and their software should be performed. To aid in this process of vendor selection, the construction firm can utilize the vendor selection analysis form shown in Figure 11.1.

Criteria	Maximum Points	Vendor 1	Vendor 2	Vendor 3	Vendor 4
Application Software					
Job cost reporting	200				
Payroll	100				
Accounts payable	50				
General ledger-financial reporting	30				
Accounts receivable	10				
Subcontractor control	60				
TOTAL	450				
Software					
Installation support	50				
User training	40				
Documentation	30				
Continuing support	40				
Firm size and stability	10				
Industry experience	30				
TOTAL	200				
Hardware					
Installation support	30				
Expansion potential	70				
Equipment performance	50				
Ease of operation	50				
Equipment maintenance	50				
Data communication capability	50				
TOTAL	300				

Figure 11.1

PROJECT MANAGEMENT SOFTWARE

To successfully manage the construction project, the construction firm has to perform several project management functions to include the following:

- Estimating
- Scheduling
- Job Cost Control
- Productivity Measurement and Improvement
- Equipment Management

While many construction firms have already computerized their financial accounting (although they may need to update it), a lessor number of construction firms have computerized all of the above project management functions.

Estimating

Estimating entails the preparation of a bid by taking off project work quantities and determining the cost of labor, material, equipment, subcontractors, and various types of overhead that are needed to put the work in place. The estimating is a time consuming function and one that entails much room for error given all the data processing that is part of the function. The use of a computer can improve both the accuracy and the amount of time it takes to prepare a project estimate.

The computer and accompanying computer software can assist estimating by means of the following:

- Computer aided design (CAD) programs
- Process math calculations and formula
- Enable the build up of data bases of past performances that should improve the forecasting and costing of estimates
- Enable "what if" analysis to study the estimate under different assumed future events

CAD applications not only enable the user to prepare computerized drawings for a project, but also enable the "reading" of the drawings to perform a computerized quantity take-off. This latter application, performing a computerized take-off of quantities is just beginning to become reality for construction firms.

As with most software, there are many vendors that supply CAD programs. However, one vendor, AutoCAD dominates the industry.

The process of using a computer to perform math calculations, build up a data base, and perform what if analysis can be performed with two different approaches to computer software. The construction firm can choose to go to what is referred to as general application software, or industry software. Approximately half of the construction firms using computers for estimating have chosen the general application software approach and half have chosen the industry software approach.

Examples of general application software include programs like EXCEL, LOTUS, ACCESS. Using these programs, the construction firm configures these general application templates to meet the firms needs and current practices. On the other hand, the firm can choose to purchase industry designed software like TIMBERLINE, WINEST, etc. Using these industry programs, the construction firm follows the designed programs in preparing their estimates.

There are arguments for and against each of these options for performing computerized estimating. Some of the plusses and minuses are summarized below:

Issue	**General Application Programs**	**Industry Programs**
Can custom design to meet current practices of the firm	Flexible to enable this but requires time and knowledge of programs	More difficult to do in that programs are pre-designed
Time to set up	Requires considerable set up time	Often ready to go after little training
Knowledge of computer needed	Need to be fairly knowledgeable about how to customize templates	Little computer knowledge required; just follow instructions.
Able to build historical data base	This is one of the primary benefits of these programs	Vendors are starting to provide limited capability
Cost	Software inexpensive. Must consider time to format.	Software more expensive but programs ready to run

If the construction firm chooses to go the industry software direction for estimating, they still must sort through the many vendors that supply these industry programs. Included in the issues that should be evaluated for these multiple vendors are the following:

- Number of work packages the program can process
- The levels of breakdown that can be used, packages, tasks, types of costs, etc.
- Historical data base that is part to the program
- Ability to build historical data base

- Flexibility of program to different types of work performed
- Ability of program to interface with other programs (scheduling, CAD, cost control, etc.)
- Cost of programs
- Maintenance and updates available

Project Planning and Scheduling

Project planning and scheduling techniques to include the critical path method (CPM) have been available to the construction industry for more than thirty years. In the early years of their use (60's and 70's) the plans and schedules and accompanying calculations were performed manually. When the planning and scheduling exercise was performed manually, one could argue that the benefit to cost ratio of the entire process of preparing and using a schedule was poor and maybe not even justified.

There is now an abundance of computer software available to significantly increase the benefit cost ratio of the planning and scheduling functions. Inexpensive programs to include Primavera, Suretrack, and Microsoft Project enable the construction firm to:

- Plot as planned project schedules
- Perform CPM calculations and determine activity float
- Plot and manage resources
- Plot and manage cash flow
- Update project in a timely and accurate manner

Ideally the computerized scheduling program interfaces with the construction firm's estimating function such that the two functions can be performed in conjunction with one another. Unfortunately, most computer software vendors provide either estimating or scheduling software, not both. However, many of the vendors have taken steps to enable their programs to be interfaced with other functions; estimating with scheduling or vice versa.

Computerized software programs for construction planning and scheduling vary in price from a few hundred dollars to the thousands of dollars. The more expensive programs normally enable the user to input more project activities and also typically have more algorithms in regard to resource management.

Some of the factors to consider in selecting a planning and scheduling software program include:

- Number of activities that can be input
- Ability to update the program
- Resource algorithms available
- Popularity of program with clients (project owners, designers, and subcontractors)
- Ability to interface with estimating software
- Ability to interface with control function

- Ease of data entry
- Number and type of reports available

Because project schedules are often communicated and shared with the project owner and designer, an important criteria is to select scheduling software that is compatible if not the same as their system. Similar to the CAD application, the planning and scheduling software availability is dominated by only a few vendors even though there are many on the market.

Job Control Software

This job control function is one of inputting job site data (labor time, quantities in place) and producing job cost control reports that report on the status of a project and project overruns or underruns.

The computerization of the job control function is made complex by the fact that often the vendors that supply general ledger software include a job control module and the vendors that supply project management estimating software also provide a job control module. Given that the vendors that supply general ledger accounting software and vendors that supply project management software don't supply both has led to many construction firms having two stand alone job control computer systems.

Ideally the construction firm should select accounting software and project management software that integrates such that there is not confusion or redundancy in the job control function. In recent years, more and more vendors are attempting to either provide both accounting and project management programs or to as least develop software where their stand alone accounting or project management program can be interfaced with that of another vendor.

FUTURE APPLICATIONS OF COMPUTERS FOR CONSTRUCTION FIRMS

Computer technology to include hardware and especially software is a rapidly changing process. Applications unheard of only ten years ago are now in place in many firms. The same will be true of the future. The construction firm needs to keep monitoring the availability of software and potential applications that provide the firm a favorable benefit to cost usage. Included in future software applications are the following:

- The use of CAD programs for complete take-off of project work quantities.
- Enabling of correlation estimating via the keeping of historical data and the factors unique to the data record that enables the estimator to custom design his estimate to the factors that are expected for the new project.
- Enable the estimator to keep the risk of the expected productivity for a work item via the filling of probability distributions to past data. This will also

enable the estimator to calculate the risk of the project estimate as well as the expected cost of the project.

- The determination of profit as a function of project risk. This entails the development of a computer model that identifies the risk elements in a project bid and adjusts the profit to be included in the bid to reflect the summation of the risk.
- Through the collection of historical data, the determination of overhead formulae for applying overhead to projects as a function of the type of project, the duration of the project, the percentage of labor, material, equipment, and subcontractor cost in the estimate.
- Full integration of accounting, scheduling, estimating, and cost control functions.
- Simulation games that enable the construction firm to simulate a project before it's occurrence with the objective of developing an action plan of performance and as a means of training job site personnel.
- Development of cost and productivity functions for individual work tasks that enable the construction firm to determine productivity and cost as a function of crew size, environmental factors, amount of work to be done, etc.
- The use of artificial intelligence programs that enable the on-site manager to determine how to best manage the resources available to him on any day.
- The use of computer technology with bar codes and video camera technology to automate the accounting function to include monitoring and costing of on-site workers to cost codes, the preparation of the payroll, the preparation of cost reports, etc.
- Multi-media applications.

USING THE COMPUTER AS A GRAPHICS TOOL

Given the graphics capability of a computer, one of the more obvious applications one might think of is using the computer to read the construction drawings (blueprints) to actually perform the quantity takeoff function. Given the many hours a contractor expends performing the takeoff function, this reading of the construction drawings to determine takeoff quantities would appear to be a high-benefit computer application.

It is in fact possible to program a computer, via the use of a graphics pen, to actually read the construction drawings and determine quantities. However, at the present time, there are two major problems relevant to making this a cost-effective application of computers to the construction industry. For one, given any degree of construction project complexity, the computer software program that needs to be programmed to read the vast amounts of different types of materials and work items that would be included on a single set of construction drawings would be extremely complex and long.

The end result would be that it would take literally thousands of hours to develop a flexible software program to read even relatively simple construction drawings. Perhaps even more importantly, the size and complexity of such software programs would require the use of relatively large computers with extensive computer memory capacity. Such a computer is relatively expensive; a computer that may be outside the reach of the average-sized contractor.

A second difficulty of developing or applying a computer software program to read construction drawings relates to the wide range of variation in the symbols and style various project designers use in preparing construction drawings. One might argue that no two architects prepare construction drawings using the exact same symbols or style. The end result is that it is difficult, if not impossible, to develop a computer software program that would successfully be able to read each and every set of construction drawings prepared by the many project designers that prepare drawings.

While the use of the computer as a graphics tool to read the drawings has not, and may not, gain widespread popularity, the use of a computer to actually prepare a design and an accompanying set of drawings has been a highly viable application. Most computer-aided design (CAD) has evolved in the manufacturing industries. For example, via the use of a computer and appropriate computer software, an automobile designer prepares futuristic car designs that minimize wind resistance, maximize fuel economy, etc. CAD is a fast growing application of computers.

Perhaps one of the advantages of using a computer for CAD is that it results in more uniform sets of construction drawings in that several designers would utilize the same CAD software program. If this trend continues, then perhaps one of the concerns about using the computer as a tool for reading drawings will diminish. In particular, the more the trend continues toward a CAD uniform set of construction drawings, the easier and more cost-effective it becomes to use the computer to read a set of drawings to determine the quantity takeoff quantities. However, we are years away, if it indeed ever happens, from witnessing the use of a computer as a tool to read drawings. While capable to do the task, the low benefit/cost ratio of the application may limit its usefulness.

While most CAD applications have been limited to the preparation of manufacturing-industry-type applications, some project designers (architects) have taken to the use of a computer to prepare construction drawings. It is not difficult to foresee the day when the majority, if not all, construction drawings are prepared via a computer and a graphics pen.

LEVELS OF COMPUTER LANGUAGE

In describing the various levels of computer software languages, it is important to remember the languages of the sender and the receiver, i.e., the computer user and the computer hardware. One can assume that the language of the user is English (or some other spoken language). On the other hand, the main "brain" of a computer, the microprocessor, is a binary number system consisting of 0 and 1.

Given the two different communication capabilities, there is a need for a communication interface so that the user can write computer software programs. Let us start our discussion of this interface by proceeding from the language of the computer to the language of the user.

As noted above, the computer microprocessor can only understand binary numbering. However, by using various combinations of 0s and 1s, various "words" and "instructions" can be communicated. This combining of 0s and 1s to form words and instructions makes up what is referred to as *machine language*. If the user had to write computer software programs using machine language, the process would be very time consuming and difficult. For example, a few relatively simple computer instructions would require the user to specify the following machine language software codes:

Instruction	*Machine Software Code*
Get a number from memory	10110110
Get another number from memory	01101101
Add the two numbers	11110101
Place the total in memory	00110110

To appreciate the difficulty of writing a machine language software program, we should note that any meaningful software program would likely entail writing hundreds or even thousands of machine language instructions and words. The task would be extremely difficult given that the user does not speak a "binary language" or has memorized the hundreds of difficult computer instructions or words.

While difficult, the fact remains that in the early years of computers, the user (called a programmer) did have to write programs using machine language. Fortunately, it is no longer necessary to understand machine language to write a program. This brings us to the next "level" of computer languages, *assembly* language. This level of computer language and the others are illustrated in Figure 11.2.

In an assembly language a short term or phrase takes the place of the string of 0 and 1 that characterize machine language. The following examples illustrate a few assembly language instructions (a program) that add two numbers:

Instruction	*Assembly Language*
Load a number from memory	LO,A,1
Load another number from memory	LO,B,10
Add the two numbers together	ADD
Place the total in a new memory location	LO,C

An assembler program internal to the computer acts as an interface between the assembly language and the machine language. In effect this go-between program changes assembly language instructions into machine language.

While assembly language is an improvement (relative to machine language) enabling a computer programmer to understand instructions like LO, ADD, etc., the language is still relatively difficult and time consuming in regard to writing a software program. Given this time and difficulty, computer specialists sought yet another level of computer software language. This effort resulted in what we today commonly refer to as *high-level languages*. High-level languages are close to (but not exactly the same as) the English language of the user. A computer

Machine language—for example, 10110110
The language by which a computer "thinks" and "stores" data.

Assembly language—for example, LO, ADD
An "intermediate" language between machine language and various high-level languages.

BASIC—for example, PRINT 23 + 56
A high-level language commonly used in personal computers. Its popularity stems from its similarity to the English language.

FORTRAN—A high-level language used primarily for engineering/scientific applications.

COBOL—A high-level language used primarily for business-type applications.

Figure 11.2 Levels and Uses of Various Computer Languages

has the ability to convert high-level languages to an assembly language, which in turn is converted to machine language.

There are several high-level languages in common use today, e.g., FORTRAN (an abbreviation for *FOR*mula *TRAN*slation) and COBOL (an abbreviation for *CO*mmon *B*usiness-*O*riented *L*anguage). However, by far the most common high-level language in use today is BASIC. BASIC is an abbreviation for *B*eginner's *A*ll-Purpose *S*ymbolic *I*nstruction *C*ode.

BASIC is easy to learn and use. A previous nonuser of a computer or a nonprogrammer can usually quickly learn how to use BASIC, including writing software programs with the language. Many off-the-shelf software programs are written in BASIC. Because of the popularity of the language, many computers are sold with a BASIC compiler built into the machine such that the user can write programs in BASIC without any complications. In other words, the computer has a program built into the machine that interprets BASIC words and instructions and converts them into machine language. This "compiler" program is built into the ROM (read-only memory) of the computer.

BASIC and other high-level languages are vast improvements on assembly and machine languages. It is much easier to understand, and most importantly, to write computer software programs using the high-level languages. For example, the following illustrates the previously noted computer software program to add two numbers using BASIC:

Instruction	*BASIC*
Get a number from memory	INPUT A
Get another number from memory	INPUT B
Add the two numbers and place the total in memory	C = A+B

Not only is it easier to understand BASIC because the words and instructions are similar to English, but there are usually far less computer statements or instructions necessary in BASIC relative to the same program written in assembly or machine languages. For example, a single BASIC instruction might represent two or three separate assembly language instructions.

The introduction of high-level languages and in particular BASIC, has enabled the noncomputer specialist to write his own application software and to modify off-the-shelf programs. It has become realistic for a construction firm to write its own software programs for estimating, scheduling, cost control, and some of the other applications of construction.

BASIC is not the only high-level language in use today. Specialty-type high-level languages in wide use include PASCAL, LOGO, and others. However, these languages are not that useful relative to construction industry applications. As such, the following discussion will be limited to BASIC and the illustration of programs written in BASIC.

In practice, there are several versions of BASIC. For example, the BASIC supplied with the IBM-PC is slightly different from the BASIC supplied with the Apple computer. However, the versions differ only ever so slightly. One might consider the different versions like different dialects of the English language. Usually, the computer programmer has little difficulty in adapting from one version of BASIC to the next.

With the intent of providing the fundamentals of BASIC, such that the reader might begin writing relatively simple construction industry software programs, or modify existing ones, this chapter will present somewhat of an overview of BASIC with an emphasis on words and instructions relative to construction industry applications.

EXAMPLE GENERAL LEDGER COMPUTER PROGRAM

To illustrate computer software programs that perform the entire financial accounting functions for a construction firm would likely require an entire book on just this topic. Software programs would need to perform general ledger functions, accounts receivable, accounts payable, payroll, and job costing. A computer program to do any one of these functions would in itself be long and complex.

While we will not illustrate programs that do each of the above-noted financial accounting functions, in Figure 11.3 we list a program written in BASIC that performs the general ledger functions. The program enables the user to set up general ledger accounts, enter financial transactions for the accounts, and print a trial balance or balance sheet. Sample output from the program is illustrated in Figure 11.4.

In the interest of presenting a relatively simple program that the reader can follow and understand, we have not concerned ourself with error routines or preferred instructions to the user that would normally be included in an off-the-shelf program.

```
10 CLS
20 INPUT "ENTER COMPANY NAME= ";NA$
30 INPUT "ENTER DATE= ";DA$
34 INPUT "ENTER C TO CONTINUE ";C$
35 CLS
40 GOSUB 200
50 GOSUB 400
60 CLS
70 PRINT "ENTER D: TO DISPLAY AN ACCOUNT"
80 PRINT "ENTER E: TO ENTER A FINANCIAL TRANSACTION"
90 PRINT "ENTER T: TO PRINT A WORKING TRIAL BALANCE"
100 PRINT "ENTER B: TO PRINT A BALANCE SHEET
110 PRINT "ENTER S: TO STOP/TERMINATE THE PROGRAM
120 INPUT CH$
130 IF (CH$="D") THEN GOSUB 600
140 IF (CH$="E") THEN GOSUB 800
150 IF (CH$="T") THEN GOSUB 1000
160 IF (CH$="B") THEN GOSUB 1200
170 IF (CH$="S") THEN 2000
180 CLS
190 GOTO 60
200 CLS
205 INPUT "ENTER NO. OF GENERAL LEDGER ACCOUNTS= ";N
210 INPUT "ENTER NO. OF ASSET ACCOUNTS= ";A
215 INPUT "ENTER NO. OF LIABILITY ACCOUNTS= ";L
220 INPUT "ENTER NO. OF EQUITY ACCOUNTS= ";Q
230 FOR J=1 TO N
235 CLS
240 PRINT "ENTER ACCOUNT NO. ";J;
245 INPUT N$(J)
250 PRINT "ENTER D IF DEBIT ACCOUNT OR C IF CREDIT ACCOUNT";
255 INPUT T$(J)
260 NEXT J
265 TA$="DEBIT"
270 TB$="CREDIT"
275 FA$="$$###,####.##"
280 FB$="$$###,####.##   $$###,####.##   $$###,####.##"
285 FC$="$$###,####.##   $$###,####.##"
290 FD$="----------------------------------------------
300 RETURN
400 CLS
402 D=0
405 PRINT "ACCOUNT BALANCES BEING INITIALIZED
410 PRINT "YOU WILL NOW INPUT ACCOUNT BALANCES FROM END OF PREVIOUS YEAR
411 INPUT "ENTER C TO CONTINUE ";C$
412 CLS
415 DIM AA(100,2)
416 DIM AB(100,2)
420 FOR K=1 TO N
425 CLS
430 PRINT N$(K);
435 IF (T$(K)="C") THEN 455
440 PRINT " ACCOUNT TYPE= ";TA$
445 INPUT "ENTER ACCOUNT BALANCE= ";AA(K,1)
447 AA(K,2)=0
450 GOTO 465
455 PRINT "ACCOUNT TYPE= ";TB$
460 INPUT "ENTER ACCOUNT BALANCE= ";AA(K,2)
462 AA(K,1)=0
465 NEXT K
470 PRINT "THE PROGRAM WILL NOW CHECK TO SEE IF THE DEBITS EQUAL THE CREDITS
472 INPUT "ENTER C TO CONTINUE ";C$
```

Figure 11.3 Sample Computer Program Written in BASIC for General Ledger Accounting

```
473 CLS
475 GOSUB 1500
478 IF (D=1) THEN 400
485 PRINT "THE PROGRAM WILL NOW CHECK TO SEE IF ASSETS=LIABILITIES PLUS NET WORT
H
486 INPUT "ENTER C TO CONTINUE ";C$
487 CLS
490 GOSUB 1600
495 IF (D=2) THEN 400
498 RETURN
600 CLS
605 GOSUB 700
608 GOSUB 1700
610 PRINT "DO YOU WANT TO PRINT MORE ACCOUNT NAMES?"
615 INPUT "ENTER Y OR N";CB$
620 IF (CB$="Y") THEN 600
625 RETURN
700 CLS
705 INPUT "ENTER NO. OF ACCOUNTS YOU WANT TO VIEW= ";NT
710 FOR R=1 TO NT
715 PRINT "NO.";R;"   ";N$(R)
720 NEXT R
725 INPUT "ENTER ACCOUNT NUMBER= ";ACC
730 RETURN
800 CLS
805 GOSUB 700
810 INPUT "ENTER D FOR DEBIT OR C FOR CREDIT ";CT$
815 INPUT "ENTER AMOUNT= ";AMT
820 IF (CT$="D") THEN AA(ACC,1)=AA(ACC,1)+AMT
825 IF (CT$="C") THEN AA(ACC,2)=AA(ACC,2)+AMT
830 INPUT "ENTER C TO INPUT OFFSETTING ACCOUNT ";C$
835 GOSUB 700
840 IF (CT$="D") THEN AA(ACC,2)=AA(ACC,2)+AMT
845 IF (CT$="C") THEN AA(ACC,1)=AA(ACC,1)+AMT
850 GOSUB 1500
852 INPUT "ENTER C TO CONTINUE ";C$
855 GOSUB 1600
860 RETURN
1000 CLS
1005 PRINT "TRIAL BALANCE"
1010 PRINT TAB(20);FD$
1015 PRINT "ACCOUNT";TAB(30);TA$;TAB(53);TB$
1020 T1=0
1025 T2=0
1030 FOR S=1 TO N
1035 IF AA(S,2)>AA(S,1) GOTO 1070
1040 PRINT N$(S);TAB(25);
1045 PRINT USING FC$;AA(S,1)-AA(S,2),0
1055 T1=AA(S,1)-AA(S,2)+T1
1060 GOTO 1090
1070 PRINT N$(S);TAB(25);
1075 PRINT USING FC$;0,AA(S,2)-AA(S,1)
1080 T2=AA(S,2)-AA(S,1)+T2
1090 NEXT S
1095 PRINT TAB(10);"TOTALS";TAB(25);
1100 PRINT USING FC$;T1,T2
1105 INPUT "ENTER C TO CONTINUE ";C$
1110 RETURN
1200 CLS
1205 PRINT "BALANCE SHEET"
```

Figure 11.3 *Continued*

```
1210 FOR I=1 TO N
1215 AB(I,1)=AA(I,1)
1220 AB(I,2)=AA(I,2)
1225 M$(I)=N$(I)
1230 NEXT I
1235 CLS
1240 PRINT TAB(15);NA$
1245 PRINT TAB(15);"BALANCE SHEET"
1250 PRINT TAB(15);DA$
1255 PRINT " ASSETS"
1260 AF=0
1265 FOR I=1 TO A
1270 PRINT M$(I);TAB(25)
1275 PRINT USING FA$;AB(I,1)-AB(I,2)
1280 AF=AF+AB(I,1)-AB(I,2)
1285 NEXT I
1290 PRINT "    TOTAL ASSETS ";TAB(35);
1295 PRINT USING FA$;AF
1300 PRINT "  LIABILITIES "
1305 LF=0
1308 R=A +L
1310 FOR I=(1 + A) TO R
1315 PRINT M$(I);TAB(25);
1320 PRINT USING FA$;AB(I,2)-AB(I,1)
1325 LF=LF + AB(I,2)-AB(I,1)
1330 NEXT I
1335 PRINT "  TOTAL LIABILITIES ";TAB(35);
1340 PRINT USING FA$;LF
1345 PRINT ""
1350 PRINT " OWNER'S EQUITY"
1355 EQ=0
1360 FOR I=A+L+1 TO N
1365 PRINT M$(I);TAB(25);
1370 PRINT USING FA$;AB(I,2)-AB(I,1)
1375 EQ=EQ+AB(I,2)-AB(I,1)
1380 NEXT I
1385 PRINT "  TOTAL OWNER'S EQUITY ";TAB(35);
1390 PRINT USING FA$;EQ
1395 PRINT ""
1400 PRINT "TOTAL LIABILITIES + OWNER'S EQUITY= ";TAB(50)
1405 PRINT USING FA$;LF +EQ
1410 INPUT "ENTER C TO CONTINUE ";C$
1420 RETURN
1500 T1=0
1505 T2=0
1510 FOR LA=1 TO N
1515 T1=T1+AA(LA,1)
1520 T2=T2+AA(LA,2)
1525 NEXT LA
1530 PRINT "DEBITS= ";
1535 PRINT USING FA$;T1
1540 PRINT "CREDITS= ";
1545 PRINT USING FA$;T2
1550 IF (T1=T2) THEN RETURN
1555 PRINT ""
1560 PRINT "DEBITS TO NOT EQUAL CREDITS"
1565 INPUT "ENTER C TO REENTER ACCOUNT BALANCES ";C$
1570 D=1

1575 RETURN
```

Figure 11.3 *Continued*

```
1600 AS=0
1605 FOR M= 1 TO A
1610 AS=AS +(AA(M,1)-AA(M,2))
1615 NEXT M
1620 LI=0
1625 FOR M=1+A TO A+L
1630 LI=LI+ (AA(M,2)-AA(M,1))
1635 NEXT M
1640 OQ=0
1645 FOR M=1+A+L TO N
1650 OQ=OQ+(AA(M,2)-AA(M,1))
1655 NEXT M
1660 PRINT "      ASSETS      LIABILITIES      OWNER'S EQUITY
1665 PRINT USING FB$;AS,LI,OQ
1667 INPUT "ENTER C TO CONTINUE ";C$
1670 IF (AS=LI+OQ) THEN RETURN
1675 PRINT "ASSETS ARE NOT EQUAL TO LIABILITIES PLUS OWNER'S EQUITY
1680 D=2
1685 INPUT "ENTER C TO REENTER ACCOUNT BALANCES
1690 RETURN
1700 CLS
1705 PRINT N$(ACC)
1710 PRINT TAB(7);FD$
1720 PRINT TAB(10);TA$;TAB(31);TB$
1725 PRINT TAB(7);FD$
1730 PRINT USING FC$;AA(ACC,1),AA(ACC,2)
1735 PRINT TAB(7);FD$
1740 PRINT "BALANCE= ";
1745 PRINT USING FC$;ABS(AA(ACC,1)-AA(ACC,2))
1750 PRINT " ";
1755 IF (AA(ACC,1)>AA(ACC,2)) THEN PRINT TA$
1760 IF (AA(ACC,2)>AA(ACC,1)) THEN PRINT TB$
1770 RETURN
2000 CLS
2005 PRINT "THIS IS THE END OF THE PROGRAM"
```

Figure 11.3 *Continued*

While we will not discuss every line of the program illustrated in Figure 11.3, we will now discuss several of the unique and more important parts of the program. Perhaps the one unique aspect of the general ledger program listed in Figure 11.4 is the use of many subroutines. A subroutine is used by a programmer if a certain routine (the instructions in the subroutine) occurs in several places in the overall program. Rather than repeat the routines several times, the programmer has the program "branch" to the subroutine when the program wants to execute the instructions. The subroutine is *called* by a GOSUB instruction.

Let us now describe how the overall program works. After having the program user input the project name and date in lines 20 and 30, the program branches to subroutines 200 and 400. In subroutine 200 (lines 200 through 300) the user informs the program about the number of accounts, if they are primarily debit or credit balance accounts, and with the use of the loop in lines 230 through 260 inputs the general ledger account names. Various variables that will subsequently be used to format output are also initialized in subroutine 200.

```
TRIAL BALANCE
                              ------------------------------------------------
ACCOUNT                              DEBIT                    CREDIT
CASH                              $9,000.00           $0.00
ACC. REC                          $5,000.00           $0.00
EQUIPMENT                         $2,000.00           $0.00
ACC. PAYABLE                          $0.00       $3,000.00
NOTE REC.                             $0.00       $2,000.00
LOAN DUE                              $0.00       $6,000.00
RET. EARNINGS                         $0.00       $5,000.00
          TOTALS                 $16,000.00      $16,000.00
ENTER C TO CONTINUE ?


             GOODWORK CONSTRUCTION
             BALANCE SHEET
             4-24-1984
 ASSETS
CASH                          $9,000.00
ACC. REC                      $5,000.00
EQUIPMENT                     $2,000.00
   TOTAL ASSETS                          $16,000.00
  LIABILITIES
ACC. PAYABLE                  $3,000.00
NOTE REC.                     $2,000.00
LOAN DUE                      $6,000.00
  TOTAL LIABILITIES                      $11,000.00

 OWNER'S EQUITY
RET. EARNINGS                 $5,000.00
  TOTAL OWNER'S EQUITY                    $5,000.00

TOTAL LIABILITIES + OWNER'S EQUITY=                          $16,000.00
ENTER C TO CONTINUE ?
```

Figure 11.4 Sample Reports from General Ledger Program

Subroutine 400 enables the user to input account balances for each of the previously defined account names. The account balances would be entered as zeros in the initial run. After the initial run, the account balances received as output from the last run would be input.

The reader should note that the program illustrated is intentionally simple such that we can easily follow it. To be an effective program for general ledger accounting, several modifications would be needed. For example, as it now stands, the user would have to redefine the general ledger accounts each time he runs the program.

To be more effective as a program, we would want to use data file programming to "store" the setup account names on a data disk. After the first run of the program we would then have the program read the data disk (on which would be the account names). This would eliminate our need to enter them each time. The same type of programming would be done in regard to the account balances. By storing the account balances on a data disk, we would not have to reenter them each time we ran the program. While we will not discuss the storing of data on a data disk in this chapter, it will be illustrated in another sample program in a later chapter.

Once the user enters the account balances in subroutine 400, the program branches to subroutines 1500 and 1600. In subroutine 1500 the program checks to determine that the sum total of all inputted debit amounts equals the sum total of all inputted credit amounts. Similarly, in subroutine 1600, the program checks that the sum of the financial entries for the asset accounts equal the liability plus the owner's equity accounts. Assuming that both of these subroutines find that entries "do balance," the program execution is returned to subroutine 400, which in turn returns to line 60.

The user is then given an option menu of displaying accounts, entering financial transactions, printing a working trial balance, or printing a balance sheet. Let us now describe the purpose of each of these program options.

If the user selects to display an account, the program branches to subroutine 600. Subroutine 600 in turn branches to subroutine 700 and 1700. In subroutine 700 the user is given an opportunity to view the previously entered general ledger account names. He also selects the account number for which he wants a display.

The program then branches to subroutine 1700. This subroutine prints the debit and credit balances for the selected account and also prints the net balance amount. After completing this, the program returns to subroutine 600, which in turn returns the user to the option menu.

If the user selects to enter financial transactions, the program branches to subroutine 800. This subroutine in turn first branches to subroutine 700, which again enables the user to identify the account name for which he wants to enter a transaction. After identifying the account, the program returns to subroutine 800. This subroutine then requests the user to enter the financial transaction. The reader should note that after inputting the transaction, subroutine 800, by branching back to subroutine 700, requests the name of the offsetting account. The reader will note that for every debit entry for an account there must also be an account credited. After a transaction is entered, subroutine 800 branches to subroutines 1500 and 1600 again to check that debits equal credits, and assets equal liabilities plus owner's equity. Subroutine 800 then returns the user to the option menu.

If the user selects to print a trial balance, the program branches to subroutine 1000. This subroutine accesses no other subroutines. Instead, via the program loop in lines 1030 to 1090, the program prints the account balances for each general ledger account. The totals are also printed and the user is returned to the options menu.

If the user selects to print a balance sheet, the program branches to subroutine 1200. Subroutine 1200 also executes without accessing another subroutine. Three program loops (lines 1265–1285, lines 1310–1330, and lines 1360–1380) print the name and account balances for the assets, liabilities, and owner's equity accounts. The subroutine then returns to the options menu. The user can select to stop/terminate the program from the options menu.

The program listed in Figure 11.3 is designed to print/display all reports on the computer menu. Modifications would be necessary to yield hardcopy printer reports such as the reports illustrated in Figure 11.4.

INTEGRATED PROJECT MANAGEMENT USING THE MICROCOMPUTER

One of the biggest advantages of using the microcomputer in the construction industry is its function as a tool for the construction estimating task. The microcomputer's use in estimating includes performing routine estimating calculations and conversions, aiding in the actual taking-off of quantities from the drawings, performing of risk analysis, and providing the constructor an almost limitless data storage capacity for filing historical data to include the keeping of past labor productivity data.

This later application—using the microcomputer to store and process historical labor productivity data—is especially useful to the construction contractor (or for that matter to the designer or project owner doing the estimating). It becomes possible to store years of past project data, and subsequently access it, on a single data disk that is inserted into the microcomputer disk drive.

The computer has enabled what is referred to as integrated estimating and project management. In addition, the microcomputer enables what the author refers to as the "fifth" level of construction estimating. Before describing such an application, let us first describe what is meant by integrated estimating and project management.

The process or concept of integrated estimating and project management simply means that project estimating, planning and scheduling, and subsequent cost control are performed in conjunction with one another. This is done by using a common unit of measure. To illustrate this common unit of work that is commonly referred to as a common data base, consider the following example:

WORK ITEM	CONCRETE WALL FORMS
1. Quantity take-off	320,000 sfca (sq ft. of contact area)
2. Assumed productivity	8.0 manhours/100 sfca
3. Calc. of req. manhours	320,000/8/100 = 400 manhours
4. Assumed labor rate	$15.00/manhour
5. Calc. est. labor cost	(400 mh) ($15.00/mh) = $6,000.00
6. Assumed crew size	5 workers
7. Calc. duration	(400 mh)/(5mh/hour) = 80 hours
8. Calc. duration (days)	(80 hours)/(8 hours/day) = 10 days
9. Assumed progress after several days	160,000 sfca in place 300 manhours expended
10. Calc. percent complete	160,000 sfca/320,000 sfca = 50% complete
11. Percent of labor effort expended	300 mh/400 mh = 75%

12. Proj. labor total hours	300 mh/.50 = 600 manhours
13. Projected labor overrun	600 mh − 400 mh = 200 manhours
14. Projected labor cost overrun	(200 mh) ($15/mh) = $3,000.00

The above process illustrates the use of a common unit of measurement, thereby integrating several project management functions. An estimate is prepared in step 5; a duration for a bar chart or a CPM schedule is prepared in step 8; and a cost control report is prepared in steps 10 through 14. After the project is complete, a new productivity would be calculated (manhours per 100 sfca) and this productivity might be used in step 2 the next time the work process is estimated. The process repeats itself each time the work item is estimated, scheduled, and controlled.

Before discussing what was previously referred to as the fifth level of estimating, let us now give an overview of the integrated computer software system illustrated as Figure 11.5. The integrated software system illustrated consists of four interrelated software programs. They are illustrated by the four disks shown with a single line. The programs are referred to as the WORK ITEM HISTORY PROGRAM, PREPARE ESTIMATE PROGRAM, the PROJECT SCHEDULING PROGRAM, and the PROJECT CONTROL PROGRAM.

The WORK ITEM HISTORY PROGRAM enables a firm to create what the author refers to as one's own Dodge Manual. The program is used to define work items that are to be part of the estimating system, e.g., concrete wall footings. This program is also used to store past productivity data from previously completed projects. This data is stored on a data disk (illustrated via the double line data disk on the right of Figure 11.5). It is possible to keep numerous past occurrences of labor productivity for a work item on a single data disk. Also, it is possible to keep this data for several hundred different work items on a single data disk. At any point in time, several different types of historical data reports are available as noted in the upper right corner of the illustration.

When faced with the preparation of a new estimate, a constructor would then load the PREPARE ESTIMATE PROGRAM. Here the constructor would input labor rates, productivity, and material costs using the same common units or work items previously set up with the WORK ITEM HISTORY PROGRAM. Most importantly, as the estimator prepared an estimate using the PREPARE PROGRAM, the estimator could access the historical work item data disk and view historical data. For example, when estimating labor productivity for a proposed project, the estimator can easily access (by hitting a few keys on the keyboard) years of past productivity data for the work item. In effect, one program (the PREPARE PROGRAM) accesses data prepared via another program (the WORK ITEM PROGRAM).

Immediately after preparing an estimate (and printing the several estimate reports noted in the lower right corner of the illustration), the user of the computer system would load the SCHEDULE PROGRAM. Given the concept of a common unit of measurement or work item, the user would input what work item (or activity) follows another, and how many workers are to be assigned to

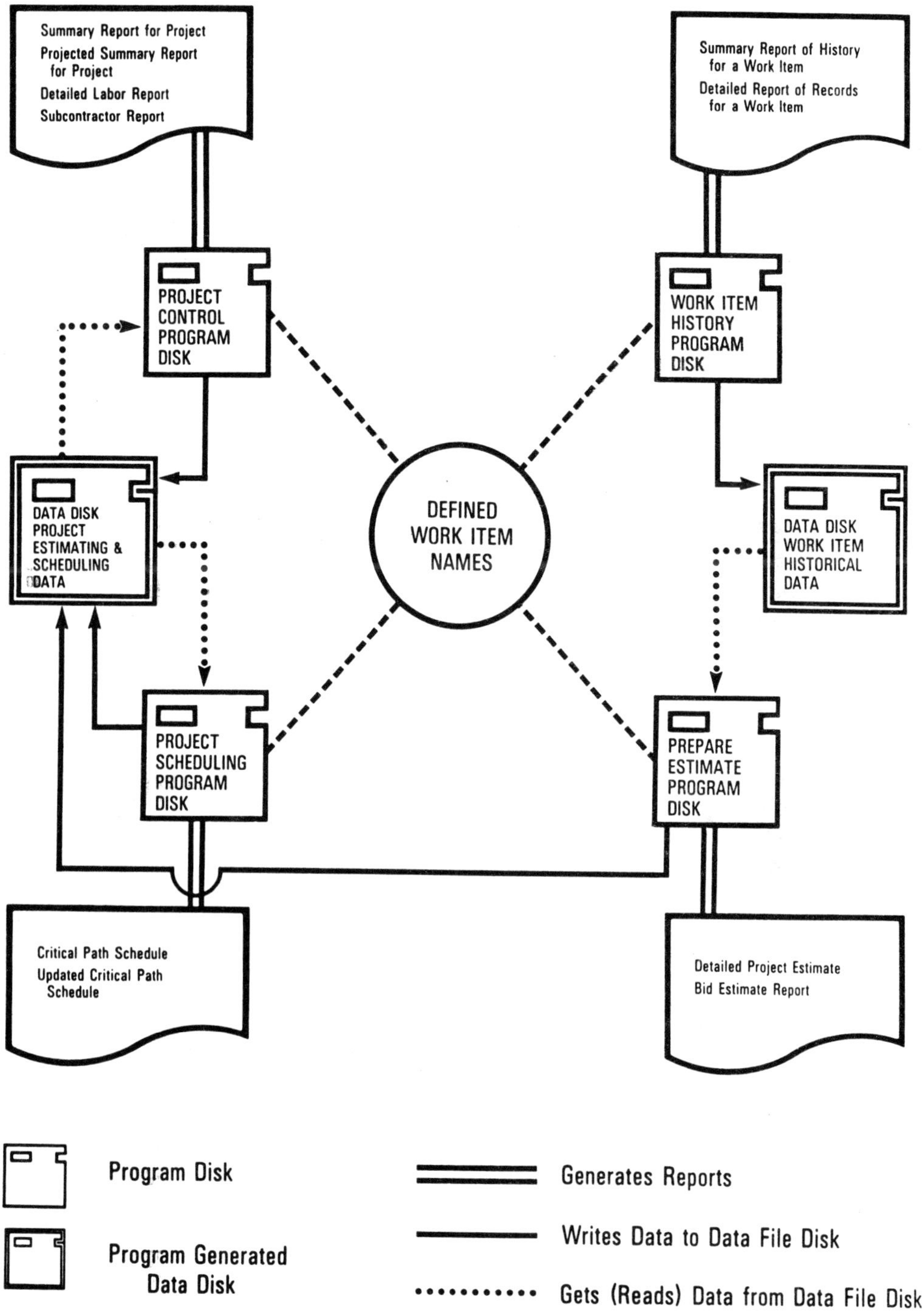
Summary Report for Project
Projected Summary Report for Project
Detailed Labor Report
Subcontractor Report
Summary Report of History for a Work Item
Detailed Report of Records for a Work Item
PROJECT CONTROL PROGRAM DISK
WORK ITEM HISTORY PROGRAM DISK
DATA DISK PROJECT ESTIMATING & SCHEDULING DATA
DEFINED WORK ITEM NAMES
DATA DISK WORK ITEM HISTORICAL DATA
PROJECT SCHEDULING PROGRAM DISK
PREPARE ESTIMATE PROGRAM DISK
Critical Path Schedule
Updated Critical Path Schedule
Detailed Project Estimate
Bid Estimate Report
Program Disk
Program Generated Data Disk
Generates Reports
Writes Data to Data File Disk
Gets (Reads) Data from Data File Disk

Figure 11.5

each work item. The SCHEDULE PROGRAM would then access the PROJECT ESTIMATING AND SCHEDULING DATA DISK shown (prepared via the PREPARE PROGRAM), read the estimated quantity of work, assumed labor productivity, and calculate the durations for the activities. The SCHEDULE PROGRAM would then be used to print the critical path calculations and an overall schedule.

If the contractor was successful in obtaining the project via his bid estimate, he would then attempt to control the project via the PROJECT CONTROL PROGRAM. This program would read the estimate data from the data disk and use the previously prepared estimating data as the basis of the control process. Labor hours expended and work completed on a work item basis would be input to the program on an ongoing basis. The various reports noted in the upper left corner of the illustration could be printed. These reports would set out labor overruns, problem areas, and projected profit on a work item basis.

When a project is complete, the system user would load the WORK ITEM HISTORY PROGRAM and input the past project data, thereby increasing the data base. The process would continue each time the constructor estimated another project.

In addition to illustrating an integrated estimating and project management system, the described program enables what we previously referred to as the fifth level of estimating. Let us describe this. The only meaningful way to predict the future is to analyze the past. Let us consider labor productivity. The author proposes that a contractor can be categorized into one of the following four types in regard to historical labor productivity:

1. The firm does not even have a total of carpenter (a sample craft) hours expended for the previous year.
2. The firm has a sum total of carpenter hours expended last year as a firm.
3. The firm has collected the total carpenter hours expended per job on projects it has completed.
4. The firm has collected historical labor productivity data on a work item basis (e.g., hours for placing wall forms).

One might argue that we've listed the four categories from worst to best. Perhaps only level four—collecting data on a work item basis—is meaningful for estimating future projects. However, given the fact that no two projects or work environments are the same, even this level (the fourth) might be criticized as being relatively weak.

The computer system described enables a fifth level of estimating. As historical labor productivity data is stored via the WORK ITEM HISTORY PROGRAM, the user can input "correlation" data such as the weather conditions, size of project, crew size, who the superintendent was, etc. Given the almost infinite data storage capacity of a microcomputer, this correlation data can be stored with the historical labor productivity data. The computer user can then "match" his expected job conditions with a previous historical record, and ask the computer the expected productivity, given the expected conditions. This better "matching" of the conditions should enable an improved potential for an accurate estimate of labor productivity—a real benefit of the microcomputer for the construction industry!

The above described application of the microcomputer to construction estimating is perhaps the most useful application of the microcomputer to the construction estimating function. The application should improve the accuracy of the overall estimating function.

12
CASH FLOW AND BUDGETING

INTRODUCTION

Every business must pay strict attention to its planning and control of cash. This is especially true in regard to the construction firm. The unique characteristics of the construction firm and industry, including weather, variable workload, sensitivity to the economy, and relatively large dollar value of the firm's product all place emphasis on the critical nature of planning and managing cash flow.

The construction firm's failure to plan and/or control its cash is high on the list of reasons for construction firm bankruptcies. Even when seemingly making money, it is a common occurrence to weekly or even daily witness the construction firm trying to "meet its bills." Last-minute calls to customers to collect receivables, delay paying vendors, or shifting cash from one bank to another place the firm in a state of risk every day.

Many construction firms boast of increased volume and a significant backlog of work. They often equate growth in sales volume with the success of their firm. But many of these so-called successful construction firms are becoming insolvent because they do not have enough cash to meet the needs of their existing volume, yet alone increased volume.

One also hears of construction firms "making money while going broke." This often refers to the firm's performing work at a profit while failing to collect cash. Accounting procedures can lead to a wide variation between financial statement profits and the balance in a firm's checkbook. Profits in the form of receivables, depreciation, and excess billings do not help the firm pay its bills. The common habit of "rolling over" the receivables and other noncash revenue from one construction project to the next eventually spells trouble at the first slowdown in volume.

No degree of accounting or financial management practices will ever totally eliminate the problems of cash management. The unique characteristics of the industry prevent a totally scientific approach to cash management by the accounting-related functions of cash flow preparation and analysis. However, the preparation of cash budgets can go a long way toward reducing cash-management problems.

Cash-flow analysis is the charting of cash movement into the production process, then into accounts receivable, and back into cash. Preparing a cash budget is merely an attempt to predict the flows into and out of cash during some future span of time. The procedures for preparing cash-flow analysis and cash budgets along with the benefits of both of these functions are discussed in this chapter.

THE CASH CYCLE

The construction firm is subject to a continual cycle of events that may increase or decrease its cash balance. Knowledge of these events and the impact of each on the firm's available cash is the first step on the road to managing cash. The diagram in Figure 12.1 illustrates the cycle cash takes through the construction firm. The cycle starts when the firm's cash is decreased in the acquisition of materials and services to build a construction project. Cash is further reduced in paying off accounts payable to suppliers.

As the construction firm builds a project, it typically makes interim billings to its customer for work performed. These billings become receivables. When customers pay, accounts receivables are reduced and the cash account increases. However, cash flows from customers may be received subsequent to

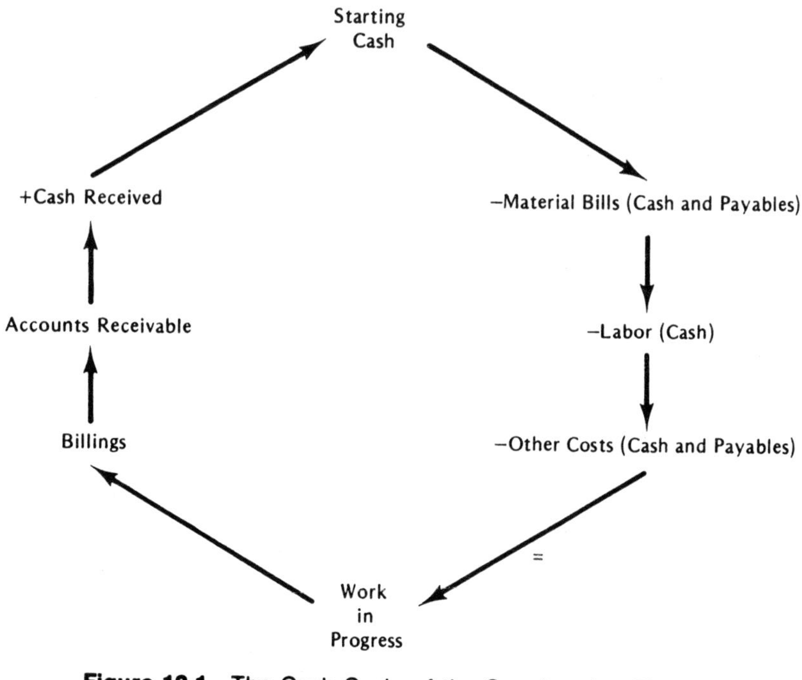

Figure 12.1 The Cash Cycle of the Construction Firm

the construction firm's payment of its bills to vendors and the payment of its labor payroll. This of course is the cash-management problem confronting the construction firm.

In addition to the typical cash operations illustrated in Figure 12.1 that affect a firm's cash balance, other less frequent events can significantly add to or subtract from the cash balance. Purchasing real estate and construction equipment can adversely affect a firm's cash position. Less frequent events such as an unfavorable legal settlement, payment of officer bonuses or dividends, or expenditures for new developments like purchasing a computer all may weaken a firm's cash position on a short-term and/or long-term basis.

Unusual events may also lead to an increase in the construction firm's cash balance. Selling fixed assets such as some of the firm's equipment fleet can create significant cash. The construction firm uses this means of creating cash as a last-resort effort to solve a cash shortage problem that stemmed from poor management of the operational cycle. When the equipment is sold as a last-resort effort, the construction firm may have to sell it at an unfavorable discounted value. Other infrequent events leading to an increase in cash include a favorable legal settlement, enactment of a tax change leading to a cash rebate, and disposal of real estate.

Ideally the construction firm should receive its cash from building a project before it expends the cash for paying its suppliers, subcontractors, and labor. This ideal is usually impossible given the payment and owner retainage clauses that typify the contractor-customer relationship. However, it is also true that, in practice, the gap in time between the construction firm's payment of its bills and collection of its bills is too excessive for sound business management. Too little attention is placed on timely billing and collection. At the same time, the typical firm fails to take advantage of accounts payable discounts and related payment practices that can lessen the negative impact of payables.

The ability to manage the cash cycle illustrated in Figure 12.1 is sometimes measured by financial ratio analysis. Specifically, inventory turnover, work-in-progress turnover, and receivable turnover are financial ratios that, in part, measure the ability to turn the production process into cash. Financial ratios were discussed in Chapter 7.

PROJECT PLANNING

Fundamental to the task of preparing a cash-flow analysis of cash received and cash disbursed on a construction project is the preparation of a project plan. Unless the firm knows when it is going to perform various segments or activities that comprise a construction project, it cannot chart its outflow of cash expenditures as a function of time.

Project planning entails defining activities necessary to complete a project and determining when each of the activities is to be performed. Project activities include elements of work such as placing concrete footing, stripping wall forms, and placing steel joists. Determining when activities are to be performed is constrained by the technical relationship between activities and the available resources of the firm. For example, the firm's stripping of concrete wall forms depends on the completion of placing and curing the concrete in the wall. Similarly, if a crane is required to perform two different activities and the construction firm is limited to using one crane, then one activity must be performed before the start up of the other activity.

In practice the project-planning effort of the construction firm varies from very detailed computer-generated project plans to virtually no plan at all. Unfortunately, more often than not, the latter is more characteristic of the planning effort than the former. The absence of planning effort is no doubt one of the main reasons for the construction firm's lack of adequate project cash-flow analysis. Without a prepared plan, an adequate cash-flow analysis is not possible.

Two project-planning management tools or models are in use by some construction firms. One is referred to as the *bar chart model* (also referred to as a Gantt chart) while the other tool or model is referred to as the *critical-path method or model* (CPM).

Bar Chart Model

A typical bar chart model for a project is shown in Figure 12.2. The defined activities of the project are listed vertically in the bar chart. In addition to columns for the quantities of work to be performed for each activity and columns for the start and finish of each activity as determined by the activity logic and overall project plan, a time scale is illustrated on the diagram. The planned time for performing an activity is shown by a horizontal bar. The bar begins at the estimated starting date of the activity and ends at the estimated finish date. In addition to the horizontal bar, an additional bar can be drawn for each activity used to indicate the actual progress of the activity. The progress bar is often cross-hatched to differentiate between the bar for planned progress and the one illustrating actual progress.

The bar chart helps the construction firm plan and control a project. In addition, the bar chart can be used to assist in scheduling labor, material, equipment, and cash. It is the application of planning models to the scheduling of cash that is discussed in following sections of this chapter.

Owing to its visual effectiveness and the simplicity of preparing a bar chart plan for a project, several construction firms prefer using the bar chart over CPM. However, bar charts have several limitations. They do not show the interdependencies of all project activities as well as CPM. In addition CPM offers more potential for scheduling techniques. In defense of the bar chart, it does provide a vehicle for cash-flow analysis. Its use by the construction firm would enhance cash-flow analysis as would the use of the more sophisticated CPM.

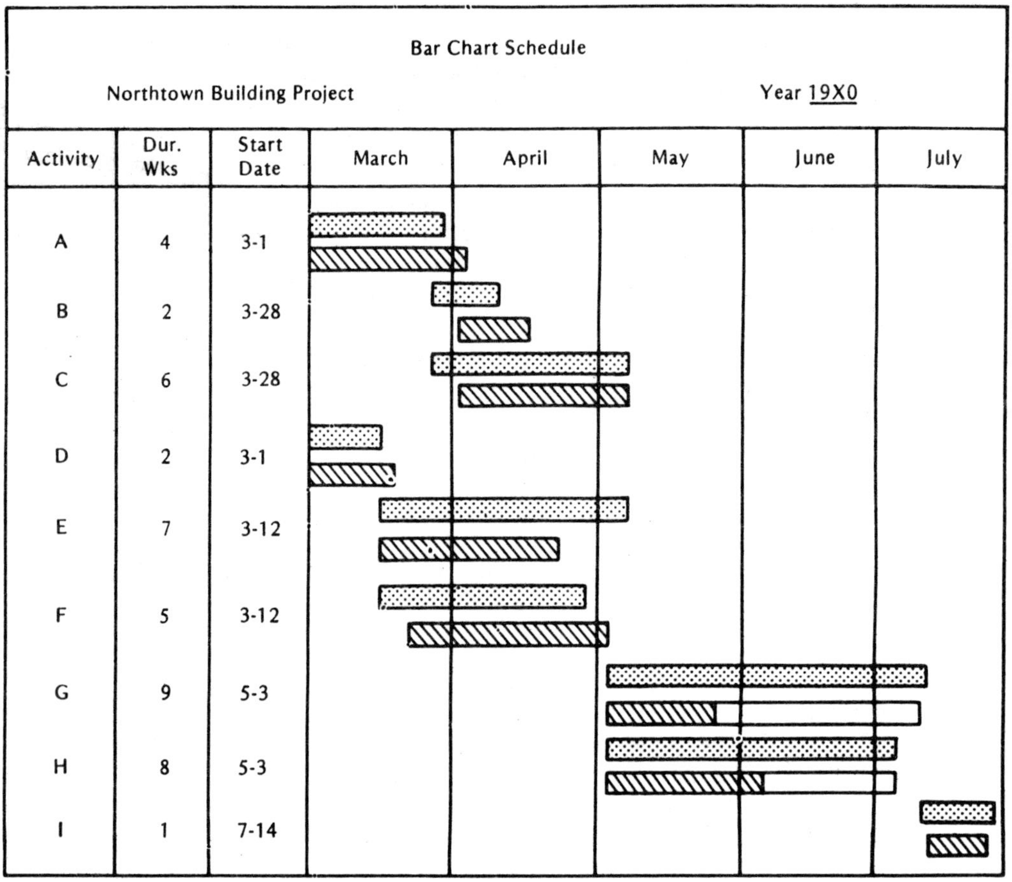

Figure 12.2 A Bar Chart Schedule

Critical-Path Method

Like the bar chart model, a critical-path method plan for a project can serve as the basis for preparing a cash-flow analysis for a project. Because of its increased sophistication, the CPM offers the user more potential applications than the bar chart model.

The CPM technique is an application of a science referred to as *network theory*. When constructing a CPM network model for planning a construction project, an *arrow-notation* network or a *circle-notation* network can be prepared. Arrow-notation CPM diagrams are in greater use and are more advantageous as a visual tool for analyzing cash flows for a construction project. For this reason, the discussion of CPM is limited to arrow notation in this chapter.

An arrow-notation CPM diagram is prepared by using arrows to represent activities. The relation, or logic, between project activities is represented by

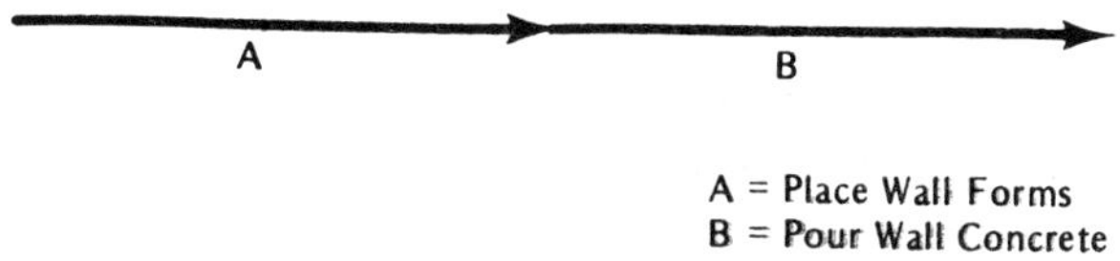

Figure 12.3 One CPM Activity Dependent on Another

connecting the tail of the arrow representing one activity to the head of the arrow representing another activity. This is illustrated in Figure 12.3. The diagram shown in Figure 12.3 represents the fact that activity B cannot start before activity A is completed. This is all the diagram represents. It does not indicate that activity B starts as soon as activity A is completed—it may or may not start as soon as A is completed. Note that A and B are merely abbreviations for a more detailed description of the activities as indicated in Figure 12.3.

If two activities have no relationship to each other, they can be shown several different ways on a CPM arrow-notation diagram. Figure 12.4 illustrates three different ways of indicating that activities C and D have no dependence on one another.

Our major interest in CPM in this chapter is its use as a basis for the analysis of a project's cash flow. However, CPM can and is used for assisting in several other management functions. Fundamental to the use of CPM for any application is an understanding of *basic CPM calculations*. These are aimed at satisfying three objectives:

1. Determining the minimum project completion time or duration.
2. Determining which project activities dictate or control the minimum project completion time. These activities are called the *critical activities* and form a path through the CPM diagram (hence the term "critical-path method").
3. Determining how much time each project activity can be delayed without affecting the minimum project completion time.

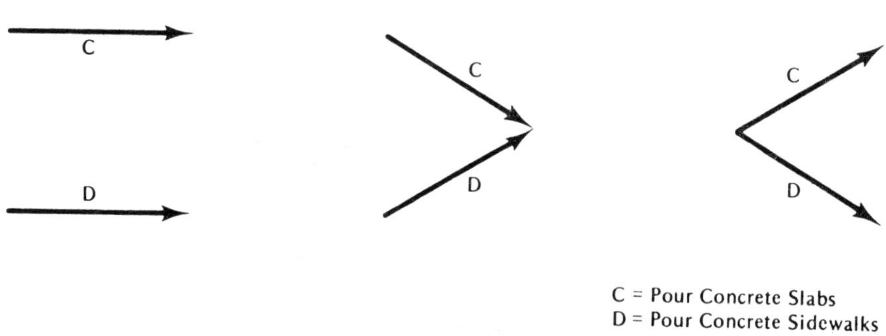

Figure 12.4 Independent CPM Activities

In order to accomplish the three basic CPM calculation objectives, it is necessary to perform a series of calculations on a CPM diagram. One set of calculations is determined from a forward pass through the CPM network, also referred to as the *earliest start schedule* since the calculations performed will yield information pertaining to the earliest time that the project activities can possibly start and finish. The second set of calculations made on the CPM diagram is called the backward pass, also referred to as the *latest start time* schedule since the calculations will yield information pertaining to the latest time activities can possibly start and finish without delaying the calculated minimum project completion time.

In order to illustrate how the three objectives of basic CPM calculations are satisfied by the two described schedules, we will perform calculations on the CPM project plan shown in Figure 12.5. The planned duration of each CPM activity is placed alongside the corresponding activity. Note that in the construction of the CPM diagram there is no intended relationship between the length of an arrow respresenting an activity and the duration of an activity.

In performing the sets of calculations on the CPM diagram, we will generate five different pieces of information about each activity:

Earliest start time for an activity	:	abbreviated EST
Earliest finish time for an activity	:	abbreviated EFT
Latest start time for an activity	:	abbreviated LST
Latest finish time for an activity	:	abbreviated LFT
Total float for an activity	:	abbreviated TF

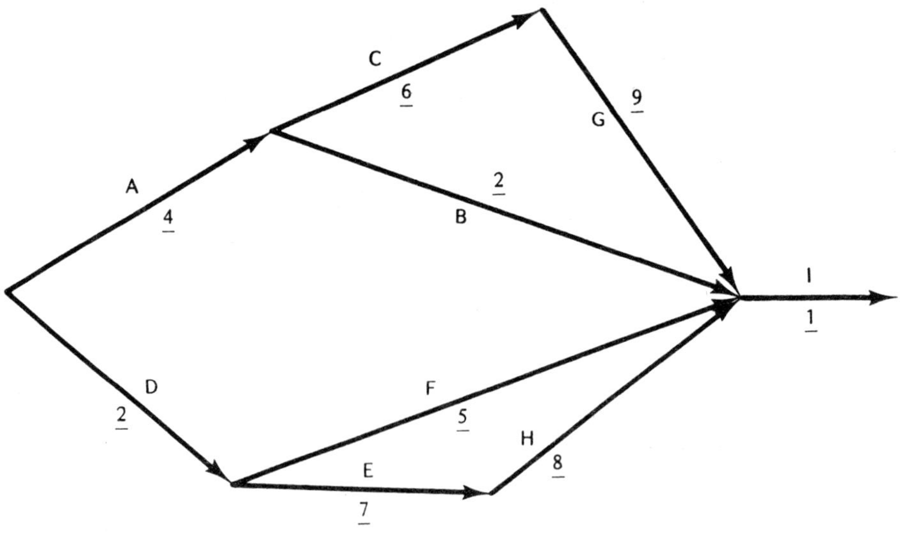

Figure 12.5 A CPM Diagram

Activity	Duration	EST	EFT	LST	LFT	TF
A	4	0	4	0	4	0
B	2	4	6	17	19	13
C	6	4	10	4	10	0
D	2	0	2	2	4	2
E	7	2	9	4	11	2
F	5	2	7	14	19	12
G	9	10	19	10	19	0
H	8	9	17	11	19	2
I	1	19	20	19	20	0

Figure 12.6 Answers for CPM Calculations

The earliest start time (EST) for an activity is defined as the earliest possible time the activity can start. Assuming a starting date for the project illustrated in Figure 12.5 as the end of week 0 (which is equivalent to the beginning of week 1), the earliest start time of activities A and D are calculated as 0. (Note: CPM activity durations might be stated in days, weeks, or months). Nothing constrains the start of activities A and D. The EST answers, along with the answers from other calculations for the CPM diagram in Figure 12.5, are illustrated in Figure 12.6.

The earliest finish time (EFT) for an activity is calculated as an activity's earliest start time plus the activity's duration. In other words, if an activity such as A can start on week 0 (the end of week 0) and it takes four weeks to complete, the soonest A can be completed is the end of the fourth week.

The EST of any other activity is calculated as the maximum EFT of activities immediately preceding the activity in question. In the case of activity C, only one activity, activity A, directly precedes it. Therefore, the EST of activity C is equal to the EFT of activity A, or the end of four weeks.

Other activity EST's and EFT's can be calculated in a similar manner. Let us consider activity I shown in Figure 12.5. Its start is constrained by completing activities B, F, G, and H. The EFT's of activities B, F, G, and H are 6, 7, 19, and 17 weeks respectively. Because activity I cannot start until all four activities are complete, activity I's EST is the end of the nineteenth week. Similarly, activity I's EFT is the end of the twentieth week. The EST's and EFT's of all the activities shown in Figure 12.5 are shown in Figure 12.6.

Because activity I is the terminating activity of the project shown in Figure 12.5, activity I's EFT also represents the minimum completion time of the project. In other words, the minimum completion time of the project is the end of the twentieth week. The first objective of the CPM calculations is achieved.

The latest start time (LST) and latest finish time (LFT) for each CPM activity are calculated from the backward pass through the CPM network. As a starting point for the calculations, the project duration is set equal to the minimum project duration (twenty weeks in the example in Figure 12.5).

The LFT for an activity is defined as the latest possible time an activity can finish without delaying the predetermined project completion time. Because activity I is a terminating activity in the CPM diagram shown in Figure 12.5, its LFT is therefore twenty. This answer is also shown in Figure 12.6.

The LST of an activity is the activity's latest finish time (LFT) minus the activity's duration. Because activity I has a duration of one week and must be completed by the end of the twentieth week (its LFT), it must be started no later than the end of the nineteenth week (or 20 − 1 = 19).

The LFT of any other activity is equal to the minimum LST of the activities immediately following the activity in question. For example, only activity I immediately follows activity G. Therefore, the (LFT) of activity G is equal to the LST of activity I or the end of the nineteenth week.

The LST's and LFT's of the remaining activities shown in Figure 12.5 are calculated in a similar manner. Let us consider activity A. It is followed immediately by activities B and C. The latest start times of activities B and C are the end of weeks seventeen and four respectively. In order for each of these activities to start no later than their LST's, activity A must be done by the smaller of the two or the end of the fourth week.

The last CPM calculation is determining each activity's *total float* which is the amount of time an activity can be delayed, assuming no other activity is delayed, without affecting the minimum completion time of a project. Total float is a function of both the earliest and latest start time schedules. Total float for an activity is the difference between the LST and EST for the activity or the difference between the LFT and EFT for the activity. Either of these calculations will yield the same total float value. The calculated total floats for the activities illustrated in Figure 12.5 are shown in Figure 12.6.

Inspection of Figure 12.6 shows that activities A, C, G, and I have total float of 0. The LST's and EST's for these activities are equal as are their LFT's and EFT's. In other words, these activities cannot be delayed. They dictate the minimum project duration and form a path through the CPM network. Therefore, the second basic CPM calculation objective, determining the critical activities, is complete. The total floats shown in Figure 12.6 for the other activities represent the possible delay times for the noncritical activities and satisfy the third and final objective of the basic CPM calculations.

The calculated activity times and total float times shown in Figure 12.6 can be used as a basis of scheduling project activities and the resources used for each activity. Knowledge of possible delay times for the activities provides the planner a means of allocating scarce resources and leveling the demand for a resource such as cash.

Time-Scale CPM

To better enable the use of a prepared CPM diagram for analyzing a project's cash flow, a *time-scale CPM* diagram or network may be prepared. In the CPM arrow-notation diagram discussed to this point, the lengths of individual arrows were not related to the duration of the activity represented by the arrow. However, when constructing a time-scale CPM network, the arrow

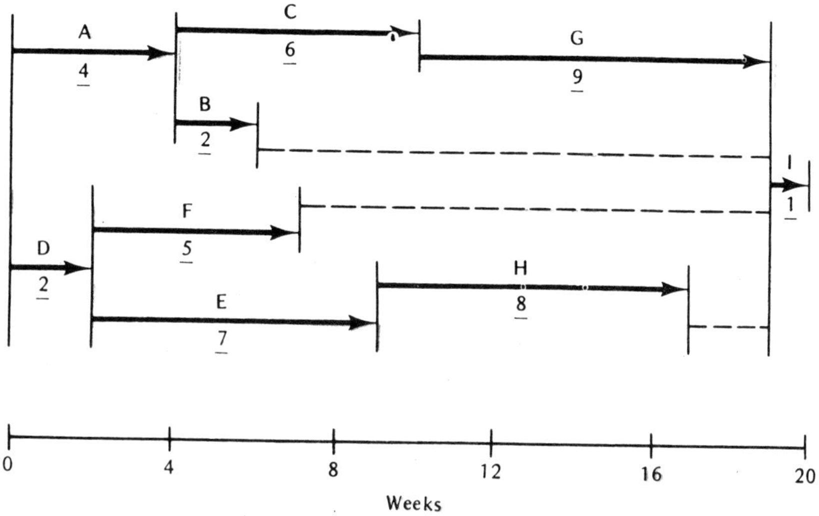

Figure 12.7 Time-Scale CPM

lengths used to represent activities are proportional in length to the various activity durations.

The time-scale CPM network is prepared by connecting activity arrows according to their defined logic. Each activity is represented by an arrow of a length dictated by the activity duration and the time scale that is placed on the horizontal axis of the time-scale CPM. Figure 12.7 illustrates a time-scale CPM network for the previously discussed CPM diagram shown in Figure 12.5.

Note that the time-scale CPM shown in Figure 12.7 corresponds to the earliest start time schedule. It therefore indicates the exact timing of each activity and is less general than the CPM diagram shown in Figure 12.5. A latest start time time-scale CPM could also be prepared for the project shown in Figure 12.5.

The time-scale CPM network or diagram shown in Figure 12.7 looks very similar to the bar chart model shown in Figure 12.2. Both have an improved visual effect over the CPM diagram shown in Figure 12.5. More important, both the time-scale CPM and the bar chart model provide a means of charting cash inflows and outflows as a function of time. This will now be illustrated in the following section. However, one should not lose sight of the additional information obtained from the CPM diagram or time-scale CPM diagram versus the bar chart model.

PROJECT PLANNING AND CASH-FLOW ANALYSIS

The project plan, be it a bar chart plan or a CPM plan, serves as the basis for charting the cash inflows and outflows for building a construction project.

Therefore, preparing such a plan is fundamental to determining project cash requirements and managing the inflows and outflows of project cash.

To illustrate the dependence of determining and analyzing cash flow on the project plan, we will consider the project represented by the CPM diagram in Figure 12.5 and the time-scale CPM diagram shown in Figure 12.7.

In addition to the activity durations that were determined, let us assume that the direct cost of performing each activity is as follows:

	Direct Cost
Activity A	$80,000
Activity B	60,000
Activity C	90,000
Activity D	50,000
Activity E	70,000
Activity F	100,000
Activity G	45,000
Activity H	160,000
Activity I	40,000
Total direct cost	$695,000

Each activity's duration is shown alongside each activity in the time-scale CPM diagram shown in Figure 12.8. The diagram represents the project's earliest start time schedule.

In preparing a cash-flow analysis for the project, let us further assume that the construction firm building the project has related overhead expenses of $2,500 per week and includes $30,000 of profit in its bid. The total contract price is calculated as follows:

Direct costs	$695,000
Overhead costs	
(20 weeks times $2,500)	50,000
Profit	30,000
Total contract amount	$775,000

Let us assume that the contract between the project owner and the construction firm states that a progress report is to be made every four weeks and billings for the work completed in that period are to be paid to the construction firm within two weeks thereafter. Let us further assume that the owner is to retain 10 percent of each progress payment which will be paid as part of the final progress payment if the work is completed satisfactorily by the construction firm.

Charting the construction costs for each of the four-week intervals is shown as the cash outflow in Figure 12.8. They are calculated as the sum of the expended direct costs for the activities worked on during the four-week period and the $2,500 per week or $10,000 per four-week overhead cost. It is

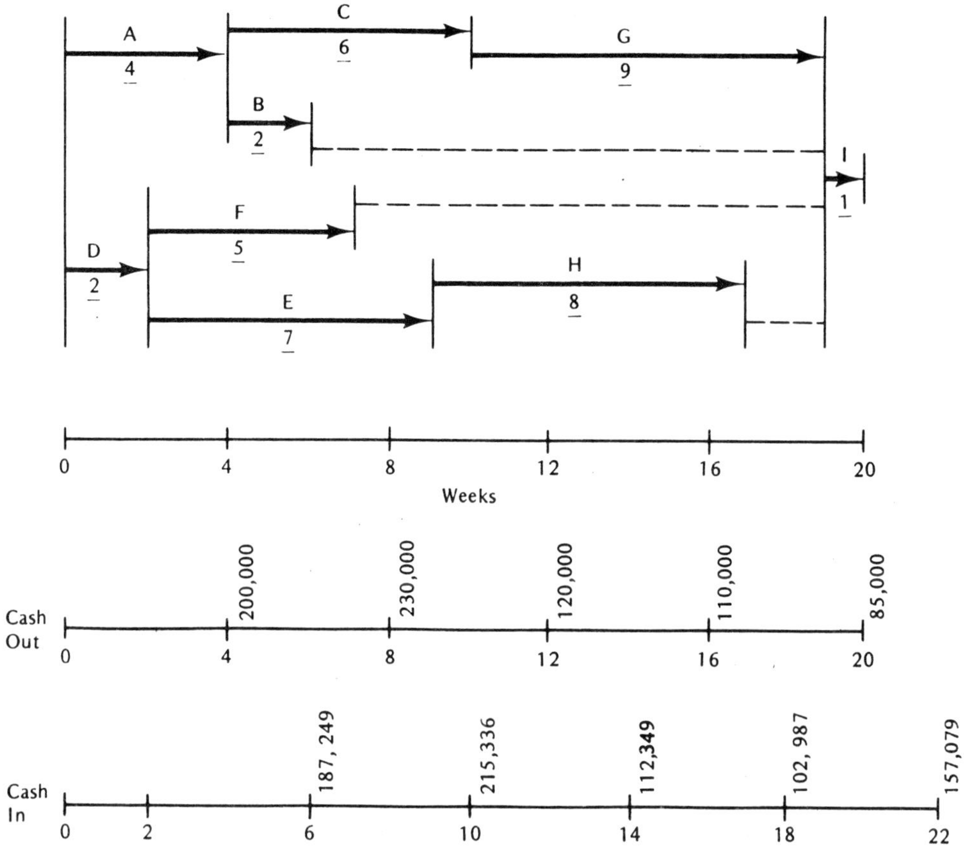

Figure 12.8 Cash-Flow Diagram

assumed that the costs expended on any activity during a time period are proportional to the percentage of work completed for the activity in the time period. For example, during the first four-week time period two weeks of a total of five weeks of duration for activity F are completed. Therefore, the assumed cost spent for activity F during the first four-week time period is two-fifths of F's total direct cost of $100,000, or $40,000.

The total cash outflow for the first four weeks is calculated as follows:

Activity A: 4/4 times $80,000	=	$ 80,000
Activity D: 2/2 times $50,000	=	50,000
Activity E: 2/7 times $70,000	=	20,000
Activity F: 2/5 times $100,000	=	40,000
Overhead costs: 4 months times $2,500	=	10,000
Total cash outflow		$200,000

The cash outflow for the other four-week intervals is calculated in a similar manner.

Admittedly, the construction firm may not have to pay all of its bills incurred in the same time period. For example, it may be possible to defer the payment of a material bill. However, given knowledge of this fact, it could be interjected into charting the timing of the cash outflows.

The cash inflows shown in Figure 12.8 are calculated by summing the costs incurred in the previous four-week period, adding a proportionate share of the construction firm's profit that it will bill with the interim progress reports, and multiplying by 90 percent to reflect the fact that the owner will retain 10 percent as a retainer. The profit billed in a given period is assumed to be calculated by multiplying the total profit by the percent of total costs expended during the progress billing period. All cash inflows are assumed to be received two weeks after the progress report is made.

The calculation of the first cash inflow received at the end of the sixth week of the project is as follows:

Direct costs and overhead costs in previous period	$200,000
Profit billed ($30,000 times $200,000/$745,000)	8,054
Total billed	$208,054
Less retainer	20,805
Total cash received	$187,249

The other cash inflows shown can be calculated in the same manner. The cash inflow received at the end of the twenty-second month includes the owner's payment of the accumulated retainer amounts.

Assuming the construction firm's cash outflows occur linearly throughout a progress report period, the cumulative cash outflows and inflows are shown in Figure 12.9. The difference between the firm's cumulative cash outflows and inflows at any point in time represents the overdraft or surplus of cash from the project. An overdraft represents the amount of cash the construction firm will have to have available from its own funds or borrowed funds in order to perform the project as scheduled. In effect, preparing the cash flow for the project charts out the cash needs for the project. Knowing these cash needs ahead of time allows the firm to secure financing well in advance so that it does not get caught in a cash shortage which could lead to contract default and even bankruptcy. Effective cash management defines financing needs well in advance of when the cash is actually needed.

The cash-flow analysis shown in Figures 12.8 and 12.9 corresponds to an earliest start time schedule. A latest start time CPM schedule could also be prepared along with a corresponding charting of each cash inflow and outflow. The cash inflows and outflows from this schedule would differ from those illustrated in Figures 12.8 and 12.9. In fact, numerous other schedules that

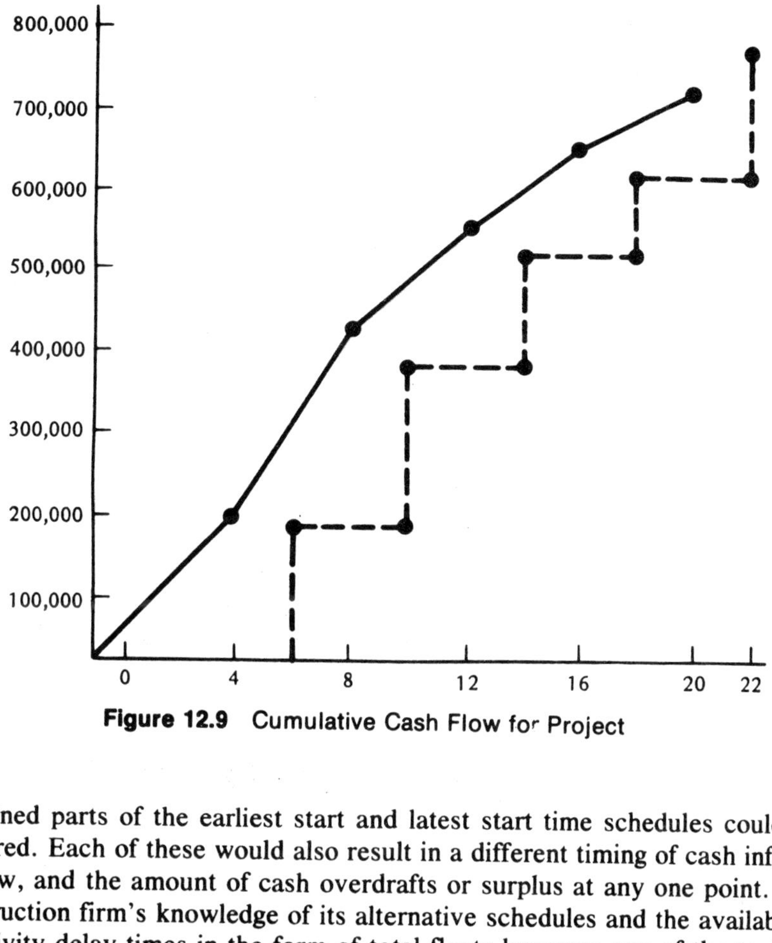

Figure 12.9 Cumulative Cash Flow for Project

combined parts of the earliest start and latest start time schedules could be prepared. Each of these would also result in a different timing of cash inflow, outflow, and the amount of cash overdrafts or surplus at any one point. The construction firm's knowledge of its alternative schedules and the availability of activity delay times in the form of total floats becomes one of the tools of effective cash management.

MANAGING CASH

Events outside the control of the construction firm will always restrict the firm's cash position. However, the construction firm can control some events that can lessen the financial impact of the external events. Specifically, the construction firm's attention to the everyday function of handling its receivables, payables, and inventory purchases can aid in managing cash. Cash management is also enhanced by an awareness of the effect of the timing of various construction activities as dictated by a bar chart or CPM plan.

Being able to control accounts receivable is a key to the construction firm's cash position at any specific point in time. The construction firm cannot afford to be in the finance business. Attention must focus on speeding up the receipt on money owed the firm. Cash collected can be invested at an interest rate that can lead to a significant increase in the firm's bottom-line profits. Equally important is the fact that, given the firm's failure to collect its receivable, it may be forced to secure borrowed funds as working capital. Borrowed funds, in turn, place another demand on the firm's cash and profits in that, associated with the borrowing of funds, is the payment of interest.

The construction firm's dependence on receivables is exemplified by the typical billing and payment retention practices of the construction project owner. Upon completing various segments of a project, the construction firm makes progress billings to the project owner. However, actual payment may be slow depending on the owner. Delays of a month or more are common. In addition, when in fact payment is made, the owner may choose to retain part of the payment (typically 10 percent) until the construction project is completed.

Control of accounts receivable entails being selective in doing business, paying attention to billing procedures, maintaining good accounting records, having workable collection procedures, and establishing an adequate provision for bad debts. One cannot overemphasize the benefits of doing work for reputable customers. While the selection of work is constrained by the competitive nature of the construction industry, the fact remains that the profitable and liquid construction firms are those that are effective in marketing their services to a preferred list of customers.

Billing dates and getting bills out in a timely manner are another area in which accounts receivable control is important. When work is completed it should be billed. All too often the construction firm focuses attention on creating new work when in fact more attention should be drawn to billing and collecting its cash for work already completed. Often the firm sets a specific day of the month as its billing date. While this may help make the billing process a routine one, it may also result in a delay in collecting cash owed it for work completed.

Accounts receivable analysis by means of adequate accounting records enhances cash collection. Too often the construction firm does not pay attention to collecting cash owed it because the accounting records do not draw attention to the status of overdue accounts.

Collection of receivables is merely a matter of continual policing of the accounts owed the firm. Telephone calls and personal letters written by the owner of the construction firm or a chief officer to the delinquent account can be effective. Collecting receivables is an unpleasant part of doing business; however, failure to collect the receivables leads to even more unpleasant events such as potential bankruptcy.

The construction firm often has more control of its accounts payable than its accounts receivable. Specifically, it can hold back payment to a vendor or possibly a subcontractor as a means of preventing a temporary cash shortage. However, the firm must be cautious in this approach to managing its cash position. Continual late payment to vendors and subcontractors leads to a very unfavorable reputation that eventually will hurt the construction firm's marketing efforts.

The firm's cash position and management can be improved by attention to purchase discounts associated with paying its vendors. Often a discount is given if early payment is made; for example, a "2/10 net 30" means the construction firm can receive a 2 percent discount if it pays the invoice within ten days. Given the large dollar value of material purchased for a project, this discount can add up to a significant dollar amount.

The benefit of the savings associated with taking advantage of cash discounts must be weighed against the need to maintain a favorable cash balance. A firm may be so conscious of taking advantage of cash discounts that it runs itself into a temporary cash shortage. The solution is a well-balanced program of taking advantage of discounts when the firm's cash position allows such practices. In order to implement this type of balanced program, the accounting records must be structured to report on key discount dates. In other words, the firm's accounts payable accounting records provide the basis for an effective accounts payable cash-management program.

The material inventory maintained by construction firms varies from virtually none to significant dollar amounts of material. More often than not most construction firms, especially the smaller ones, purchase materials for a specific project. As a general rule the construction firm is better off if it does not stockpile substantial material inventories at the expense of weakening its cash position. One of the favorable financial characteristics of the construction industry is that the firm does not have to have a significant cash investment in inventory in order to carry out its operations.

There are occasions when it becomes advantageous to purchase some material as inventory. The feasibility of this depends on several factors including the costs of ordering and material storage and the possible lower price associated with buying material in large quantities. However, one should not lose sight of the effect of early purchase on the firm's cash position. Often this consideration far outweighs the consideration of sophisticated inventory models aimed at determining the most economical order quantity and order point.

In an earlier section of this chapter the relationship between cash inflows and outflows and a project plan and schedule was illustrated. Specifically it was noted that, depending on when construction activities (such as pouring concrete walls) were performed, timing of cash inflows and outflows to the construction firm would vary. For example, a significantly different cash flow results as a function of time if a firm implements an earliest start time CPM schedule versus a latest start time CPM schedule.

Using total floats generated in CPM calculations discussed in an earlier section of this chapter provides the construction firm a means of further managing its cash position. Delaying the start of a construction activity while not delaying the total project duration by using activity total floats (possible delay times) can prove a means of avoiding a temporary cash shortage. In fact one may adjust or even prepare a total project plan to be compatible with the cash position objectives of the firm. In effect, the planning and scheduling of project activities can be used as a means of assisting in cash management and vice versa.

Another cash-flow management device used by construction firms is using several checking accounts. For example, the firm might establish a checking account for its general expenses at one bank; another checking account for writing payroll checks at another bank. The firm then transfers funds from its general expense account to its payroll account by writing a check payable to the payroll account from the general expense account. Given a temporary cash shortage in regard to meeting its weekly payroll, the firm writes the check from the general expense account to the payroll account on the day (or even the day after) it distributes the payroll checks. The check is written from the general expense account even though there are insufficient funds to cover the check. However, because the check takes a few days to clear the payroll account bank and return to the expense account bank, the construction firm creates a few days of float in regard to its ability to meet its payroll. The hope is that cash is received within a few days to cover the insufficient funds check.

The described practice is commonly referred to as *kiting*. While used by firms, kiting is obviously looked upon with disfavor by lending institutions. The practice often leads to a confrontation with the bank and does little to enhance the reputation of the construction firm. Kiting also raises the question "What happens if the firm cannot raise funds during the float period that are necessary to cover the insufficient funds?" The answer of course is that the firm is in trouble and as a result, the bank may call various notes it holds which can lead to even more financial problems for the construction firm.

While kiting is a poor excuse for the failure to practice good cash management, several firms still hold open the kiting possibility by establishing two checking accounts. This gives the firm the potential for one or two days' delay in meeting its cash requirements given an unexpected event. Holding this potential open can be viewed as good cash management as long as the firm does not become dependent on the kiting practice. If it frequently depends on the practice, the firm probably has more severe and permanent financial problems ahead of it.

CASH BUDGET FOR THE FIRM

In a previous section of this chapter, preparing or charting the construction firm's cash inflows and outflows via a project plan was illustrated. This charting provides the firm a means of managing cash on the project. Charting cash flow for a specific project serves another important purpose: the project cash-flow analysis becomes part of the overall construction firm cash-flow analysis or budget.

Preparing or charting cash flows for a firm's total operations is commonly referred to as a *cash budget*. Regardless of whether the charting of total firm cash inflows is referred to as cash-flow analysis or cash budgeting, it may be used to accomplish several management functions. For one, the cash budget for total operations can be used to analyze cash needs on a short-term or long-term basis. While the charting of cash flows for a project establishes cash overdrafts or surpluses for a specific project, the cash budget establishes cash overdrafts or surpluses for the total company. Knowing these cash overdrafts or surpluses in advance aids the construction firm in securing needed funds in advance, planning investment opportunities for temporary surpluses of cash, and taking steps that affect operations that can result in a leveling of cash needs at a specific point in time.

The cash-flow analysis or budget for total firm operations also serves as an aid in planning. Specifically, the cash budget can be used to establish expectations for a future period. These expectations become the construction firm's plan for the future. In this sense, the cash budget can serve as a motivating force for total company operations.

Another increasingly important function that the total operations budget serves is to satisfy the needs of lending institutions considering lending money to the construction firm. The lending institution may want to analyze the firm's cash flow to determine the construction firm's ability to repay the loan under consideration. The relationship between the construction firm and third parties such as lending institutions was discussed in Chapter 7.

Cash budgets may be prepared to cover different spans of time. A monthly budget might be prepared with the main objective of guiding the actions of the production process. On the other hand, a yearly cash budget might be used by upper management for mapping out growth and capital expenditures.

The cash budget that integrates all the expected cash inflows and outflows of the firm is part of the master budget preparation. The basic steps in preparing a master budget that focuses on total cash inflows and outflows as a function of time will now be illustrated by means of an example. The master or cash budget illustrated is for a one-year span of time. However, the various steps and schedules comprising the operating segment of the master budget are only shown for a quarter of the year. The schedules that comprise the master budget are:

1. Contracted work budget
2. Direct materials budget
3. Direct labor budget
4. Job overhead budget
5. General overhead budget
6. Budgeted statement of cash inflows and outflows.

Each of the first five budgets listed is a support schedule for the statement of cash inflows and outflows. The statement of cash inflows and outflows is

SAMPLE CONSTRUCTION CO., INC.
Contracted Work Budget
for the Second Quarter of the 19X0 Fiscal Year

	Previously contracted work performed this period	New contracts signed this period	Work performed that is contracted this period	Total work this period
Project A	$ 25,000			$ 25,000
Project B		$525,000	$112,000	112,000
Project C	135,000			135,000
Project D		215,000		0
Projece E		110,000	110,000	110,000
				$382,000

Figure 12.10 Contracted Work Budget

also commonly referred to as the statement of cash receipts and disbursements. For example, the contracted work budget shown in Figure 12.10 provides a means of determining cash inflows. This is done by estimating the amount of work to be performed from past contracts and new contracts during the period in question. This can be done by using the procedures described for preparing a project's cash flows as was illustrated in Figure 12.8. In the example, this is done quarterly and the contracted work budget shown is for the second quarter.

The construction firm will not receive cash payment during a given time period for all the work performed during that period. There may be a time lag between the time the work is completed and the time the owner bills the firm for the work. In addition, the owner may be slow paying for the work or he may in fact retain part of the payment until the entire project is judged substantially complete. As such, the dollar value shown for the work performed in the statement of cash receipts and disbursements shown in Figure 12.10 are adjusted in order to determine the cash received.

The direct material and labor budgets for the example in question are shown in Figures 12.11 and 12.12, respectively. These budgets are determined

SAMPLE CONSTRUCTION CO., INC.
Direct Material Budget
for the Second Quarter of the 19X0 Fiscal Year

	Accured material cost to be paid	Material purchased this period	Material purchased and paid for this period	Total cash paid
Project A	$2,000	$ 8,250	$ 7,150	$ 9,150
Project B	0	44,000	44,000	44,000
Project C	0	12,000	6,500	6,500
Project D	0	4,000	0	0
Project E	0	4,000	2,000	2,000
				$61,650

Figure 12.11 Direct Material Budget

SAMPLE CONSTRUCTION CO., INC.
Direct Labor Budget
for the Second Quarter of 19X0 Fiscal Year

	Accrued payroll paid this period	Labor cost this period	Labor hours this period to be paid this period	Total cash paid
Project A	$ 9,250	$ 9,250	$ 8,500	$ 17,750
Project B	0	43,000	17,000	17,000
Project C	15,000	29,750	26,750	41,750
Project D	0	0	0	0
Project E	0	52,000	52,000	52,000
				$128,500

Figure 12.12 Direct Labor Budget

on the basis of the estimated work completed during the time period as indicated in the contract work budget. It may be appropriate to prepare support schedules of the various types of materials used and labor crafts employed. Both direct material and labor costs are integrated into the disbursements segment of the statement of cash receipts and disbursements.

The job overhead and general overhead budgets are shown in Figure 12.13 and 12.14 respectively. In order to determine rates for applying the overhead costs to individual jobs, job overhead costs are estimated for a given volume of work (total cost of work performed of $100,000), and annual general overhead costs are estimated. A job overhead rate of 17 percent of total cost of work performed is found by dividing the sum of the estimated job overhead costs by the $100,000 base. Similarly, a monthly general overhead amount of cost to be allocated is determined by dividing the estimated annual costs by twelve months. Using the two bases described, job overhead and general overhead are integrated into the disbursements segment of the statement of cash receipts and disbursements.

SAMPLE CONSTRUCTION CO., INC.
Job Overhead Budget
for the Fiscal Year Ending
December 31, 19X0

For Activity Level of Total Cost of
Work Performed of $100,000

	Amount
Supplies	$ 500
Supervision	8,000
Payroll fringe benefits	2,000
Equipment	6,000
Maintenance	500
	$17,000
Job overhead rate (percent of total work performed) ($17,000/$100,000)	17%

Figure 12.13 Job Overhead Budget

SAMPLE CONSTRUCTION CO., INC.
General Overhead Budget
for the Fiscal Year Ending December 31, 19X0

	Annual Amount
Salaries	$110,000
Depreciation	25,000
Property taxes	12,500
Property insurance	5,500
Interest on mortgage	2,000
Utilities	12,000
Maintenance	85,000
	$252,000
Monthly overhead rate: ($252,000/12)	$ 21,000

Figure 12.14 General Overhead Budget

SAMPLE CONSTRUCTION CO., INC.
Budgeted Statement of Cash Receipts and Disbursements
for the Fiscal Year Ending December 31, 19X0

	Quarters				For Year
	1	2	3	4	
Cash Balance, beginning	$ 5,000	$ 5,560	$ 28,670	$ 4,020	
Work performed	242,000	382,000	248,000	142,000	$1,014,000
	$247,000	$387,560	$276,670	$146,020	
Less amount of cash retained by owner	10,000	25,000	43,150	8,450	
a. Total available for expenses	$237,000	$362,560	$233,520	$137,570	
Less disbursements:					
Materials	$ 51,500	$ 61,650	$ 56,500	$ 20,540	$ 190,190
Labor	81,400	128,500	62,840	31,000	303,740
Job overhead	41,140	64,940	42,160	24,140	172,380
Applied fixed overhead	63,000	63,000	63,000	63,000	252,000
b. Total disbursements	$237,040	$318,090	$224,500	$138,680	$ 918,310
Minimum cash balance desired	5,000	5,000	5,000	5,000	
Total cash needed	$242,040	$323,090	$229,500	$143,680	
Excess of total cash available over total cash needed before financing (deficiency)	($ 5,040)	$ 39,470	$ 4,020	($ 6,110)	
Financing:					
Borrowing (beginning)	$ 11,200	$ 0	$ 0	$ 15,000	$ 26,200
Repayments	0	(10,000)	0	0	(10,000)
Interest	(600)	(800)	0	(1,100)	(2,500)
c. Financing effect	$ 10,600	($ 10,800)	$ 0	$ 13,900	$ 13,700
Cash balance	$ 5,560	$ 28,670	$ 4,020	$ 7,790	

Figure 12.15 Statement of Cash Receipts and Disbursements

The schedules shown in Figures 12.10 through 12.14 support the preparation of the cash receipts and disbursements statement shown in Figure 12.15. While the statement of cash receipts and disbursements in Figure 12.15 is for a year's duration, several of the calculations in the schedules shown in Figures 12.10 through 12.14 were for a single quarter or three-month period. Subcalculations for the other three quarters that support the statement of cash receipts and disbursements in Figure 12.15 are not shown. However, the calculations would be made in a similar manner to those made in Figures 12.10 through 12.14.

The statement of budgeted cash receipts and disbursements in Figure 12.15 aids in avoiding unnecessary idle cash and even more importantly focuses on potential cash deficiencies. The importance of mapping the firm's cash flow cannot be overemphasized. It is of such importance that the larger manufacturing firms prepare a similar statement for a time span of only a week.

The previously presented budgets (e.g., direct material costs) comprise a substantial portion of the statement of cash receipts and disbursements. However, recognition of beginning cash balance, minimum desired cash balance, and financing effects (amount borrowed, repaid, and interest) must also be recognized in determining the ending cash balance. This is also illustrated in Figure 12.15. The wide variations in the ending cash balance for the example shown are common in the construction industry. The variable environment, unique nature of the product, and duration and method of payment from the project owner are all factors leading to nonuniform cash recipts and disbursements. This being the case, the statement of cash receipts and disbursements takes on added significance.

CASH FLOW AND CHANGING CONDITIONS

Construction firms often attempt to make an argument against any planning effort based on the fact that construction is subject to many uncertain events that defy prediction. They often give the same reason when arguing against preparing a detailed cash-flow analysis or budget.

This argument is weak because the alternative they offer usually relates to "seat of the pants" management. It is also true that other industries are confronted with uncertainties. Nonetheless, firms in these other industries continue to pay close attention to planning the production process and preparing and analyzing cash flows. What these firms, and the construction firm, must do is attempt to better predict the uncertain events and incorporate them into the planning and cash-flow functions.

Computers can be used very effectively to defeat the problem of uncertain events in regard to preparing a plan and cash-flow analysis. While the previous chapters addressed applications of computers to construction and construction accounting, another relevant area of application relates to *financial modeling* and the analysis of cash flow. Using financial modeling, the construction firm inputs planning and cash-flow assumptions into a computer programmed to

'SAMPLE CONTRACTOR CONTRACTS DATA 000 OMITTED'

		JAN	FEB	MAR	APR	MAY	JUN
1Ø A CONTRACT	1ØØ						
11 A MATERIAL				1Ø	1Ø	1Ø	
12 A SUBCONTRACT			5		5		
13 A LABOR		5	5	1Ø	1Ø	1Ø	
14 A OVERHEAD		1	1	2	2	2	
2Ø B CONTRACT	2ØØ						
21 B MATERIAL				1Ø	2Ø	1Ø	
22 B SUBCONTRACT						1Ø	3Ø
23 B LABOR				1Ø	2Ø	2Ø	3Ø
24 B OVERHEAD				2	5	5	7
3Ø C CONTRACT	4ØØ						
31 C MATERIAL						2Ø	4Ø
32 C SUBCONTRACT						2Ø	2Ø
33 C LABOR						5	5
34 C OVERHEAD						1	1

'SAMPLE CONTRACTOR CONTRACTS DATA 000 OMITTED'

	JUL	AUG	SEP	OCT	NOV	DEC	TOT YR
1Ø A CONTRACT							
11 A MATERIAL							
12 A SUBCONTRACT							
13 A LABOR							
14 A OVERHEAD							
2Ø B CONTRACT							
21 B MATERIAL							
22 B SUBCONTRACT							
23 B LABOR							
24 B OVERHEAD							
3Ø C CONTRACT							
31 C MATERIAL	4Ø	2Ø	2Ø	2Ø	2Ø	2Ø	
32 C SUBCONTRACT	2Ø	2Ø	2Ø				
33 C LABOR	5	5	1Ø	1Ø	1Ø	1Ø	
34 C OVERHEAD	1	1	2	2	2	2	

Figure 12.16 Assumed Project Data for Financial Modeling

prepare a charting of cash inflows and outflows in much the same manner that was used to prepare a manual cash-flow charting in the previous sections of this chapter. An example computer input data and the resulting computer output data from such a computer system are shown in Figures 12.16 and 12.17 respectively. As may be observed from Figure 12.17, projected financial statement data as well as cash-flow charting is printed as computer output.

Once the construction firm has built the financial model illustrated in Figure 12.17, the computer program may be used to analyze any possible future event and determine its impact on the cash flow and financial statements. This may be done merely by inputting the change into the computer via a computer card or similar input device. For example, let us assume that it is possible a labor strike might occur in the month of May in the year being considered. Using financial modeling, it is possible to look into the future and

'SAMPLE CONTRACTOR MASTER ASSUMPTIONS' 000

		JAN	FEB	MAR	APR	MAY	JUN
51 SALES		7	13	50	81	124	146
57 GROSS PROFIT		1	1	5	8	11	12
63 OH OV UN APPLIE		2	2	-2	-3	-5	-5
66 PROFIT AFTER TAX	20	-1	0	5	9	12	13
114 ACCOUNTS RECEI			6	17	56	117	184
115 RETAIN RECEIV		1	2	7	15	27	42
159 TOTAL EQUITY	70	69	69	74	83	94	107
194 CURR CASH FLOW	30	-1	-7	-3	-19	-22	-19
198 CUMULATIVE CAS	30	29	22	19	0	-23	-41

'SAMPLE CONTRACTOR MASTER ASSUMPTIONS'

	JUL	AUG	SEP	OCT	NOV	DEC	TOT YR
51 SALES	71	49	56	35	35	35	700
57 GROSS PROFIT	4	3	4	2	2	2	55
63 OH OV UN APPLIE	3	3	2	2	2	2	0
66 PROFIT AFTER TAX	1	0	2	1	1	1	41
114 ACCOUNTS RECEI	243	195	108	95	82	62	62
115 RETAIN RECEIV	39	24	30	33	37	40	-30
159 TOTAL EQUITY	108	108	110	110	111	111	50
194 CURR CASH FLOW	-23	35	64	-9	-9	17	5
198 CUMULATIVE CAS	-64	-30	34	26	17	35	

COMMAND: This is certain significant data taken from the foregoing statements.

Figure 12.17 Output Data from Financial Modeling Assuming Initial Plan

'SAMPLE CONTRACTOR MONTH DELAY IN WORK IN MAY' 000

		JAN	FEB	MAR	APR	MAY	JUN
51 SALES		7	13	50	81		124
57 GROSS PROFIT		1	1	5	8		11
63 OH OV UN APPLIE		2	2	-2	-3	4	-5
66 PROFIT AFTER TAX		-1	0	5	9	-3	12
114 ACCOUNTS RECEI			6	17	56	117	72
115 RETAIN RECEIV		1	2	7	15	15	27
159 TOTAL EQUITY	70	69	69	74	83	80	91
194 CURR CASH FLOW		-1	-7	-3	-19	-29	24
198 CUMULATIVE CAS	30	29	22	19	0	-29	-6

'SAMPLE CONTRACTOR MONTH DELAY IN WORK IN MAY'

	JUL	AUG	SEP	OCT	NOV	DEC	TOT YR
51 SALES	146	71	49	56	35	69	700
57 GROSS PROFIT	12	4	3	4	2	4	55
63 OH OV UN APPLIE	-5	3	3	2	2	-1	0
66 PROFIT AFTER TAX	13	1	0	2	1	4	41
114 ACCOUNTS RECEI	112	243	195	108	95	82	
115 RETAIN RECEIV	42	39	24	30	33	40	
159 TOTAL EQUITY	104	105	105	107	107	111	
194 CURR CASH FLOW	4	-65	35	64	-9	-7	-51
198 CUMULATIVE CAS	-2	-67	-33	31	23	15	

COMMAND: The same data lines are printed above assuming a strike closes down all projects during May. Short-term borrowing needs go from a high of 64,000 in July to 67,000 in August. All work is still completed by December 31, 19X0

Figure 12.18 Financial Modeling Output Given an Uncertainty

determine what this unexpected or unpredictable event will do to the cash flow shown in Figure 12.17. The revised financial statements and cash flows for this possible future event are illustrated in Figure 12.18. Given the built financial model and the input data regarding the possible future event, the computer generates the output data shown in Figure 12.18 in a matter of seconds.

Similar types of possible uncertain or unpredictable events could be analyzed in a matter of minutes using the computer-based financial modeling process. Admittedly the computer is only doing what also could be done manually. However, the time required to generate revised cash flows and financial statements would probably result in an effort that outweighed the benefit. It is the computer's capability that allows us to analyze efficiently the results of possible future events. In effect, the computer-based financial modeling program provides the construction firm a means of analyzing possible uncertain events and, therefore, in great part defeat the argument that planning including cash-flow analysis is not advantageous because it does not recognize the uncertainty of future events affecting the construction process.

13
BREAK-EVEN ANALYSIS AND OVERHEAD ALLOCATION

INTRODUCTION

A typical income (profit or loss) statement for a construction firm was illustrated in Chapter 6. The profitability of the construction firm depends on every line item on the financial statement. Given this fact, the construction firm must decide on what items to focus on in order to best increase profits and reduce the risk of losing money. For example, given a set volume of work, should the construction firm place all its emphasis on controlling its costs of production or should it focus on minimizing its overhead costs such as its office administration costs?

The difficulty of choosing a specific approach to increase total profits relates to the difficulty of measuring the results of a specific approach and the long-term effects of any one approach. For example, a reduction in general and administrative expense may result in an immediate increase in profits. However, a reduction may result in a decrease in marketing effort leading to a reduction in volume and revenue. Similarly, a reduction in general and administrative expense may lead to less management support for the production process. This lack of support, including cost-control reports and economical purchasing of material, may lead to added production costs that may offset the reduced overhead (general and administrative) expense. While the reduction of general and administrative expense may be justified, it is not always easy to measure the actual dollar benefit obtained from this or any other action.

In a broad sense, the line items comprising the construction firm's income statement may be grouped as follows:

	Revenue
Minus:	Cost of sales
Equal:	Gross Profit
Minus:	Overhead
Equal:	Net profit

The gross profit divided by revenue is commonly referred to as *gross margin*.

This chapter addresses the relationships among the elements comprising the income statment. Specifically, the concepts of break-even analysis and overhead allocation are discussed along with other relationships that exist among income statement line items. The overall objective of the chapter is to provide the construction firm short-term decision-making potential through the analysis of cost-accounting data.

COST-ACCOUNTING TERMINOLOGY

In order to understand the discussion that is presented in following sections of this chapter, it is necessary to first learn some of the language of cost accounting. This is especially true because in practice misuse of various cost-accounting terms has led to interpretation problems.

The very term *cost* is subject to many interpretations. Cost in an accounting sense is dollars exchanged for goods or services. Dollars paid for material, for labor, or for a bond or insurance are examples of costs to the construction firm. A properly designed cost-accounting system assigns the various types of costs that occur to certain defined *cost objects*. A cost object is an activity or part of an organization for which a separate determination of cost is needed. Cost objects are defined in a manner consistent with the decision-making needs of management; for example, if the construction firm desires to have each project superintendent responsible for individual job overheads, then a job overhead cost object should be set up for each individual job. Similarly, segregating overtime labor hours from normal working hours may be the result of management's desire to analyze overtime policies. It may choose to allocate such overtime labor costs to job overhead rather than to direct cost. Regardless of its decision or policy as to the given cost, the firm's very decision to segregate the cost results in creating a cost object. Various construction work items such as concrete slab work, footings, masonry walls, and so forth, are commonly segregated as to data collection. Each of the work items is thus identified as a cost object. Cost objects can be identified as individual work items or even segments of one's business.

There are numerous classifications of the term cost. These classifications often depend on the nature of the cost as to the product produced. The benefit of classifying costs is that the classifications can serve as a means of analyzing a given cost with the objective of managing the cost. Several classifications of costs will now be defined.

Costs that vary directly with changes in activity are called *variable costs*. Examples of variable costs are costs of material and labor used in the production process and equipment hours expended in the manufacturing process. *Fixed costs* are those that vary with the passage of time despite changes in the level of activity. A secretary's wages and the salary of an estimator or a superintendent employed the full year regardless of the availability of company jobs may be considered fixed costs. It should be noted that a fixed cost may vary if the level of activity changes substantially. For example, if a construction firm reorganizes such that it reduces its volume by 50 percent, it may find it necessary to lay off an estimator or two. As such, the fixed cost is no longer fixed. The end result is that, when speaking about a fixed cost, one must recognize the existence of the relevant range of business activity. The relevant range is that level of activity for which the firm budgets and expects to operate. As such, the definition of fixed cost is valid only for the firm's relevant range of activity. To illustrate the problem of fixed costs not being fixed over unexpected activity levels, the term *semifixed* is introduced.

It should be noted that, what is a variable cost to one firm, might in fact be a fixed cost to another firm. For example, one construction firm may hire and fire job superintendents as a function of workload, whereas another firm may keep a given number of superintendents on its payroll regardless of workload level.

An important classification in regard to how costs are reported in the financial statements of a firm is identifying costs as product or period costs. Costs expended in transforming materials into useful products are referred to as *product costs*. These types of costs may be thought of as "attaching" to the product. Carpenter and iron-worker wages, concrete and steel costs, and even job superintendent's (assuming they are allocated to the supervision of the production process) wages are product costs. In general, production-related costs are identified as product costs. Product costs are sometimes referred to as inventoriable costs.

Period costs do not directly result from manufacturing the product. They are costs that relate to selling the product and the overall general administrative costs of operating the firm. They do not attach to the product produced. Secretarial wages, estimator's wages, and office equipment are examples of construction firm period costs. Note that if the secretary or estimator is assigned to a given job these labor costs may be considered product costs.

While it is true that most period costs are fixed in nature, there are exceptions. Personnel responsible for finding work may be paid a commission based on the dollar volume of work contracted. This cost, while not be attached to the work itself, is in fact a variable cost.

The concept of product and period cost has implications as to the financial statements and tax liabilities of the firm. Whereas product costs are visualized as attached to the product, they are identified as part of a product inventory that the firm maintains or holds at the end of a reporting period. When using the completed-contract method of revenue recognition, these costs are not viewed as expenses to the firm until the inventory is sold; instead, they are temporarily viewed as assets. On the other hand, period costs do not attach to the manufactured product and, as such, are often viewed as expenses in the period in which they occur. The difference between the two accounting procedures is very important in regard to construction work because of the rather common long duration of a construction project. That is, the construction project, which can be viewed as inventory or work-in-progress, may be in that status for two or three years. Rather significant differences in financial statements and tax implications result from the alternatives of viewing a cost as a product or period cost. These differences are in part illustrated in Chapters 6 and 17.

Similar to classifying a cost as a product or period cost is the concept of a direct cost, indirect cost, and overhead cost. In reality all costs are direct costs to some cost object. Necessary to the definition of a direct cost is the definition of the cost object. If a cost is traced to a defined cost object, it is a direct cost in regard to that cost object. If it is not traced to the defined cost object, it is an indirect cost to the cost object. For example, a secretary's wage is a direct cost to the construction company. The wage is usually not traced to a specific project and is therefore an indirect cost to a project.

For the construction industry, the use of the term direct cost is usually reserved to mean a cost traced to a specific construction project. Project labor and material are examples of direct costs of this type. Equipment costs may or may not be traced to a specific project. In the former case they would be identified as a direct cost and in the later they would be identified as an indirect cost.

The construction industry usually reserves the term indirect cost for those costs that are traced to the building of all projects taken as a whole. In other words, they are construction-oriented costs but are not commonly traced to building a specific project. Labor payroll taxes, supervision costs, and, to a certain extent, equipment costs are examples of indirect costs. As noted earlier, some firms trace equipment to a specific project, in which case the cost is considered a direct cost.

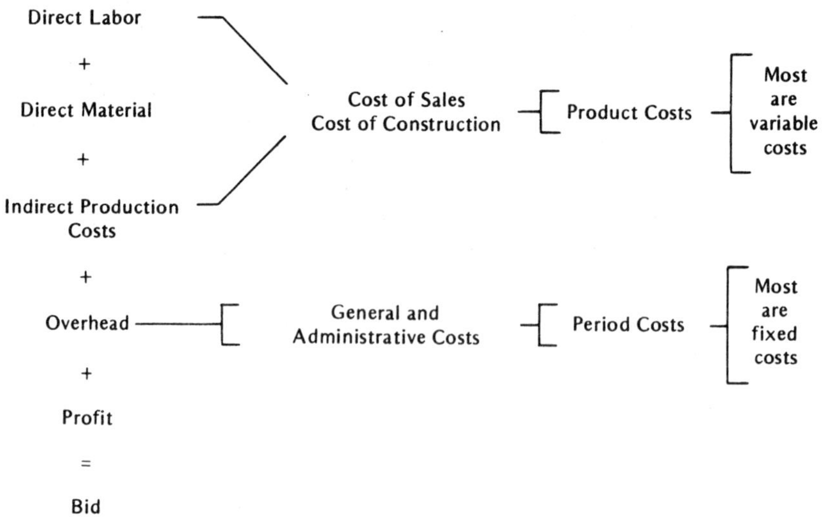

Figure 13.1 Classification of Costs

In the construction industry the term *overhead cost* is normally used to mean the firm's costs that are not commonly identified as project costs. In effect, they are costs incurred by the construction firm that support the production process. Specifically, the costs of maintaining the home office, executive salaries, and marketing or selling expenses are usually referred to as overhead costs.

The sum of direct costs and indirect costs is commonly referred to as the *cost of sales* or the *cost of construction* on the construction firm's income statement. This is illustrated in Figure 13.1. The overhead costs are commonly referred to as the *costs of operations* or *general and administrative costs* on the income statement. This is also illustrated in Figure 13.1

The relationships of some of the many classifications of costs are also illustrated in Figure 13.1. Note that a single cost may be referred to by several different names depending on the classification used. For example, a secretary's cost may be considered a fixed cost, a period cost, an overhead cost, and a general and administrative cost.

METHODS FOR INCREASING PROFITS

A construction firm's success is measured by its profitability. Some individuals might argue that the objective or accomplishments of the construction firm include improving its public image and serving a community and employees. However, these seemingly nonmonetary objectives are usually all tied to making money. While profits might seem a selfish or self-serving objective, in reality a profitable construction firm and industry serves the best interests of many other individuals and the country as a whole.

The profitability of the individual construction firm can be expressed in different ways. For example, one commonly refers to *return of equity* or *earning power* when discussing profitability. A firm able to generate $100,000 of bottom-line annual profits on an investment of $400,000 is, in effect, obtaining a rate of return of 25 percent on its investment. The higher its return, the more successful the firm might be evaluated.

Rate of return or earning power is a meaningful method employed by external parties to evaluate the construction firm. Using this calculated rate of return, the external party might evaluate a construction firm relative to another construction firm or relative to firms in other industries.

The individual construction firm is usually much more concerned about its total bottom-line profits (referred to as *net income* or *profit after taxes*) than its return on equity. More often than not the owners of the construction firm have come up from the construction ranks and are committed to operating a construction firm. Therefore, a comparison of the firm's rate of return or return on equity to a similar financial measure of a nonconstruction firm is somewhat meaningless to the firm. Relative to comparing its rate of return to other construction firms, the individual firm may not have access to financial data of its competitors. Even when it does, the unique characteristics of each construction firm may lead to limited use from the comparison.

The end result is that the individual construction firm often measures its success year in and year out by its bottom-line or net profits. Usually net profits are a measure of the money that is made available to the owners of the firm. Because of the possibility of *paper profits* in the form of depreciation, net profits and free cash available to the owners of the firm may on occasion not have a one-to-one relationship. However, it usually follows that the higher the bottom-line profits of the firm, the more money available to the owners for luxury vacations, expensive automobiles, and bigger and better houses.

Given the construction firm's objective of increasing bottom-line or net profits, there are essentially three different approaches taken to improve the profits. These may be classified as follows:

1. Increased volume approach
2. Increased gross margin approach
3. Control of overhead approach

While the construction firm can take all three approaches simultaneously, each firm often limits itself to one approach. While focusing on only one is not to be recommended, at least it is better than no approach.

Increased Volume

Most construction firms take the increased volume approach as their means to increase their profits (we are using profits to mean bottom-line profits or net profits after tax). The firm assumes that the more volume they do, the more profits it will generate.

The firm that takes the volume approach often argues that their gross margin or revenue minus costs is controlled by competition. They also argue that their overhead costs are not a variable in that they must maintain "their team" in order to carry out construction activities.

The fact that the construction firm has so often equated increased profits with increased volume has no doubt led to many equating size of firm with success. However, volume is often overemphasized as a means of increasing total profits. Too often the construction firm fails to control its costs on its projects already underway at the expense of going out and finding more work.

Added volume can lead to substantial increases in total profits if the construction firm is successful in maintaining its profit margin and controlling its overhead costs. On the other hand, increased volume that leads to a decreased profit margin may actually lead to smaller total profits. Similarly, increased volume that leads to substantial increases in overhead costs may also lead to less total profits. The three described possibilities are illustrated in Figure 13.2. It is obvious from Figure 13.2 that merely increasing volume is not always the correct approach to increasing total profits. In fact, many construction firms would do themselves well to lessen their volume approach.

	How Achieved	Also Affects
Increased Volume	Increased marketing Diversification Increased bidding Lower bids	Overhead (possibly higher) Gross margin
Gross Margin	Increased productivity More selective in choice of work	May have to limit volume to do more profitable work May increase overhead
Decreased Overhead	Eliminate expenditures not needed Restrict work performed	May adversely affect volume

Figure 13.2 Methods for Increasing Profits

Increased Gross Margin

The increased gross margin approach to increasing profits can return significant bottom-line profits. As noted earlier, the construction firm often argues that its gross margin is dictated by competition. In reality, gross margins for construction firms vary significantly. For example, for general contractors the gross margin may be 10 to 20 percent. This 10 percent difference in gross margin on a construction volume as small as $1 million equates to a potential difference of $100,000 in bottom-line profits.

The increased gross margin approach to increasing total profits addresses both the revenue and cost of sales components of the construction firm's income statement. Gross margin is calculated as follows:

	Revenue
minus:	Cost of sales
equals:	Gross profit
divided by:	Revenue
equals:	Gross margin

Gross margin is also referred to in practice as *gross profit margin*.

One means of increasing gross margin is for the construction firm to decrease its cost of doing a given volume of work. For example, an increase in manhour output would lead to a reduced unit cost of construction with the end result being increased total profits. All too often the construction firm takes the approach that it cannot do anything about field costs. It gives arguments that relate to labor unions dictating costs, costs being dictated by weather, material shortages, etc.

Given the large percentage of nonproductive time that characterizes field work (some studies suggest nonproductive time accounts for as high as 50 percent of all field time), the construction firm is writing off a significant profit potential when it ignores controlling or reducing its construction costs. Numerous examples of cost reductions can be detected and implemented if the firm will take the time to be innovative as to field methods.

Even if one accepts the weak argument that construction costs are determined once the project is defined, the gross margin approach can still be used for increasing total profits. The key is to take on work that allows for a significant profit margin. In other words, instead of merely seeking more volume, the construction firm should seek out volume that includes a price conducive of increased or significant gross margin.

The competitive nature of the normal lump sum construction contract weakens the construction firm's ability to secure contracts with an improved profit margin. It follows that the ability to market one's services outside the competitive lump sum process may be the key to securing higher gross margin contracts. In other words, the salesmanship of the firm becomes a part of the increased gross margin approach to increasing profits.

Control of Overhead

Many of the construction firm's overhead costs tend to be fixed costs. Examples include cost of maintaining the company office, cost of the clerical staff, advertising expense, and the cost of dues and subscriptions. The controlling overhead costs approach to increasing total profits entails keeping the firm's overhead costs less than the gross profits. The smaller the overhead costs are relative to the firm's gross profits, the larger the total profits.

The construction firm's difficulty in increasing or maintaining total profits often relates to the variable volume of the firm from one year to the next. The competitive nature of the construction industry and the industry's volume dependence on the overall economy are two leading causes for the individual firm's volume variability. While the construction firm's volume tends to be quite variable, its overhead costs from one period to the next tend to be relatively static with any change usually being additive.

Given a decreased or "flat" volume of construction work, the firm must address reducing and controlling its overhead costs. If it fails to do this, not only will decreased profits result, but the firm may actually put itself in a state of potential financial failure. An attempt to compensate for a decreased volume by decreased construction costs will usually not be totally effective in the short run. The benefits of implementing improved field methods tend to result in gradual benefits, the sum of which may be substantial over the long run.

The fixed nature of most overhead costs does make their reduction somewhat difficult. However, as was pointed out in an earlier section of this chapter, what is a fixed cost for one volume of activity in effect becomes a variable cost for a different volume of activity. While three clerical employees might be needed to handle duties associated with the firm performing four million dollars of work, two staff members may be able to handle a reduced volume of two million dollars. Some might argue that the volume of the firm will probably return to four million and therefore the third clerical staff member should be retained to fill the expected increase. Admittedly, this policy has its advantages. However, it also follows that retaining the excess capacity during the reduced volume may lead to financial difficulties that may prevent the firm from returning to the four million volume level.

An effective approach to overhead control for the construction firm is a *marginal overhead budget* approach. This approach is similar to the management approach of *zero-based budgeting*. When using the marginal overhead budget approach, the construction firm establishes the minimum amounts of various overhead items it needs to support an expected volume of work. Each overhead item should be justified. The firm does not get locked into an overhead that was justified five years prior. A construction firm doing two million dollars of volume cannot afford an overhead characteristic of a four million dollar volume firm! It needs to be able to be somewhat flexible with its overhead costs and it needs to continually justify its overhead costs.

BREAK-EVEN ANALYSIS AND CONTRIBUTION

The cost-accounting concepts of break-even analysis and contribution provide a means of interrelating the three previously discussed approaches to construction firm profits. These approaches considered volume, gross margin, and overhead. Break-even analysis and contribution also prove to be useful concepts when it comes to evaluating the feasibility of a construction firm bidding below its total costs to cover some of its overhead.

The basic equation that serves as the basis of break-even analysis and contribution is as follows:

$$\text{profit} = \text{revenue} - \text{variable expenses} - \text{fixed expenses}$$

Using this equation it is possible to calculate a break-even volume or revenue for a construction firm, commonly referred to as the firm's *break-even point*. The break-even point or volume is the level of volume at which the firm's revenue exactly equals its total costs. At this volume, the construction firm neither makes money nor loses it.

Break-even analysis is a useful means for the construction firm to determine what level of volume is needed to cover its planned overhead expenses. In order to perform this analysis, we usually assume that the construction firm's costs of sales are variable expenses and its operating or general and administrative costs are fixed costs. While there are exceptions to these assumptions, most construction costs are variable, and most operating costs may be considered fixed within a given range of volume.

The break-even point calculation for the construction firm assumes the firm has estimated its overhead or fixed expenses for the period in question. Let us assume this amount is \$240,000 for an upcoming year for a given construction firm. The analysis also assumes that the construction firm can predict its gross margin on work to be performed. In reality this prediction is not difficult given previous year performance. Without an innovative approach to decreasing construction field costs and securing more profitable projects, a construction firm's gross margin does not vary significantly from one year to the next. For purposes of example, let us assume a construction firm is able to attain a gross margin of 12 percent.

Given the estimated annual overhead expenses and the firm's gross margin, the necessary break-even point or volume needed to cover the overhead is calculated as follows:

At break-even point:

$$\text{revenue} = \text{cost of sales} + \text{operating expense}$$

but

$$\text{gross margin} = (\text{revenue} - \text{cost of sales})/\text{revenue}$$

therefore, at break-even point

$$\text{gross margin} = \text{operating expenses}/\text{revenue}$$

or

$$\text{revenue} = \text{operating expenses}/\text{gross margin}$$

In the example of the $240,000 overhead and 12 percent gross margin, the break-even volume is calculated as follows:

$$\text{break-even volume} = \frac{\$240{,}000}{.12} = \$2{,}000{,}000$$

This calculation yields the fact that the construction firm is going to have to secure at least $2 million of volume in the one-year period to prevent a loss. Similarly, if the required annual volume is judged unfeasible, the calculation of the break-even volume draws attention to the fact that the construction firm will probably have to reduce its overhead to prevent a loss.

Establishing a required volume needed to cover overhead in effect defines a minimum goal for the firm. Setting such a goal often motivates the firm to achieve it and also serves as the basis for justifying certain marketing plans and expenditures. Periodically the break-even point should be recalculated. This is in recognition of changes in overhead expenditures and modifications in the gross margin.

The concept of *contribution* is also useful in profit analysis. Contribution is defined as follows:

$$\text{contribution} = \text{revenue} - \text{variable expense}$$

A specific construction project yields the construction firm a positive contribution as long as the dollar contract amount is greater than the cost of construction (remember we identified the cost of construction or sales as mainly a variable cost). As long as a project has positive contribution, it contributes

Assume firm's monthly overhead equals $40,000 Direct costs of project equal $180,000	Firm Considering Bidding Project of One Month Duration Alternative 1 Bid high (Very little chance of getting contract)	 Alternative 2 Bid low (Very good change of getting contract)	 Alternative 3 Don't Bid
Bid	$230,000	$200,000	
Costs:			
Direct	180,000	180,000	
Fixed	40,000	40,000	40,000
Profit (Loss)	$ 10,000	($ 20,000)	($40,000)
Contribution to overhead and profit	$ 50,000	$ 20,000	0

Figure 13.3 Concept of Bidding Below Total Costs

to covering some of the firm's overhead. For example, let us assume a construction firm contracts to build a project for $2,000,000 and subsequently its cost of construction (including direct and indirect costs) is $1,800,000. A $200,000 contribution results that helps to cover some of the firm's overhead.

Having introduced the concept of contribution, we can understand the common practice of some construction firms occasionally signing a contract to build a project for less than total costs. By total costs is meant the costs of construction and an allocated percentage of the firm's overhead costs. This practice is illustrated in Figure 13.3.

Obviously a construction firm should never bid below its estimate of construction costs. This type of project would have a negative contribution as to both project profits and company profits. If a firm's total costs exceed a contract amount, the firm can obtain a profitable contribution as long as the costs of construction are less than the contract revenue. Even then the construction firm has to avoid the practice of bidding below cost from becoming habit forming. A continual practice of bidding below total cost means the firm is not covering its overhead costs. Eventually the problem may compound to result in more severe financial results such as bankruptcy.

OVERHEAD ALLOCATION

One of the weakest areas of good construction firm management or accounting is overhead allocation which is part of the estimating process. The lack of adequate overhead allocation procedures is one of the many reasons for construction firm bankruptcies. All too often the construction firm spends hundreds of hours to accurately estimate direct labor and material costs only to then proceed by adding a large percent (e.g., 30 or 40 percent) to cover all other costs including overhead. The result is that the effort expended attempting to accurately estimate direct costs is negated by the crudeness of the method used for estimating all other costs.

The construction firm incurs several different types of costs in carrying out its construction business. Essentially these costs are one of the following three types:

1. Costs directly related to a specific project
2. Costs directly related to building projects in general
3. Costs incurred by the firm that support the production process but are not directly related to production

Costs directly related to a specific project are considered direct costs to a specific project and are identified in the estimate for the project. These include direct labor and material and should never be allocated to a project as they are clearly not overhead costs.

Costs directly related to building projects in general are often referred to as indirect costs or sometimes as *job overhead costs*. Examples of job overhead costs might include supervision costs and equipment costs or expenses. Job overhead costs are considered traceable to all projects, but not easily traceable to any one specific project.

In practice construction firms have on occasion recognized job overhead-related costs in the project estimate by using an allocation process; for example, a construction firm might multiply the sum of a project's labor and material cost by 10 percent to determine the job overhead cost to apply to a specific project.

The described process of allocating job overhead costs to a project can lead to an inaccurate estimate. The process assumes that job overhead costs are the same percentage of the direct costs for each project. This is usually not the case. For example, assuming supervision is handled as a job overhead cost, it is true that the amount of necessary supervision on projects varies substantially. The amount of supervision required often depends on the complexity or uniqueness of the job.

The correct method of recognizing job overhead types of costs in a project estimate is to identify each job overhead cost for a specific project and add them for inclusion in the total project estimate. In other words, job overhead costs should not be allocated. They should be handled as a direct cost to a project when estimating the project's costs.

In practice certain job overhead costs may be more easily handled by allocating them to various projects. For example, the construction firm may choose to use an allocation process for equipment rather than identify the equipment to be used on a specific project and the amount of expected use on the specific project. While this procedure may prove to be efficient as to the time required to recognize a project's equipment costs, the construction firm should be reminded that the potential for accurate estimates diminishes anytime a cost is treated on an allocation basis. Job overhead costs are, by the name itself, traceable to projects. The more detailed the construction firm is in identifying specific job overhead costs, the more likely will accurate estimates result.

Costs incurred by the firm that support the production process but are not directly related to the production process need to be allocated to a project. These costs were referred to as general and administrative costs or expenses in previous sections of this chapter. They are also commonly referred to simply as *overhead* costs, or as *company* or *office* overhead. Examples of these costs include the costs of maintaining the home office, entertainment expenses, and marketing costs or expenses.

Two somewhat separate questions must be addressed when applying general and administrative (G and A) costs or overhead to specific projects. First, the construction firm must decide on the basis for the overhead allocation process. Second, once an overhead basis is chosen, there still is the question as to the mechanics of determining the amount to be applied to a specific project.

The objective of any allocation of expense is to attempt to apply costs to the cost object in an amount that matches the total costs incurred because of the existence of the cost object. In regard to project estimating, the cost object is the construction project.

Too often total direct cost, including labor and material costs (and equipment if it is treated as a direct cost), is taken for granted as the best basis for applying G and A costs to projects. While this may prove an accurate basis for some firms, other allocation bases may prove more accurate for other construction firms.

Some construction firms find that they attain a better matching of applied and actual cost if they apply G and A costs to specific projects as a function of only the direct labor cost of the project. This is the second most common method in use.

One might also make a good argument for applying G and A costs to specific projects as a function of the expected duration of the projects. Most G and A costs are fixed in nature. The total dollar amount of these types of costs is often a function of time only. For example, many of the costs of maintaining a company office are fixed. The cost of maintaining the office for two months is approximately twice the cost of maintaining it for one month.

It can be argued that the longer a project takes to complete, the more G and A costs are incurred and the more should be applied to the project. This is a defensible argument and while not in wide use, many construction firms could probably get a better matching of actual and applied overhead if they would recognize duration in their G and A allocation process.

The mechanics of overhead allocation are relatively simple. However, in spite of the simplicity, construction firms continue to ignore the process in favor of an antiquated process. Too often the firm will use the same percentage for overhead allocation year in and year out without any periodic review or analysis of the percentage. For example, a construction firm might add 15 percent of total direct costs to each estimate for a number of years without ever analyzing the overhead percentage. The danger of this process is that a firm's overhead costs, volume, and gross margin change yearly, each at a different rate.

The objective of the allocation or application of G and A costs to projects is to apply every dollar of G and A costs, no more or no less, to all projects over a defined period of time. If the firm uses an allocation basis that falls short of applying $50,000 of G and A, a profit of $30,000 is actually a loss of $20,000. If the firm falls short of applying some of its overhead, the unapplied amount is referred to as underapplied overhead. If the firm actually applies more overhead to projects than incurred, the excess applied is referred to as overapplied overhead.

Given the basis by which overhead as G and A costs is to be applied, the process involved requires two estimates to determine the application rate. An estimate of the G and A costs for the time period in question and an estimate of the dollar amount of the overhead basis must be forecasted or estimated.

As a minimum, the construction firm should analyze its G and A application rate annually. To illustrate the mechanics of overhead allocation, let us assume a construction firm allocated its G and A overhead costs to projects on the basis of the sum of direct labor and material costs, and that the firm reviews and establishes its G and A application rate annually. The example being considered is illustrated in Figure 13.4.

The first step of the allocation process illustrated in Figure 13.4 is determining the estimate of the coming year's G and A costs. It is these costs that are to be applied in total to projects constructed during the year. The estimate of a coming year's G and A costs or expenses is not as difficult as it might seem. Usually the components that make up the total G and A costs do not vary significantly from one year to the next. Therefore determining the estimate of the coming year's G and A costs can often be attained by merely multiplying the prior year's G and A costs by an inflation factor. Obviously any major increase or decrease of G and A costs stemming from a planned expansion or contraction would also have to be acknowledged in the estimate.

As a means of determining an estimate of the firm's direct labor and material costs for the coming year, volume is projected along with the firm's gross profit margin. These two variables are then used to estimate the coming year's direct labor and material costs. This "backing into" the estimate of direct labor and material costs as a function of volume is commonplace because the amount of the direct labor and material costs is in great part determined by the dollar volume of work performed.

Once the volume is projected ($4,000,000 in Figure 13.4), the gross margin is used to calculate the direct labor and material costs. In Figure 13.4 the total cost of sales is assumed to consist only of the direct labor and material costs.

Step 1 Estimate of Annual Overhead (General and Administrative Expense)

Last Year's G&A	$270,000
10% Inflation	27,000
Firm growth	23,000
Estimated G&A	$320,000

Step 2 Estimate of $ of Cost Basis for Allocation

Estimated volume	$4,000,000
Gross margin	
	20% = $800,000
Labor and Matl. $	$3,200,000

Step 3 Overhead Allocation Rate

$$\frac{\text{overhead costs estimated (G \& A)}}{\text{labor and material estimate}} = \frac{320{,}000}{3{,}200{,}000} = 10\%$$

Step 4 Cost to Apply to a Specific Project

Estimated labor and matl. costs = $500,000	
Overhead to apply	
Labor and matl. costs 500,000	
times allocation rate 10%	50,000
Costs	$550,000

Figure 13.4 Overhead Allocation Process

If equipment or other costs were assumed part of the cost of sales, these costs would have to be subtracted from the expected volume to yield the expected direct labor and material costs.

The calculations shown in Figure 13.4 yield an application rate of 10 percent. Therefore, in the year in question, each time a project is estimated, an overhead cost is applied to the project equal in amount to 10 percent times the project's estimated direct labor and material costs. For example, for the $500,000 project in Figure 13.4, the applied G and A cost is 10 percent multiplied by $500,000, or $50,000.

It is advantageous for the construction firm to review periodically the calculated overhead rate at various times during the year. If it is apparent after four months into the year that the firm's estimate of annual volume is too high, an upward adjustment in the overhead rate is probably justified.

The constraint to good overhead allocation is the competitive nature of the construction industry. Apart from a firm's accurately calculated overhead rate is the fact that the construction firm still has to be low enough in its bid to secure the project contract. It is possible that the firm's allocation process results in project bids that are noncompetitive. However, it does not follow that the firm should make a bid that contains an allocation rate less than the firm's calculated rate. What more likely follows is that the construction firm needs to lessen its total overhead costs to a point where it is competitive.

ABSORPTION VERSUS DIRECT COSTING

The previous section addressed the allocation of overhead costs to individual projects. It was suggested that a construction firm's general and administrative overhead (e.g., fixed costs) be allocated to individual projects such that the sum of the costs of the individual projects includes the sum of all the firm's overhead costs.

In cost-accounting terminology, the described methods for handling overhead (i.e., allocate all the overhead to individual projects) is referred to as absorption costing. As such, all costs become "inventory costs" while the projects are in the work-in-progress state. In effect, overhead costs become an asset until the project is completed and turned over to the owner.

An alternative to the absorption-costing procedure is direct costing (also referred to as contribution costing). Direct costing emphasizes the fact that fixed overhead is of a different nature than direct costs or variable overhead. Fixed costs are costs that occur independent of activity and must be recognized during a given period. As such, direct costing treats these fixed overhead costs as period costs. They are not considered to attach to the product (the construction project). Therefore, they are not considered to be part of work-in-progress when a project has a duration in excess of the accounting period in question. Instead, the fixed overhead costs are expensed in the period in which they occur.

Much of the argument for direct costing is centered around the different decisions that relate to creating and controlling variable overhead costs versus fixed overhead costs. Fixed costs generally originate in the firm's decisions as to the size of its company and planned growth. As such, they are committed costs. On the other hand, variable costs originate because of the daily operation of the firm. Responsibility for these costs is centered on manufacturing personnel. In the construction industry, the personnel responsible for these variable overhead costs would probably be job foremen and superintendents. On the other hand, upper management is generally responsible for the committed costs. Direct costing emphasizes these different levels of responsibility by separately recognizing the two types of costs.

From an accounting point of view, the important difference between absorption costing and direct costing is the different income effects of the two costing methods. This difference is high-lighted in Figure 13.5. As shown, reported net income is lower when using direct costing. Absorption costing yields a higher net income because fixed overhead costs are made part of inventory instead of being expensed as they are in direct costing. Note should be made that, over several accounting periods, the difference between the reported incomes using the two costing procedures will tend to be eliminated. This is especially the case when volume tends to be relatively constant. However, during periods of wide variation in sales or work performed (e.g., construction project work completed), the reported income using the two procedures will vary substantially.

Absorption Costing			
Modulars sold: 1,000 at $1,000.00			$1,000,000
Cost of units sold			
Variable: 1,100 units at	$600.00	$660,000	
Fixed manuf.	200.00	220,000	
Less ending Inventory 100 units	800.00	80,000	800,000
Gross Margin			$ 200,000
Less selling and administrative (including variable and fixed)			90,000
Net income			$ 110,000

Direct Costing		
Modulars sold 1,000 at $1,000.00		$1,000,000
Variable manuf. costs	$660,000	
Less ending inventory 100 units at 600	60,000	
Variable manuf. costs for units sold	$600,000	
Add variable selling and administrative	40,000	$ 640,000
Contribution margin less fixed costs:		$ 360,000
Fixed manuf.	220,000	
Fixed selling and manuf.	50,000	270,000
Net income		$ 90,000

Figure 13.5 Comparison of Absorption and Direct Costing

Several construction firms handle fixed overhead (i.e., G and A overhead) in a manner that approaches direct costing. For example, some construction firms do not allocate any G and A overhead to the cost of individual projects. Instead, they merely use a larger profit margin for their projects to cover such overhead costs as are recognized as period costs. The costs are not recognized as part of project work-in-progress. This procedure has the advantage of recognizing and holding project personnel responsible for only those costs within their control. On the other hand, there is the disadvantage that there is no assurance that profit margins are set such that all company G and A overhead will be recovered.

Part 4.
AUDITING

CHAPTERS

14
FINANCIAL AUDITING

INTRODUCTION

The purpose of the independent financial audit performed by a certified public accountant is to express an opinion as to whether or not the financial statements of the firm being audited fairly present the firm's financial position and the results of the firm's operations for the period specified. Audited financial statements assure a third party that an independent party, the certified public accountant, has reviewed and passed judgment on the validity of the statements. We will refer to the financial audit merely as an audit throughout this chapter.

Audited financial statements is a topic especially relevant to the construction industry in that firms in the industry are very dependent on external parties. These external parties include sureties or bonding companies, lending institutions, and occasionally material and equipment vendors. External parties use the audited financial statements in their analysis of their willingness to extend credit or financial support to the construction firm. Without the audit opinion of the independent public accountant, the financial statements are open for question because they probably will have been prepared by the same individuals seeking the financial assistance or insurance.

The audit examination process entails several accounting audit steps and procedures. The actual steps and procedures required by the independent public accountant in great part depend on the type of firm being audited and the financial and accounting controls of the firm.

The construction firm presents several unique auditing problems. First, many construction firms lack good financial and accounting internal controls. Second, the question of revenue recognition in the construction industry is complicated by the existence of long-term contracts. Particularly troublesome to the audit function is determining the percentage of completion for a project. These unique construction auditing problems along with auditing in general are discussed in this chapter.

AUDITING AND THE INDEPENDENT PUBLIC ACCOUNTANT

The construction firm's first audit usually is initiated as a result of external party demands. For example, a homebuilder may expand to include commercial construction. As part of this expansion, the construction firm gets more involved in the competitive bidding process. Sooner or later the potential project owner requires the construction firm to obtain a performance bond from a surety company. The surety or bonding company in turn probably will require the construction firm to submit audited financial statements as a prerequisite for obtaining bonding. A similar process initiating the audit might be generated by the lending institution.

Once the construction firm is subject to an audit, the requirement usually becomes an annual event. The audit process becomes part of the preparation of wrapping up the year end and serves as the source of much of the information required for preparing the annual federal income tax return.

Requiring construction firms to have an audit of their financial statements is increasing. This is partly due to the construction firm's increasing dependency on external parties and financial credit. In addition there is a growing tendency to have several separate but equal prime contracts for a single project versus the alternative of using a single general contractor who in turn contracts with several subcontractors. For example, in the relatively recently used construction management (CM) process, many specialty contractors including electrical and plumbing contractors are becoming prime contractors. More often than not, prime contractors have to provide their own individual performance bond with the result that the firms often need to have an audit.

Faced with requiring an audit, the construction firm may for the first time turn to using a certified public accountant. Prior to the need for an audit, the construction firm may have performed all of its accounting internally including preparing financial statements. As an alternative, the firm may have employed the services of a bookkeeping firm to carry out accounting-related services such as preparing tax returns.

Most state laws limit the preparation of audited financial statements to certified public accountants. Certified public accountant (CPA) is a designation granted by each of the states to persons who qualify by passing the Uniform CPA Examination and meeting both education and experience requirements. In effect, the purpose of the CPA designation is to ensure third parties and the construction firm of the independent public accountant's ability to perform his functions. Not all independent public accountants are CPA's. However, preparing audited financial statements is usually limited to CPA's. While a non-CPA can prepare financial statements for the construction firm, the statements are usually not viewed with the same degree of confidence by external parties as are audited financial statements.

Many construction firms employ the services of a CPA independent of the firm's need for audited financial statements. This is because the services of a CPA are not limited to performing audits. Tax planning and tax return preparations are common services of a CPA firm. Several of the larger CPA firms also have experience in offering specialized management services to include cash flow, project planning, marketing programs, and financial planning.

While services of the CPA firm can vary depending on the skills of the firm, auditing remains the primary service of the CPA firm. Ideally the audit function leads to the CPA giving an *unqualified opinion* regarding the financial statements of the construction firm. The unqualified opinion in effect indicates that the reader of the financial statements can be assured of the fact that the financial statements are accurately and fairly represented. In order to give an unqualified opinion, the CPA has to perform various audit steps and procedures aimed at testing the validity of the financial statements. Some of these steps are discussed in this chapter.

The accounting profession has adopted a standard form of unqualified opinion. The wording of this standardized opinion is illustrated in Figure 14.1.

The unqualified opinion shown in Figure 14.1 contains two paragraphs. The first paragraph is referred to as the *scope* paragraph. The scope paragraph indicates what financial statements were audited and indicates that the audit was performed using accepted accounting principles and procedures. The second paragraph is referred to as the *opinion* paragraph. It is in this paragraph that the auditor states that the statements are presented fairly.

Not all audits lead to an unqualified opinion. Other types of opinions are qualified by including the "subject to," "except for," or "disclaimer" opinion. While each of these will not be described here, suffice it to say that they are

To the Board of Directors
SAMPLE CONSTRUCTION CO., INC.

We have examined the balance sheet of Sample Construction Co., Inc., as of December 31, 19—, and the related statements of operations, retained income, and source and application of funds for the year then ended. Our examination was made in accordance with generally accepted auditing standards, and accordingly included such tests of accounting records and such other auditing procedures as we considered necessary in the circumstances.

In our opinion, the accompanying balance sheet and statements of operations, retained income, and source and application of funds present fairly the financial position of Sample Construction Co., Inc., at December 31, 19—, and the results of its operations and source and application of funds for the year then ended, in conformity with generally accepted accounting principles applied to a basis consistent with that of the preceding year.

James J. Adrian
Certified Public Accountant

Figure 14.1 Unqualified Audit Opinion

not desirable and generally weaken the construction firm's ability to carry out its business dealings with external parties.

In doing an audit the CPA will perform audit steps that are in accordance with generally accepted auditing standards. Specifically the accounting profession holds out ten different auditing standards as the acceptable level of quality that must be maintained in performing an audit. These standards address both the quality of field work auditing steps or procedures and financial reporting auditing steps or procedures. Even with the standards the actual auditing steps performed on a specific audit will vary depending on the auditor's evaluation and judgment.

In addition to the term standard, the phrase generally accepted accounting principles is extremely important in performing an audit. What are generally accepted accounting principles are established by the accounting profession and include methods for recognizing revenue, taking depreciation, etc. In effect, when the auditor expresses an opinion that the construction firm's financial statements are presented fairly, in effect he is indicating that the accounting presentation is consistent with defined generally accepted accounting principles. The auditor is not passing judgment on the benefit or validity of a recognized generally accepted accounting principle. He is merely indicating that the construction firm is in conformance with the principle.

In performing an audit the construction firm will usually start with an evaluation of the internal control practices of the construction firm. Internal control may be defined as follows:

> Internal control is the firm's plan of organization adopted within the firm to safeguard its assets, check the accuracy and reliability of its accounting records, and encourage adherence to predetermined managerial policies.

Specific examples of internal control include taking steps to avoid fraud or theft in the accounting process and implementing security steps to prevent misuse or theft of construction equipment.

Performing an internal control evaluation plays a major role in the auditor's defining a work program for auditing a specific firm. The weaker the internal controls implemented by the construction firm, the more detailed the auditing steps required. Internal controls for the construction firm are discussed in greater detail in the following chapter.

The auditor will prepare an audit work program which will include the extent and amount of detail of the individual audit work steps. It will consider the results of the analysis of internal control and the unique characteristics of the construction firm being audited.

Once the audit work program is developed, the auditor will proceed to an account by account analysis of accounts to be presented on the financial statements. In carrying out the analysis of individual accounts, the auditor will use several different auditing techniques for gathering and verifying financial data. Included are inspection, confirmation, inquiry, and comparison.

AUDIT PROCESS

1. Review last year's audit
2. Evaluate firm's internal controls
3. Prepare audit work program
4. Analyze individual accounts
5. Prepare work papers
6. Prepare financial statements
7. Review financial statements with firm
8. Prepare management letter

Figure 14.2 The Audit Process

Inspection or examination entails observing documents pertaining to specific accounting transactions that have occurred. For example, the auditor might inspect invoices from vendors to assure himself that payables are properly recorded in the accounting books of record.

Confirmation is a commonly used auditor technique. The process of confirming or confirmation relates to gathering evidence to support an account balance by means of a direct request to a third party. The most common auditing use of confirmation is in connection with the auditor's verification of accounts receivable. A letter is written to the individual or company owing the construction firm money asking the individual or company to confirm the correctness of the account as shown by the construction firm's records and stated in the letter. If the individual or company is asked to acknowledge the confirmation as right or wrong, the confirmation is referred to as a *positive* confirmation. If the individual or company is to respond only if the confirmation shows an incorrect balance, the process is referred to as a *negative* confirmation.

Inquiry is the process by which the auditor seeks financial and accounting data by directly asking a person who is likely to be able to supply the information. Inquiry of project superintendents may lead to disclosure of certain favorable or unfavorable project costs that may affect the amount of revenue to be recognized in a given accounting period.

Yet another audit technique available to the auditor is comparison. Comparing account balances at two different points in time, such as last year's balance versus this year's balance, can lead to detecting invalid data. Further audit tests would then be implemented to carry the analysis further.

The auditor will usually prepare a set of work papers in analyzing financial statement account balances. This step in the audit process along with others is illustrated in Figure 14.2. Once audit work papers are prepared and reviewed, they serve as the basis for preparing the audited financial statements.

UNIQUE CONSTRUCTION AUDITING PROBLEMS

The nature of the construction firm and the building process causes construction accounting to be quite unlike accounting in other types of firms. The result is that the CPA auditor is confronted with several unique auditing problems and required procedures when auditing the construction firm. The uniqueness of the construction firm in regard to auditing procedures is evidenced by the fact that the American Institute of Certified Public Accountants (AICPA) has authored a special guide for assisting the auditor in auditing the construction firm.

As noted in the previous section of this chapter, the auditor usually starts an audit engagement by evaluating the firm's internal controls. The better the internal controls, the less audit testing required. The weaker the internal controls, the less the auditor can rely on accounting records and therefore must expand the audit program and audit steps.

An unfavorable characteristic of most construction firms is that they have weak internal controls. In part this is because the typical construction firm is small as to the number of employees. Therefore, there is little opportunity for segregation of duties. For example, good internal accounting controls would have two different employees make out the bills and receive money, or make out purchase orders and subsequently pay the vendors. Because the construction firm may have a single employee, or even just a single part-time employee, for carrying out the clerical and accounting functions, the ideal office internal control procedures may not be possible or practical.

Examples of inadequate internal controls by the construction firm are not limited to the small firm. Too often, the construction firm tends to discount the value of accounting in favor of spending its time on sales and production. Examples of these weak internal controls resulting from a lack of attention include a less than structured approach to project estimating and control, failure to periodically review profit or loss of an ongoing project, and a lack of recordkeeping.

In addition to making the audit process more efficient and economical, the construction firm increases its overall operating efficiency if good internal control practices are implemented. Internal controls and operational efficiency are discussed in the following chapter.

In addition to the weak internal controls that characterize the construction firm, the auditor is faced with several other problem areas. Included are the construction firm's practices relating to allocation of overhead to projects, indirect charges on cost plus type of work, and handling of equipment costs. The methods employed to allocate overhead costs to projects vary considerably in the construction industry. Some firms write off all overhead or general and administrative expense as a period cost. Others attach some of these expenses to the project as a product cost. This has the effect of recognizing an asset versus an expense when recognized as a period cost. The auditor must determine if proper treatment of the costs is made, and if the firm is consistent in its treatment.

Cost plus work can create accounting problems for both the construction firm and the auditor. There is always a question of what indirect costs occur because of the project. Depending on what indirect costs are identified to a project, the very profitability of the project can vary, and the profit of the firm reported in a specific period can vary. For example, if the completed-contract method of recognizing revenue is used, indirect costs charged to a project may be recognized as an asset at year end. If the costs were not attached to the project, they probably would be expensed in the period incurred.

Construction equipment creates several different potential problems for the auditor. Construction firms often rent equipment with an option to buy with rental payments applying against the purchase price. Equipment rental charges for a specific project have to be analyzed in order to determine that the rates are fair and do not reflect a future purchase price. Gross profit on the project can be misstated by acquiring assets in this manner and charging the entire cost against the single project.

An equally troublesome auditing problem occurs when the construction firm owns its equipment. Many of these firms charge an expense to projects for the use of the equipment. In theory this is good accounting in that it potentially identifies actual project cost. The audit difficulty that arises relates to how and what charge is actually made to the project for use of the equipment. In other words, what should be the proper equipment rate charge? Some firms charge their equipment to projects at competing rental rates, others charge it at a rate that reflects its purchase cost, operating costs, and profits, still other firms use another method for determining the rates to be used. The auditor must consider these different possibilities in evaluating individual project profitability.

Other difficulties associated with auditing the construction firm relate to the specific characteristics of the firm. For example, some firms may have to buy significant dollar amounts of material or inventory to put in place for a project. Given this fact a question of when revenue is recognized occurs. Should revenue be recognized as the material is purchased or when it is installed? Similar types of auditing problems occur with other aspects of the construction process including project payrolls, subcontractor payments, and recognition of retainer income.

While all the discussed unique characteristics or processes of the construction firm create audit difficulties, no area creates more problems or uncertainty for the auditor than determining the percentage of completion, which is part of the percentage-of-completion revenue-recognition method. This method of recognizing revenue is used for long-term construction contracts and was discussed in Chapter 4. The percentage-of-completion method is the most frequently used method of recognizing revenue for long-term construction projects. The audit difficulty associated with using this method relates to the fact that the amount of profit recognized for a specific project at a point in time is very dependent on the estimated percentage of completion at that point in time. Too often the determination of percentage of completion is made arbitrarily with little or no regard to work actually performed and remaining. The wide variation in profits as a function of a few percentage points difference in the percentage of completion was illustrated in Chapter 8.

Determining the percentage of completion usually depends on calculating the cost expended to date and the estimate of costs to complete. Both of these areas can present problems for the auditor. The lack of good accounting records can prevent the auditor from establishing costs to date. The problem is made more complex and complicated by various possible accounting treatments of project equipment and indirect costs.

Even more troublesome than the determining of project costs to date is determining a project's cost to complete. Like determining incurred costs to date, it can have a major impact on calculating the percentage of completion. Many construction firms cannot give an accurate estimate of the cost to complete at any point in time during the building of a project. This is evidenced in part by the high failure rate in the construction industry. Many uncertain events such as weather, material availability, and labor productivity all affect the costs to complete a project.

The auditor uses several different audit steps to assist him in attempting to establish the percentage of completion for a project. In addition to evaluating the construction firm's own opinion by analyzing bids and past costs, the auditor will obtain percentage-of-completion confirmations from project owners. The auditor might also visit a project to evaluate its percentage of completion. In spite of any audit technique used, the percentage of completion remains somewhat of an uncertain variable for the construction firm and auditor. It is probably the most challenging area of construction firm auditing. Suggested audit steps for determining the percentage of completion are discussed in a later section of this chapter.

AUDITING BALANCE SHEET AND INCOME STATEMENT ACCOUNTS

The audit is aimed at giving an opinion on the fairness or accuracy of the financial statements. Therefore, in effect the auditor is passing judgment on the accounts that appear on both the balance sheet and income statement. While certain audit engagements may limit themselves to an audit of the balance sheet (especially first-time audits of a firm), most audits address all accounts that make up the balance sheet and income statement. These financial statements along with a statement of changes in financial position were discussed in Chapter 6. Because the accounts that make up the statements of changes in financial position are either on the balance sheet or income statement, the auditor is in effect auditing the statement of changes in financial position when the other financial statements are audited.

The auditor has different audit objectives and uses different audit procedures for the different accounts being audited. In addition, the desired internal controls that in part dictate the required audit program vary for the different accounts being audited. While each auditor or auditing firm defines its own audit work program (also called *audit program*) as deemed necessary, some common procedures should be part of any audit program. The audit program is the step by step instructions that are to be performed in auditing the construction firm. As each step is performed, the individual who performs the step places his or her initials by the step in the audit program and also indicates the date the step was performed.

Some of the audit objectives of specific types of accounts along with the more common audit procedures for auditing the accounts will now be discussed. Additionally, a sample audit program is illustrated for the accounts discussed. Proper internal controls for the accounts will be discussed in the following chapter.

Auditing Cash

The auditor spends considerable audit time in examining cash. While cash may not be a significant asset relative to other assets on the firm's book, the liquid nature of cash draws attention to the relatively high risk associated with the asset. The liquidity of cash enhances fraud. Additional audit time is directed toward cash because of the relationship between cash and several other financial statement accounts. For example, purchase of capital assets such as trucks can be analyzed by inspecting the related cash transaction.

The audit objectives regarding cash are as follows:

1. Determine that the cash balance is correct.
2. Determine that cash is in the accounts and locations where indicated.
3. Determine that cash is properly cut off for the period being audited.

In order to determine that the cash balance is correct and in proper accounts and locations, the auditor performs various audit steps or procedures. Included in these are counting the cash on hand, confirming bank balances, proving the accuracy of the firm's bank reconciliation, and tracing representative transactions from origin through cash disbursement.

In order to determine that a proper cut-off has been made, the auditor performs tests to determine that deposits in transit reach the bank promptly. Also the auditor performs tests by ascertaining that checks do not remain outstanding for an unreasonable length of time. An example of an audit program for auditing cash is illustrated in Figure 14.3. The program is not meant to be complete, but does represent significant audit program steps.

Auditing Receivables

Unfortunately for the construction firm, receivables often make up a substantial portion of its assets. Because of the significant dollar amount of the receivables and because there may be a question of their collectability, the auditor pays special attention to receivables when auditing the construction

Cash	Initial	Date
1. Determine locations, custodians, and probable amounts of all cash funds and undeposited receipts, and count all cash funds and undeposited receipts.	_____	_____
2. Test petty cash transactions during year.	_____	_____
3. Obtain and verify or prepare reconciliations of all bank accounts.	_____	_____
4. Obtain independent bank confirmations.		
5. Obtain cut-off statement directly from bank and check all in-transit items.	_____	_____
6. Determine the propriety of the cash cut-off.	_____	_____
7. Cash receipts detail:	_____	_____
a. For a test period reconcile total receipts per cash book with total credits per bank statement.	_____	_____
b. On a statistical sampling or other valid test basis examine receipt entries; trace to duplicate deposit ticket, bank statement, and accounts receivable ledger.	_____	_____
c. Foot cash receipts journal for a test period and trace general ledger postings.	_____	_____
d. Test discounts.	_____	_____

Figure 14.3 Audit Program for Cash

firm. For example, it is suggested that the auditor should confirm *all* significant receivables due the construction firm from project owners.

Audit objectives related to receivables are as follows:

1. Determine reasonableness of accounts receivable balances.
2. Review cut-off recorded receivables.
3. Determine collectability of receivables.

The above list is not meant to be an exclusive list of objectives, but represents three major objectives.

The reasonableness of the accounts receivable balances is accomplished mainly by confirmations. Additionally, subsequent receipt at the cut-off date of the financial statements is used as a test. Also, inspecting evidence of work performed that supports a receivable can be used as further evidence for a receivable accuracy.

Review of the cut-off is performed by ascertaining the validity of recorded receivables and analyzing any subsequently unearned revenue. The cut-off is especially important in construction because of the significant dollar value of a single billing and corresponding receivable.

Accounts receivable	Initial	Date
1. Obtain and check to or prepare from detail ledger accounts an aged list of accounts receivable balances. Reconcile the total with the general ledger control accounts.	______	______
2. Classify balances on list as to customers, officers and employees, parent and subsidiary companies, and others. Exclude consignments.	______	______
3. Communicate directly with debtors by either positive request for confirmation or negative request for confirmation.	______	______
4. Check replies to requests for confirmation and investigate differences.	______	______
5. Test collections subsequent to balance sheet date particularly for receivables on which no confirmation was requested and/or received. Examine invoices and shipping documents for accounts not paid.	______	______
6. Scan general ledger control for the period to ascertain propriety of unusual transactions and material charge-offs.	______	______
7. Discuss collectibility of accounts with responsible officials, consider review of applicable correspondence, and review accounts written off.	______	______
8. Schedule, analyze, and determine adequacy of allowance for doubtful accounts.	______	______
9. Prepare notes for management letter.	______	______

Figure 14.4 Audit Program for Receivables

The collectability of receivables is evaluated by aging the construction firm's receivable. Old receivables become questionable as to collectability. Individual delinquent accounts can be analyzed as a further test on the collectability of receivables. An example of an audit program for receivables is illustrated in Figure 14.4

Inventories and investments seldom make up significant dollar amounts on the construction firm's financial statements. For that reason we will not discuss audit objectives or procedures. This is not to imply that the auditor omits them in his audit program.

Auditing Fixed Assets

While fixed assets such as the construction firm's equipment and home office are very large in terms of dollar value, they usually create fewer audit difficulties than current assets. The reason being that fixed assets cause fewer problems in that they are by their nature more fixed both as to location and in terms of turnover through the firm. Audit objectives for fixed assets include the following:

1. Establish existence of fixed assets.
2. Determine ownership of fixed assets.
3. Establish accuracy of depreciation charges.

The large dollar value associated with each piece of construction equipment makes it essential to establish the existence of a fixed asset. A single piece of construction equipment may have a value in excess of $100,000. Therefore, major assets should be analyzed. Source documents relating to the purchase should be traced through the accounting records. In order to establish ownership of the assets, the auditor inspects contracts, deeds, and tax-related documents. An example of an audit program for fixed assets is illustrated in Figure 14.5.

Auditing Accounts Payable

The construction firm is very dependent on liabilities, especially short-term ones. Included in the liabilities are amounts due material vendors and lending

Property and equipment	Initial	Date
1. Obtain and verify or prepare a schedule of changes in fixed assets and related accumulated depreciation accounts for the period. Compare totals to ledger control.	______	______
2. Inspect new properties if practicable.	______	______
3. Vouch additions and retirements over $________, and test items under this amount during period.	______	______
4. Vouch charges over $____________ to repairs and maintenance or other related expense account during the period.	______	______
5. Update permanent depreciation schedule or test clients' plant ledger or schedule for current year additions and retirements, and compute current year depreciation expense.	______	______
6. Reconcile additions to accumulated depreciation accounts with related expense accounts.	______	______
7. Ascertain that depreciation rates used during the period appear to be reasonably adequate.	______	______
8. Ascertain that all major retirements during the period under review have been reflected in the accounts.	______	______
9. Examine leases, abstract for or update permanent file, consider capitalization, and obtain necessary footnote information	______	______
10. Prepare notes for management letter.	______	______

Figure 14.5 Audit Program for Fixed Assets

institutions. Audit objectives related to the auditing of liabilities include the following:

1. Determine that recorded liabilities are correct.
2. Establish the existence of any unrecorded liabilities.
3. Relate liabilities to other accounts.

Confirmations can be used to determine that recorded liabilities are correct in dollar amount. In addition, the auditor can review and analyze interest expense accounting entries for establishing the accuracy of a payable. An attorney's letter is requested to pass judgment on any possible outstanding lawsuits relative to recognizing a payable or contingent liability.

Establishing unrecorded liabilities is somewhat troublesome for the auditor. A single unrecorded liability can have a significant dollar impact on both the balance sheet and income statement. The auditor reviews subsequent transactions after the financial statement cut-off date in an attempt to identify any unrecorded liability. He also reviews minutes of board meetings for any actions leading to purchases that may not be recorded. Additionally, the auditor obtains a *representation* letter from the construction firm. In effect this letter is proof of the fact that the auditor cannot totally be assured of the nonexistence of unrecorded liabilities. In the representation letter, the construction firm says that it has disclosed all information including liabilities to the auditor.

Relating liabilities to other accounts is done by tracing source documents of financial transactions. In addition to providing evidence of the existence of a liability, tracing the source documents helps verify the related account transaction.

An example of an audit program for accounts payables is illustrated in Figure 14.6. The program shown limits itself to accounts payables. Other liabilities such as notes payable and accrued expenses would be somewhat similar.

Auditing Equity Accounts

Owner's equity accounts include both the investment of the owner and profits held in the firm. The investment may be in the form of common stock and the profits retained may be in the form of retained earnings. Audit objectives related to the auditing of owner's equity accounts include the following:

1. Determine that legal requirements of equity stock have been observed.
2. Relate equity changes to other financial statement accounts.
3. Examine officer board meetings to determine authorization for events and transactions.

All three of these audit objectives can be attained by reviewing board meeting minutes and tracing individual journal entries. Tracing each journal entry for the equity accounts is possible because of the relatively few equity transactions that take place in a period of a year. An example of an audit program for the construction firm's equity investment (also referred to as capital or stock) and retained earnings is illustrated in Figure 14.7.

Auditing Revenue Transactions

When auditing the balance sheet accounts, the auditor is testing several income-related accounts. For example, tracing a material vendor's invoice to verify a payable also establishes the existence of an expense. The result is that audit steps limited exclusively to either revenue or expense are somewhat limited.

The objectives of audit steps regarding revenue transactions are as follows:

1. Determine accuracy of account balances.
2. Determine that all revenues are recorded.
3. Determine that all recorded revenue is earned.

The accuracy of the account balances is established by tracing source documents including billings and subsequent collections. Month to month revenues are analyzed to identify any unusual items or any marked changes in revenue trends.

Accounts payable	Initial	Date
1. Obtain and verify or prepare lists of accounts payable classified as trade creditors, officers and employees, parent and subsidiary companies, and others. Reconcile with general ledger accounts.	______	______
2. Investigate large, irregular, old, or disputed balances.	______	______
3. Reclassify consignments and major debit balances.	______	______
4. Test balances with monthly statements and/or vendors' invoices and consider requesting confirmations from principal suppliers.	______	______
5. Foot accounts payable journal for a test period and trace general ledger postings.	______	______
6. Search for material unrecorded liabilities; for the period immediately following balance sheet, examine unentered invoices and vouchers, voucher register entries, cash book entries, etc.	______	______
7. Prepare notes for management letter.	______	______

Figure 14.6 Audit Program for Accounts Payable

Capital stock and retained earnings	Inital	Date
1. Capital stock		
a. Obtain and verify or prepare schedule of each class of capital stock and show privileges and/or restrictions.	______	______
b. Verify outstanding stock by reference to open stubs in stock certificate book.	______	______
c. Note that all canceled certificates have been accounted for.	______	______
d. Foot stockholders register and reconcile total with general ledger control.	______	______
e. Vouch changes in capital structure during the period.	______	______
f. Obtain and verify or prepare schedule of treasury stock and examine or confirm certificates	______	______
g. Ascertain amounts of dividends in arrears on cumulative preferred stock.	______	______
h. Reconcile dividend payments and rates with outstanding stock.	______	______
2. Retained earnings		
a. Obtain and verify or prepare schedule of each retained earning or other capital account per the general ledger.	______	______
b. Determine authorization and verify propriety of charges and credits to account for the period.	______	______
3. Prepare notes for management letter.	______	______

Figure 14.7 Audit Program for Equity Accounts

Establishing that all revenues are recorded is sometimes difficult. The best approach is a creative consideration of possible sources of miscellaneous revenue that may not have been recorded. Furthermore, tests can be made on gross margin percentages and revenue trends to possibly detect an unrecorded revenue transaction. Customer prepayments, which result in unearned revenue, can usually be identified by tracing source documents. Overbillings that result in unearned revenue are discussed in a following section of this chapter.

Auditing Expense Transactions

Related to revenue transactions are expense transactions. The construction firm might be witness to over a hundred or more expenses of its own within a given day or week. Because of the frequency of expense transactions, the

Income and expense accounts	Initial	Date
1. Obtain and verify or prepare sales workpapers as are deemed appropriate and necessary to the type of business of the client. Supplemental detail audit programs should be used whenever possible.	______	______
2. Obtain and verify or prepare schedules and vouch significant amounts of such expense accounts as are deemed necessary.	______	______
3. Vouch invoices for a selected period if previous coverage not sufficient.	______	______
4. Compare expense and income accounts not analyzed in detail with those of preceding year and ascertain propriety of significant changes.	______	______
5. Scan expense and income accounts not analyzed and ascertain propriety of unusual entries (credits to expense accounts and debits to income accounts.)	______	______
6. On a statistical sampling or other valid test basis, schedule and analyze payroll for the period.		
a. For employees paid on an hourly basis, test actual hours paid to timecards or other supporting evidence.	______	______
b. Test rates of pay to approved schedules of hourly rates or salary schedules.	______	______
c. Test computations of gross pay, payroll tax deductions, net extensions, distributions, footings, etc.	______	______
d. Test names on pay records to other personnel records or other satisfactory evidence of employment. Consider attending and/or controlling a pay-off or perform such other "ghost" detection procedures as are considered desirable.	______	______
e. Foot payroll journal for a test period and trace general ledger postings.	______	______
7. Prepare notes for management letter.	______	______

Figure 14.8 Audit Program for Revenue and Expense

auditor is limited to testing select transactions. The objectives of audit steps regarding expense transactions are as follows:

1. Determine accuracy of account balances.
2. Determine that expenses have not been capitalized and vice versa.
3. Determine that all losses are recorded.

The accuracy of the expense accounts is in great part established by testing and tracing specific expense transactions. Using computers, the transactions to be tested can be chosen by random sampling. Expense trends and unusual transactions are also analyzed to determine the expense account accuracy.

Determining that expense accounts are not capitalized and vice versa is accomplished by analyzing significant dollar-sized transactions. For example, all expense transactions greater than $300 may be listed (called scheduling in accounting terminology) and analyzed. Unrecorded losses may occur because of damage to equipment, or building, or the selling of an asset at an unfavorable price. Each related asset account has to be analyzed as a means of recognizing any loss.

In many instances the auditor does his revenue and expense audit work simultaneously. An example of an audit program for revenue (also referred to as income) and expenses is illustrated in Figure 14.8.

AUDITING WORK IN PROGRESS

As noted earlier, the major audit problem encountered in the examining of a construction firm's financial statements is in the audit of contracts in progress. While this is true regardless of whether the firm uses the completed-contract or percentage-of-completion revenue-recognition method, it is the percentage-of-completion method that is especially troublesome.

The audit problem associated with using the completed-contract method centers around the question of completion. Because no revenue or expense is identified until a project is complete, the actual date of completion becomes a very important date. If a project is near completion at the end of a firm's year end cut-off for financial statements, a few days difference in the completion date can potentially shift significant revenue and expense (and resulting profit or loss) from one year to another. The term *substantially* complete is often used as a guide in assisting the auditor to identify the project-completion date. The problem is that the term substantially complete is somewhat subjective.

The problem of identifying project completion is compounded by the fact that, in theory, auditors and the IRS interpret completion differently. Project completion for financial reporting and calculating taxable income are discussed in Chapters 4 and 17 respectively.

The majority of construction firms use the percentage-of-completion method for financial reporting. The main reason for its use centers around a better matching of revenue and expense than the completed-contract method. The percentage-of-completion method recognizes income (profit or loss) on a project as the project progresses. The auditor's difficulty relates to the question of the project's profitability at any point in time.

Several different acceptable methods are used by construction firms for determining the percentage of completion and the resulting income to be recognized. The most common method of determining the percentage of completion is by calculating the percentage that incurred costs to date bear to estimated total cost after giving effect to estimates of cost to complete based upon most recent information. Using this method, it is recognized that cost, especially during the early stages of the construction project, might exclude all or a portion of the cost of such items as materials and subcontracts if it appears that such an exclusion would result in a more meaningful periodic allocation of income. This qualification takes into account situations in which substantial quantities of materials may have been accumulated on the project site, but not used. It also covers such situations in which engineering and architectural fees have been incurred that may be out of proportion to the actual work performed.

When the percentage-of-completion method is used for recognizing revenue for a project, the objectives of the audit work relating to the project are as follows:

1. Determine contract amount and billing amounts.
2. Determine accuracy of recorded costs to date.
3. Determine accuracy of estimated costs to complete.

The auditor uses confirmations to determine information about billings and contract amount. For all significant projects in progress, the auditor should obtain confirmation of contract amount. The auditor should also include confirmation of billings and payments to date on each confirmation request. An example of an audit program for establishing contract amount and billings is illustrated in Figure 14.9.

To verify the accuracy of contract costs to date, the auditor utilizes many of the audit steps that would be utilized for auditing the completed cost of any project. In great part, the audit work will relate to tracing source documents to determine if project costs are being recorded properly. Attention also focuses on any unrecorded liabilities and the validity of recorded payables. An abbreviated audit program for establishing the accuracy of project costs to date is illustrated in Figure 14.10.

	Initial	Date
1. For contracts in progress, compare total estimated contract price to copy of contract and approved change orders.	______	______
2. Trace billings on significant contracts to invoices.	______	______
3. Confirm all contracts using the positive form on all significant contracts.	______	______
4. Confirm several significant contracts that were in process at the end of the previous year, but which have no receivable balance as of the current year.	______	______
5. Investigate disputes and accounts that are past due.	______	______

Figure 14.9 Audit Program for Contract Amount and Billings

	Initial	Date
1. In order to determine that the costs incurred to date are proper, the following accounts payable work are performed:	______	______
a. Obtain contract payables trial balance at audit date.	______	______
b. Select a number of projects to be used in connection with confirmation work.	______	______
c. For each of these projects, confirm all subcontract and material suppliers amounts.	______	______
2. Obtain a schedule that details costs incurred to date into labor, material and subcontract amounts, or other project cost detail maintained by client.	______	______
3. Trace cost incurred to contract cost cards on all contracts and examine supporting documents for cost incurred.	______	______
4. Vouch all items over a certain amount included in accounts payable.	______	______
5. Perform a search for unrecorded liabilities as follows:		
a. Agree information on the listing to cash disbursements register.	______	______
b. Ascertain that all disbursements have been included on the listing.	______	______

Figure 14.10 Audit Program for Costs to Date

Undoubtedly, determining the accuracy of the construction firm's computed cost to complete causes the auditor the most difficulty. The auditor uses both internal sources of construction firm information and external sources when establishing the cost to complete. Included in the internal sources is inspection of the original estimate to make a comparative analysis of actual costs incurred to date with estimated costs used in the estimate. The more accurate the estimated cost relative to the actual costs, the more the auditor can rely on the estimate of estimated remaining costs. The auditor also discusses the costs to complete with the construction firm. This discussion may result in a more objective evaluation of the cost to complete by the construction firm.

The auditor may also make a project site visit as part of establishing the cost to complete. With the typical auditor's limited construction knowledge, it is unlikely that he can be precise in "observing" the percentage of completion. However, by visiting the project site, a reasonable range of percentage of completion can be established. Additionally, the project site visit can lead to on-site discussions with project managers and superintendents that might surface important information about the project status and cost to complete.

The more an auditor knows about the building process, the better qualified he is to evaluate the construction firm's cost to complete. Therefore, the auditor's work program depends somewhat on the skills and construction knowledge of the auditor. An abbreviated audit program for determining the accuracy of the percentage of completion is illustrated in Figure 14.11. The audit program shown does not include some of the more innovative audit steps that might be used by the auditor possessing a degree of construction know-how.

Also of concern to the auditor are events that take place after the date of the financial statement cut-off but before the audited statements are published. Financial statements for a December 31 year end might not be published by the auditor until February or even later. During this time period, events may have occurred that adversely affect the profit of projects in process on December 31. Additionally the construction firm may have contracted new projects during this period that may have a significant impact on the future profitability of the firm.

Both of the possible events cited should be of concern to the auditor. In the first case, a situation in which events occur after the financial statement date for a project in process at that date, it is important for the auditor to establish the date of the events that affect the profitability. If the events indeed occurred after the financial statement date (December 31), the auditor does

	Initial	Date
1. Review with the firm's personnel the additional costs to complete the contracts.	______	______
2. Determine the current actual total costs incurred on projects in progress at previous audit date and compare to the cost estimates used at that date. If contract is still in process, compare previous audit date estimate to estimate currently used.	______	______
3. For a number of contracts, secure bid sheets and related supporting schedules and divide into work subcontracted and work to be done by the client.		
To determine the accuracy of current estimated cost perform the following:		
a. For work subcontracted out, compare original estimated cost to copy of subcontract awarded. Determine that effect of differences has been considered in current estimate of total cost.	______	______
b. For work to be completed by firm, compare original estimated cost to cost incurred to date, and, to the extent data is available, determine that cost and progress experience to date has been considered in firm's estimate of the additional cost to be incurred.	______	______
4. Review results of audit work with management and on-site field managers. Obtain management representation letter on reasonableness of estimated costs to complete and extent of progress on contracts in process.	______	______

Figure 14.11 Audit Program for Costs to Complete

not have to consider them in his financial statement presentation. On the other hand, if the decrease in profitability of the project actually results from events prior to the financial statement date (December 31), the published financial statements should include the events and the resulting lessened profitability.

Normally any contract commitments made subsequent to the financial statement date (December 31) do not have to be disclosed in the published financial statements. However, if the auditor judges the commitments to have a major adverse affect on the ability of the construction firm to continue as a going concern, most auditors would agree that this should be disclosed in the financial statements as an accompanying note. However, this will put the auditor in an unfavorable light with his client, the construction firm. This illustrates the unusual role of the auditor—employed and paid by a client to report on the client.

AUDITED FINANCIAL STATEMENTS

The presentation and form of financial statements for the construction firm were discussed in Chapter 6. Other than the fact that audited financial statements are to include an opinion statement and statement of accounting policies and notes, audited and unaudited financial statements potentially look alike. The major difference in audited versus unaudited financial statements is the amount of work performed by the auditor in determining that the financial statements are correct. Given the additional work and testing performed by the auditor in performing an audit, it follows that the reader of the audited financial statements puts more confidence in them.

Published audited financial statements should include the following information:

1. CPA/auditor's opinion
2. Balance sheet (statement of financial position)
3. Income statement (profit and loss statement)
4. Statement of changes in financial position
5. Optional statements or schedules
   a. Schedule of operating expense
   b. Schedule of work in progress
   c. Others needed for adequate reporting
6. Summary of accounting policies
7. Notes to financial statements

The above information is presented in the published, audited financial statements in an order as listed. An example of a table of contents from a set of audited financial statements illustrating the typical order of information presented is shown in Figure 14.12.

Following the optional table of contents, the first information presented is the CPA/auditor's opinion statement. Ideally, the auditor is able to express

SAMPLE CONSTRUCTION CO., INC.
ANYWHERE, U.S.A.
FINANCIAL STATEMENTS
and
ACCOUNTANTS' REPORT
December 31, 19X0

TABLE OF CONTENTS

Figure 14.12 Table of Contents for Audited Financial Statements

an unqualified opinion regarding the fairness of the financial statements that follow. The typical two-paragraph unqualified opinion was illustrated in Figure 14.1. If there are events or circumstances that prevent the auditor from giving an unqualified opinion, a third or middle paragraph is usually part of the opinion. Events that might prevent the auditor from giving an unqualified opinion include the construction firm's poor internal controls, the auditor's inability to observe beginning of year work in progress (often occurs in a first-time audit), or the auditor's nonagreement with certain account balances of the construction firm.

The opinion page is followed by the three required financial statements: the balance sheet, the income statement, and the statement of changes in financial position. Examples of these three financial statements were illustrated in Chapter 6. Any additional statements or schedules that support good financial disclosure follow the three standard and required financial statements. These statements or schedules, while optional, often assist the external party who is attempting to interpret the financial statements. Because one of the major objectives of the audited statements is to help the external party interpret the financial statements, one might argue that the optional statements or schedules are necessary. For example, many would argue that a schedule of the construction firm's work in progress should be a required part of the published, audited financial statements. The schedule of work in progress along with other optional schedules was illustrated in Chapter 6.

Following required and optional financial statements and schedules, the auditor is to include a statement as to the summary of accounting policies. Numerous different accounting policies, procedures, and methods are available to the construction firm for recognizing revenue, expense, and asset-related accounting transactions. The purpose of the auditor's disclosure of accounting policies used by the construction firm is to identify the accounting policies used that dictate the financial results reported. An example of a set of accounting policies disclosed in audited financial statements is shown in Figure 14.13.

A very important part of the audited financial statements is the disclosure of the notes to the financial statements. The purpose of the notes is to clarify various line items presented in the financial statements.

The auditor has a degree of discretion in deciding what financial data in the financial statements need further disclosure in the notes to the financial statements. The auditor should consider the needs of the external party financial statement reader. Usually many of the reported notes relate to the notes payable section of the balance sheet. Specifically, what security is pledged for outstanding notes is disclosed. This is important information to a external party considering offering the construction firm additional credit or loans. An example of a set of notes disclosed in audited financial statements is shown in Figure 14.14.

In addition to further clarifying line item information presented on the financial statements, notes to the financial statements are also used to inform the reader of any unusual event that could affect the ongoing profitability of the construction firm. For example, any unusual information about a construc-

SAMPLE CONSTRUCTION CO., INC.
SUMMARY OF ACCOUNTING POLICIES
December 31, 19X0

a. The Company maintains its books on the accural basis of accounting; income is recognized on the percentage-of-completion method, and cost and expense are recorded when liabilities are incurred.

b. The Company uses the direct write-off method of recognizing bad debt losses. No allowance for uncollectible accounts has been provided since the amount of such allowance would not be significant.

c. Inventories are carried at the "lower of cost or market value," cost being determined on the first-in, first-out basis of accounting.

d. Depreciation is calculated on the double-declining balance, 150% declining balance, and straight-line method using the following lives:

Machinery and equipment	3–10 years
Office furniture and equipment	2–5 years
Autos and trucks	3–10 years

The Company uses the same method of depreciation in determining taxable income.

e. Investment credit on purchased equipment is accounted for on the flow-through method, i.e., as a direct reduction of income taxes in the year in which the assets are placed in service.

Figure 14.13 Example of Disclosed Accounting Policies

SAMPLE CONSTRUCTION CO., INC.
NOTES TO FINANCIAL STATEMENTS
December 31, 19X0

Note 1 Fabricators Co., Inc., Steel Erectors, Inc., Investment Co., a partnership, and Redi-Mix and Trucking Co., Inc. are all under common ownership.

Note 2 Equipment contracts payable in the amount of $109,148 are secured by equipment with a cost of $144,563.

Monthly Payment Requirements	Maturity Date
$1,450	May 1, 19X2
$2,125	May 15, 19X4

Note 3 A bank note payable in the amount of $50,203 is secured by property and equipment with a cost of $146,373. The note requires monthly principal payments of $4,735, including interest at 8½% per annum. Final payment is due February 5, 19X1

Another bank note payable of $7,200 is secured by personal guarantee of the Company's officers. The note requires monthly principal payments of $1,700 including interest at 9% per annum. Final payment is due July 6, 19X2

Note 4 The Company rents land and buildings for its principal site of operation from Investment Co. (see Note 1). There is no lease agreement.

Note 5 The Company adopted a pension plan on October 1, 19X0. Approval by the Internal Revenue Service is presently pending. Contributions to the plan are made by the Company on behalf of those employees deemed eligible under the provisions of the pension plan trust agreement. Contribution the plan for the year ended December 31, 19X0 was $24,793. The actuarial cost method used to determine pension costs provides for full funding of the plan. Since the plan does not incorporate past service credits, no part of the annual provision relates to past service costs and thereby represents normal cost only. Based on the actuarial cost method used to compute contributions, there are no unfunded amounts in the plan.

Note 6 In May 19X0 an individual purchased 25 shares of capital stock for $10,000 which is shown as follows:

	Capital Stock Issued		Capital Contributed in excess of Par
	No. of Shares	Amount	
Beginning balance, January 31, 19X0	925	$92,500	$52,500
Additions—sale of capital stock	25	2,500	7,500
Ending balance December 31, 19X0	950	$95,000	$60,000

Earnings per share is calculated on the weighted average method of shares of stock outstanding during the year.

Figure 14.14 Example of Notes to Financial Statements

tion project, such as a quaranteed maximum provision of a cost plus contract, should be disclosed. Another example of information to be disclosed is the construction firm's involvement in a joint venture.

While not considered part of the audited financial statements, many auditors give the construction firm a *management letter* as part of the audit engagement. This letter is not made part of the financial statements because the intent is only to give it to the construction firm. Often the management letter cites inefficiencies in the construction firm's financial and accounting processes. Most construction firms choose to keep this information confidential in regard to external parties such as the surety and lending institutions.

In performing the audit work program, the auditor comes across several construction firm financial and accounting inefficiencies or areas of improvement. For example, there may be a more efficient means of doing the payroll-related accounting than the practices currently used by the firm being audited. The auditor may assist the firm by drawing the firm's attention to these areas. It does this by means of the formal management letter. The auditor sometimes also receives a benefit in that the construction firm may engage the auditor to help it remove the inefficiency or make the improvement being suggested. The management letter should follow every audit of the construction firm.

15
MANAGEMENT AUDITING

INTRODUCTION

Recent years have seen an increasing interest in management auditing. Unlike auditing that was discussed in the previous chapter, management auditing provides information to the construction firm for its own use, information about its accounting, financial, and operational characteristics. There is no intent to disclose the results of a management audit to external parties such as sureties and lending institutions.

Management auditing can be defined as the appraisal of a firm's accounting, financial, and other operations with the objective of improving the effectiveness and efficiency of each of these. The emphasis is on identifying areas of improvement rather than on historic financial results. While not part of the audit carried out by a CPA/auditor aimed at publishing financial statements, the management audit can result in recommendations that, if implemented, can lessen the cost of the CPA/auditor and also improve the financial results that are subsequently published in audited financial statements.

The process of management auditing as discussed in this chapter can be performed by the owner of the construction firm, by an employee, or by a contracted external party. The contracted external party might be the construction firm's CPA/auditor or a consultant. The frequency of management auditing might vary from an ongoing process to an annual process. Following sections of this chapter illustrate the process and benefits of management auditing independent of who performs the function.

OBJECTIVES OF MANAGEMENT AUDITING

Management auditing is a process of evaluation. The more we evaluate any set of procedures or practices, the more likely we are to be able to find inefficiencies that can be reduced or eliminated. Because we sometimes find it difficult to evaluate ourselves or our own firm, some firms have made an argument for occasionally contracting a external party to evaluate the firm by means of a management audit of its accounting, finance, and operational characteristics. Other firms have found that they can be objective about performing their own internal audit if they take the time to carry out the process formally.

One can cite many reasons for justifying a firm having an ongoing or interim formal management audit performed. In the accounting area alone, many construction firms lack good management accounting controls and often use an inefficient means of bookkeeping. For example, one clerical worker might be in charge of receiving cash, writing checks, making out bills, and depositing money in the bank. Another firm's bookkeeper might be spending excess hours posting accounting journal entries to three separate documents, when in fact a bookkeeping system might be implemented that enables a one-write process.

Duplication of effort and poor segregation of duties is another weakness of many construction firms. For example, four owners of a construction firm might all perform the marketing, estimating, production, and control function of the firm. Analysis of the firm by means of management auditing may lead to the conclusion that the four owners would be much more effective and efficient if each of them were to specialize as to one of the four functions noted.

Analysis of the firm's financial practices may lead to detection of several costly practices or lack of practices. For example, the firm's accounts payable system may be such that the construction firm is unable to identify purchase discount dates and therefore is unable to take advantage of the potential discounts. Additionally it may be that the firm's receivables practices do not enhance timely collection of its revenue.

The need for an objective evaluation of the effectiveness and efficiency of the construction firm's accounting, financial, and operational practices is increased as the firm changes its size or type of operation. A construction firm doing ten million dollars of annual volume needs different accounting, financial, and operational practices than it did when the firm was doing one million dollars of annual volume. Too often a firm changes in size or type of work performed without the necessary accompanying changes in all segments of its business.

Much of the ability to perform a quality management audit depends on the innovative characteristics of the individual or individuals performing the audit as well as knowledge of specific management auditing steps. Some individuals are better at identifying inefficiencies than others. Obviously an individual becomes better at noting inefficiencies and/or citing improvement potential as he gains experience and familiarity with the specific industry characteristics.

Independent of these "art" rather than "science" characteristics of the successful management audit, there are some specific processes and/or procedures used by the management auditor in the evaluation. Specifically, regardless of whether the person performing the management audit is part of the construction firm or a contracted external party, the following practices will be included in the work activities:

1. Evaluate the soundness, accuracy, and application of accounting and financial controls.
2. Determine whether assets are accounted for and safeguarded from potential losses.
3. Evaluate the performance of personnel as to effectiveness and efficiency.
4. Evaluate the extent of compliance of the firm with its own and external established policies, plans, and procedures.

The first two practices noted are often considered part of *internal control auditing*. The third practice noted can be considered part of *operational auditing*, and the fourth practice noted is commonly considered part of *compliance auditing*. We will consider internal control, operational, and compliance auditing as part of the broader management auditing process.

Internal control auditing is the evaluation of internal controls used by the construction firm to enhance project control and protect its assets. As noted in the previous chapter, the construction firm is characterized by poor internal controls. The result is a threat of financial loss of assets as well as difficulty associated with performing the financial audit discussed in Chapter 14.

The operational audit expands on an analysis of the accounting and financial functions to include an evaluation of marketing or sales and production business functions. The operational audit concentrates on seeking out aspects of operations in which inefficiency and excessive costs can be reduced by implementing operating controls.

The compliance audit concerns itself with ascertaining whether company and external party policies, procedures, and controls are carried out. Some of these policies, procedures, and controls might be established as a result of the internal or operational audit. However, established policies, procedures, or controls are of no value unless they are actually followed in practice.

The results of the management audit, including internal control, operational, and compliance auditing, are written up as a report sometimes referred to as the *management audit report*. The management audit report is not to be confused with the management letter that follows a financial audit. The management audit report is in great part a series of audit findings, each followed by a recommendation. A finding is a write-up of a specific inefficiency observed in the management audit. The individual performing the management audit follows the finding with a recommendation aimed at reducing or eliminating the efficiency. An example of a written-up finding is as follows:

Finding: Cash is occasionally paid directly to material vendors or directly to a laid off worker.

Recommendation: All expenditures should be paid by check and each check coded to an expense account code.

Regardless of whether the management audit is performed by in-house construction firm personnel or contracted to consultants or accountants, a formal report including findings and recommendations should be part of the process.

INTERNAL CONTROL AUDIT FOR ACCOUNTING/FINANCE

The CPA/auditor performs an internal control review as part of establishing an audit program for the financial audit. The CPA/auditor internal control evaluation is an AICPA mandatory part of an audit aimed at publishing financial statements. However, the detail or extent of this internal control review usually would not be expected to be as thorough as that performed as part of the internal control audit of internal controls.

Internal controls are not limited to controls for the accounting or financial functions. The construction firm also vitally needs internal controls in its estimate/bid process and control process. The construction firm puts every asset it owns on the line when it bids on a construction project and subsequently attempts to control the project time and cost. Internal controls for accounting and finance practices are discussed in this section. Internal control practices for the estimate/bid and control processes are discussed in the following section of this chapter.

The internal control audit is in effect an evaluation of whether or not ideal internal controls are in use by the firm. This is true regardless of whether the internal control audit is performed by in-house firm personnel or by a external party. The ideal internal controls for various types of construction firm accounts will now be discussed.

Cash

As is true of the financial audit, cash draws the attention of the internal control audit. The liquidity of the cash and the relatively large amount of free cash the construction firm keeps available for building projects draws special attention to the construction firm's need for internal controls of cash. The following is a list of preferred internal controls or practices to be used by the construction firm for cash receipts or revenue:

1. Cash-receiving activities are centralized in as few hands as possible.
2. The receipt of cash is provable by other records.
3. Persons receiving cash have no access to accounting records. Incoming receipts are controlled by other than those having access to cash or the accounting records.
4. The bank has been instructed not to cash checks payable to the company.
5. All cash receipts are deposited intact.

Ideally the construction firm should attempt to segregate as many cash receipts and cash disbursement functions to as many separate individuals as possible. However, as a practical matter this is made difficult because of the small number of employees including accounting and finance employees employed by the construction firm. Given this potentially troublesome internal control concern, the owner or owners of the construction firm has to pay strict attention to implementing alternative controls. The construction firm's close surveillance can defeat the potential problems associated with a lack of segregation of duties.

Some preferred internal controls for distributing the cash of the construction firm are as follows:

1. All disbursements (other than petty cash) are made by check.
2. All checks are countersigned.
3. No checks are made payable to cash.
4. All checks are prenumbered.
5. No counter checks are permitted.
6. All disbursements are properly substantiated. Supporting documents include evidence of receipt and approval.
7. All such supporting documents are canceled in such a manner as to preclude their use a second time.
8. Monthly bank reconciliations are made by someone other than the person writing the checks or recording disbursements.
9. All checks are protectographed.
10. Petty cash funds are maintained on an imprest basis with the same standard of developing documentary evidence as for other disbursements.

Each of these practices is readily available to the construction firm and can be implemented regardless of the size or number of employees of the firm.

Receivables

As noted in the previous chapter in the discussion of financial auditing, the construction firm commonly carries a significant dollar amount of receivables on its balance sheet. All too often the firm falls victim to a lack of control of the receivables with subsequent receipt of late payment or recognition of large write-offs for uncollectables. Following is a list of preferred internal controls or practices for receivables, both accounts receivables and notes receivables:

1. Each entry to the accounts receivable ledger is supported by documentary evidence.
2. All noncash credits, such as credit memos, allowances, bad debts, etc. are properly authorized.
3. Subsidiary ledgers are balanced regularly.
4. Postings are made by an individual other than those having access to incoming receipts.

5. Statements are mailed monthly by someone other than the bookkeeper or cashier.
6. Notes and other investments on hand are checked regularly with the controlling account.
7. This checking is done by someone other than the person receiving cash or recording the transaction.
8. Partial payments are endorsed on the back of notes.
9. Note renewals are properly authorized.
10. Discounted notes are credited to a note receivable discount account.

Internal controls as they relate to receivables are necessary in order to prevent the construction firm from being in the banking business. The construction firm that gives too much credit by not collecting its receivables will soon find itself unable to meet its own financial commitments.

Fixed Assets

Failure to implement adequate internal controls for fixed assets is evidenced by the fact that on occasion construction firms have lost major pieces of equipment by theft from project sites. The lost equipment has included scrapers as well as trucks. Obviously loss of equipment of this scale is rare for the typical construction firm. However, for a smaller construction firm, even the loss of a small piece of equipment can have a significant negative affect on the firm's net worth.

Internal control of fixed assets in great part entails asset recordkeeping and reports. However, other practices, such as controlling the authority to make asset acquisitions, are fundamental to controlling significant and crippling cash-flow expenditures for fixed assets. Some preferred internal controls for fixed assets follow:

1. Detailed subsidiary records of fixed assets and reserves for depreciation are maintained.
2. These records are periodically compared with fixed assets on hand.
3. All capital expenditures are authorized by responsible officers.
4. The accounting personnel are capable of distinguishing between capital expenditures and maintenance and repair items.
5. Retirements are under satisfactory accounting control.

Given the large dollar value associated with a single piece of construction equipment, it is essential that adequate fixed-asset internal controls be implemented.

Accounts Payable

Internal controls of accounts payable and purchases are interrelated. The initial control on a firm's payables starts with the very purchase of the goods or services that create the payable. Violations of good internal controls for accounts payable and purchasing occur daily at the construction project site and in the construction firm's office. For example, many construction firms give their field personnel a free rein when it comes to purchasing material or supplies for building a project. While this free rein might enhance project efficiency in that the field personnel can order and receive material when needed, there also exists a significant problem should field personnel prove dishonest or fraudulent in their purchasing of material.

Good internal controls for accounts payable and purchasing entails detailed accounting records. These preferred internal controls along with others for accounts payable and purchases are as follows:

1. Prenumbered purchase orders are used for all purchases.
2. The responsibility for receiving incoming merchandise is established with one individual.
3. Prenumbered receiving tickets are prepared for all incoming merchandise.
4. A numerical file of receiving tickets (or a comparable record) is maintained.
5. Persons responsible for purchasing and receiving merchandise do not approve invoices for payment or handle disbursements.
6. Invoice prices, extensions, additions, and freight charges are checked.
7. Invoices are compared with purchase orders and receiving tickets prior to payment.
8. An approved list of vendors is maintained.
9. A voucher or purchase register and an accounts payable subsidiary ledger are maintained.
10. Suppliers' monthly statements are regularly compared with recorded liabilities.
11. Distributions to purchase and expense accounts are established by responsible employees.
12. Periodic physical checks of the inventory records are conducted by persons other than those keeping the inventory records.
13. The inventory is taken under the supervision of responsible officials.

Good internal controls over accounts payable and purchases is necessary if the construction firm is to minimize the cost of performing its services.

Payroll

The large dollar value associated with the construction firm's employment of labor, draws need to internal controls for the payroll function. All too often a construction firm overpays an employee, or pays for an employee who already has been laid off or fired. Less frequent in occurrence, but even more financially damaging to the construction firm, is its falling victim to a fraudulent bookkeeper who has been stealing from the firm through its payroll account or process.

The following is a list of a few internal controls related to the payroll process:

1. Written authorizations are on file for all employees appearing on payrolls and for all salary and wage-rate changes.
2. All salary and wage payments are made by checks signed and distributed by persons other than those preparing the payroll.
3. All payroll computations are independently checked and the payroll bank account is reconciled by someone other than the person preparing the payroll or signing payroll checks.

Like other areas discussed, internal controls for the payroll process are only effective if they are implemented continuously as part of the construction firm's daily operations or business.

INTERNAL CONTROLS FOR PROJECT ESTIMATE AND CONTROL

The CPA/auditor spends considerable time and expense (which is in turn charged back to the construction firm) when evaluating the accounting and financial internal controls as part of the financial audit. However, more often than not he spends little time in evaluating the construction firm's internal controls as they relate to the firm's estimating, bidding, and controlling of construction projects. This is ironic given that poor project estimating/bidding and control are the most common reasons for construction firm bankruptcy. At the same time fraud, often resulting from a failure to implement adequate accounting and financial internal controls, is relatively low on the list of reasons for construction firm bankruptcies.

The management audit cannot be expected to disclose information about a construction firm's inability to predict actual costs or the firm's inability to implement the most productive construction method in a given situation. The individual or individuals performing the internal control audit portion of the management audit may not know how many cubic yards of concrete finishers can place in an hour, or whether pumping concrete is more productive than using a crane for a given type of construction pour.

The internal control audit can disclose several nontechnical inefficiencies that can prove to be as detrimental to the profitability of the construction project and firm as an error in productivity information. Given the large dollar value of the typical construction project and the resulting potential dollar loss if a single error is made, it becomes vital to the construction firm to implement estimating and bidding controls on a continual basis. Examples of preferred internal controls for project estimating/bidding are as follows:

1. All items on the estimate summary should be completed or crossed out if not applicable.
2. Rule-of-thumb cost checks should be incorporated in the estimate summary.
3. Detailed estimate sheets should be accumulated in support of the estimate summary.
4. Approvals should be required for each step in the estimate process.
5. Cost estimates should be obtained from more than one subcontractor for each phase of work to be subcontracted.
6. The construction firm should use financially stable and high-quality subcontractors.
7. Estimate-bid forms and procedures should be periodically reviewed for appropriateness.
8. Both successful and unsuccessful bids should be analyzed by comparison with bids submitted by other construction firms.
9. Quality and cost estimates should be subsequently compared with actual quantitites and costs.
10. Historical unit costs or productivity records should be accumulated for use in estimating and bidding.
11. Unit costs or productivity data should be adjusted to provide for conditions on the current project.

All too often a construction firm creates potential for profit on a project by means of a good estimate/bid, only to fail to obtain the profit because of poor project control of time and cost. As is true of the estimating process, the internal control audit cannot be expected to inform the constructor how to control project time and cost. However, there are certain accounting-related practices that can enhance the project control function. The objective of internal control auditing as it relates to control of project time and cost is evaluating the degree of implementation of preferred practices. Examples of good internal controls that relate to the ongoing control of project time and costs are as follows:

1. Labor, equipment, and subcontractors should be scheduled using bar charts and/or the critical-path method (CPM).
2. Reports should be generated to indicate project costs incurred, units completed, and costs to complete the project phase or work item.
3. Project progress should be measured against the job plan.
4. Time sheets should be designed to accumulate hours worked by project phase or work item.
5. Time sheets should be approved by project foremen or superintendents.
6. Material invoices should be matched with receiving reports before payment.

7. Material invoices should be account-coded by project phases or work item as defined in the project estimate.
8. Equipment rental or usage rates should be established for equipment used on a project.
9. Equipment used on each project should be charged to a project phase or work item.
10. Units of work completed and to be completed by project phase or work phase item should be reported weekly or monthly.

The above list is not meant to be an inclusive one. Any internal control or check that the construction firm can implement that can potentially eliminate a single costly error is advantageous. To a certain extent, what might be a good internal control for one firm might not be an adequate control for another firm. Each firm has its own characteristics including type and number of personnel that can dictate the need for some controls. However, the internal control auditor has to be careful not to put too much weight on personality traits, such as good character, as an alternative or substitute for good control practices that are independent of the people involved.

OPERATIONAL AUDITING

Every firm, including the construction firm, contains varying degrees of inefficiencies. For example, some industrial-engineering studies have indicated that approximately 50 percent of all construction field labor time is for nonproductive time. Few if any industrywide studies have been performed on the inefficiencies or nonproductive time that occurs in the general and administrative or office-related duties of the construction firm including accounting. However, it would be rare to find a firm that could not improve its daily office routines. In some cases the improvement in office routines would lead to increased field production in that more timely and meaningful management reports could be made available to the field personnel.

The benefit of detecting inefficiencies and improving the operational procedures of the construction firm is that they can have a significant impact on the profitability of the construction firm. The bottom-line profit margin of most construction firms averages less than 3 percent. At the same time, both production costs and general and administrative overhead costs consist in great part of labor-related costs. The result is that a mere marginal increase in efficiency in either production or general and administrative procedures can significantly multiply the firm's profit margin.

Some individuals would argue that the operational auditor needs a great degree of experience in the area being audited in order to detect inefficiencies. In reality some of the most objective evaluations can be made by an individual who knows little about a given process. In many cases, what should appear obvious proves to be overlooked because an individual experienced in the process already is "locked into" seeing a process that contains inefficiencies.

Specific inefficiencies and nonproductive time in construction field methods are not discussed here because each delay is somewhat unique to a given construction project. However, attention to crew, method layout, and field communication processes all can lead to improved efficiency and lower costs of production.

The operational auditing of the general and administrative functions can be far reaching in scope. We will limit ourselves to the operational auditing of the accounting function. Specifically we will address the efficiency of various general accounting procedures and also specific procedures that relate to select company accounts.

Attention to clerical and bookkeeping procedures such as typing, copying, transferring, and summarizing data can surface wasted efforts and time-consuming delays. Firms tend to get locked into methods that later become antiquated as the firm increases its size or implements other automated procedures. Examples of areas in which the operational auditor can usually find inefficiencies are as follows:

1. Duplication of activity such as reports that are handwritten and then typed.
2. Nonessential activities being performed such as reports that are issued but not used and statistical summaries that are maintained but never reported to anyone.
3. Inefficient transcription of data such as copying data.
4. Extra copies of documents prepared when some copies are never used.
5. In posting accounting data, the source information is not put in the same sequence as the records to which they are posted.
6. Unnecessary detail in management reports such as listing numbers to pennies and tenths of hours.
7. Too much reliance on automated data processing when some hand entry may prove to be more timely and economical.
8. Inadequate frequency of reports to include printing reports more frequently than a manager can use them.
9. Failure to produce summary reports for top management and more detailed reports that serve the needs of the production personnel.
10. Inefficient handling of nonroutine (exception) transactions. Often it is best to handle these separately outside the routine transactions rather than upset the normal flow for the routine transactions.

Other procedures relating to specific accounts also can result in improved operational efficiency. It is difficult to generalize as to efficient practices for each firm. What might be a good practice may prove time consuming or wasteful for another firm. However, some of the following accounting practices can lead to increased efficiency for many construction firms:

1. Using open-invoice system for receivables. High turnover bills are put in file until cash is received instead of posting each bill.
2. Using form letters for handling routine receivables and other correspondence.
3. Balance receivables during the month instead of at the end of the month in order to save time in peak periods.
4. Using copy of purchase order form filed numerically as a substitute to replace a written purchase order log.
5. Prepare purchase order form in longhand for orders placed by phone rather than type afterwards.
6. Eliminate accounts payable ledger and/or voucher register, and/or detail posted cash disbursements journal for payables.
7. Using a nonmechanized method to simultaneously prepare payroll register, earnings records, and checks.
8. Using combination timecard and labor distribution card for payroll and job costing.
9. Using estimates for monthly depreciation closing entries instead of making manual repetitive calculations each month.
10. Eliminating duplicate records to include equipment records, and two sets of books for financial and taxable income.

The above list illustrates one approach to operational auditing. That is, given a predefined preferred practice or situation, the operational auditor can determine if the construction firm is implementing the preferred practices. A second approach that can prove equally effective is critiquing existing practices of the construction firm apart from a defined preferred practice or situation. The second approach has the advantage that there are a few preferred practices that can be held out as ideal for each firm. Therefore, it may prove advantageous to evaluate what is, rather than what should be.

As is true of the internal control audit, the operational audit should be followed by a write-up of findings and recommendations. The findings and recommendations serve as the base for changes that lead to increased efficiency and, hopefully, improved profits for the construction firm.

COMPLIANCE AUDITING

The third aspect of what we defined as management auditing is *compliance auditing*. Unlike internal control auditing and operational auditing, each of which are in great part the ability to foresee weakenesses or improvement areas, compliance auditing is more a verification process. Using inquiry and observation, the compliance auditor determines if established firm policies, procedures, and controls are being implemented according to plan.

Compliance auditing is similar to a safety inspection. An OSHA (Occupational Safety and Health Act) inspector will occasionally visit the construction firm's project site to determine whether the firm's safety practices conform or comply with the safety requirements as defined in federal registers. If the construction firm does not comply with the established standards, it is cited (possibly fined) and expected to make corrections or improvements aimed at complying with the standards and thereby enhancing construction project safety.

Numerous other areas of construction firm operations can and should be evaluated as to compliance with defined acceptable practices. For example, the best and most accurate project cost system that can possibly be designed fails if the project field personnel do not take the time or required effort to properly fill out the source documents such as timecards, daily reports, purchase orders, and change orders. The compliance auditor would test for the proper filling out of the cost system source documents by observing various project superintendents, assistant superintendents, and perhaps foremen who have been given the responsibility of being responsible for accurate source document data. The compliance auditor would also inspect historic source documents prepared in the last few months. This inspection would indicate if the field personnel were delinquent or negligent in their source-document reporting. If they were, the construction firm could then take the appropriate action necessary to ensure accurate source-document reporting.

What a firm or management says it is doing and what it is actually doing may be entirely two different things. Compliance auditing does not question what we should be doing; it merely reports on a comparison of what the firm indicates it is or should be doing and what actually is being done.

The construction firm can be effective in performing the compliance audit with its own employees. When this is done the process becomes a self-evaluation. The construction firm that can evaluate itself on an ongoing basis probably improves its efficiency and effectiveness of operations the most. As was true of the other two defined areas of managerial auditing, the compliance audit has an objective of evaluating rather than policing. When one performs a management audit, the results are disclosed to the construction firm itself. The findings are not intended for external-party use.

Part 5.
TAX PLANNING

CHAPTERS

16
INITIAL TAX-PLANNING DECISIONS

INTRODUCTION

Regardless of the size of the construction firm, the firm's owner can be assured of having at least one partner, the Internal Revenue Service (IRS). The IRS, along with state taxing bodies, receives a share of the profits generated by the construction firm. Normally the more profits the firm generates, the more taxes are paid to taxing bodies.

The major objective of tax planning is tax deferral and, if possible, tax avoidance. Some would argue that tax planning can only defer taxes, that the tax is only moved from one period to the next. For example, if revenue from a project is deferred from one year, it will have to be paid the next year. However, it is also true that a continual deferral of a tax in effect results in an avoidance in that the deferral is carried from one period to the next forever.

Even if one recognizes that the major benefit of tax planning is tax deferral from one period to the next, the value of the deferral should not be discounted. Given the high cost of capital associated with operating a construction firm, and the time value of money (the later one pays an expense, the less the effective cost), tax deferral can result in a significant dollar savings. Additionally, the tax deferral can result in deferring cash outflow in the early years of the construction firm. These early years are normally years when cash availability is critical for the construction firm.

While sometimes overlooked, another objective of tax planning that should be considered is matching the construction firm's ability to pay tax with its obligation to pay tax. On occasion a construction firm has placed emphasis on tax deferral and later, when the tax became due, found itself out of cash and unable to pay the deferred tax.

Tax planning is often viewed as an annual, last-minute effort aimed at reducing the firm's tax liability. While annual tax planning is to be recommended, it is also true that some initial one-time decisions that the construction firm makes play a major role in the firm's ongoing annual tax liability. These types of initial or one-time tax planning considerations are discussed in this chapter. The following chapters discuss tax planning that tends to be more annual in occurrence.

LEGAL ORGANIZATIONAL STRUCTURE

Several different forms of legal organizational structure are available to the construction firm. The choice made by the firm as to its legal organizational structure affects the tax liability of the firm year in and year out. Because of the continuing effect of the initial choice, it becomes important that the construction firm evaluate the immediate and ongoing effect of its initial choice when weighing the alternatives available.

The most common forms of legal organizational structure available to the construction firm include the following:

1. Proprietorship
2. Partnership
3. Corporation
4. Subchapter S Corporation

Less used legal organizational structures include limited partnerships and joint ventures.

While tax consequence is a major factor to be considered in selecting a legal organizational structure, it is not the only factor. In particular the choice of legal organizational structure also has an effect on the liability of the firm's owners, the firm's ability to secure loans, the degree of governmental control, and in some cases the firm's ability to centralize the management decision-making process. The emphasis of the discussion of legal organizational structure in this chapter is on tax consequences only.

Proprietorship

The tax consequence of a proprietorship is relatively easy to explain. All of the income generated by a construction firm structured as a proprietorship gets funneled to the owner's personal income tax return. Specifically, the construction firm owner lists the revenue and expense from his construction firm on schedule C of a form 1040 personal income tax return. The result is that income earned from the owner's construction firm gets taxed at the rates of individuals.

Because income from a proprietorship is taxed at individual rates, it makes little difference whether the owner of the firm takes money out of the firm as a regular salary, by means of occasional draws, or as profits at the end of the year. The result is that in practice various owners do use each of these methods of "paying themselves" for their services to the construction firm.

One of the difficulties associated with the fact that the proprietor's construction firm and the proprietor himself are treated as one as to tax calculations is that, because of this, the firm owner tends to mix the financial activities of the firm with his personal financial activities. There is little attémpt to differentiate between the two. Merging or mixing firm and personal transactions means that the firm's profitability cannot be singled out and meaningful management reports cannot be generated.

Tax rates for individuals (and therefore construction firms having a proprietorship legal organizational structure) increase as the calculated taxable income increases. While the tax rates for small amounts of taxable income are relatively small (e.g., 10 percent), they increase rapidly as taxable income increases and reach a maximum of 50 percent.

For small construction firms that have relatively small annual calculated taxable income (e.g., $20,000), the effective tax rates are smaller for a proprietorship versus a corporate legal structure. However, as taxable income increases, the proprietorship tax rates increase, while the corporate tax rates stay fixed with the result often being a lower tax rate for the corporate structure.

Perhaps as important as tax rates is that some tax saving devices are available to one legal structure and not the other. Specifically, several devices available to corporations are not available to the proprietorship. Some of these are discussed in a following discussion on corporate legal organizational structure.

Partnership

In spite of the many potential problems associated with individuals forming a partnership to carry out a business, the partnership legal organizational structure continues to be used by some construction firms. In addition to the personality conflicts common to partnerships, the potential accounting and tax problems that evolve when a partner dies or resigns from the partnership or the partnership dissolves are troublesome. Usually a partnership legal organizational structure is a poor substitute for a corporate structure.

The partnership structure serves merely as a funnel of income to individual partners. Partnership income is not taxed to the partnership; rather, all income is funneled to partners who are then taxed as individual taxpayers. For this reason, there is an internal revenue provision that requires that the income distributions to partners be made in a manner that does not attempt to manipulate tax payments. For example, it is not permissible to distribute all capital gain income (which is taxed at a lesser rate) to a high-income partner, and all ordinary income to a relatively low-income partner for the purpose of minimizing total tax expense. Although the IRS permits much freedom in regard to partnership income distribution, they are particularly in disfavor of distribution plans that are not consistent from one year to the next.

There are alternative salary plans that may be used in the calculated total income distributions to the partners. The income of the partnership may be distributed on the bases of capital investment, then salaries, with any remaining income to be distributed equally. For example, two partners A and B may agree to an income distribution plan whereby each is to receive 5% interest on their beginning of the year capital investment, a $12,000 salary for A and a $8,000 salary for B, with remaining income to be divided equally. The income is to be distributed in the order of interest, then salary. Further, the agreement should state what the distribution is to be should there be more income than that required to pay interest but less than that required to pay full salaries. For example, the salaries may be paid on a ratio basis in that case. The actual income distribution, assuming total income of $50,000, beginning of year capital investments of A and B as $60,000 and $100,000 would be as follows:

	Partner A	Partner B
Interest		
A: (.05) (60,000)	$ 3,000	
B: (.05) (100,000)		$ 5,000
Salaries	12,000	8,000
Remaining (50,000 − 28,000)	11,000	11,000
Total	$26,000	$24,000

Because of the almost infinite combinations of possible ways to distribute partnership income, it is absolutely necessary that the agreement be clear and be such that it covers all possible amounts to be distributed.

As previously indicated, partnership income is distributed to the partners who in turn include their distributions in their individual tax returns. Thus the partnership income may be taxed at different rates. Each partner reflects his share of partnership income on his own individual annual income tax form. A partnership income tax return is also required to be filed annually. However, it is merely an information return and has no tax implications.

One of the more complex partnership tax transactions that may cause disputes among partners is the tax implications that arise when a partner turns over a nonmonetary asset to the partnership as part of his investment capital and the asset is later sold at a profit or loss. The difficulty takes place when a partner contributes an asset that has value (the tax base) for tax purposes less than or greater than the fair market value of the asset. During recent inflationary years, the fair market value has often exceeded the tax base of the asset. For example, a construction contractor in joining a partnership with another partner may contribute a piece of construction equipment with a fair market value of $20,000. However, at the time the construction contractor contributed the piece of equipment, it may have had a tax base of $10,000. This difference in fair market value and tax base may be due to prior accelerated depreciation or merely inflation of equipment prices.

The tax question arises when the equipment is later sold. For example, assume that the partnership later sells the piece of construction equipment for

$30,000. This results in a $20,000 gain as to tax liability. Typically, the tax expense is identified with the partnership and the expense is distributed to the partners in the predetermined profit and loss ratio. The inequity of this procedure is that, from the partnership's point of view, only a $10,000 gain is realized in that the construction contractor was credited with a $20,000 capital contribution. A more fair distribution of the tax expense of the gain would be to recognize a $10,000 personal gain for the construction contractor and a $10,000 company gain for the partnership with the tax expense allocated separately for the two gains. However, often the entire gain is allocated to the partnership. Clearly, the existence of such a tax distribution and liability is grounds for dispute and should be understood by the partners before the partnership agreement. This is merely one of the potential areas of dispute that can occur in a partnership legal organizational structure.

Corporation

Most construction firms' decision to incorporate centers around a potentially more favorable liability position for the firm's owners and a lower potential tax liability. The more favorable liability question is usually overemphasized in that usually the owner of a corporate construction company will have to pledge his personal assets as a means of obtaining bonds and loans and therefore has the same liability as a proprietorship. The result is that tax aspects become a major consideration in the decision to incorporate.

The corporate tax consideration is not favorable for every construction firm. If the firm is small and thus has little taxable income, a corporate structure may actually result in a higher effective tax rate and tax liabiltty. However, as the firm's income increases, the corporate tax rate structure does become more favorable.

Unlike proprietorship or individual tax rates, corporate tax rates are somewhat fixed. The actual rates on corporate income have varied with the passage of different tax laws. However, usually there have been two or three increments of fixed rates that are applied to the corporation.

As discussed previously, the income tax expense for a proprietorship or a partnership is funneled through the tax returns of the individual owners. On the other hand, the corporation pays income tax as a separate entity. In addition, income that is distributed to owners is again taxed to each owner as an individual tax expense.

At first glance, this double taxation for the corporation may seem to be unfavorable and in fact it may be. However, two points are noteworthy before judgment is passed: first, the income tax rate differs for the proprietorship and the corporation. For the individual, the rates increase to as much as 50 percent for active income and 70 percent for passive income. The corporate rates peak at a fixed rate less than the individual rates associated with high income. A second and more significant point to be made is that only the profits of the construction firm that are in turn distributed to the owners get taxed twice.

With this in mind the construction firm can retain some of its profits for planned growth and an improved working capital position that can improve the firm's bonding capacity position.

The entire question of double taxation can be avoided by setting the owner's or owners' salaries at a rate equivalent to what would be paid as a profit distribution. The salary is considered an expense to the corporation and therefore is not taxed as profits. The result is a significant tax savings relative to distributing the profits as a profit distribution (dividends). The tax difference between salary and profit distribution is illustrated in Figure 16.1 in which a corporate effective tax rate of 30 percent and an individual effective tax rate of 40 percent are assumed.

One of the difficulties of taking the profits out of the corporation as salary is that the firm may not be able to predict its profits in advance in order to set the appropriate salaries. This is especially true of the construction firm that has significant volume changes from one year to the next, each of which is difficult to forecast. However, using a bonus plan provides the corporate construction firm a means of distributing salary after the close of the firm's year at which time the total profits are known. The bonus plan or clause should be written into the corporate by-laws. Specifically, a plan that allows for the amounts of distribution to be tied to generated profits can help defeat an IRS view or argument that a distributed bonus is unjust compensation.

Yet another means used for the owner of the corporate construction firm to avoid potential double taxation is to retain ownership of some assets of the firm in the name of the owner personally and in turn rent the asset to the

	Paid as Salary	Paid as Distribution of Profits
Company profits	$80,000	$80,000
– salary	40,000	20,000
Profits after salary distribution	$40,000	$60,000
Profits distributed	–	20,000
Total compensation to owners (before tax)	40,000	40,000
Tax Effect		
Corporate tax (30 Percent)	$12,000	$18,000
Tax on individual (40 Percent)	16,000	16,000
TOTAL TAX PAID	$28,000	$34,000

Figure 16.1 Tax Effect of Salary Versus Profit Distribution

corporation. For example, the owner of a corporate construction firm might buy as an individual a building to be used as his construction firm's main office. He then rents the building to the corporation at a rate that reflects a profit. The corporation reflects the rate as an expense on its books with the result that some of the construction firm's profits are paid out as a corporate expense in the form of rent to the owner. No double taxation occurs because the corporation recognizes the rental charge as an expense in calculating its taxable income.

The IRS does look at the justification for salaries, distributed bonuses, or rental charges. For example, the IRS would not permit the construction firm to pay a $50,000 salary to the son of the firm's owner for periodic sweeping of the company office floors. The salary and any bonus are supposed to be *just compensation*. However, just compensation is a relative term so the corporate construction firm has considerable freedom in setting salaries and bonuses as a means of avoiding double taxation.

The point at which the corporate tax rates become more favorable than individual tax rates varies from case to case because of some of the variables that make up the individual tax rates. The firm's profits to be distributed and various allowable distribution and allowable deductions affect the comparison.

Apart from the tax rate consideration are some of the tax devices or "loopholes" that are advantageous to the corporate legal organizational structure. For example, the corporate structure can take advantage of the tax benefits of a medical expense reimbursement plan or hospitalization and health plan. As an individual taxpayer (or proprietor), an individual has to have his medical bills exceed an IRS predetermined minimum before he can get a tax benefit from the expenditures. As long as the expenditures are less than the minimum, the individual gets no deduction for them on his tax return. On the other hand, if the incorporated construction firm sets up its own medical plan, some medical expenses of the owners and their dependents might be recognized as a taxable expense on the books of the construction firm. The construction firm merely reimburses the individuals for their medical expenses and is allowed to take each dollar of expense as a deduction in calculating taxable income independent of any minimum.

Other fringe benefits to the owners and/or employees that can be made available in the corporate structure include a tax-free death benefit payment to a survivor, a wage continuation plan in the event of illness, group life insurance, and deferred compensation plans. Another tax advantage of the corporation relates to the sale of the business. A gain on the sale of an owner's stock interest share in a corporation will usually be eligible for capital gain treatment (which results in a lower tax rate). On the sale of a partnership or proprietorship, the amount realized is allocated among the various assets sold, usually resulting in part of the gain being taxable as ordinary income.

Another potential benefit of the corporation is that it is free to choose its taxable year end as any date it desires. This can be used to the advantage of the construction firm in that it can pick a date that best matches its ability to pay the tax and also that reflects the firm in the best light as to financial reporting.

The corporate structure can present a few tax problems not characteristic of the proprietorship or partnership. The major one is that the IRS may attack the corporation's retaining of what they refer to as unreasonable surplus accumulations or excess earnings. They may impose a penalty tax on these earnings because in their view they should not have been sheltered from the double taxation that would occur if they were distributed. Unreasonable surplus accumulation or excess earnings are discussed in a following section of this chapter.

Subchapter S Corporation

Several years ago, the federal government became convinced that small, closely held firms needed a tax alternative to either being a corporation or a proprietorship. For these small, closely held businesses, adopting a corporate legal organizational structure might result in a higher effective tax rate than the rates applicable to a proprietorship. At the same time the proprietorship does not offer some of the planning devices of a corporation or the potential lessened liability for the owners of the construction firm. The federal income tax agencies, in an attempt to help small, closely held businesses devised the Subchapter S corporation. The use of this structure for taxing purposes is limited to small, closely held businesses as defined by the IRS.

In general, the major effect of a firm's election to become a Subchapter S corporation is to eliminate the corporation as a separate tax-paying entity. All of the income generated by the Subchapter S corporation is taxed directly to the owners of the company.

There are two major tax differences between the Subchapter S corporation and the corporation. First, both distributed and nondistributed incomes from the Subchapter S corporation are funneled directly to the individual owners of the firm for tax purposes. Therefore, there is no potential for double taxation (tax corporate profit and tax the individuals receiving the profits).

The second major difference is that the tax rates relevant to the Subchapter S corporation income are the relevant rates applicable to the individuals receiving income. This is contrasted with the fixed rates relevant to corporations. For many smaller construction firms, the taxable income is such that the individual tax rates turn out to be less than the applicable corporate rates.

There are several tax planning implications that follow from using the Subchapter S designation. For example, the Subchapter S corporation might be used in early years of a business as a means of funneling early year losses directly to the tax returns of the firm's owners. As the firm starts to generate significant income in later years, the firm might then change its structure to a corporation in order to take advantage of the more favorable tax rates. Other examples of using the Subchapter S corporation as a tax-planning device are discussed in the following section of this chapter.

The IRS imposes several guidelines or requirements to be met in being eligible for a Subchapter S corporation and once elected how it operates. A maximum number of owners is stipulated, and the percentage of allowable passive income to total income are two of the many provisions. These provisions change with the different tax laws in effect at a specific point in time. It is therefore necessary that the construction firm choosing a Subchapter S designation check the requirements relevant at the time of inception of its election of its legal structure.

TAX PLANNING AND LEGAL STRUCTURE

While it is meaningful to contrast the tax differences of alternative legal organizational structures, the choice of one method over another somewhat depends on the set of circumstances that prevail for the construction firm and its owners at a specific point in time. What is a good tax organizational structure for a firm at a specific point in time may not be a good structure at another point in time. Recognizing the relevant set of circumstances at a specific point in time that pertain to choosing a tax structure is an important part of the tax-planning effort.

In an earlier section of this chapter, reference was made to the fact that a Subchapter S corporation often proves to be beneficial to the construction firm just starting or in its initial years of operation. This is because any losses incurred (which are often typical during the initial years of any business) get funneled directly to the individual's tax return under the Subchapter S corporation structure. These losses can be directly set off against any other income of the individual owners to yield a reduced individual tax liability. If the construction firm is a corporation, the tax losses stay in the corporation and get carried forward to following years. However, given the time value of money and the fact that typically the owner needs all the cash he can get (including cash saved by a reduced tax liability) in early years of the construction firm, the Subchapter S corporation proves advantageous.

As an example of how outside circumstances can dictate the best tax structure at a specific point in time, let us consider a construction firm, the owners of which have substantial outside income in the form of real estate rental income. Assuming the construction firm is generating profits, the corporate structure is preferred in that the Subchapter S corporation would funnel the construction firm's income directly to the individuals who are already at a high taxable income rate because of their outside real estate rental income.

Another tax-planning vehicle in use is setting up several interrelated companies, some of which are Subchapter S corporations and some of which are corporations. By means of intercompany exchange and profit recognition, the owners of all the companies are able to manage their tax liability. To illustrate this concept, let us assume the simplest situation, one owner in control of two construction-related firms, one of which is tax structured as a corporation, and one of which is a Subchapter S corporation. Using interrelated company transactions, the owner can somewhat level the incomes of the corporation, Subchapter S corporation, and his individual income to minimize the aggregate tax liability. For example, given a significant owner's outside income, the owner will attempt to have the Subchapter S corporation report losses, while directing and retaining as much of the profits from operations into the corporation. The result is that the Subchapter S corporation's losses are used to offset the income of the individual owner, while the construction profits are taxed at a favorable tax rate in the corporation.

The IRS does not turn its head in light of an individual or individuals using interrelated companies to manipulate tax liability. However, as is true of several areas of taxation, while the IRS can be viewed in a policing role, the tax law still offers the construction firm and its owner a significant degree of maneuverability.

UNREASONABLE SURPLUS OR EXCESS EARNINGS

As noted in an earlier section one of the potential tax problems of the corporate tax structure is the IRS's position against unreasonable surplus or excess earnings. The IRS is especially attentive to the small, closely held corporation as to excess earnings. This is because they often take the view that the only reason for this type of firm's choice of corporate structure is to avoid tax.

The IRS feels that the excess earnings should be distributed and therefore taxed twice, once to the corporation and once to the individual to whom the distribution is made. As an alternative, they argue that the excess earnings that are retained should be taxed at the applicable individual rate, which is usually higher than the corporate tax rate applied to the sheltered excess retained earnings. With this in mind, internal revenue agents have often picked the construction firm as a prime target for IRS excess earning audits and related imposed tax penalties.

The construction firm has two very strong arguments against the IRS in defending its accumulated surplus or excess earnings. For one, most construction firms are undercapitalized. As noted in Chapter 7, the current position and debt to equity financial ratios are usually considered less than desirable for most construction firms. The construction firm is usually deficient in available cash for operations, let alone having excess cash for growth and research and development activities. The result is that the incorporated construction firm should usually be able to defend some if not all its excess earnings based on a need to improve its financial strength in an industry characterized as having many financial weaknesses.

A second argument the construction firm can take in defense of its excess earnings relates to an indemnity clause often found in the construction firm's agreement with its bonding agent. Few owners of construction firms are ever able to free themselves of the indemnity agreement. The clause is the agreement by which the owner of the construction firm pledges his own assets as security for a bond for a project it builds. If the incorporated construction firm goes bankrupt while building a project, the indemnity clause or agreement gives the surety or bonding company the right to offset the owner's personal assets against outstanding claims before the surety company is liable for any claims.

The presence of the commonplace indemnity clause in the construction process is by itself an indication of the weakness that typifies most construction firms' financial position. Based on this fact, once again the construction firm should be able to successfully argue for its need to build up excess earnings. It should argue that the build-up of the excess earnings is needed to eliminate the indemnity agreement, an agreement that applies to few other industries.

ESTATE-PLANNING CONSIDERATIONS

The owner of every construction firm usually has an objective of building up an estate that can serve as retirement income or be passed on to a younger generation. The objectives of estate planning are to maximize the cash available to the owners of the firm upon retirement or sale of the firm. Much of this effort centers around minimizing the tax consequences of a built-up amount of income and minimizing the tax consequences of selling or transferring ownership of the construction firm. Estate planning must recognize the high tax rates associated with transfer of estates. If attention is not given to effective tax planning, high estate taxes can almost eliminate an estate that has taken the owner of the construction firm years to build.

It is difficult to generalize as to the most effective estate planning for every owner of a construction firm. The personal assets of the owner and his family have to be considered in order to specify an effective estate plan. However, usually the corporate organizational structure offers the owner of the construction firm the most estate-planning benefits. Examples of some of the estate-planning considerations that pertain to a corporate structure are as follows:

1. Gifts of stock can be made to children at a time when the value of the stock is low, thus minimizing gift taxes, while placing the growth potential in the younger generation.
2. There is an opportunity for piecemeal sale or gift of the firm to the one who is ultimately to take over, while the initial owner can still retain control and avoid personal liability.
3. The corporate existence does not cease upon the owner's or shareholder's death and the executor can generally continue the business without securing court approval.
4. If the corporate business is continued, the ultimate disposition is of stock and not an undivided interest in business assets, thereby facilitating distribution.
5. Qualified survivor annuities payable to a beneficiary under a qualified pension or profit-sharing plan are not included in the taxable estate of the decedent.

6. Group term life insurance proceeds are not included in the employee's taxable estate if no incidents of ownership are retained.
7. Employee death benefits are not includable in the employee's taxable estate if he has no right to the benefit himself and has no right to designate the beneficiary.
8. The use of a bona fide buy-sell agreement can be used to fix the value of corporate shares for estate tax valuation.
9. There exists a possibility of deferring the payment of estate tax by paying it in up to ten annual installments if the closely held corporate stock constitutes a specified portion of the estate.
10. Partial stock redemptions are possible at capital gains rates to the extent of funeral and administration expenses and death taxes.

Each of the listed estate-planning considerations is by itself somewhat complicated. Suffice it to say that the owner of the construction firm needs to consult professional advice as to his own situation. However, the fact remains that more flexible estate planning is another argument that can be made for the corporate organizational structure.

The use of trusts is common in estate planning. A trust is a distinct tax entity for which a tax return must be filed. The major reason for creating a trust is to avoid or decrease the effect of progressive estate taxes. A second reason for the trust is that the creator of the trust may want to protect the beneficiaries of his estate from financial ignorance or inexperience, or spendthrift habits of the beneficiaries by placing his estate in the hands of a competent *fiduciary*.

The creator (grantor) of a trust places income-generating assets, such as real property or cash, in a trust that is overseen by the designated fiduciary. The designated fiduciary is often a financial institution. Tax savings result because the income generated by the assets gets divided among the beneficiaries. Because of the division and the lower tax rates normally applicable to the beneficiaries, the effective tax rate and related tax liability may be significantly lower than would have resulted if the grantor retained outright ownership.

Trusts are available to the owner of the construction firm regardless of whether the firm is structured as a proprietorship, partnership, corporation, or Subchapter S corporation. However, fiduciaries often prefer the grantor to be a corporation in that this structure may lessen the liability of the fiduciary.

Numerous types of trusts are available to the owner of the construction firm. Usually the trust creator must have only limited control of the trust's assets if the potential tax savings are to be realized. Otherwise the IRS treats the trust as a sham, created for the purpose of artificially reducing the creator's tax.

17
TAX PLANNING AND REVENUE RECOGNITION

INTRODUCTION

One of the most talked about tax topics regarding the construction firm is the method of revenue recognition used by the construction firm. The construction firm has available to it several different revenue-recognition methods. The methods include the cash, accrual, percentage-of-completion, and completed-contract methods. Each of these can result in a different tax liability in a given year.

The use of alternative revenue-recognition methods for financial reporting was discussed in Chapter 3. However, there is no necessity to use the same revenue-recognition method for financial reporting and determining tax liability. Often it is preferable to use separate methods for the two purposes. For example, it may be advantageous to use the completed-contract method for determining tax liability while using the percentage-of-completion method for financial reporting.

Most accounting methods available for calculating financial statement income are also allowable for determining tax liability and vice versa. Auditors place more restrictions on the choice of accounting methods than do tax laws. For example, even though the cash method may be available for calculating taxable income, the method is not regarded by CPA's as an acceptable method for reporting financial results. Both auditors and tax laws require consistency in using a method for a given purpose, be it financial reporting or calculating taxable income.

This chapter illustrates the tax differences of the alternative revenue-recognition methods available for use by the construction firm. In addition, tax strategy as to the use of the methods and other revenue-related tax effects are discussed.

CASH AND ACCRUAL METHODS

The tax advantage of the cash method of accounting is that it results in a great deal of tax-planning potential. By prepaying or deferring year-end expenses and by deferring billings, it is possible to increase or decrease the taxable income in any one year. Being able to increase or decrease taxable income in any one year can reduce the total tax liability by changing the tax rate of a given year; it also provides the firm a means of deferring the tax due to a following year. Even if the sum total tax liability for a number of years is equal, an advantage of deferring the tax due results because of the time value of money.

The cash method will lessen the tax liability in a given year if the amounts billed and uncollected are in excess of costs and expenses incurred but not paid. For the small construction firm, the cash method may actually result in a better matching of ability to pay to the occurrence of the actual liability. Postponing the recognition of revenue until the cash is received results in the cash being received before the related tax on the revenue becomes due.

The cash method of accounting has certain disadvantages. In order to lessen the tax liability by means of early payment of disbursements, the contractor has to have adequate financing which may or may not be the case. Also on the negative side is the fact that such early payment may have the effect that the contractor is financing the construction project for the owner.

While taxes deferred from one year to the next are at least worth the interest at which the money can be invested or borrowed, the fact remains that deferring tax will merely result in carrying the tax liability over to the next year. It is not possible to defer the tax permanently because the firm must implement its chosen accounting method on a consistent basis.

The accrual method of accounting permits less flexibility in tax planning than the cash method. All receivables and payables are recorded as incurred. If there are more payables than receivables, the accrual method of accounting will result in a lower tax liability than would be due under the cash method. On the other hand, if there are more receivables than payables, the accrual method of accounting will result in a higher tax liability than would be due using the cash method.

For the construction firm that has chosen the accrual method of accounting for calculating taxable income, the most significant tax-planning question is whether retentions on billings should be included in taxable income. Recent IRS cases indicate that they will allow retentions on billings to be excluded or included from taxable income as long as the chosen practice is applied on a consistent basis. In order to defer the tax liability and gain the benefits of the time value of money, retentions on billings should be excluded in calculating taxable income. It is worth noting that the IRS has been liberal in its approving of requests from contractors to change from the accrual method with inclusion of retentions to the accrual method with exclusion of retentions. As is true of other changes in methods, the firm must apply for the change by filing form 3115 (discussed in a following section of this chapter).

While the accrual method does imply a better matching than the cash method, the concept may be overridden by adherence to the practice of recognizing revenue when one has a legal right to the money. A unique industry characteristic that brings out this point is the industry's practice of overbilling by front-ending the profit on select work performed. When using the accrual method of accounting, the IRS requires that the overbilling be recognized in taxable income because the money is constructively received. This is true in spite of the fact that the firm has not really "earned" the overbilled amount of money. Thus, while overbillings have the advantage of yielding the firm money before it is earned, they have the disadvantage of being taxable before they are earned. The construction firm does not get the best of both worlds.

LONG-TERM CONTRACT METHODS

In addition to the cash and accrual revenue-recognition methods, the IRS regulations permit the construction firm to use long-term contract revenue-recognition methods for calculating tax liability. Both the percentage-of-completion and completed-contract revenue-recognition methods are identified as acceptable long-term contract methods.

In order to be eligible for treatment as a long-term contract method, a contract must be for the construction or manufacturing of a project that normally requires more than twelve months to complete. If a building normally would take thirteen months to construct but because of prudent management is finished in eleven months, the project income can be recognized using a long-term contract method.

As an exception to the twelve-month requirement for long-term contract, the tax courts have ruled that a project that overlaps a firm's year end can be considered a long-term contract and therefore eligible for long-term treatment. For example, if a construction firm has a year end of December 31 and starts a five-month project in October, income from the project at year end can be reflected using a long-term contract revenue-recognition method.

Contracts for services such as architectural design may or may not be eligible for treatment as long-term contracts. The terms of the contract dictate correct treatment.

The contractor who has contracts exceeding a twelve-month duration can choose a long-term contract accounting method for these contracts and choose another accounting method such as the cash method for reporting taxable income for projects of less than a twelve-month duration. The IRS requires the firm to be consistent in its use of any tax method. The construction firm is not permitted to manipulate its tax liability through variable use of available revenue-recognition methods such as long-term contract methods.

Long-term contract methods have widespread usage by the construction firm. Different tax effects result from using the percentage-of-completion method and completed-contract method.

Percentage-of-Completion Method

Using the percentage-of-completion method, the firm reports as income that part of the construction contract price which represents the percentage of the entire contract completed during the year. The percentage completed can be determined in several ways. Two procedures for calculating the percentage are acceptable under current tax laws. The first and more widely used method calculates the percentage of completion as the percentage of costs incurred in the year in question to the estimated total costs of the project. When using this method a more accurate percentage of completion is usually determined if the firm annually evaluates (and revises if necessary) the estimated total costs to complete a project rather than merely assume that the original estimate of total costs is correct. When making such a revision, the tax laws require that appropriate documentation showing the basis of such revision be available at the firm's place of business for inspection.

The second acceptable tax method for calculating the percentage of completion is based on calculating the percentage of work done. Note that this percentage may be made independent of costs. For example, a contractor constructing ten miles of roadway might assume the project is 20 percent complete after two miles are paved. Such a procedure is acceptable as long as the contractor obtains and retains certificates of architects or engineers showing the percentage completed during the year.

Compared to the completed-contract method to be discussed in the next section, the percentage-of-completion method usually has the advantage of better reflecting the annual income earned. Using the percentage-of-completion method results in a reportable income that will not fluctuate as significantly as it would using the completed-contract method. As explained in a later section, this more level annual income may result in a smaller effective tax liability from year to year for the firm.

The percentage-of-completion method has the disadvantage that the reportable income is based on an estimate. As such, if the estimate is in error, the method may over- or underestimate income. If overstated, the firm pays too much tax. While over the life of the project the firm will "recapture" this overpayment of tax, it will not recapture the time value of money opportunity interest cost associated with early payment.

The most often stated disadvantage of the percentage-of-completion method is that it frequently does not permit the deferral of income taxes to the extent that the cash, accrual, or completed-contract methods do. This is usually the argument given by the firm that chooses an alternative accounting revenue-recognition method.

Completed-Contract Method

Using the completed-contract method, income is reported in the year in which the construction project is completed and accepted. Both revenue and expenses are deferred as to their inclusion in income until this point in time.

By deferring the recognition of income, the tax liability is also deferred. However, eventually the tax liability must be paid. The result is that over a period of time the tax benefits of adopting the completed-contract method diminish. The tax benefit can be viewed as a one-time initial benefit. This initial tax deferral benefit can be extremely important to the new firm which often has early year cash-flow difficulties.

One of the most important problems associated with using the completed-contract method is determining the end of a project. This is an important point in time in that it dictates the taxable year in which income is to be recognized. The tax courts have held that the time for recognition is when the project is substantially completed. This differs from the IRS regulations that indicate income should be recognized when the project is completed and accepted. Substantial completion and completed are terms open to interpretation. What is completed in the eyes of the contractor may not be completed in the opinion of the owner. Technically, substantial completion implies that the project is completed to the point that the owner can utilize it for the purpose intended. However, even with this definition the point in time may be difficult to pinpoint. In many instances the owner's agent, the architect or engineer, may pass judgment as to substantial completion.

There can be inconsistency in the IRS regulations and the rulings of the tax courts. For example, the fact that final payment is being held (and therefore the project has not been accepted) by the owner does not necessarily mean that the contractor has not reached substantial completion. Similarly, one cannot assume in all cases that final payment is indicative of substantial completion having been performed.

It should be obvious that the exact point in time at which a project should be considered complete is a theoretical problem. As a practical matter, the later the point in time used, the more the tax benefit. Normally the contractor will not have difficulty defending his selection of the point in time a project is completed if he is consistent in his approach.

Another significant question that sometimes occurs in using the completed-contract method for tax purposes is the treatment of overhead costs. Overhead costs can be classified as either job overhead or company (i.e., general) overhead. Job overhead costs are those that directly relate to projects. These types of overhead costs should be treated in the same way that direct labor and direct material are treated. That is, when using the completed-contract method, the job overhead costs should be attached to a project and only considered as an expense when the project is ruled complete and income is recognized.

Other types of overhead costs are not as easily identified with a single project. For example, the salary of an estimator or the costs of maintaining the central office, such as utility bills, may not be easily traceable to a single project. These types of overhead costs are commonly referred to as company overhead. Even when using the completed-contract method, the tax law allows these company overhead costs to be treated as period costs. As such for purposes of calculating taxable income, the company overhead costs can be recognized in the year in which they occur.

While most overhead costs are clearly job overhead costs and others are clearly company overhead costs, a firm may have some overhead costs that have characteristics of both types. For example, the salary of a job superintendent who divides his time among several ongoing projects might be treated as a job overhead cost by one firm and a company overhead cost by yet another firm. When in doubt and a case can be made for recognizing the cost as a company overhead cost, the contractor gains tax deferral benefits by recognizing the cost as a period cost (a company overhead cost). As with other methods it is important that the contractor be consistent in his method application. The IRS takes a dim view of inconsistent methods.

Frequent mention has been made of the contractor's right to utilize alternative financial reporting accounting methods for tax purposes. As is true of most tax laws, there are exceptions. A case in point is the treatment of sales tax on material (an overhead cost). When using the completed-contract method for financial reporting, the contractor may choose to either recognize the sales tax as a period cost or attach it to the project and as such defer it. However, tax law requires that sales tax be recognized in the year in which it occurred (a period cost).

A potential disadvantage of the completed-contract method is the possibility of having the firm's income of a few years concentrated in one year for tax purposes with the result being a higher tax rate. For example, assume an incorporated contractor performed a project that took two years to complete. Let us further assume the following:

	% Completion Profits	*Completed Contract Profits*
Year 19X0	\$70,000	
Year 19X1	70,000	\$140,000

For purpose of illustration, let us assume the following corporate tax rates:

First	\$25,000	17%
Next	25,000	20%
Next	25,000	30%
Next	25,000	40%
Greater than	100,000	46%

If the corporation had used the percentage-of-completion method of accounting, the total tax liability to the firm would have been

Year 19X0		*Year 19X1*	
First		First	
$25,000 × .17 =	$4,250	$25,000 × .17 =	$4,250
Next		Next	
$25,000 × .20 =	5,000	$25,000 × .20 =	5,000
Next		Next	
$20,000 × .30 =	6,000	$20,000 × .30 =	6,000
	$15,250		$15,250
TOTAL	= $15,250	+ $15,250	= $30,500

If the corporation had used the completed-contract method of accounting, the total tax liability would have been

Year 19X0	*Year 19X1*	
$0	First	
	$25,000 × .17 =	$ 4,250
	Next	
	$25,000 × .20 =	5,000
	Next	
	$25,000 × .30 =	7,500
	Next	
	$25,000 × .40 =	10,000
	Next	
	$40,000 × .46 =	18,400
$0		$45,150

TOTAL = $0 + $45,150 = $45,150

Obviously the example has been constructed to illustrate the considerably increased tax liability of the completed-contract method that results because of the income concentration in one time period. While the example may be exaggerated, it does point out that, in certain select situations, the benefits of tax deferral may be outweighed by a higher effective tax rate.

Perhaps the greatest disadvantage of the completed-contract method is that, when using the method for calculating taxable income, losses may be recognized only when the project is complete. This can result in reversing the tax deferral effects. That is, while the method is chosen to defer taxes, the fact that losses cannot be recognized until the project is completed results in a deferral of the tax benefits.

TAX DIFFERENCES OF REVENUE-RECOGNITION METHODS

In order to illustrate the income tax implications of the alternative accounting methods available to the construction firm, we will consider financial data for the Sample Construction Company. While the dollar amounts may not be typical of each firm, they are representative of data common to many construction firms.

In 19X0 Sample Construction Company was in its first year of operation. During that year the firm received and started work on its first construction project. The firm has chosen December 31 as its taxable year end. Because the project it has started is expected to have a duration exceeding twelve months, the firm can select a long-term contract method or the cash or accrual accounting method.

Financial data regarding the project started in 19X0 is as follows:

Total project contract amount		$4,000,000
Total project estimated cost		3,600,000
Total estimated gross profit		$ 400,000
Total billed as of 12/31/X0		
Gross	$2,000,000	
Less retainer of 10%	200,000	$1,800,000
Total cash received as of 12/31/X0		$1,400,000
Contract costs incurred as of 12/31/X0		
Paid	$1,400,000	
Unpaid	200,000	$1,600,000
General overhead as of 12/31/X0		
Paid	$ 40,000	
Unpaid	20,000	$ 60,000

In order to determine the tax implications of the choice of accounting method in the firm's first income tax liability calcuation, the taxable income or loss will now be calculated. While the tax effect for following years is also relevant to the choice of methods, the first year effect is especially important to a new firm because the new firm typically is sensitive to the need for cash.

Should the firm select the cash method of accounting, the taxable income would be calculated as follows:

Cash Method

Cash revenues	$1,400,000
Cash costs	1,400,000
Gross profit	0
General overhead	$ 40,000
Taxable loss	$ (40,000)

The taxable income is calculated by only considering the cash transactions. The resulting taxable loss would result in no tax being due.

If the accrual method is chosen, the contractor has a choice of including or excluding retainers in its calculation of taxable income. As noted, the exclusion of the retainer will result in less tax liability for the tax-paying entity. Let us first calculate the taxable income with the assumption that retainers are included in taxable income.

Accrual Method—
Including Retainer

Revenues	$2,000,000
Contract costs	1,600,000
Gross profit	$ 400,000
General overhead	60,000
Taxable income	$ 340,000

If retainers are excluded from the revenues the taxable income would be as follows.

Accrual Method—
Excluding Retainers

Revenues	$1,800,000
Contract costs	1,600,000
Gross profit	$ 200,000
General overhead	60,000
Taxable income	$ 140,000

It should be evident that excluding the contract retainer can have a dramatic effect on the calculated taxable income. The significantly higher taxable income using the accrual method versus the cash method is because the uncollected billings (i.e., receivables) far exceed the unpaid construction costs (payables). Had the payables exceeded the receivables, the taxable income would have been less if an accrual method were used.

Turning our attention to the long-term contract methods, let us first consider the percentage-of-completion method. While several methods are available for determining the percentage of completion, let us assume the contractor selects to determine the percentage complete on the basis of a ratio of costs incurred to total estimated costs. This percentage is calculated as $1,600,000 divided by $3,600,000 times 100 or 44.4 percent. Using this percentage, the calculation of taxable income is made as follows:

Percentage-of-Completion
Method

Revenue (.444 × $4,000,000)	$1,776,000
Contract costs	1,600,000
Gross profit	$ 176,000
General overhead	60,000
Taxable income	$ 116,000

Finally let us consider the tax effects of the completed contract method. The taxable income is calculated as follows:

Completed-Contract Method

Revenues	$ 0
Contract costs	0
Gross profit	$ 0
General overhead	60,000
Taxable loss	$ (60,000)

Since the single project that Sample Construction Company worked on during 19X0 was not complete by year end, no revenue or costs (direct expenses) are reflected in the taxable income. However, the general overhead costs are treated as period costs and recognized in the year incurred.

Let us summarize the first-year taxable incomes or losses for the different accounting methods:

	Income	*Loss*
Cash method		$40,000
Accrual method—including retainer	$340,000	
Accrual method—excluding retainer	140,000	
Percentage-of-completion method	116,000	
Completed-contract method		60,000

Obviously the calculated incomes and losses are influenced by the financial data selection. Regardless of the data given, the accrual method excluding retainages will result in less of a tax liability than the accrual method that includes retainages, and the completed-contract method results in less taxable income than the percentage-of-completion method (in the first year).

PRACTICAL CONSIDERATIONS OF REVENUE-RECOGNITION METHODS

The question arises as to what revenue recognition method should be used for calculating taxable income and for reporting financial income for a specific construction firm. No one method may be best for every firm.

The choice of revenue-recognition method for calculating taxable income should be made independent of the method used for calculating financial income. Too often it is argued that two sets of books must be kept in order to use one method for taxable income and one method for financial reporting. In reality, simple accounting entries can be made at year end that enable the firm to switch its accounting records to another accounting method.

Many construction firms use the cash method of accounting for tax purposes. This choice of methods is sometimes made in recognition of the potential of manipulating taxable income through early payment of expenses at year end. While this manipulation can work to the construction firm's advantage, it can also prove detrimental with the result that the cash method is a bad choice of methods. In particular the following points are areas of caution for the cash method:

1. This method of tax reporting is diametrically opposed to the contractor's typical cash management posture—collect contract revenues as early as possible through unbalanced bids and pay contract costs as late as possible.
2. The purported flexibility is only available to the extent that the contractor has and maintains a flexible cash position. Banks and savings and loan associations thrive on this method because of their cash reserves. This method is of less use to the construction firm that is in the unpleasant position of not having the cash necessary to capitalize on this flexibility.
3. Concern over reducing tax liability can lead to crash year-end actions that are inconsistent with sound business management.

If these areas of potential difficulties can be controlled, the cash method does provide the construction firm tax-planning benefits. Assuming sound business judgment is applied in addition to the concern for tax planning, the cash method may be preferred to the accrual method for projects not eligible for long-term contract treatment.

A word of caution should be made in regard to the cash method of accounting. In an earlier section mention was made of the fact that the IRS could challenge the use of an accounting method if the method does not clearly reflect income. A case in point is the IRS's rather frequent challenge of a taxpayer's use of the cash method when the method is accompanied by a continuing build-up of receivables or if the firm has considerable year-end work in progress. In an attempt to speed up its tax collection, the IRS may argue that the cash method accompanied by a large and sudden build-up of receivables does not clearly reflect income. The firm can best argue against such a stance by showing evidence of matching income and taxes over a period of years.

The IRS will often disallow the cash method for the construction firm when the firm carries an inventory of material. When material is present, the IRS argues that it is too easy to manipulate income by buying material inventory before it is needed for a project.

The IRS also restricts the use of the completed-contract method. While tax regulations are subject to change, current tax law is such that the completed-contract method may be limited to smaller contracts.

In spite of restrictions on its use, the completed-contract method is often identified as the preferable tax method for revenue-recognition for long-term contracts. The method defers tax liability until a project is completed. At a minimum this deferral is worth the interest income associated with temporarily in-

vesting the cash equivalent to tax liability. However, the total tax liability of the firm will be equal over the life of the firm regardless of the tax method chosen: what is deferred one year is due in a following year.

The completed-contract method can result in wide swings in taxable income from one year to the next. This is especially true of the methods used by the relatively small construction firm. The firm's income may be subject to a high tax rate in one year (e.g., 40 percent) and a relatively small rate in yet another year. The end result is two potentially unfavorable tax results. First, the total tax liability of the firm may be greater than if the firm leveled the taxable income for each year. Second, a large tax liability in a given year may result in a hardship on the construction firm's cash flow.

For a relatively small construction firm that has taxable income in the $0 to $100,000 range, reporting income on a percentage-completion method may be preferable. This is especially true if the firm is a corporation. Current tax rates for corporations are relatively low for taxable incomes of one hundred thousand dollars or less. Taxable income above one hundred thousand dollars gets taxed at a much higher rate. Through the use of the percentage-of-completion method and tax planning it is possible to level taxable income at approximately one hundred thousand dollars or less annually. The result is a substantially lower effective tax rate for the percentage-of-completion method compared to the completed-contract method.

As the construction firm's taxable income increases beyond the one hundred thousand dollar level, the advantage of leveling taxable income diminishes. This is the reason that the completed-contract method for reporting taxable income is often recommended for the relatively large firm. In this case the deferral of a tax liability starts to outweigh the benefits of a more level taxable income.

Perhaps more important than the temporary deferral of taxes associated with the completed-contract method is the potential to manipulate revenue recognition at year end through tax planning. Flexibility can be provided through judicious use of several techniques including:

1. Management of physical completion of contracts
2. Construction management contracts
3. Combination or segmentation of contracts
4. Change orders
5. Changing year ends

Earlier discussion indicated that the firm must be consistent in its determination of the completion (acceptance) of projects for tax recognition when using the completed-contract method. However, there is nothing to prevent the contractor from planning resources available to a project such that project completion is delayed (or expedited if that is the contractor's objective). Project plans, schedules, and progress reports provide the firm a means of allocating resources to projects in a manner that is compatible with the firm's tax-planning objectives.

Construction-management contracts are usually written such that the contract calls for a service rather than a manufacturing of a project. Therefore, the typical construction-management contract (often referred to as CM) may not qualify for a long-term accounting method even if the services overlap a year end or extend beyond a year's duration. The result is that it is possible for a construction firm to use two different accounting methods for projects of equal duration. Depending on its immediate tax-planning objective, the firm can attempt to enter into a CM contract or a traditional construction contract.

It is somewhat common for an owner to build a large project through a series of phases. For examples, school building complexes may be let to contractors through phase A, which may be offices, phase B, which may be classrooms, etc. If a single contractor is successful in obtaining contracts for more than one phase, the question arises as to whether the contracts should be treated as one for tax purposes or treated as severed contracts. Assuming the contractor is utilizing the completed-contract method, there are tax deferral benefits for aggregating the contracts. The firm can argue that the reason it obtained the second phase was due in great part to its success in obtaining the first phase. While such an argument may be with merit, the IRS is somewhat strict in its treatment of aggregated and severed contracts. In particular, if under normal operating circumstances contracts would be separate, the contractor cannot freely aggregate the contracts. The same policy applies to a single contract: it cannot be severed by the contractor if such a severing is uncommon for the type of contract in question.

The IRS's firm stance on aggregated and severed contracts limits tax planning. However, the regulations do not prevent some leeway. Through planning, negotiations with a potential project owner, and using the completed-contract method, the contractor can obtain tax-planning benefits.

The use of change orders provides the contractor with significant tax-planning possibilities. These possibilities are especially relevant when the completed-contract method of revenue recognition is utilized. Change orders become part of the contract to which they are associated. Therefore, if the contract is of long-term duration and the completed-contract method is utilized, revenue recognition for the change order is deferred until project completion. This treatment is more favorable than having to treat revenue from each change order in the period incurred. Theoretically, by using change orders it becomes possible for a contractor to perform work for an owner indefinitely with an indefinite deferral of revenue and tax. No doubt the IRS would treat such an obvious manipulation as one not purely reflecting income. Nonetheless, change orders provide the contractor with tax-planning potential.

The choice of the construction firm's year end increases in significance when using the completed-contract method. A contractor in a geographic location affected by widely varying seasons commonly finishes a project at a certain time of the year. For example, a contractor in the midwest may complete a large number of projects in October. By choosing September 30 as the year end, the firm can defer taxes on its completed projects by eleven months. Such a deferral may significantly alleviate many cash-flow problems inherent to the construction firm.

The completed-contract method is not without its disadvantages. For example, it is often argued that the method can shift income all to one period with the result being a higher tax bracket and therefore a larger dollar tax liability. This argument is only valid for a proprietorship or partnership and the argument is often overemphasized. More often than not, the completed-contract method does not result in a widely fluctuating yearly taxable income. The result is that in some cases the tax-planning advantages of the completed-contract method outweigh the disadvantages.

When attempting to select the most advantageous method, one should remember that, over the lifetime of the business, the total taxable income will be the same regardless of the accounting method used. Thus attention has to center on the benefits of tax deferral. As noted earlier, available cash is usually of concern to the new firm. As such, a method such as the cash method or the completed-contract method may be advantageous in first-year tax deferral.

Using the completed-contract method in a firm's first year of business can result in a taxable loss in the first year. In order to take advantage of the benefits of the loss, the firm must turn a profit in the immediately following years.

Because many firms tend to grow in revenues and income as they grow in age, firms commonly find themselves moving to a higher tax rate as a function of time. The result is that income that is deferred may be taxed at a higher rate when the income is deferred. This potential disadvantage of the completed-contract method of accounting must be weighed against the tax deferral benefits of the method.

CHANGING REVENUE-RECOGNITION METHODS

In earlier sections mention was made of the fact that the contractor can request a change in its accounting methods used in determining taxable income. The change can be made only upon receiving the permission of the commissioner of Internal Revenue.

The benefits of different accounting methods were highlighted in the earlier sections of this chapter. It should be noted that there are certain procedural factors that can actually make the change difficult and in select instances the change may have distinct disadvantages.

The contractor initiates its request for a change by filing Form 3115 with the commissioner of Internal Revenue in Washington, D.C. The form must be filed within 180 days after the beginning of the year of the change. If the commissioner approves the change, a letter setting forth the conditions is sent to the contractor. The contractor in turn attaches a copy of the commissioner's letter to its tax return for the year of the change.

The Internal Revenue Service will permit authorized changes. For example, the contractor will usually have little difficulty in receiving the right to change from the accrual method of accounting that includes retainers to the accrual method of accounting that excludes retainers. While a change will be granted, the IRS requires that any tax effects resulting from a change be spread over ten years or the number of years the original accounting method was employed, whichever is less. This reduces the benefit that the contractor would receive if all the benefits could be received immediately.

The completed-contract method of accounting is often chosen because of its potential tax benefits. However, there are some potentially substantial disadvantages associated with switching to the completed-contract method from another method. In particular the contractor switching to the completed-contract method for tax purposes must report *all* income from projects completed in the year of change. The result is that there may be a double reporting of income on contracts in progress at the beginning of the year of the change. Thus, if a contractor would have a project in progress at the beginning of the tax change year, and the firm recognized $50,000 of income for the prior year, theoretically the $50,000 would have to be recognized again with the result being a double tax on the $50,000. To partially offset this disadvantage to the contractor, the IRS allows the double-reported income to be deducted over a period of ten years. Note that, while the contractor is permitted to eventually deduct all the double-taxed income, the deductions occur in the future and as such the contractor is penalized because of the time value of money effects.

Let us illustrate this potential time value of money disadvantage by assuming a contractor switches from the percentage-of-completion method to the completed-contract method. A contractor requests permission for an accounting change in early 19X1 and receives permission to change for the year 19X1. In 19X0 the contractor utilized the percentage-completion method. During 19X0 the contractor worked on three projects, none of which were completed by year end. However, because the percentage-of-completion method was used for 19X0, $300,000 of income was recognized for the 19X0 taxable year. This $300,000 was based on the percentage of total work done in 19X0 on the contracts.

In 19X1 the contractor completed the three projects started in 19X0 and received an additional profit of $200,000 for a total of $500,000 from the three projects. During 19X1 three other projects were started but not completed until 19X2. Ignoring the work completed in 19X1, the dollar amount of income using the completed-contract method for the following years was as follows:

	Completed contract income
19X2	$200,000
19X3	300,000
19X4	200,000
19X5	300,000
19X6	200,000
19X7	300,000
19X8	200,000
19X9	300,000
19X10	200,000

Year	Percentage of completion	Completed contract	Deduction adjustment	Taxable income
19X0	$300,000			$300,000
19X1		$500,000	($30,000)	$470,000
19X2		200,000	(30,000)	170,000
19X3		300,000	(30,000)	270,000
19X4		200,000	(30,000)	170,000
19X5		300,000	(30,000)	270,000
19X6		200,000	(30,000)	170,000
19X7		300,000	(30,000)	270,000
19X8		200,000	(30,000)	170,000
19X9		300,000	(30,000)	270,000
19X10		200,000	(30,000)	170,000

Figure 17.1 Effect of Changing to Completed-Contract Method

Because of the IRS's requirement to recognize all income in the year the project is completed, the taxable incomes reportable must be adjusted as shown in Figure 17.1.

It can be observed in Figure 17.1 that in 19X1 the firm has to report $300,000 of taxable income that was recognized and taxed for the year 19X0. The double tax on this amount is returned to the contractor through the ten $30,000 downward income adjustments for each of the ten years. However, the contractor loses a substantial amount of interest associated with the early double taxation. Additionally, it should be noted that the double recognition of income in the year of the accounting change may have the effect of placing the contractor in a high income tax rate bracket. The high tax rate bracket may be greater than the tax rate at which the contractor receives the adjustment reduction. The result can be that the contractor may not be returned all of the double tax even when ignoring the negative aspect of the loss of interest.

The fact that there are potential procedural disadvantages of changing accounting methods does not imply that these disadvantages always or ever outweigh the advantages of the change in question. What should be clear is that a wise initial choice of accounting method is most advantageous.

TAXABLE INCOME AND FINANCIAL REPORTING DIFFERENCES

The Internal Revenue Service's regulations on methods of calculating taxable income are not totally consistent with Industry Audit Guides published by the American Institute of Certified Public Accountants (AICPA) for reporting income. Most of the differences are ones of degree of emphasis and application. The guide published by the AICPA for reporting income in the financial statements of the firm also addresses some reporting principles and procedures not relevant to calculating taxable income.

If the construction firm requires an audit, the CPA performing the audit must satisfy the guidelines established for his profession. As such, the AICPA audit guides become the basis for proper finanical accounting and the use of an accounting method. Naturally a firm that is not required to have an audit is less constrained in its choice or use of an accounting method for financial reporting. However, even this firm may have to abide by the AICPA guidelines in order to have its financial statements be acceptable to outside parties such as banks and sureties.

In general, tax law regulations are more lenient in regard to the choice and use of accounting methods than are the AICPA auditing guides for financial reporting. For example, the tax rules place few constraints on the construction firm in its selection of the completed-contract method. However, the AICPA audit guide for financial reporting almost restricts the use of the completed-contract method to those instances for which there is no reasonably dependable estimate of the extent of project progress because of inherent hazards.

Another example of the more stringent accounting method requirements of financial reporting relates to the basis for determining the percentage of completion in the percentage-of-completion method. The tax rules are vague as to the basis that can be used to determine the percentage of completion. The tax rules have been interpreted to allow the percentage of completion to be calculated on a basis of amounts billed, on a cost-ratio calculation, or a ratio of production (e.g., cubic yards of concrete poured to total estimated). The AICPA audit guides specifically state that billings are not a suitable basis for income or profit allocation. The reason behind the Institute's position centers around the fact that billings may have no real relationship to performance under a contract. Often the project owner, knowingly or unknowingly, permits early billings with amounts being in excess of the amount of work actually performed. When the contractor does this over billing it is said to be front end loading or unbalancing the bid. Even if the owner is aware of the front-ending, he may permit the contractor to do it as a means of providing the contractor working capital with the owner receiving long-term benefits such as a lower project bid and good owner-contractor relations.

The AICPA audit guide, like the tax regulations, implies that the preferable method of establishing the percentage of completion is to determine the ratio that incurred costs to date bear to estimated total costs after giving effect to estimates of costs to complete based upon most recent information. The Institute also suggests that the contractor may be justified in excluding certain costs in determining the cost ratio. For example, if substantial quantities of materials are initially accumulated on a job site but not used, the direct cost to date to the contractor may not be indicative of performance. The same situation may occur if a large dollar amount for architect or engineering fees are received at an early date. In these cases the exclusion of these costs from the calculation of the ratio of costs complete to total estimated costs will likely result in a more meaningful periodic recognition of income.

While a ratio of costs appears preferable for determining the percentage of completion, the AICPA, like the tax regulations, indicates that the percentage of completion can be determined from another measure of progress.

This is interpreted to mean that an architect or engineer's estimate of progress (e.g., he estimates the project as 30 percent complete), or a measure of work, such as cubic yards of excavation performed relative to the total estimated, can be used in determining percentage of completion.

As to the completed-contract method, the AICPA indicates that a project is substantially complete (i.e., for purpose of recognizing income) if remaining costs are not significant in amount. This differs in part from the regulations regarding income recognition established by the IRS. The AICPA's position on defining substantial completion and the point of income recognition is that this definition discourages a deliberate postponement of income recognition by deferring the performance on some minor part of the work.

The tax regulations allow the contractor using the completed-contract method to write off general overhead costs (e.g., general and administrative costs) as a period cost (i.e., expense in year incurred and not "attached" to a project and deferred). Because of the benefits of early recognition of expenses, the contractor using the completed contract should, and more often than not does, recognize the general overhead costs as period costs. The AICPA also allows recognition of general overhead costs as a period cost when using the completed-contract method. However, the AICPA does state that, when the completed-contract method is used, it may be appropriate to allocate general and administrative expenses (i.e., general overhead) to contract costs (i.e., product costs) rather than periodic income. Their reasoning is that this may result in a better matching of costs and revenues, particularly in years when no contracts are completed.

Tax law provisions state that, when using the completed-contract method of accounting, losses may be recognized only when contracts are completed. On the other hand, the AICPA requires that when estimates of cost to complete and extent of progress toward completion indicate a loss on a contract in progress, such a loss should be recognized in the financial statements. This applies to both the percentage-of-completion and the completed-contract methods of accounting. This AICPA provision is consistent with the conservatism principle of accounting. The end result is that losses are treated differently in computing taxable income and financial reporting when using the completed contract method.

The provision for a potential loss on a project is necessary only when the *direct* costs (excludes company overhead) are expected to exceed total contract price. This is the case if company overhead costs are treated as period costs. If the company overhead costs are attached to projects (as AICPA recommends they sometimes should), then the provision for a loss should recognize company overhead costs.

18
DEPRECIATION AND RELATED TAX BENEFITS

INTRODUCTION

Depreciation is probably one of the least understood but most important aspects of taxation for a firm that utilizes capital assets. Depreciation is essentially an accounting device. The importance of depreciation in the financial affairs of the firm is in its effect on income taxes, which are subsequently reflected in the cash-flow position of the firm.

Depreciation can be defined as the accounting process of allocating the cost of a tangible operational fixed asset against the periodic revenue created from the asset. Examples of tangible operational assets include machinery, tools, and buildings.

Fixed assets are normally acquired for operational purposes rather than for sale. They are purchased because of their future revenue-generating potential. Because it is expected that revenue will be generated for a relatively long period (e.g., in excess of a year), the firm is not allowed to expense the purchase immediately. Instead, a portion of the total purchase cost is periodically expensed or depreciated by allocating it against the generated revenue.

A firm can utilize different depreciation methods for calculating financial income and taxable income. Depreciation serves the following purposes:

1. It provides the firm a tax expense similar to the expense it would obtain if it rented the asset.
2. It provides the firm an incentive to invest in fixed assets. This investment creates jobs and has positive national economic implications.
3. The depreciation expense creates a "reserve" for replacing the asset at the end of its useful life.

It is doubtful if the last purpose listed is accomplished. During inflationary periods the cost of replacing a fixed asset at the end of its useful life usually far exceeds the initial cost of the asset. This is especially true if the life of the asset is relatively long (e.g., five years or more). The reserve that in effect is established through depreciation is insufficient to replace the asset.

The concept of investment tax credit and capital gain treatment are somewhat closely related to depreciation. Both of these devices are also accounting based and significantly affect income taxes and, therefore, cash flow. These devices along with depreciation are discussed in this chapter.

IMPORTANCE OF DEPRECIATION

In order to appreciate the implication of various available depreciation methods, and constraints and exceptions to the methods, it is necessary to first understand the economic importance of depreciation. Depreciation affects the economic worth of an investment in two ways. First, depreciation results in a yearly cash transaction. This transaction is in the form of a reduced tax liability through a "noncash" annual expense (depreciation is an allowable expense for tax purposes but it does not require the expending of cash).

Depreciation also affects the timing of cash transactions. Alternative depreciation methods allow for different amounts of depreciation expense to be recognized in different years. Because next year's receipts are worth less than this year's, depreciation can have an effect on the present value of future cash receipts.

In order to illustrate the importance of the tax and timing effects of depreciation, assume that a contractor is considering an investment in a concrete batch plant. The initial cash outlay is estimated at $600,000. The contractor estimates that the new concrete batch plant will yield a net cash return before taxes of about $100,000 a year for twenty years, ignoring the effects of depreciation. Let us further assume that the contractor has an effective tax rate of 40 percent. Therefore, the contractor's after-tax return will be $60,000 per year. This return also neglects the effect of depreciation.

On the basis of the after-tax return of $60,000, the contractor might precede to analyze the batch plant expenditure based on the following comparison:

Initial cash outlay	$ 600,000
Expected cash inflows (20 × $60,000)	$1,200,000

A decision based on this comparison may prove incorrect. The comparison fails to recognize several essential factors. For one, the time value of money is ignored. The $600,000 is spent immediately but the annual returns are spread over twenty years. A cash inflow in a later year is not worth as much to the contractor as an equal inflow received at the present time. The future cash inflows must be discounted in the analysis. Using time value of money and assuming a 10 percent interest factor table, the total cash inflows of $1,200,000 are discounted to a present value of $510,840 (i.e., $60,000 times 8.514). If this

$510,840 is compared to the $600,000 cost of the batch plant, the investment appears to be unprofitable. However, this comparison is also deficient. It lacks the recognition of depreciation.

Let us assume that at the end of twenty years the batch plant will have little or no salvage value. In that case the entire $600,000 of initial investment will be depreciated against taxable income. With a 40 percent income tax rate, total income taxes over the twenty years will be reduced by $240,000 (i.e., 40 percent times $600,000).

Similar to the annual cash revenue inflows, the dollar benefits obtained through depreciation are not all received immediately. They must be discounted in order to calculate their economic value. Let us assume that the batch plant is depreciated on a straight-line basis over twenty years. The present value of the depreciation benefits can then be calculated as follows:

Depreciation per year ($600,000/20 yrs.)	$30,000
times tax rate	40%
Tax savings per year	$12,000
Present value of 20 payments of $12,000 each at 10%	$102,168

The above calculation assumes that the firm has taxable income for which the depreciation benefits can be offset.

Having recognized the effects of time value of money and depreciation, a valid comparison can be made of the batch plant purchase. This is as follows:

Initial cash outlay		$600,000
Present value of cash inflows (ignoring depreciation)	$510,840	
Present value of depreciation benefits	102,168	
Present value of cash inflows		613,008

While the outflow and inflow are nearly equal, the analysis does indicate a favorable return in that the cash inflows slightly exceed the cash outflow. The contractor's evaluation of other factors such as risk in the economic projections may lead to nonpurchase. However, theoretically the purchase appears profitable.

The example has illustrated how depreciation benefits can affect the real worth of an investment. Failure to recognize depreciation benefits would have led to the conclusion that the investment was unwarranted.

The calculation of depreciation benefits was made on the basis of straight-line depreciation. Use of available accelerated-depreciation methods would have led to even more benefits. Also the benefit of possible investment credit was ignored. Finally, it may be that the asset could be depreciated in less than twenty years. This would also add to a greater calculated present value of cash inflows. This is because both the depreciation amount and the timing of their recognition affect the present value of depreciation benefits.

DEPRECIATION METHODS

Several methods are in use for depreciating assets. These methods range from those requiring only simple mathematics to methods based on interest factors. Depreciation methods are commonly classified as methods that depreciate an asset as a function of time or use. These two types of depreciation are in recognition of the fact that some assets wear out as a function of time whereas others wear out as a function of use. Hybrid time-and-use depreciation methods can be developed for assets that depreciate as a function of both time and use.

In practice, most construction firms utilize time depreciation methods regardless of whether the asset in question wears out as a function of time or use. Depreciation methods that are a function of use commonly require detailed asset production recordkeeping. The result is that the firm often chooses depreciation methods that are a function of time because they are easier methods to apply.

Several commonly used depreciation methods are discussed in the following paragraphs. In presenting these methods, P will be used to represent the initial cost of the depreciable asset, L the salvage value, n the life of the asset, and D the depreciation rate in a given time period.

Straight-Line Depreciation

The straight-line depreciation method is the simplest means of depreciating a piece of equipment as a function of time. It is the depreciation method used most widely by contractors. The asset is merely depreciated equally over its expected life. If we let P equal the initial cost, n the expected life, and L the salvage value after a life of n, then the depreciation charge per unit of n time is as follows.

$$\text{depreciation charge per unit of time} = (P - L)/n$$

Usually n is given in years, so that the depreciation charge per unit of time becomes the annual depreciation charge. For example, let us assume that the initial cost of a depreciable asset is \$12,000. Its estimated salvage value after its expected life of five years is \$2,000. The annual depreciation charge is calculated as follows:

$$\text{annual depreciation charge} = (\$12{,}000 - \$2{,}000)/5 = \$2{,}000$$

Sum-of-the-Digits Depreciation

As previously mentioned, a contractor can usually optimize his tax benefits if he can depreciate his assets at such a rate that the asset is depreciated more in its early years than in its later years. In other words, he would like to depreciate his assets so that the depreciation charge for the first year (from this point on, we will assume the interval of time to be a year) is more than the depreciation charge for the second year, and so on. One such time depreciation method that does this is referred to as the sum-of-the-digits depreciation method. Consider the previous example in which we purchased an asset for \$12,000 with an expected life of five years and a salvage value at that time of \$2,000. Using the sum of the digits depreciation method, we sum all the digits between 0 and n. In this example, $n = 5$, so the sum of the digits from 0 to 5 equals $1 + 2 + 3 + 4 + 5$, which equals 15. The sum of the digits will always be given by the formula, $n(n + 1)/2$. The depreciation charge for any given year is now found by multiplying $(P - L)$ by the fraction derived from subtracting the depreciation year from $n + 1$ and dividing the result by the sum of the digits as calculated from $n(n + 1)/2$. For example, if we are calculating the depreciation charge for the first year in our example, it would be as follows:

$$\text{depreciation charge for first year} = (\$12{,}000 - \$2{,}000)(5)/15 = \$3{,}333.33$$

The 5 in the above expression is derived from subtracting 1 from the sum of $n + 1$. If we let m represent the year for which we are calculating the depreciation charge, then the depreciation charge for that year may be calculated from the following general formula:

$$\text{depreciation charge for } m\text{th year} = 2(P - L)(n + 1 - m)/(n(n + 1))$$

In the example, the depreciation charge for the second year therefore becomes the following:

$$\text{depreciation charge for second year} = 2(\$10{,}000)(5 + 1 - 2)/30$$

The depreciation charge for the remaining years may be found in a similar manner. It will be found that each year the depreciation charge decreases from the previous year.

Declining-Balance Depreciation

As an alternative to the sum-of-the-digits depreciation method, a contractor may use the declining-balance depreciation method for accelerated or fast write-off of his depreciable assets. Using the declining-balance depreciation method, the depreciation charge for a given year is derived by taking a constant percentage of the previous year's undepreciated balance. This method requires a nonzero salvage value since theoretically an undepreciated value of zero would never be reached.

Let us assume a depreciation rate of 30 percent is to be used. Let us further assume the same asset data used in the previous examples of depreciation methods. Specifically, P is \$12,000, n is 5 years, and L is \$2,000. The depreciation rate referred to as D is 30 percent.

The depreciation charge for the first year is calculated as follows:

$$\$12{,}000 \times 0.30 = \$3{,}600$$

The depreciation charge for the second year is found in a similar manner:

$$(\$12{,}000 - 3{,}600) \times 0.30 = \$2{,}520$$

The depreciation charge for the remaining years may be found in a similar manner. Note that, because of the arbitrary use of a depreciation rate, it will be necessary to adjust later year depreciation amounts in order to reach the exact salvage value after five years.

Constant Unit Use Charge Depreciation

A construction contractor also has several use depreciation methods available for depreciating his depreciable assets. Even though much of a contractor's assets depreciate (wear out) with use, contractors have a tendency to depreciate the equipment as a function of time. This is partly because depreciation methods that are a function of use require the contractor to keep close track of the production performed by his equipment. It is suggested that the contractor keep these records. He is thus able to use the more accurate use depreciation methods when they are applicable and is also aided in his cost-control program.

The most basic and practical use depreciation method is referred to as the constant unit use charge method. In this method all of the production units produced or performed by an asset are charged at the same rate. For example, let us assume that a contractor buys an earth-moving piece of construction equipment for \$12,000. The manufacturer informs the contractor that the expected life of the equipment is 1,000,000 cubic yards of earth removal. At that time, the equipment's salvage value is estimated to be \$2,000. Using the constant unit use charge depreciation method, a depreciation rate, or cost per unit of use, is calculated as follows:

$$\text{depreciation rate} = D = (P - L)/n$$

In the example above, the depreciation rate is calculated as follows:

$$\begin{aligned}\text{depreciation rate} &= \text{D} = (\$12{,}000 - \$2{,}000)/(1{,}000{,}000 \text{ cu yd})\\ &= \$0.01/\text{cu yd}\end{aligned}$$

The depreciation charge for the equipment for any given year is then calculated by multiplying the depreciation rate by the number of production units produced or performed in that year. In the example, let us assume that 120,000 cubic yards of earth were moved by the equipment in a given year. The depreciation charge for that year is then calculated as follows:

$$\begin{aligned}\text{depreciation charge} &= (\$0.01)/(\text{cu yd}) \times (120{,}000 \text{ cu yd})\\ &= \$1{,}200\end{aligned}$$

The depreciation for other years may be found in a similar manner.

Declining Unit Use Depreciation

By means of a use depreciation method, a contractor can also accelerate its depreciation charge of its assets. One such use depreciation method is called the declining unit use charge method. In this method, early production units are assigned a higher depreciation rate than later production units. Let us assume we want to depreciate the first 500,000 cubic yards of production in the previous example at twice the rate as the final 500,000 cubic yards of expected life of production. We must first determine an equivalent number of production units by doubling the first 500,000. Thus we have a total of 2 × (500,000) plus 500,000 or 1,500,000 production units. The depreciation rate for the first 500,000 units is found by dividing ($P - L$) by 1,500,000 and multiplying the result by 2. This is done as follows:

depreciation rate (first 500,000 units)
= [($12,000 − $2,000)/1,500,000 cu yd] × 2 = 0.0133 cu yd

The depreciation charge for any given year is found by multiplying the production units produced or performed in the year by the respective depreciation rate for those units. In our example, assume that prior to the fourth year, 400,000 cubic yards of production have been performed. We are interested in calculating the depreciation charge for the fourth year in which 200,000 cubic yards of earth are moved by the equipment. The depreciation charge for the year is found by multiplying 100,000 units (part of the first 500,000 units) by the depreciation rate of $0.0133 per unit, and adding it to the product of 100,000 units (part of the last 500,000 units) and the depreciation rate of $0.00666 per unit. The result is as follows:

depreciation charge (fourth year) = (100,000) × (0.0133) + (100,000) × (0.00666) = $2,000

The depreciation charge for any other year is found in a similar manner.

USE OF DEPRECIATION METHODS

All assets are not eligible for depreciation. Specifically two types of assets are eligible for depreciation. The Internal Revenue Code allows for a reasonable allowance for depreciation for the exhaustion, wear, and tear of the following:

1. property used in trade or business
2. property held for the production of income.

The construction firm's buildings and equipment qualify as property used in trade or business.

Excluded from assets qualifying for depreciation are land (i.e., supposedly it does not wear out) and assets held for personal use and enjoyment. For example, the construction firm owner's residence or pleasure automobile do not qualify for depreciation.

ACCEPTABLE METHODS

The Internal Revenue Code restricts the taxpayer in its use of depreciation methods. Specifically for those assets that qualify for depreciation, the code provides for use of the following methods:

1. straight-line method
2. declining-balance method using a rate not exceeding twice the rate that would have been used had the depreciation been computed using the straight-line method.
3. sum-of-the-digits method.
4. any other consistent method which, when added to all allowances for the period commencing with the taxpayer's use of property and including the taxable year, does not during the first two-thirds of the useful life of the property exceed the total of such allowance which would have been used had such allowance been computed using double-declining balance depreciation.

Both the straight-line and sum-of-the-digits depreciation methods are singled out as acceptable methods by the IRS. The declining-balance method is also identified as being acceptable. However, constraints are placed on the use of the method. Specifically, the declining-balance depreciation rate is limited to not exceeding twice the straight-line rate. Therefore, it has become common to talk about *double-declining depreciation*. This method assumes a depreciation rate equal to twice the straight-line rate. For example, for an asset that has a life of ten years, the straight line rate is 10% (1/10). Double declining-balance depreciation would utilize a depreciation rate of 20 percent.

As noted under the description of allowable methods, the Code also allows other consistent use of a depreciation method. The method described in number 4 above in effect provides for using any depreciation method for which the accumulated depreciation during the first two-thirds of the life does not exceed the accumulated depreciation for the same period had the double-declining depreciation method been used.

Because of the possibility of using the depreciation method characterized in 4, the taxpayer may devise a hybrid depreciation method. However, in practice few of these hybrid methods are utilized. Instead most firms make use of straight-line, declining-balance (i.e. especially double-declining balance), or sum-of-the-digits depreciation methods.

The term consistency is especially important in the selection and use of depreciation methods. A firm is not free to change depreciation methods at will for the purpose of limiting its tax liability. Rather it must continue to utilize an acceptable selected method consistently. If it desires to change methods it must obtain permission from the IRS. Permission is not granted if the request is made solely on the basis of reducing or limiting tax liability.

It is permissible to utilize different depreciation methods for different types of assets. For example, a contractor may choose to depreciate its equipment using straight-line depreciation and depreciate its buildings using double-declining depreciation. However, once a method is chosen for a given class of assets, the firm must be consistent in its use of the method.

As an alternative to calculating a separate depreciation charge for each of its assets, the contractor has an option to group its assets for the purpose of calculating the depreciation charge. The grouping of assets for calculating depreciation saves clerical time. Additionally the IRS has provided the taxpayers the advantage of shortened depreciation lives when grouping its assets. The taxpayer is interested in utilizing a shortest asset life as possible. Because of time the value of money concepts, the sooner the firm can depreciate its assets, the larger is the value of the depreciation benefits.

As indicated in an earlier section, one of the purposes of depreciation is to promote industry's investment in assets. Consistent with this intent, Congress has devised a depreciation provision aimed at aiding the small business in its purchase of assets. This provision is often referred to as *first-year depreciation*. Because of limitations on the use of the provision, its use has significance only to the small business firm. Many construction firms qualify as such a firm.

Using the first year depreciation provision, in the year of acquisition, an allowance equal to 20 percent of the cost of qualified property may be deducted in addition to depreciation deducted under the normal methods. Specifics of the provision are subject to variation as a function of the wishes of Congress.

The first-year depreciation is in addition to the regular depreciation. For example, let us assume an asset has a cost of $15,000 a life of ten years, no salvage, and the asset is depreciated using straight-line depreciation. The regular first-year depreciation would be $1,500. If the asset qualifies for additional first-year depreciation, the additional first-year allowable depreciation would be $2,000 (i.e., assuming $2,000 is the maximum). Therefore the total first-year depreciation would be $3,500. Over the life of the asset, the total depreciation amount is limited to the $15,000 cost of the asset. Therefore, depreciation charges less than the regular $1,500 must be recognized in the later years of the life of the asset. Usually this is done by eliminating the excess $2,000 from the last year's depreciation charge.

To qualify the first-year depreciation an asset must be *tangible personnel* property that has an estimated useful life of at least six years from the date of acquisition. Excluded from assets that qualify are real property (e.g., buildings) and intangible property (e.g., purchased goodwill). Production-oriented equipment such as cranes, scrapers, etc. qualify for the additional depreciation charge in the first year of purchase. This depreciation charge can lead to increased cash flow which is often critical for the small firm, especially the small firm in its early years of business.

RESTRICTIONS ON ACCELERATED METHODS

Accelerated depreciation methods include the sum-of-the-digits and declining-balance depreciation methods. These depreciation methods have the benefit of returning cash-flow benefits quicker to the firm.

While giving the taxpayer the right to use these advantageous depreciation methods, the IRS has also placed restrictions on using the methods. Specifically, in order to use an accelerated-depreciation method, the taxpayer must meet the following tests:

1. The property must have a useful life of three years or more.
2. The property must be tangible, i.e., buildings or equipment are tangible, goodwill is intangible.

Somewhat less significant are restrictions relating to the date of purchase. Because the relevant dates are the early 1950's, they have little significance as to current practices.

The permission to use accelerated depreciation methods has traditionally been used by Congress as a tool for regulating the economy. Provisions currently exist that are aimed directly at residential and commercial construction. In addition to the restrictions cited above, the following provisions relate to these types of construction:

1. Double-declining methods may be used on new residential rental property.
2. New nonresidential rental or used residential buildings are restricted to 150 declining-balance depreciation.
3. Used nonresidential rental property is subject to a maximum of 125 declining-balance depreciation.

For a building to qualify as residential property, at least 80 percent of the gross rents must come from the dwelling units. Depreciation on a building which is used partly for business (e.g., a contractor uses part of a building for his house and part for his business) is limited to the depreciation on the segment used for business.

INVESTMENT CREDIT

The tax advantages of purchasing assets are not limited to utilizing depreciation deductions. From time to time Congress has attempted to stimulate economic growth by granting an incentive to firms to purchase capital assets. The presence of this incentive and the degree of the incentive have varied over time. One incentive is referred to as an *investment credit*.

In effect the investment credit is computed by applying a percentage times the qualified investment made by the taxpayer during the year. The investment credit is a credit subtracted from the gross tax liability to arrive at the net tax liability. Therefore, a dollar of investment credit is worth more to the taxpayer than is a dollar deduction for depreciation. Given a tax rate of 40 percent, a $1 depreciation deduction reduces the tax by $0.40, while a $1 investment credit reduces the tax by $1. In addition, the investment credit deduction has no effect on present or future depreciation deductions. Unlike depreciation which may have to be recaptured as income in later years when the asset is sold, investment credit deductions do not have to be recaptured.

The purpose of the investment credit is to promote investment by firms and therefore increase the rate of economic growth and employment. However, Congress has recognized that investment in some types of assets have little to no effect on the rate of economic growth or employment. Therefore, only certain types of assets qualify for investment credit. Those types that are permitted include the following:

1. Tangible personal property subject to the depreciation deduction, e.g., trucks, cranes, generators.
2. Tangible real property subject to depreciation that is used in manufacturing or production. Buildings other than those that are part of the manufacturing process are excluded. For example, a contractor's office building is excluded. Remodeling of a building may be eligible.

Land is excluded from being eligible for investment tax credit. While investment in used property (e.g., purchase of a used crane) qualifies for the investment credit, used property is subject to more limitations as to the investment credit amount.

The dollar value of investment credit the taxpayer is entitled to depends on the percentage rate in effect and the useful life of the asset. Assets in some industries have a relatively short life (e.g., trucks), while some industries use assets that have a relatively long life (e.g., manufacturing plants). If recognizing the life of an asset was not included in the investment credit calculation, an industry with assets with a short life would have distinct advantages.

To reduce the potential inequity of unequal asset lives, the portion of the cost of a qualified asset included in the qualified investment (used for calculating the credit) depends on the estimated useful life of the property. In particular the percentage of cost included in the qualified investment is calculated as follows:

Estimated useful life	*% of cost that qualifies*
Less than 3 years	0
3 years or more but less than 5 years	$33^1/_3$
5 years or more but less than 7 years	$66^2/_3$
7 years or more	100

Let us assume a contractor purchases the following four qualified assets. The qualified investment is calculated as follows.

Asset	*Cost*	*Life*	*%*	*Qualified Investment*
Company car	$ 5,000	2	0	$ 0
Dump truck	4,500	4	$33^1/_3$	1,500
Copy machine	6,000	6	$66^2/_3$	4,000
Batch plant eqp.	10,000	10	100	10,000
	$25,500			$15,550

The investment credit for the year is calculated by multiplying the qualified investment of $15,500 times the applicable investment credit percentage in effect at the time. For example, if the applicable rate is 10 percent the investment credit for the year would be $1,550 (i.e., $15,550 × 10%). The $1,550 is subtracted directly from the firm's tax liability. In effect the contractor is returned part of its investment.

CAPITAL GAINS

Part of the government's justification of depreciation and investment credit allowances is based on the incentive they create to purchase qualified assets. Another incentive to purchasing assets is favorable tax treatment that may be applied to the sale of select types of assets. This favorable treatment is in the form of *capital gain treatment*. Similar to investment credit provisions, the existence of capital gain treatment and the method of application have varied over time. It is often used in an attempt to regulate the economy.

The benefit of capital gain treatment is that a taxable gain that qualifies for capital gain treatment is taxed at a reduced rate relative to the tax rate charged for a nonqualified gain.

For example, let us assume a contractor sold a piece of equipment and the sale resulted in a taxable gain of $60,000. Let us further assume that the contractor was in the 40 percent income tax bracket. If the asset sale did not qualify for capital gain treatment the tax and net proceeds from the sale would be as follows:

Gain from sale	$60,000
Tax (ordinary gain)	
.40 × $60,000	24,000
Net proceeds after tax	$36,000

On the other hand, let us assume the asset sale did qualify for capital gain treatment. Let us further assume that the capital gain tax rate is forty percent of the ordinary rate. The resulting tax and net proceeds from the sale would be as follows:

Gain from sale	$60,000
Tax (capital gain)	
.16 × $60,000	9,600
Net proceeds after tax	$50,400

The net effect is a tax savings of $14,400 from the capital gain treatment. This savings does not have to be repaid in future years. In effect the IRS is giving the taxpayer a rebate for part of the purchase cost of qualified assets.

In order for a qualified asset to be eligible for capital gain treatment, the asset must be held for a specified period of time. The necessary time period is a year.

Only certain types of assets of the construction firm are eligible for capital gain treatment. Excluded are assets that are purchased as inventory items. For example, if the construction firm purchases an oversupply of masonry blocks and later sells the blocks to another firm at a significant profit, the gain is not eligible for the favorable capital gain treatment. This is true regardless of the time of ownership because inventory items are excluded from capital gain treatment.

An asset used directly in the production process, but not installed, is eligible for capital gain treatment. Therefore, the construction firm's equipment is eligible. Another significant asset eligible for the favorable capital gain treatment is investment real property or real estate.

Capital gain treatment can be relatively complicated. For example, if the construction firm uses accelerated methods in depreciating its assets, a portion of the depreciation must be recaptured when the asset is sold. This recaptured depreciation decreases the amount of gain eligible for capital gain treatment. Other examples of the complexity of capital gain treatment include the availability of an alternative capital gain tax rate available to corporations and capital gain carrybacks and carryovers. Independent of these complexities, the fact remains that capital gain tax treatment adds to the economics of the construction firm's purchase of qualified assets.

TAX CONSEQUENCES OF FIXED ASSETS

The tax consequences of fixed assets can significantly affect the financial well-being of the construction firm and its owner or owners. How the firm structures the depreciable assets into the construction firm, its subsidiaries, or affiliated companies, or into the personal assets of the owner or owners of the construction firm affects the annual and total tax benefits resulting from depreciation and related benefits such as investment tax credit and capital gain treatment.

Often the construction firm evolves out of a small proprietorship in which the owner runs the firm out of his garage. As the firm makes the transition to a corporation, one of the initial questions that must be addressed is what personal assets of the individual should be put into the corporation. The depreciable assets placed in the corporate construction firm yield depreciation benefit in that a depreciation expense can be recognized. On the other hand, if an asset such as the owner's automobile is kept as a personal asset, no depreciation expense would probably be recognized.

While it is obvious that the owner's giving of his personal depreciable assets to the incorporated construction firm yield tax benefits in the form of depreciation, there are also disadvantages associated with this practice. The major disadvantage often cited is that the owner's assets are no longer free from the liability associated with the construction operations. Another disadvantage of major depreciable assets in the construction firm relates to the potential negative effect the assets (and the resulting liabilities) have on the firm's financial statements. This was discussed in Chapter 8.

In earlier chapters, including Chapter 8, reference was made to the fact that several construction firms make the mistake of over-investing their profits from construction operations into real estate such as apartments. The reason behind their investment usually relates to the potentially high rate of return associated with the investment. Much of the high rate of return results from the tax benefits from the recognized depreciation expense.

Earlier chapters stressed the fact that the construction firm's investment in real estate often creates a cash liquidity problem for the construction firm apart from the rate of return received from the investment. Mention also was made that debt associated with the investment in real estate by the construction firm adversely affects some important financial ratios of the firm. This was because accounting treatment of an investment in real property that is to be rented requires the recognition of a short-term liability associated with the loan for the property, but no recognition is made of any short-term asset such as future rent receipts. The result is an adverse effect on the firm's current position as reflected on the financial statements.

Another difficulty of real estate being on the books of the construction firm is the tax difficulties associated with selling the real property. Specifically, if the real property is sold at a gain (as often occurs), the corporation has to pay the tax associated with the gain. In turn when the profits are distributed to the owners, the profits are taxed again.

Obviously good tax planning would not allow the investment property to be purchased through the incorporated construction firm in the first place. However, what happens if the construction firm already reflects the investment property in the corporation?

To illustrate how innovative tax strategy can be used to remove the equipment from the corporation without a major tax consequence, let us consider a construction firm with the following balance sheet and related financial data illustrated in Figure 18.1. The data shown illustrate that the construction firm has significant investments in depreciable real estate, all of which is in the corporation.

ASSETS		LIABILITIES	
Current assets		Current liabilities	
Cash	$50,000	Accounts Payable	$50,000
		Real Estate—Note	
Investments		Current Portion	20,000
Real estate			
(Apartments)	100,000	Long-term liabilities	100,000
Fixed assets		TOTAL LIABILITIES	$170,000
Equipment	50,000		
		Net worth	30,000
TOTAL ASSETS	$200,000		
		TOTAL LIABILITIES AND NET WORTH	$200,000

Figure 18.1 Balance Sheet with Real Estate

Let us assume that the real estate shown in Figure 18.1 has appreciated 100 percent from the date of purchase to the present time. If the property is sold to a third party, a significant tax from the gain on the sale results. Additionally the corporation and its owner would lose the rental income from the property and the interst and depreciation tax write-offs.

To avoid the tax gain consequences, remove the negative impact of the real estate on the construction firm's balance sheet, and maintain the benefits of ownership, the construction firm can sell the real estate to the owner or owners of the firm on an installment basis. The sale price can be at the market value that favorably increases the basis of the property for the owners. The corporate tax from the gain is spread over a ten-year period, the period of the installment sale.

In order to provide cash to the owner or owners of the construction firm to enable them to make the installment payments, their salary from the construction firm is increased. What happens is that the increased salary is paid to the owners and they in turn pay the installment payments back to the construction company. In effect they merely exchange the same cash.

The resulting sale of the real estate to the owners has placed the ownership of the real property outside the corporation. Therefore, the negative aspect of the firm paying tax on the rental income and in turn the owner's paying tax on the corporation distribution is eliminated. Secondly, the short-term liability that previously appeared on the construction firm's balance sheet with no offsetting current asset is removed. The tax strategy is just one example of how the advantageous use of the tax laws can "create profits" by managing tax liability. This of course is what tax planning is all about.

Part 6.
VALUE ADDED SERVICES

CHAPTERS

19
IMPLEMENTING PROGRAMS FOR INCREASING JOB SITE PRODUCTIVITY

CONSTRUCTION PRODUCTIVITY DEFINED

Productivity is commonly defined as follows:

$$Productivity = \frac{Units\ of\ work\ placed}{Man\text{-}hour\ of\ effort}$$

Examples would be square feet of contact area of forms placed per man-hours, or number of panels placed per man-hour.

As an alternative, some individuals refer to productivity as the reciprocal of the above; i.e. man-hours per unit of work placed. In particular, construction estimators often use this latter definition. The former definition (units or work placed per man-hour) is the correct definition; it is the one accepted by the government.

It should be noted that while the above definition is a widely accepted definition, it can be misleading in that man-hours is in the denominator. This might lead one to believe that the only way to increase productivity is to work harder, to make more labor effort. In reality there are many ways to increase productivity without working harder. The theme of the improvement ideas and programs set forth in this unit are to work smarter, not harder.

The construction process is characterized as requiring a high degree of on-site labor cost. As such, it is common to think of productivity as the efficiency by which labor places material and equipment at the job site.

The process can be modeled as follows:

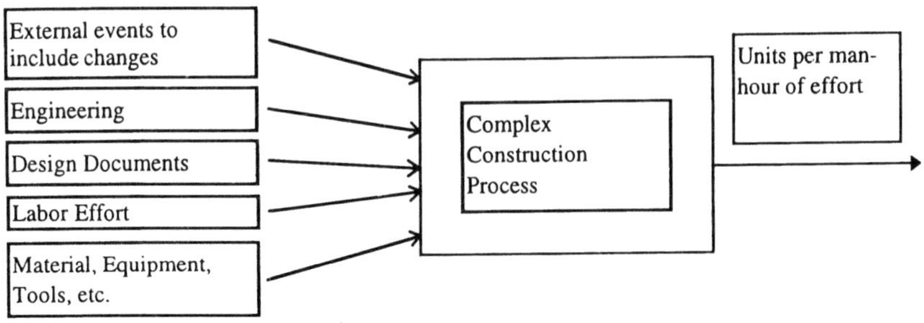

The units of output produced per man-hour of effort or input (or alternatively, the man-hours required per unit of work produced) is very sensitive to many input factors to include the amount and quality of labor, the availability of materials, equipment, and tools, and required engineering tasks such as the preparation of shop drawings.

Given the above definition of productivity, the United Stated Department of Commerce has measured the average annual increases in construction productivity to be less than one percent a year for the last ten years. This is illustrated in Figure 19.1. The average annual increase in construction productivity of 0.8 percent compares to a 2 to 3 percent annual increase for all US industries.

Unfortunately during the same time period when construction productivity has been nearly flat, construction costs have risen. During the past ten to fifteen years, construction costs have risen each and every year, sometimes in excess of five percent in a given year. These increasing costs and flat productivity has put downward pressure on the profitability of many construction firms. Given the fierce competition of the bidding process, the construction firm may not be able to pass on added material and labor costs to the project owner. As shown in Figure 19.1, for many firms this decreasing profitability owing to the failure to increase productivity while costs have increased has resulted in the risk of the bid exceeding the planned profitability in the bid.

Another way of looking at productivity in the construction industry is to look at the composition of the eight hour work day. Documented job site studies performed by the author indicate that between forty and sixty percent of a typical construction day is for non-productive time. One can consider non-productive time to include time associated with workers waiting for instructions, doing redo work, taking advantage of a lack of supervision, double handling of material, etc. In addition, non-productive time includes a certain amount of what can be referred to as unnecessary support time such as a worker carrying boards from one location to another merely because the material was not effectively stored in the proper location in the job site layout process. An example of such a work day is illustrated in Figure 19.2.

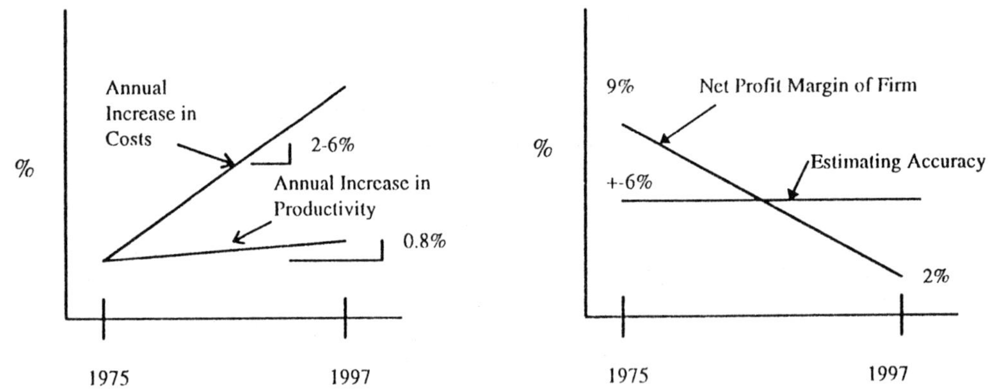

Figure 19.1

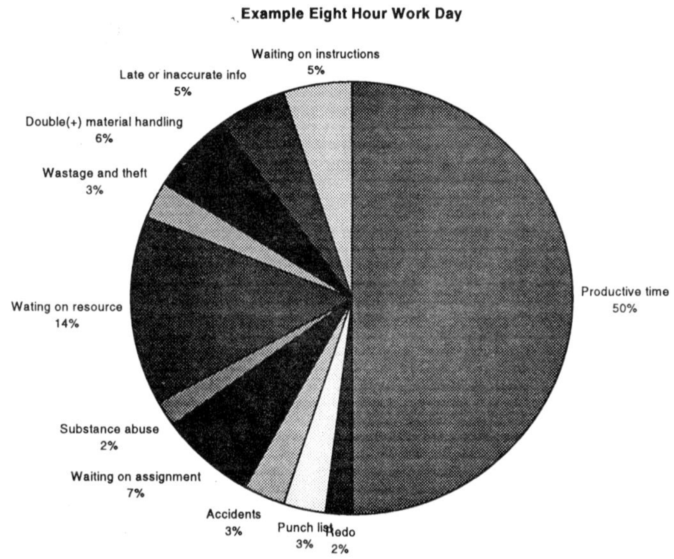

Figure 19.2

OPPORTUNITY TO INCREASE CONSTRUCTION PRODUCTIVITY

It is not being suggested that the solution to the problem of low construction industry productivity or non-productive time is an easy problem to solve. The construction process is a difficult one. Problems such as a variable environment to include precipitation, temperature variations, and the complexity of the building process itself are just a few of the problems that most non-construction industries do not have to confront.

Independent of the difficulties associated with improving construction productivity, it should be pointed out that tremendous opportunity exists to improve productivity. If the construction process can be correctly identified as having fifty percent non-productive time, it can also be viewed as having an opportunity to increase productivity by fifty percent.

It is unrealistic to believe that the construction supervisor can eliminate all construction non-productive time. However, a mere small increase in productivity on the order of five percent can have a significant impact on the profitability of the construction firm. Shown below in Figure 19.3 is a breakdown of a typical construction bid for a building project. Subcontractors are consolidated in the overall estimate illustrated. The two percent profit or $20,000 is a typical profit margin in the bid if one deletes the company overhead component from the overall bid/estimate.

A five percent increase in productivity would have the effect of decreasing the overall project labor cost by five percent. As illustrated in Figure 19.3, a five percent increase in productivity and a corresponding five percent decrease in labor costs would result in a profit contribution equal to the initial planned profit.

The end result is that a mere five percent increase in productivity can have the result of doubling the profits of the construction firm.

Potential Impact of Productivity Increase on Profitability for Example Building Construction Project

Bid Cost Component	Cost %	$1M Project
Field Labor Cost	40	$400,000
Material Cost	35	350,000
Equipment Cost	7	70,000
Job Overhead (General Conditions)	8	80,000
Company Overhead	8	80,000
Profit	2	20,000
TOTAL	100	$1,000,000

Assume a 5% Increase in Construction Productivity
Labor Cost Savings = (5%) x ($400,000 of labor cost) = $20,000
NOTE: A 5% Increase Doubles the Planned Profits

Figure 19.3

TEN STEP PROGRAM TO INCREASE PRODUCTIVITY

There is no quick fix for increasing job site productivity. However, by implementing proactive programs and procedures, small steps can be made toward significant increases in productivity. The key is to not accept the inefficiencies of the past (the defects in Figure 19.2) as the benchmarks for the future.

With the objective of increasing productivity and profits, this unit proposes a ten step process for aiding the construction firm increase productivity. The ten steps are as follows:

Ten Step Program for Increasing Job Site Productivity

1. Planning Prior to the Start of Construction
2. Implementing Personnel Management Procedures
3. Planning and Scheduling
4. Material Management
5. Implementing an Emphasis on Cost and Risk
6. Implementing TQM philosophy
7. Improve Safety
8. Improving Equipment Productivity
9. Communications, Field Recordkeeping, and the Job Cost System
10. Quality and Pride in Work

1. Planning Prior to the Start of Construction

The construction firm expends considerable time estimating a project and preparing a bid. If successful, they are awarded a contract to construct the project. However there typically is a time period between when the contractor is awarded the project and when the contractor receives the notice to proceed construction. Often during this time period the construction firm does very little in the way of preplanning or taking steps to enhance project productivity. The lack of actions by the contractor during the time period between receiving a contract and the start of construction has led the author to refer to this as the dormant phase of the construction project.

As evidence of the dormant phase of the construction phase, very little is typically done in regard to preplanning the job site layout. Instead of being planned, job site layouts often evolve as the job progresses. Given the fact that the very layout of the job has a considerable impact on productivity (distances walked, double handling of material, etc.), safety, and communications, the contractor misses an opportunity to favorably impact productivity right from the start of the project. What is being suggested is that the contractor's management staff spends time evaluating alternative job site layout plans before construction starts.

As example of the need to plan the job site layout, consider the job site layout for an example project shown in Figure 19.4. The job site layout has several defects that would likely lead to low productivity, safety problems, possible theft, and communication problems. The participant will notice the poor choice of locating the equipment and material. The job site layout shown in Figure 19.5 is an improved job site layout for the same project.

Planning a productive job site layout is only one of several actions that the construction firm should perform during the time period between getting a project and starting the project. Other steps include preparing a project plan and schedule and developing a plan for processing change orders, etc.

It is suggested that a checklist be developed for the construction firm that lists each step that the construction firm should perform in the dormant phase. The purpose of the list is to remind the firm of what should be done and to hold individuals responsible for performing each of the steps.

2. Implementing Personnel Management Procedures

The construction process is very dependent of the efforts of the construction workers. As noted earlier in this unit, labor costs on a building construction project average around forty percent.

The high dependence on labor efforts is compounded by the fact that many construction workers may view themselves as working for a job rather than a firm. Whereas a tool and die worker in a factor, a retail clerk at a merchandiser, or a receptionist at an office may work for a firm for an entire lifetime, a construction craftsman may work for several contractors in a given year. One might argue that the construction worker doesn't view himself as working for a firm; instead he may view himself working on jobs.

The end result is that the construction firm and the construction supervisor must take special effort to be attentive to the personnel needs of the workers. The author proposes that the construction firm take specific steps to pay attention to the following three needs of each and every worker.

a. Pride in work
b. Measuring system of performance
c. An effective communication system

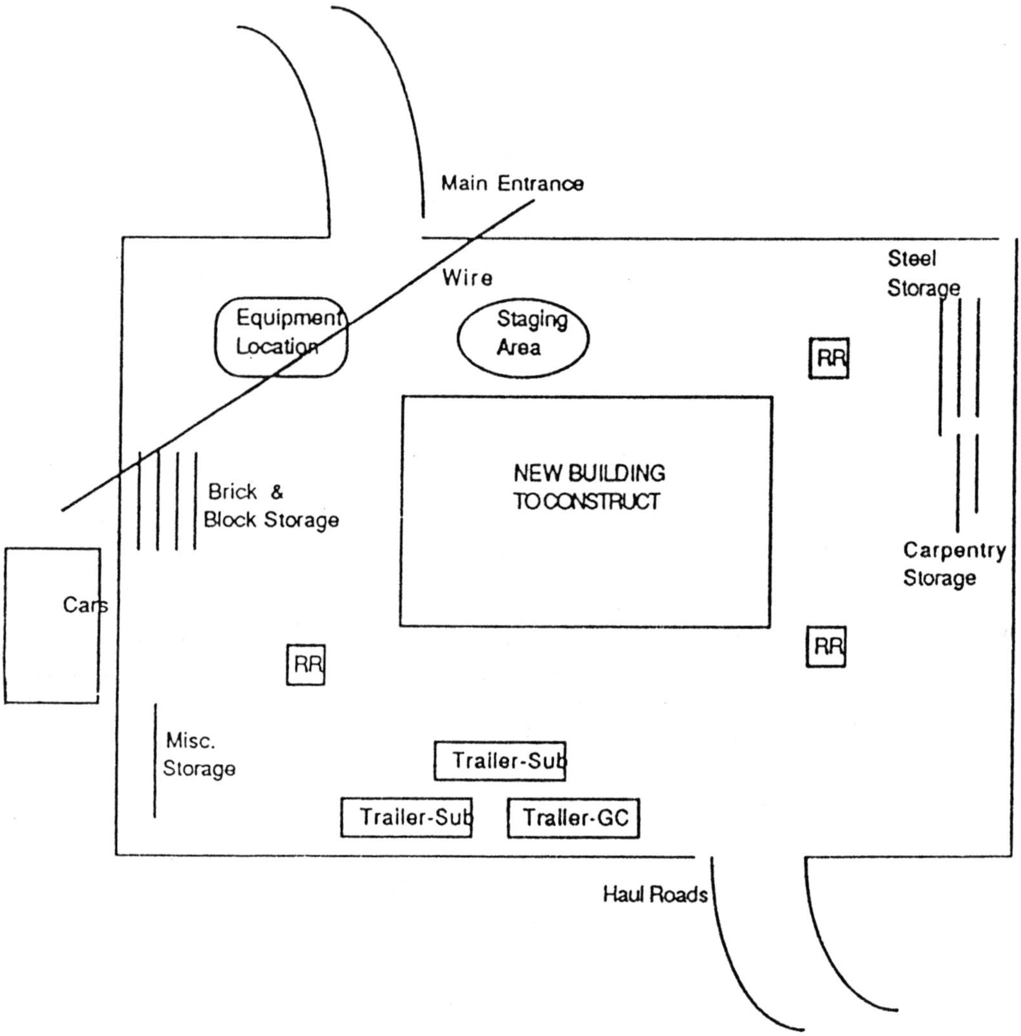

JOB SITE LAYOUT FOR AN EXAMPLE BUILDING CONSTRUCTION PROJECT

Figure 19.4

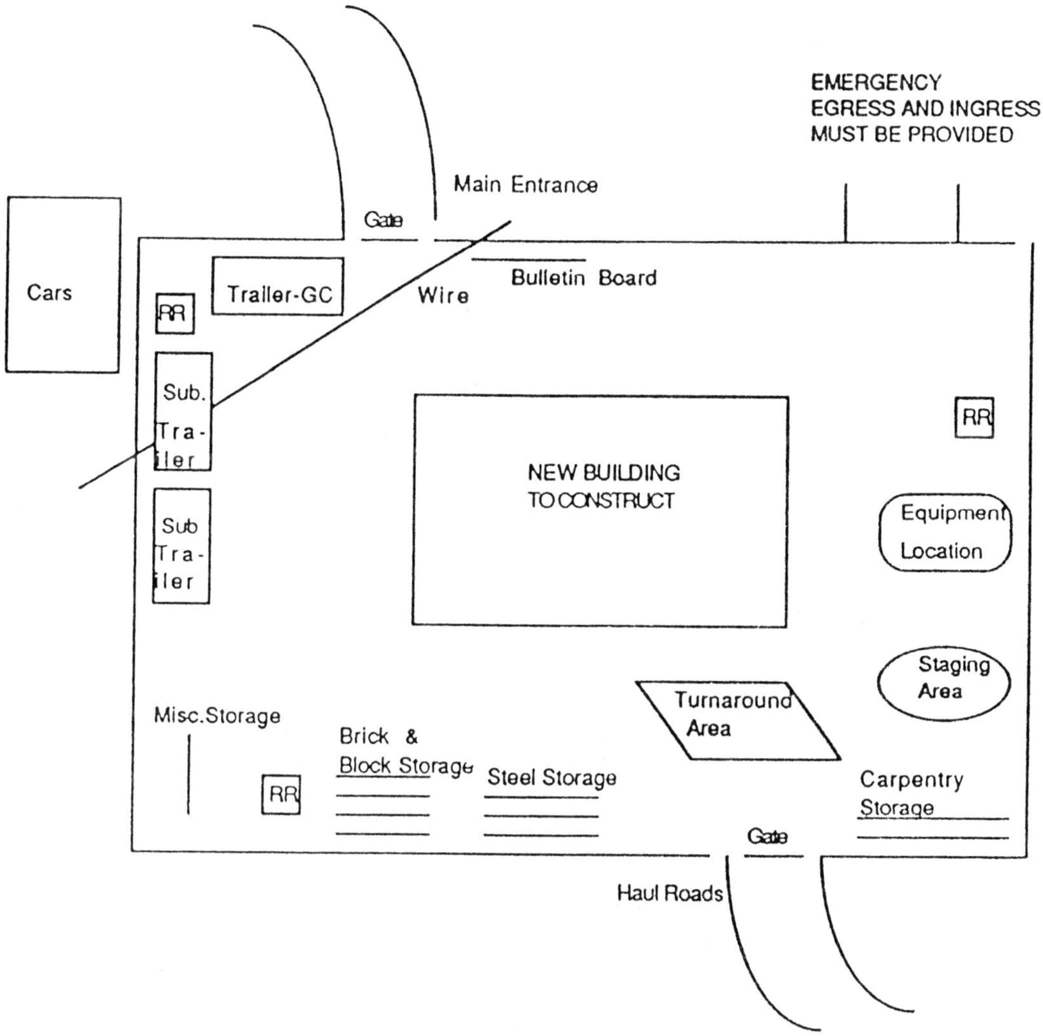

PROPOSED CHANGED JOB SITE LAYOUT FOR
BUILDING CONSTRUCTION PROJECT

Figure 19.5

Pride in work in great part includes recognition and giving the workers a sense of accomplishment. Personnel management actions such as a mere pat on the back, placing the names of workers on a sign at the job site, and asking workers for suggestions can all be actions in a long term commitment to productivity improvement.

An effective measuring system entails giving workers a basis of measuring his own individual performance. This includes communicating what is expected of the worker, and communicating how he is doing relative to the plan. The plan and subsequent performance system should be communicated both at a job level as well as an individual level. Leaving the worker in the dark as to what is expected of him and how the project is to progress and how it is progressing does not accommodate a positive worker attitude.

The construction firm should consider sharing information regarding man-hour budgets and expected productivity for specific work tasks, project schedules, and project progress with the workers. The alternative is to assume that the workers don't care. This negative assumption promotes a we versus they attitude that is sure to result in less satisfactory productivity.

The providing of workers a communication channel is addressed as a separate productivity program step. However it should be noted that effective communication is a two way street. A construction supervisor who simply tells his workers what to do rather than also occasionally ask them for ideas is likely to witness less than desirable productivity from the workers.

3. Planning and Scheduling

There is a significant amount of literature of the topics of planning and scheduling of construction work. There is little doubt that the industry has made more use of formalized schedules such as the critical path method (CPM). This use has been enhanced by the availability of software programs that have lowered the time and cost to prepare such schedules.

There are actually three somewhat different types of plans or schedule that can be used by the supervisor to improve on-site productivity.

a. Short interval planning or a one day plan
b. One to three week revolving plan and schedule
c. Master schedule (for example a critical path diagram; CPM)

The use of a short interval schedule and a one to three week look ahead schedule for productivity improvement have not had as much attention in the literature as have the preparation and use of a master schedule. An example Short Interval Scheduling form and a One to Three Week Look Ahead Revolving Schedule are shown in Figures 19.6 and 19.7.

Job site productivity can be significantly increased if the supervisor would plan the next day's work one day ahead of time. The use of a short interval schedule form and the one to three week look ahead schedule can be the difference between a productive work day and the construction team waiting on materials, looking for tools, or waiting on equipment.

SHORT INTERVAL JOB SCHEDULING FORM				
Job Name______		Date______	Individual______	
Work Planned Tomorrow	Quantity to Be Done	Tools Needed	Material Needed	Eq. Needed

Other Considerations:______________________________

Other Resources Needed:______________________________

Concerns: ______________________________

Figure 19.6

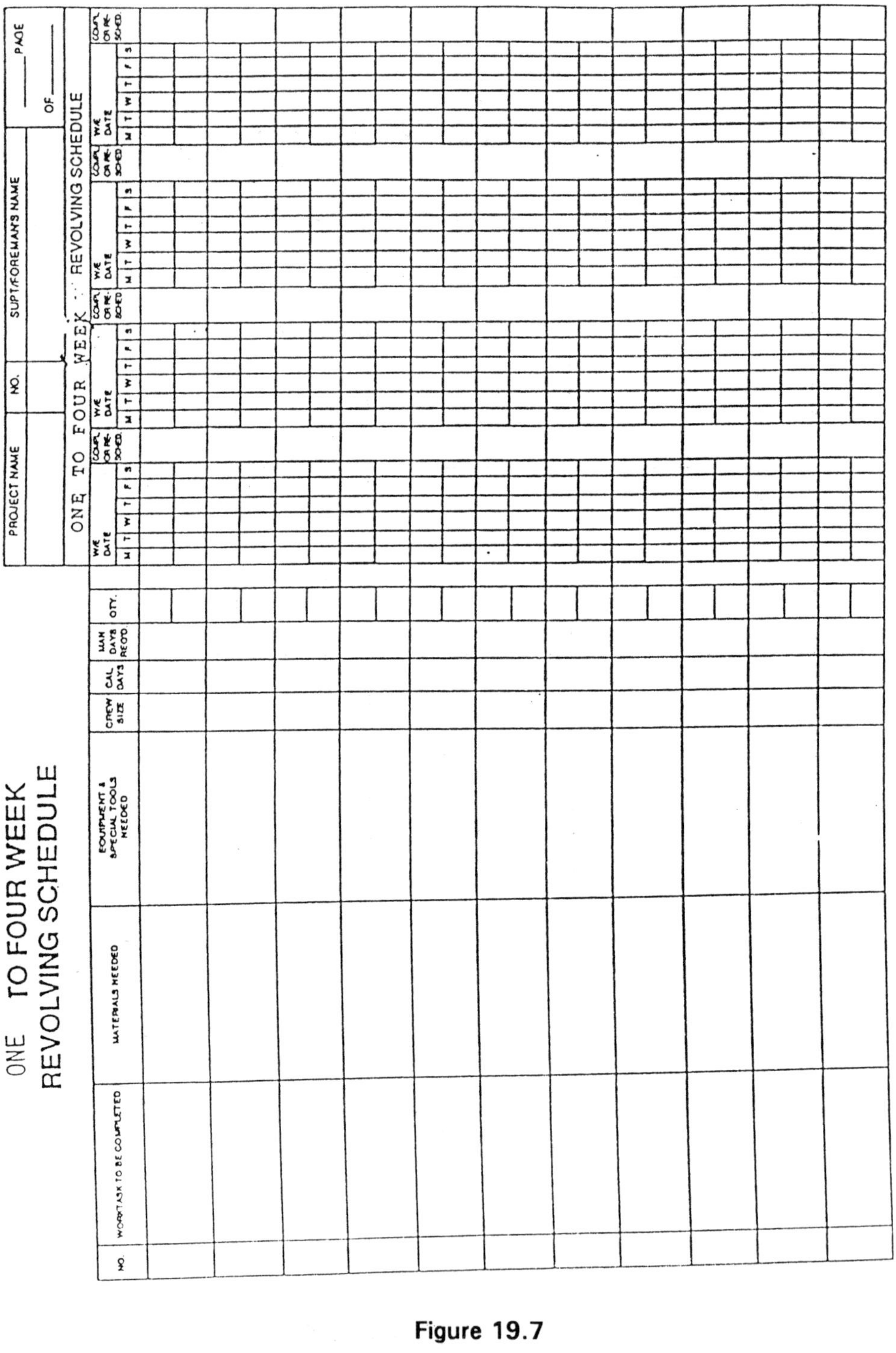

ONE TO FOUR WEEK
REVOLVING SCHEDULE

PROJECT NAME	NO.	SUPT/FOREMAN'S NAME	____ PAGE OF ____

ONE TO FOUR WEEK REVOLVING SCHEDULE

NO.	WORK TASK TO BE COMPLETED	MATERIALS NEEDED	EQUIPMENT & SPECIAL TOOLS NEEDED	CREW SIZE	CAL DAYS	MAN DAYS REQ'D	QTY.	W/E DATE M T W T F S	COMPL OR RE-SCHED.	W/E DATE M T W T F S	COMPL OR RE-SCHED.	W/E DATE M T W T F S	COMPL OR RE-SCHED.	W/E DATE M T W T F S	COMPL OR RE-SCHED.

Figure 19.7

The overall project schedule (a CPM often done with the aid of computer software program) also helps productivity. Because things go wrong and things change, it is also important to update the project schedule on a timely basis.

4. Material Management

Studies performed by the author indicate that it is not unusual for the construction worker to handle material two, three, or more times at a job site before placing it in it's final location at a project. Multiple material handlings at the job site cause wasted time and wasted labor effort.

Labor effort and productivity are tied to material handling and material management. The goal should be to handle material the least number of times as possible. In addition to negatively affecting productivity, multiple material handling increases safety problems and material wastage.

A program for effective handling of materials at the job site should include the following programs.

Steps for Improving Material Handling

1. Prepare an effective job site layout.
2. Order material on a just in time basis when effective.
3. Place material near location of placement.
4. Fabricate material off site if possible.
5. Document all material obstructions.
6. Hold individuals responsible for material theft and wastage.
7. Make workers knowledgeable of the cost of materials.
8. Investigate incidences of multiple material handling.

5. Implementing an Emphasis on Cost and Risk

The author would suggest that the construction firm and construction supervisor expend considerable time policing the construction process; making sure that everyone is working hard. However, working hard may not be working smart.

In an attempt to change the construction supervisor from being only a reactive manager to a proactive manager, the author proposes the implementation of a management approach he refers to as "MORE". More stands for the following:

Measurement of productivity
Opportunity for improvement
Risk emphasis
Evaluate cost

Measurement

How many labor hours were expended on the construction project for punch list work? How many hours did a piece of equipment do work on a specific project versus how many hours was the equipment standing idle? How many hours was a laborer in a non-productive work state versus that of a carpenter on the same project? How many instances were there of double handling of materials on a specific project? These are questions that the constructor can not normally answer. The reason he or she cannot answer the above questions is that the construction supervisor does not pay attention to measuring things. Instead he or she watches and gets used to inefficiencies. Inefficiencies become standards.

In the MORE approach, the construction supervisor is asked to measure things that he or she has taken for granted. Once a week the supervisor is to measure something, be it the distance material is moved, be it the amount of times foremen are waiting on material, be it the number of times work is done twice (redo work), be it the number of incidences of theft, or anything that affects productivity. The measurement can be done by timing things with a wristwatch or by merely taking random visual samples of the work states of labor or equipment.

The key is to force the supervisor to become proactive by forcing the measurement process. This attention to measurement will not require added personnel or added time for the supervisor. As part of the normal supervising duties, they are merely required to measure something. This should not take added time. Instead of merely watching, they are to measure and record their results. To force this measurement, supervisors are required to submit to the main office, one write up of measurement every two weeks. Depending on what they measure, they might take measurements daily as a basis for this biweekly write-up, or they may only take them once during two week period.

The premise of the measurement component of MORE is that measurement is fundamental to improvement. The measurement component will draw one's attention to inefficiencies and improvement potential.

Opportunity for Improvement

The second component of MORE is the focus on challenging the work process for opportunity to improve. Biweekly, the supervisor is required to write up one example of an alternative way of doing a work task that is in process or will be in process at his or her job site.

Almost always, there is more than one way to accomplish a work task. Different crew sizes, the use of varying types of equipment, the use of alternative concrete forming systems, the substitution of different materials, and even the alternative times when a work task can be performed enable the construction supervisor to choose between several ways of accomplishing a work task. Each of the alternative ways of doing the work function will result in a different time and cost. In addition, depending on how a work task is performed, following work tasks may be affected positively or negatively. The process of challenging a work process looking for opportunity to improve is a three step process:

1. Familiarize oneself with the existing methods.
2. Conceptualize an alternative method. Sketch the proposed method on a pad of paper to better describe the proposed method.
3. Make total cost, unit cost, and duration calculations to compare the alternative methods.

The requirement to make the above type of analysis on an on-going basis (for example, biweekly) will force the supervisor to become conscious of looking for better ways to do things. His or her ability to determine a better work method is not guaranteed. However, the mere fact that the supervisor will take the time to consider alternatives will likely result in finding opportunity for improvement.

Risk Emphasis

The construction process is subject to considerable uncertainty and risk. The productivity, cost, and duration of a work process is dependent on the unpredictable weather, variation in worker skills and attitudes, unexpected equipment breakdowns, and changes in the scope of work.

Risk can be thought of as possible variation from expected results. Consider the two construction methods illustrated in Figure 19.8.

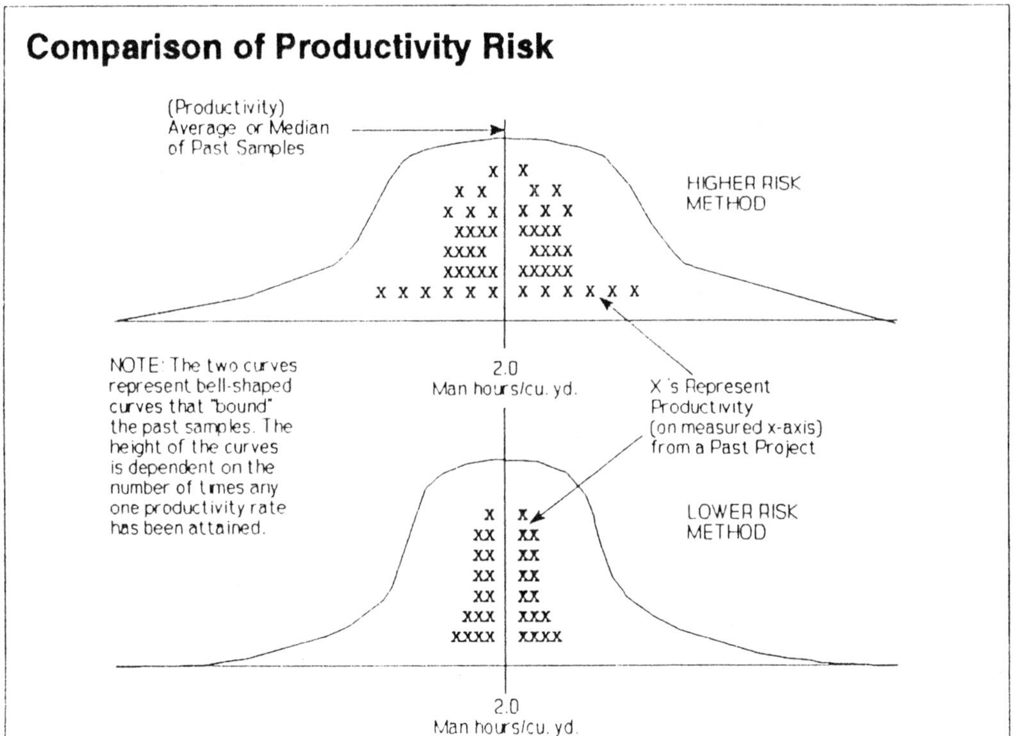

Figure 19.8

Assume that a construction supervisor has collected past project productivity data regarding two alternative ways of placing concrete (for example, using a concrete pump versus placing it with a crane bucket). The points shown under the two bell shaped curves represent the amount of concrete placed per man-hour on past projects. Using bell shaped curves representative of what is referred to as a normal distribution in probability theory, the past samples are grouped by the curves shown. While the past project data implies that both methods of placing the concrete have the same expected average productivity, the past project data implies that the samples for Method 1 have varied more from the average than those of Method 2. Method 1 has more productivity risk.

The construction supervisor must pay attention to productivity risk as well as production and the cost of production (see fourth element of MORE) when managing construction. Consider the following steps necessary to construct a concrete foundation wall:

Form walls
Place reinforcing
Place concrete

Most everyone would agree that the work task above that has the most variation in units of work placed per time period would be the forming of the concrete work task. Owing to the difficulty of placing the forming tie, breaking the form from the wall in the stripping operation, or bracing the form itself, the square feet of contact area of forms placed varies significantly in any fifteen minute time period.

While most constructors would agree that the forming operation has the most variation in the production process and is therefore the riskiest work task, the fact remains that it is the placement of the concrete itself that gets the most attention of the construction supervisor. The day they are placing the concrete, everyone in sight is at the job site watching the concrete fall from the concrete chute into the wall. On the other hand, the forming operation often goes unsupervised. An analysis of the job cost ledgers for projects would illustrate that the risk in the project schedule and project cost is more with the forming operation than the placement operation.

In the MORE approach, the supervisor is to focus on productivity risk as well as production itself. Past project data is accumulated that tracks productivity variation as well as average productivity. As a tool for the construction supervisor, the work tasks that are part of the project estimate are categorized and prioritized by productivity risk. The intent is to draw the supervisor's attention to work tasks that must be closely planned and supervised. As part of his or her daily planning, the supervisor is to use a worksheet to prioritize the risk of work tasks to be done during the day.

Evaluate cost

The observer of the construction process may view the process as one of using different types of trained workers to place concrete, steel, bricks, lumber, etc. The author would propose that everything that is being done in the construction process actually can be viewed as handling and placing money. Concrete, steel, bricks, lumber, laborers, carpenters, and equipment can all be viewed in terms of dollars. In fact, one might propose that the supervisor is not managing concrete or steel placement, he or she is really managing money.

The supervisor's need to know the cost of things and resources such as labor is critical to his or her ability to properly manage. Consider two construction work tasks that may be scheduled for the same work day; the bulk excavation of dirt or soil, and the placement of concrete. In many locations the unit cost per cubic yard of bulk excavation is on the order of $3 to $10. On the other hand, the cost per cubic yard to place concrete may be in excess of $50. Risk aside, if the supervisor can only be in one of two places, supervising the bulk excavation or supervising the placement of concrete, he or she had better be at the more expensive cost operation, the placement of concrete.

The above example of the supervisor being at the more expensive of the two operations appears obvious. However, sometimes it is not so obvious. The supervisor must know the cost of things if he or she is going to allocate management time.

All too often there is a gap between the passing of cost information from the office to job site supervisors. The supervisor may not have reviewed the estimate to determine what things cost and what are the high cost work tasks for the project. In the MORE approach, the supervisor's attention is focused on the cost of things and the cost of work tasks. This is accomplished in several ways. For one, the cost estimate is shared with all supervisors. Secondly, each supervisor is equipped with an industry cost book such as a Means Estimating Manual. Daily the supervisor is asked to look up the cost of things that he or she is doing or seeing at the job site.

In addition, the cost of high cost materials and work tasks are posted on visible signs at the job site such that all job site personnel become attentive to the evaluation of cost. Attention to the cost of things and work methods is also reiterated via the unit cost write ups that are made in the biweekly comparison of alternative work methods (the second component of (MORE).

6. Implementing TQM Philosophy

Consistent with the author's program of MORE, is the implementation of Total Quality Management concepts to increase job site productivity. There is a significant potential for the construction firm to improve productivity as well as overall operations through the implementation of a TQM program.

> **TQM is a management philosophy of involving everyone in an organization in controlling and continuously improving the process of how work is done, in order to meet customer expectations of quality.**

The four key elements of the above definition are:

- *Customer satisfaction or expectations.*
- *Involvement of everyone or empowerment of workers.*
- *Continuous or on-going improvement.*
- *Focus on the process.*

These four key elements of TQM are illustrated in Figure 19.9.

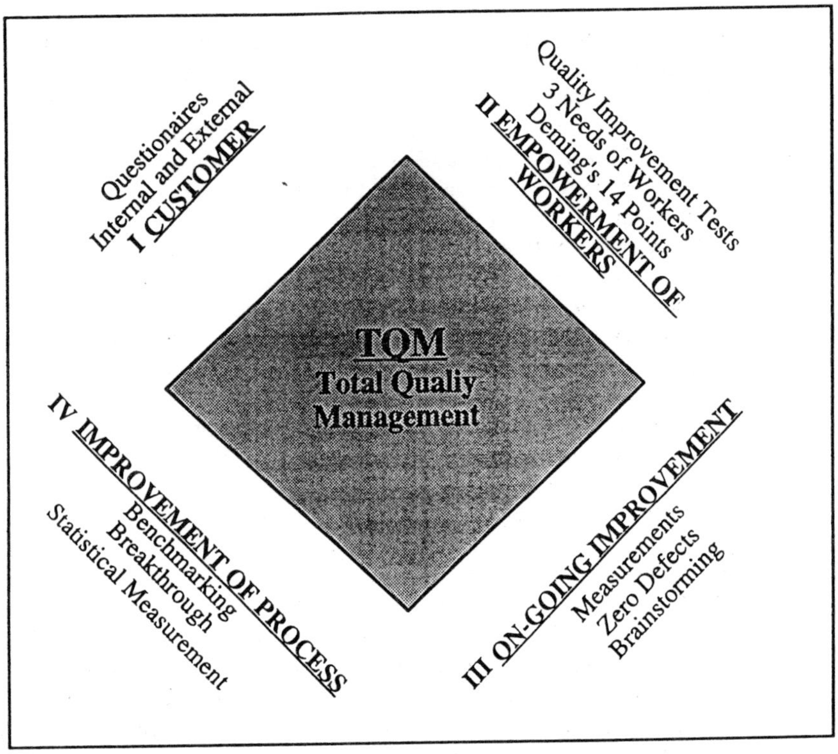

Figure 19.9

Private corporations have also seen their business environment change. In the last twenty years corporations have seen the business environment shift from one of a seller's market to a buyer's market. When products were in short supply, businesses did not have to be overly concerned about the quality of their product or the need to control costs. However, as the availability of products have become abundant, the consumer (the customer) can make increased demands for quality, price, and service.

The international scene has also forced change on American businesses. Non-US countries initially ventured into and perhaps captured the clothing and steel business from US corporations. Thereafter they successfully took a significant share of the ship building and electronic industries. Subsequently, they scored again by making large inroads in the US auto industry. Clearly, to stem the tide, US businesses must try to implement new management and work philosophies. One outgrowth of this search for means to compete is the TQM philosophy.

The question is sometimes asked, what is the difference between TQM and traditional management? A response includes the following:

- Building in quality vs. inspecting for it afterwards
- Employee involvement and authority vs. management authority only
- Focus on process improvement vs. blaming employees
- Continuous improvement vs. one time improvement

On-Going Continuous Improvement

A distinguishing element of TQM is a focus on on-going continuous improvement. At first glance this appears to be a relatively obvious goal, to continue to try to improve. However, the TQM philosophy uses a specific step-by-step process to accomplish on-going continuous improvement. This entails the following nine steps:

1. Identify a process that needs improvement.
2. Develop a cross disciplined team to study the process and improve it.
3. Define data to collect about the process such that process can be improved.
4. Collect data regarding process (measure).
5. Analyze data and brainstorm for improvement.
6. Determine recommendations for implementations.
7. Implement recommendations for improvement of process.
8. Collect data again (measure) to verify improvement and to identify additional improvement ideas.
9. Return to step five and continue to cycle for on-going improvement (ideally reach zero defects).

This nine step iterative cycle is illustrated in Figure 19.10. The following four features characterize the on-going improvement cycle.

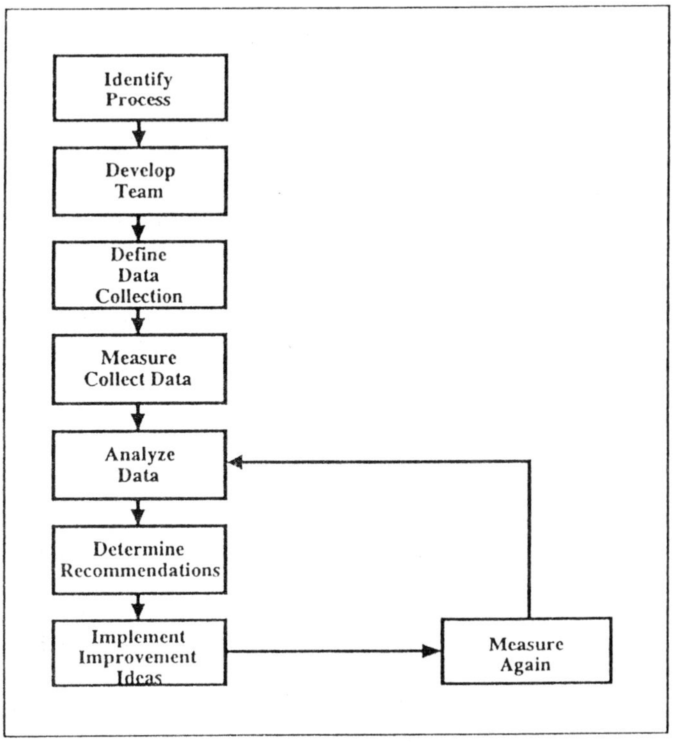

Figure 19.10

Focus on process
Measurement of process
Brainstorming for improvement
Verify and measure again

7. Improve Safety

Studies have proven that the construction firm has one of the highest accident rates per number of worker hours expended. This is due in part to the difficulty of the work and the conditions in which many projects are constructed.

Regardless of the reasons for the many construction accidents that occur at job sites, the fact remains that they have an adverse affect on construction productivity. In addition to the detrimental effect of the injury for the worker himself, accidents are likely to cause low worker morale, work disruptions related to the accident, and higher insurance premiums.

More often than not, a productive job is a safe job. A worker is as likely or more likely to get hurt when he is non-productive versus when he is performing productive work. A worker in a state of boredom or in a lackadaisical state may find his mind wandering or be careless to the point of putting himself in an accident prone situation. An effective safety program that complies with safety regulations and promotes safety to the workers is compatible with the firm's productivity improvement program.

8. Improving Equipment Productivity

Depending on the type of construction project, the equipment cost component may be as high as forty percent of the total project cost or as little as one or two percent. Highway and bridge projects as well as industrial type projects require a significant use of equipment.

Equipment can be viewed similar to a worker; they both are tools of placing material and doing work. However, more often than not, the hourly cost to own or rent a piece of construction equipment is significantly higher than the wage rate of a worker. It follows that it is even more important to keep a piece of equipment productive. If the equipment is standing idle at the job site or is in transit to or from the job or from one location to another, it can be viewed as being in a nonproductive state.

Ten ideas or steps for increasing the productivity of equipment are as follows:

1. Develop an equipment estimating control system that charges a job for the use of a piece of equipment and keeps track of the costs of owning the equipment.
2. Indicate the hourly cost of ownership on each piece of equipment.
3. Monitor productive and non-productive (standby) usage for each piece of equipment.
4. Charge the supervisor a higher rate for non-productive equipment time than for productive time for the equipment.

5. Rent equipment if the firm's volume of work is variable.
6. View equipment like a worker; equipment hours should be budgeted and use compared against the budget.
7. The project should be charged for the use of equipment; not costs for equipment expenditures when the equipment is on the job.
8. Give recognition to supervisors that have a high productive to standby equipment use ratio.
9. Make individual pieces of equipment profit centers.
10. Keep equipment available and in proper working conditions.

9. Communications, Field Recordkeeping, and the Job Cost System

Job site productivity is dependent on effective written and oral communications. Poor communications leads to unnecessary redo work, poor worker attitudes, and an inability to properly monitor the work process. Oral communications at a job site are complicated by the fact that communications are carried out in the open and at a relatively noisy job process, and by the fact that the individuals communicating may have different vocabularies and have different communicating skills.

Effective communications entails listening as well as talking. All too often the supervisor only talks at the worker instead of asking the worker for ideas or listening to his concerns. On occasion the person who knows how to form the walls or place steel may not be the supervisor but instead the craftsman. Failure to take advantage of the workers knowledge runs the risk of not only taking advantage of an improved construction method but also may adversely affect the work attitude of the craftsman. Knowing a better way to do something but not being asked one's ideals tends to promote an "I don't care attitude".

Effective supervisor communications also entails taking the time to properly explain the work process to the worker. The construction craftsman may think he is suppose to know how to do something that is told to him even if he doesn't. Given confusion as to what to do, rather than ask for an explanation, the worker may proceed to do the work incorrectly.

The construction industry has been characterized for many years as an industry with inadequate written communications at the job site. Inaccurate time cards, late reports, failure to give the worker or supervisor written feedback, and lost or misplaced documents are typical of the construction job site. Part of the reason for this written communication inadequacies relates to the decentralized nature of the work process. Unlike most industries that create and monitor their communication system to include their cost accounting process at the same place they make their product, the construction industry is such that written communication is often created at the job site, transferred to the contractor's main office, and hopefully communicated back to the job site. This process results in untimely and sometimes incorrect results.

The construction supervisor often complains about bad record keeping they get at the job site; but in fact he himself may promote bad record keeping. The use of a weekly timecard that requires foremen to keep track of workers' hours charged to specific work tasks is likely to be filled out weekly rather than daily. The result will be that the foreman cannot remember on Friday what the worker did on Monday. A daily timecard would ensure more accurate data.

Preprinting time cards with work codes may improve the proper charging of labor hours. In addition, the use of daily reports that require supervisors merely to check items like weather conditions rather than describe the weather conditions is more likely to be legible and lessen the time for the recording process.

In critiquing the contractor's written communication process or system, one should remember the following three rules for improving the accuracy and timeliness of the job site record keeping process.

a. An individual that is required to fill out a form should be showed where the data goes and how it is used.
b. An individual that is required to fill out a form should be shown by example that the data was in fact used.
c. Any individual that fills out a form or inputs data should be given a subsequent feedback or report.

10. Improved Productivity Through Quality and Pride in Work

Last but not least in importance to a program for productivity improvement is the need to be attentive to performing high quality work. Poor quality construction can negatively impact the productivity program by:

1. creating an environment in which workers know that a less than desirable quality is accepted and therefore perhaps a less than good work effort is also acceptable
2. a tendency to have the worker lose pride in his work effort
3. the possibility for the need to do redo work that directly increases the required number of worker hours to do the finished work.

By giving attention to making the project safe, and by being attentive to the performance of high quality work, the supervisor can serve the objective of making a project look like a firm to the worker rather than look just like another job. Supervisor efforts to keep a project safe and efforts to maintain high quality will lead to increased productivity. Pride in work is critical to productivity improvement as well as quality.

20
QUANTIFICATION OF CHANGE ORDERS AND CLAIMS

BASE BID WORK

When the construction contractor agrees to construct a project for an owner, the contractor agrees to what is referred to as the **base bid** work. The base bid work is the work called out in the initial contract documents. The contract documents consist of the following:

- Drawings
- Specifications
- General Conditions
- Special Conditions
- Addendum
- Agreement Form

The base bid work is most identified by the drawings and specifications. The base bid work is what the project designer foreseen as the work required to complete the project. The work consists of excavation, concrete, carpentry, steel, and other types of work. Given the review and understanding of the base bid work, the contractor agrees to a bilateral contract.

CHANGE ORDER WORK

During the construction process, the contractor is often called upon to do added work that is not called out on the initial contract documents. This added work is referred to as **change order** work.

At any point in time during the construction process or after a project is complete, a change order can be in one of these states:

1. Agreed to in scope and dollar amount by the project owner and contractor.
2. In process; i.e. either the project owner or contractor has not completed the paperwork or settled on the final dollar amount or scope of work.

3. In dispute; the project owner or contractor cannot agree to the scope of work or the dollar value for the work.

The first two situations create little problem, the contract is merely adjusted to reflect the change and the costs are either segmented to the change order or combined with the base bid work. The third situation noted above often results in a dispute and what is referred to as a claim.

Change orders can occur for a variety of reasons to include the following:

- Owner or designer change of opinion or preference
- Code changes
- Schedule slippage
- Unexpected weather conditions
- Change in owner available funding
- Design error or omission

The change order process is characterized by three separate steps and three accompanying documents shown as follows:

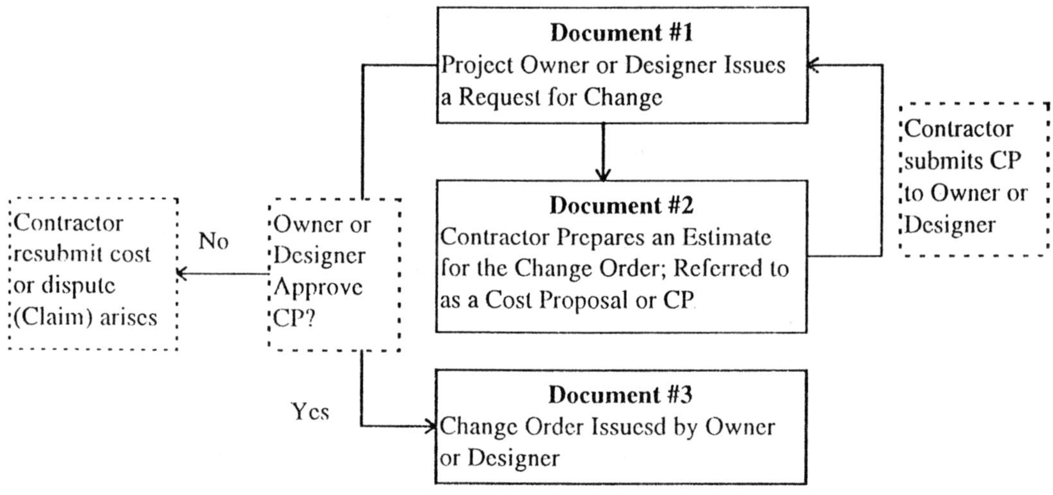

It should be noted that a single change order is often issued to cover several cost proposals. The project owner or designer may wait on reviewing several cost proposals before approving them via a single change order.

Ideally the contractor segments change order work (the price and cost) from the base bid work. This segmentation aids quantification if there is a dispute and also is consistent with contract law (in contract law each change order is a separate contract and should have its own documents; drawings, specifications, etc.). However, more often than not, the contractor merely recognizes change orders as adjustments to the base bid contract. For example, consider the following example:

Example

Initial base bid contract =	$1,200,000
Estimated construction cost of base bid contract =	$900,000
Change order agreed to during project =	$300,000
Contractor anticipated cost of change order work =	$200,000

Assume at year end (after the change order has been issued) that the contract is in process and the following information is known:

Cost expended to date =	$600,000
Estimated cost to complete =	$600,000

Assuming that the contractor uses the percentage of completion method and that cost-to-cost is used as the basis of percent complete, the earned revenue would be calculated as follows:

Percent complete = $600,000/($600,000+$600,000)=	50%
Earned Revenue = ($1,200,000 + $300,000) x .5 =	$750,000
Cost to Date =	$600,000
Earned Profit =	$150,000

As an alternative, the contractor may have segmented the change order work as a separate contract. In this case the percent complete for both the base bid work and the change order work are calculated separately.

The result will be that a different amount of total earned profit will be reported versus the earned profit that would be reported if the base bid and change order work are segmented. Both methods are acceptable in regard to proper accounting methods.

The contractor process of preparing a cost estimate for a change order is similar to that for a base bid estimate. However, the contractor should always consider the following two additional issues or costs when preparing the cost proposal for a change order:

1. The cause and effect cost that the added change order work may have on the base bid work; this is commonly referred to as impact.
2. The effect the added change order work may have on the overall project schedule to include the sequencing of activities and the projected completion date.

Some of the impact type costs of change order work may include the following:

- Dilution of crew size needed to perform work.
- Dilution of supervision needed to properly supervise base bid and change order work.
- Shifting of base bid work into the winter months.
- The need for more and less skilled labor forces.
- The changing of sequencing of work.

A consideration of these and other related change order costs should be made such that change orders are costed properly.

CONSTRUCTION CLAIM

A construction claim is defined as a request for more money (over and above the base bid work) for work that the contractor alleges they did over and above the base bid work or for base bid work performed under conditions that the contractor did not anticipate and for which they are not responsible.

The following points are of notice:

- The contractor initiates a construction claim; however, the project owner often counter claims for lack of workmanship or timely performance.
- A claim can arise either because of additional work or because of changed conditions.
- A change order is not a claim but a change order that is not agreed to can become a claim.

Claims can be of one of four types:

Scope of Work Claim
(In this type of claim, the contractor alleges that he has to do work that is not required as base bid work, or that the has do base bid work under unexpected conditions).
Example possible causes:
Unresolved change order
Vagueness in the contract drawings or specifications
Shifting of work into an unfavorable weather season

Delay Claim
(In this type of claim, the contractor alleges that the schedule changed that led to delays in the contractor getting his work done).
Example possible causes:
Prior contractor non-performance
Owner or designer delays
Owner material purchases that led to delays

Acceleration Claim
(In this type of claim, the contractor alleges that he had to hurry up or accelerate the schedule by adding more workers, working overtime, or working a second shift; all of which added cost).
Example possible causes:
Prior schedule slippage and owner directive to correct.
Unexpected delays that are now being recovered.
Need to expedite the schedule owing to changed deadlines.

Changing Site Condition Claim
(Similar to the scope of work claim except that the work in question is underground; referred to as the substructure).
Example possible causes:
Uncovering of unusual site conditions; timbers, burial grounds.
Unexpected amount of water affecting substructure work.
Inadequate borings to disclose type of soil.

Each construction claim seems to be unique as to the issues and the causation. Many claims are of the type that they consist of several of the above components; e.g. a specific claim may be both a scope of work claim and a delay claim.

Construction claims often do not get resolved quickly; they may hang on for years. The end result is that several issues need to be addressed to include the following:

FINANCIAL TREATMENT OF CLAIMS

Because it may takes months or even years to resolve an outstanding claim(s) on a completed project, the contractor and accountant are faced with the issue as to how to handle the construction claim on the year end financial statements.

The Statement of Position 81-1 states the following:

"Recognition of amounts of additional contract revenue relating to claims is appropriate only if it is probable that the claim will result in additional contract revenue and if the amount can be reliably estimated. These two requirements are satisfied by the existence of all of the following conditions:

a. The contract or other evidence provides a legal basis for the claim; or a legal opinion has been obtained, stating that under the circumstances there is a reasonable basis to support the claim.
b. Additional costs are caused by circumstances that were unforeseen at the contract date and are not the result of deficiencies in the contractor's performance.
c. Costs associated with the claim are identifiable or otherwise determinable and are reasonable in view of the work performed.

d. The evidence supporting the claim is objective and verifiable, not based on management's feel for the situation or on unsupported representations.

If the foregoing requirements are met, revenue from a claim should be recorded only to the extent that contract costs relating to the claim have been incurred. The amounts recorded, if material, should be disclosed in the notes to the financial statements. Costs attributable to claims should be treated as costs of contract performance as incurred."

The problem of not reporting the claim as revenue relates to showing the costs with no offsetting revenue which may in fact jeopardize the contractor's bonding capacity or equity.

QUANTIFICATION OF CLAIM AMOUNT

The process of resolving a claim usually entails the contractor putting together a document referred to as a Request for Equitable Adjustment (REA). This document typically includes two sections:

Entitlement
Quantification of damages

The entitlement section essentially is a legal section. It includes the facts or the story of the claim issue. It recites the issues and often cites legal cases as a basis of the entitlement.

The quantification of damages lists each component of the damages with an accompanying explanation. The matrix on the following page sets out a guide for the participant in putting together the damages.

The matrix includes each of the possible damage components for each of the types of claims listed. The legend used is as follows:

x = most likely should be included in claim damage amount
o = possibly should be included in claim damage amount; subject to dispute
= (blank) most likely should not be included in claim damage amount

It should be noted that three of the components are usually a very high percentage of the total dollar claim amount; these three components are the following:

1. Lost labor productivity owing to impact
2. Owned equipment costs
3. Company overhead costs

	Type of Claim Cost Component	Delay claim	Scope or Work Claim	Acceleration Claim	Changing site condition Cl.
1	Additional direct labor		x		x
2	Loss of productivity of labor	x	x	x	x
3	Increased labor rate	x	o	x	o
4	Additional material quantity		x	o	o
5	Additional material unit price	x	x	o	o
6	Additional subcontractor work		x		o
7	Additional subcontractor cost	x	o	o	x
8	Equipment rental cost	o	x	x	x
9	Cost for owned-equipment use	x	x	o	x
10	Cost for increase in eq. rates	o		o	o
11	Job overhead costs (variable)	o	x	o	x
12	Job overhead costs (fixed)	x			o
13	Company overhead (variable)	o	o	o	o
14	Company overhead (fixed)	x	o		o
15	Interest or finance costs	x	o	o	o
16	Profit	o	x	o	x
17	Loss of opportunity profit	o	o	o	o

The quantification of the claim amount entails determining the dollar amount for each of the "x" and "o" cells. Items 2 (loss of productivity), 9-10 (owned equipment), and 13-14 (company overhead) are typically not only the largest dollar components, but the most difficult to quantify.

Quantifying Lost Labor Productivity

The following methods are possible methods by which the lost labor productivity and associated labor costs can be quantified. They are present with the intent that the participant will be able to utilize this methods for quantifying the lost field labor productivity of man-hours. Once the man-hours are determined, they can be converted to a cost amount for the claim.

Discrete Method

In this method, the construction job site personnel record alleged productivity inefficiencies to the daily time card:

Daily Timecard	
Description	Hrs
Place ¾" conduit	2.0
Place ½' emb. conduit	2.5
Place ¾" emb. conduit	2.5
Waiting on drawings	0.5
Wait on materials	0.5
Total	8.0

Comments: Any alleged lost labor hours and/or productivity are traced right to the timecard and the sum can be calculated.

Measured Mile Method:

In this method, the productivity achieved during the alleged troublesome period is compared to the productivity achieved when there was no trouble or impact.

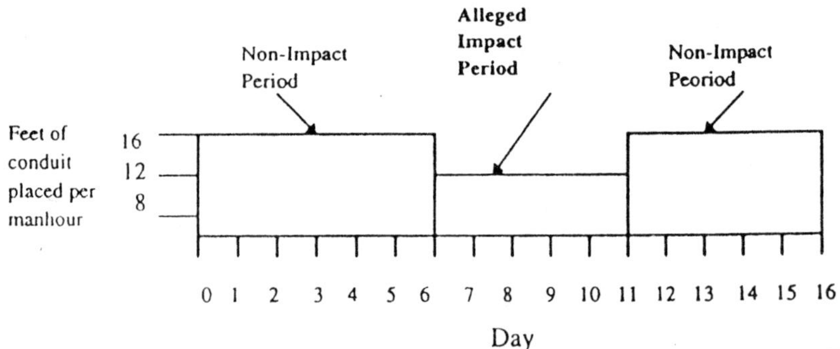

Calculation of Alleged Lost Productivity Impact
Assume Productivity drops from 16 ft. per hour to 12 ft. per hour
Assume labor rate equals $30/hr and 5 workers.
Damages equal (25%)($30/hr)(5 days)(8 hour/day)(5 workers)=$1,500

Comments: The method presents a graphical or mathematical means of illustrating alleged lost labor productivity. The method assumes that the work performed in the non-impact periods and the work performed in the "alleged" impact period were similar.

Total Cost Method:

In this method, the "alleged" labor cost damage is calculated as the difference between the actual project labor cost or hours and the estimated labor cost or hours.

Example	
Actual Project Labor Hours to Place 1,000′ of 3/4″ galvanized conduit =	650.0 mh
Estimated Project Labor Hours to Place 1,000 ′ of 3/4″ galvanized conduit =	480.0 mh
Difference	170.0 mh
times Project Labor Rate	$30.00/hr.
Total Claim Damage	$5,100.00

Comments: Method provides relatively easy calculation that can be made after the completion of the project. The method is based on four assumptions:

1. *The "total cost" method assumes that the estimating process was correct and that the resulting estimate dollar amount is correct.*
2. *The "total cost" method assumes that the recorded project labor cost and hours is correct.*
3. *The "total cost" method assumes that all the reasons for the overrun in the labor cost damage are the fault of the project owner or designer.*
4. *The "total cost" method assumes that the labor rate used in the calculation is a fair and equitable rate and represents what the contractor paid.*

Industrial Engineering Approach
In this approach, industrial engineering models such as time study, the method productivity delay model (MPDM), or time and motion studies are used to "measure" the lost productivity as it occurs. This "scientific" approach can be used when there is instant problem recognition. The user of this method must have knowledge of the industrial engineering models and how to use the models.

Earned Value Approach
This method, while not considered as a method of quantifying alleged lost labor productivity for a construction claim, is presented here in that it has been used for this purpose. In the earned value approach, the calculation of added labor hours is determined by comparing (for select time periods), the hours it took to do a group of activities versus the budgeted (or earned hours) for those activities.

To illustrate the Earned Value Method, consider the data shown below that represents the planned work durations, planned work days, and planned man-hours relative to the actual durations, work days, and man-hours.

Activity	Planned Duration	Planned Work Days	Planned Man-hours	Planned MH/Day & Crew	Actual Duration	Actual Work Days	Actual Manners	Actual MH/Day & Crew
A	4	1–4	128	32–4	4	10–13	148	37–4.6
B	6	1–6	288	48–6	6	1–6	192	32–4
C	2	1–2	64	32–4	2	5–6	60	30–3.75
D	6	5–10	240	40–5	6	14–16, 18–20	290	48.3–6+
E	12	7–18	384	32–4	13	7–19	424	32.6–4+
F	12	3–14	288	24–3	12	7–18	328	27.3–3.4
G	4	19–23	160	40–5	4	20–23	154	38.5–4.8
H	4	23–26	192	48–6	3	24–26	180	60–7.5
I	2	23–24	128	64–8	2	25–26	118	59–7.4
J	8	23–26	256	32–4	7	20–26	280	40–5
Total			2,128				2,174	

Assume the planned schedule per the contractor's submitted "as planned schedule" was as follows:

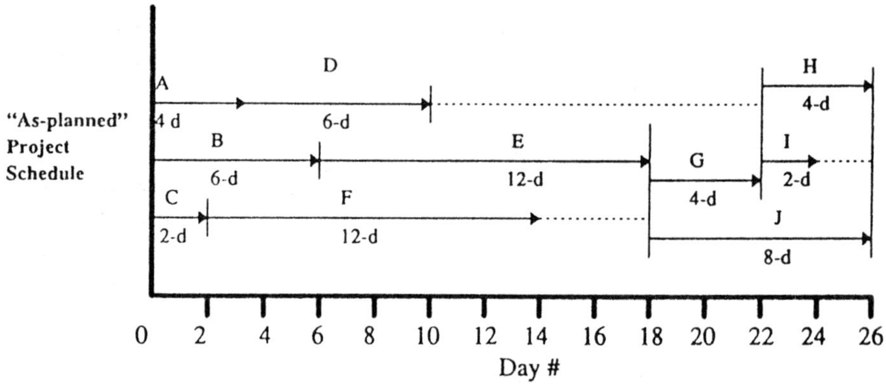

Let us further assume that the contractor alleges labor impact during days 11 through 20. Let us further assume that for whatever reason, project activities are delayed and shifted and the "as built" project schedule for the above illustrated project is as illustrated below:

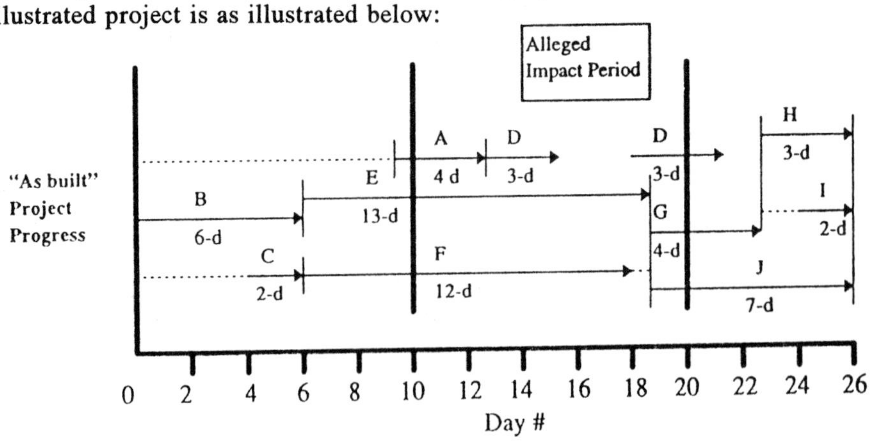

The "alleged" lost productivity calculated using the Earned Value Method is as follows:

Activity	Planned MH	Earned MH (% in impact time period)	Actual MH	Actual MH During Impact Time	Alleged Lost MH's
A	128	96	148	111	15
D	240	200	290	242	42
E	384	266	424	294	28
F	288	192	328	219	27
G	260	40	154	39	(1)
J	256	37	280	40	3
Total		831		945	114

The "Earned MH" and "Actual MH During Impact Time" columns (Col. 3 and 5) are calculated through a linear interpolation of the time in the impact period of the "Planned MH" and "Actual MH" columns.

<u>Comments</u>: *This EVM method of calculating damages is similar to the above noted cost method. It is based on more assumptions and may result in a larger damage calculation than even the cost method yields.*

For one, the earned value method assumes the following (the same assumptions used in the cost method):

1. *The method assumes that the estimating process was correct and that the resulting estimate number is correct.*
2. *The method assumes that the recorded project labor cost and hours is correct.*
3. *The method assumes that all the reasons for the overrun in the labor cost damage are the fault of the project owner or designer.*
4. *The method assumes that the labor rate used in the calculation is a fair and equitable rate and represents what the contractor should have paid.*

Secondly, the earned value method also assumes the following:

5. *That in preparing the estimate, the estimator took into account the sequencing of the project activities when determining the productivity for each activity. For example, in the planned schedule shown above, activities A, B, and C were to take place at the same time. However, for whatever reason, when the project was built, A, B, and C were not done at the same time. The productivity for each activity could be different under the two different schemes.*
6. *The earned value method assumes that once an activity starts, that an equal amount of work is performed every day until the activity is*

complete. This assumption is made in calculating the earned hours from the initial estimate. For example, in the analysis above, it is assumed that 8/12's of activity F's hours would be earned in the impact period, just because the schedule shows 8/12's of the working days occurred in the impact period.

7. *Similar to #6 above, the method ignores the fact that an activity once started, may stop, and then start again. Observe activity D shown in the "as built" schedule. The earned hours for activity D would not take into account the fact that for a few days, nothing is done. The method focuses on the start and completion day.*
8. *The earned value method assumes that the project estimate for each and every activity ties to the planned duration for the activity in the "as planned" schedule.*
9. *The method does not give any credit for time periods when the contractor "beat the budget". For the above example, it may be that the reason the contractor expended 96 fewer hours than budgeted for activity B is not independent of overruns in the impact period. In effect, the earned value method assumes that the activities are pushed into the "impact period" by activities outside the impact period, but doesn't offset any of the productivity savings from these activities in the damage calculation. In the above example, the earned value calculations result in a 114 manhour damage request, even though the total overrun in manhours for the project is only 46 manhours.*

Expert Approach

In this method, a productivity expert(s) reviews the project conditions, project correspondence and project documentation, and applies industry productivity knowledge and data to the "alleged" issues at hand to determine a reasonable lost labor productivity damage.

Example:

Description	Range of Impact on Productivity per Industry Publications	Severity on Example Project	Estimated Impact on Example Project	On-Site Labor Hours During Relevant Time Frame	Calculation of Expected Lost Labor Hours
Weather temperature	(10–30%)	small	10%	280	82.0
Inadequate scheduling	(5–15%)	severe	15%	940	141.0
Inadequate supervision	(10–25%)	average	16%	244	39.0
Worker morale	(5–30%)	significant	25%	128	32.0
Interference by other trades	(10–30%)	small	10%	540	54.0
Inadequate skills of workers	(10–30%)	significant	28%	98	27.4

<u>Comments</u>: When using the expert witness approach, the calculations and the resulting labor cost damages are only as creditable as the individual that has reviewed the issues and documents and made the calculations.

Owner Equipment Costs

An issue in dispute in claim resolution as well as for determining change order payment is the issue as to how much the contractor is entitled to for his owned equipment when added work has been done or when the work has been delayed. This issue is made critical by the fact that the hourly cost for several types of equipment may approach $100 per hour or more.

Two separate situations may initiate this issue of owned equipment costs. For one, the contractor may have had to do added work; i.e. change order work. The project owner may take the position as long as the project took the same duration as what was planned that the contractor is not entitled to added costs for his owned equipment. The owner's position is predicated on the assumption that the owned equipment costs is a sunk cost, it was there anyway.

The second situation relates to a delay in a project that required the contractor to have the equipment at the project longer than anticipated. The owner may take the position that unless the contractor can show that there was another project waiting the availability of the equipment, that the equipment is a sunk cost and therefore the contractor is not entitled to added compensation.

To resolve the above issues, both the project owner and the contractor have argued for cost reimbursement for owned equipment using one of the following rates:

- Rental rates as published by industry guide estimating books (referred to as blue book rates)
- Sunk cost (owner position that equipment sunk cost and therefore contractor entitled to $).
- Estimating rates
- Actual ownership costs

The actual rates are the most appropriate and equitable rate. Both of the above issues (added work or added duration) can be resolved if the contractor keeps track of the ownership costs of owning a specific piece of equipment. The costs of ownership include the following:

$$\text{Equipment cost} = \frac{\text{Depreciation} + \text{Maintenance} + \text{Operating} + \text{Insurance} + \text{Finance Cost} + \text{Tax} + \text{Replacemnt cost (inflation)}}{\text{Hours Used}}$$

Some the above costs are a function of equipment use:

- Depreciation (note: equipment wears out more as a function of use than of time)
- Maintenance
- Operating

Other cost components are more a function of time:

- Insurance
- Finance cost
- Tax (if there is a property tax component)
- Replacement cost

If the contractor knows each of the above cost components by having kept records, the contractor can justify requesting cost components that are a function of use when the contractor has an added work but not added time issue. Similarly, when the contractor is delayed with his equipment, even though the contractor did not do any added work, he can claim for the cost components that are a function of time.

Company Overhead Damage

When a contractor submits a claim or a change order for payment, he often includes a cost component for the firm's company overhead (company overhead includes officer salaries, home office rent, etc.) The amount of this claim component is often large and disputed.

Given the fact that most company overhead costs are a function of time (i.e. fixed costs), a company overhead cost component seems most appropriate to a delay claim. Nonetheless, it often included in most claims using one of the following procedures for quantification:

Industry average rates as published in industry publications
Company rate per financial statements
Company overhead rate used in estimate
Using the Eichleay Formula

The Eichleay formula is a process of allocating company overhead based on volume and time. Consider the example on the following page.

The example can be considered the contractor version of Eichleay. Even if the owner agrees with the entitlement using Eichleay, the project owner will likely argue that the company overhead should be calculated by using the actual duration rather than the planned duration. This would result in dividing the $50,000 by 55 weeks instead of 50 weeks.

Example:
Project 101:

Contract amount	= $1,000,000
Planned duration	= 50 weeks
Delay	= 5 weeks (for reasons outside control of contractor)
Company volume in time period	= $10,000,000
Company overhead in time period	= $500,000

The contractor would calculate the company overhead damage (using Eichleay) as follows:

Project 101 contract/Total company volume	= $1,000,000/$10,000,000
	= 10%
Company overhead allocable to Project 100	= (.10) ($500,000)
	= $50,000
Company overhead planned per week	= $50,000/50 weeks
	= $1,000/week
Company overhead damage	= (5 weeks) x $1,000/week
	= $5,000

RESOLUTION OF CLAIMS

Historically construction claims have been settled by litigation or arbitration. The two processes are contrasted as follows

Issue	Litigation	Arbitration
Speed		Suppose to be faster because of less legal maneuvering
Most thorough	Claims to be most thorough because law is followed.	
Appeal process	Can be appealed	Usually not able to appeal
Cost		As a rule lower cost because may be quicker
Type of evidence	Written evidence overrides oral testimony or intent	Most all evidence admissible
Result	More of a winner and a loser	Often a sharing of blame and accompanying award.

In recent years in an attempt to reduce expensive and time consuming litigation, other means of resolving disputes have evolved.

Mediation
In this process, an outside party tries to get the parties to agree to a settlement. Unlike in arbitration where the arbitrator(s) make the award, in mediation, the mediator is more of a referee; the disputing parties make the award.

Alternative Disputes Boards
In this process, the project owner and contractor agree to one or three individuals that will serve as independent arbitrators on all disputes on a project. Unlike arbitration, the board members are identified early in the project. Unlike arbitration, their judgments are not usually viewed as final; they can be overridden by a court. However, their judgment is accepted by the court and therefore often both parties accept the rulings of the dispute board.

RECORD KEEPING TO PREVENT CLAIM

Given the high cost of resolving claims, and the time delays associated with their resolution, it can be argued that the best claim is no claim. The prevention of claims is facilitated by good recordkeeping; both by the project owner (or designer) and the contractor. One can argue that recordkeeping is not complete unless one can play the project back like a movie when it is complete.

Recordkeeping entails the use of timecards, daily reports, minutes of meetings, job cost reports, updated schedules, etc. Recordkeeping can aid in preparing a claim as well as pinpointing responsibility and preventing claims or disputes.

21
VALUATION OF THE CONSTRUCTION FIRM

REASONS FOR DETERMINING THE VALUATION OF THE CONSTRUCTION FIRM

The 1980's and the 1990's have seen an increase in the need for the owners of construction firms to have valuations of their construction firms. Perhaps the main reason for this increase in the need for valuations has been the increased use of employee stock ownership plans (ESOP's). These plans became popular owing to tax law changes.

Perhaps another reason for the increasing number of valuations relates to the fact that many construction firms are closely held. When the owner is ready to retire, there may be no alternative but to sell the firm; as such, the need for a valuation of the firm as a basis of the sale. In fact, given the trend of the industry towards a more business and computerized approach, some owners of firms, perhaps intimidated by these new approaches to construction may be retiring earlier.

Additional reasons why a valuation of a construction firm may be needed include the following:

Sale of stock to outside investors
Setting value for ESOP transactions
For making a decision as to if the firm should go public
For the purpose of purchasing the minority owners
For tax planning purposes such as estate taxes and gifts

The valuation of the typically closely held construction firm is complicated by the fact that these types of companies, lacking publicly held and traded stock, have no visible means of measuring worth. Instead, many construction firms operate from one year to the next without having a clear understanding of the worth of the firm.

Value of a firm can be defined as what an individual, fully informed of all facts, at an arms length transaction and under no pressure, is willing to pay for the firm. Factors that effect the value of a firm include:

The type of business
The earnings capability of the firm
The economic outlook for the industry
The book value of the firm or stock
The market value of competing type firms
The dividend paying ability or history of the firm

In practice, there are several alternative methods that can be utilized to value the construction firm. To illustrate these methods, let us assume the following example construction firm.

ASSETS		LIABILITIES	
Current assets	$450,000	Current liabilities	$200,000
Fixed assets		Long term liabilities	
Buildings	140,000	Buildings	100,000
Equipment	110,000	Equipment	75,000
Total Fixed Assets	$250,000	Total Long Term Liabilities	175,000
		Total Liabilities	375,000
		Net Worth	325,000
Total Assets	$700,000	Total Worth & Liabilities	700,000

Total number of shares outstanding	1,500
Book value per share (net worth/shares)	$216.67 per share

Earnings for Years Ended December 31	(19X1-19X5)
YEAR	NET EARNINGS
19X1	$86,000
19X2	$94,000
19X3	$110,000
19X4	$96,000
19X5	$128,000

In order to value the firm, a capitalization rate must be determined. This is commonly done by first determining a price to earnings ratio (P/E) that is appropriate for the firm. P/E ratios are published for publicly traded firms in the financial pages of most newspapers.

For our example, let us assume that a P/E of 10.25 is average for a firm. This P/E ratio is adjusted for considerations such as the following:

Management depth of the owners
Financial strength of the firm
Past experience and performance
Diversification of the firm

Given the high risk of most construction firms and their relatively weak financial strength, the average P/E ratio for other firms is usually discounted for the construction firm. Let us assume that for our example, consideration of the above factors has led to a P/E ratio of 7.0. The capitalization factor for the valuation is determined by dividing the P/E ratio into 1. In our example, the capitalization rate is determined as 1/7 or 14.28 percent.

The determination of the appropriate P/E ratio and capitalization rate should not be taken lightly. It's determination is dependent on the knowledge and skill of the professional person making the valuation. Any error on the high or low side can lead to a misleading valuation.

Once the capitalization rate is determined, several valuation methods can be used to value the firm. We will now illustrate commonly used methods.

The Weighted Average of Past Earnings Method

This method is illustrated in Figure 21.1. This method gives more weight to recent earnings as illustrated in the calculations.

Year	Earnings	Weight	Total
19X1	$86,000	1	$86,000
19X2	$94,000	2	198,000
19X3	$110,000	3	330,000
19X4	$96,000	4	384,000
19X5	$128,000	5	640,000
Totals		15	1,638,000
Average weighed earnings			$109,200
x P/E ratio (7)			
= Valuation of the Firm			$764,400
divided by 1,500 shares			
= Market value per share			$509.33

Figure 21.1 Weighted Average Method

Once the average weighed earnings are determined ($109,200 in our example), they are multiplied by the acceptable P/E ratio to determine the valuation of the firm

The Arithmetic Average of Past Earnings Method

This method is illustrated in Figure 21.2. The method is the same as the previous method except that each of the past year's earnings are weighted equally.

Year	Earnings
19X1	$86,000
19X2	$94,000
19X3	$110,000
19X4	$96,000
19X5	$128,000
Total Earnings	$524,000

Average Earnings	$104,800
x P/E ratio	7.00
=Market Value	$733,600
Number of shares	1,500
=Value per share	$489.06

Figure 21.2 Arithmetic Average Method

Last Fiscal Year Earnings Method

A third method of valuation is referred to as the Last Fiscal Year Earnings Method. This method is similar to the two previous methods except that the valuation is based only on the last year's earnings. The method is illustrated in Figure 21.3.

Year	Earnings
19X5	$128,000
x P/E ratio	7.00
=Market Value	$896,000
Number of shares	1,500
Value per share	$597.33

Figure 21.3 Last Year Earning Method

Projected Earnings Method

This Projected Earnings Method is illustrated in Figure 21.4. The method is somewhat subjective in that the valuation is based on a forecast of earnings for the next year. As such, the method is subject to all the uncertainties of the construction process.

Year	Earnings
Projected for 19X6	$140,800
x P/E ratio	7
= Market value	$985,600
Number of shares	1,500
Value per share	$657.07

Figure 21.4 Projected Earnings Method

Present Value of Future Earnings Method

The present value of future earnings method is based on the assumption about earnings for several future earnings; in our example for the next five years. The method is illustrated in Figure 21.5.

Year	Earnings	Book Value
19X5	$128,000	$325,000
19X6	140,800	465,800
19X7	154,880	620,680
19X8	170,368	791,048
19X9	187,405	978,453
19X10	206,145	1,184,598

(assumes earnings grow at 10%)

Book value 19X10	$1,184,598
x Present Value Factor for Capitalization Rae of 14.27% =	0.5131
=Valuation	$607,817
divided by 1,500 shares	
= Market value per share	$405.21

Figure 21.5 Present Value Future Earnings Method

The book value or net worth of the company is adjusted accordingly. In our example, we have assumed a 10% increase in earnings per year. Using the assumed P/E ratio, the capitalized factor is used to discount the book value back to the present time to determine the valuation.

Liquidation Method

The last method illustrated is the liquidation method. This method is illustrated in Figure 21.6.

Description	Amount
Working Capital	$250,000
(current assets minus current liabilities)	
Building	$180,000
* Market value	
Equipment	$100,000
* Market value	
Gross Liquidation Value	$530,000
-Liquidation costs (15%)	-79,500
VALUATION	$450,000
Number of shares	1,500
Market value per share	$300.33

* Assumes following market values
Building $230,000
Equipment $125,000

Figure 21.6 Liquidation Method

In the liquidation method, the value of the firm is determined by calculating the liquidating value of the assets on the firm's balance sheet. In addition to the free working capital (current assets minus current liabilities), the liquidating value of the fixed assets (building and equipment in our example) are determined by subtracting the debt on these assets from the current market value (note: market value is used, not cost).

Comparison of Methods

The six different methods of valuation illustrated yield quite different results. The question is which method should be used? One solution would be to average the six methods. Using the six methods we have illustrated for the valuation of the example construction firm, we have obtained the following six valuations:

METHOD	Valuation
Weighted Average Method	$764,400
Arithmetic Average Method	$733,600
Last Year Earning Method	$896,000
Projected Earnings Method	$985,000
Present Value Method	$607,817
Liquidation Method	$450,000
AVERAGE	$739,470

The participant should be cautioned that the results are very dependent on the example financial data we have assumed. However, it should be observed that the various methods yield quite different results. The average may not be the best method of determining the valuation.

Normally, in valuing construction firms, the methods based on past earnings and the liquidation method are given more creditability than the methods that are based on future earnings. This is because of the uncertainty of future earnings in the construction process.

The best method of valuation can be only made for a specific firm when all the factors relevant are weighted by the person making the valuation. The experience and the knowledge of the construction firm and the construction industry are critical to this determination. This of course is the argument that can be made for obtaining the services of a competent professional to determine the valuation. This professional has to be knowledgeable about which method is best for the situation and also needs to know how to calculate an appropriate capitalization rate. Knowledge of valuation methods, the construction industry and firm, accounting and financial methods in order to determine the strength of reported earnings, method of estimating value of fixed assets such as equipment, and the ability to forecast future work and earnings are all required to determine an accurate valuation.

INDEX